DRIVING
THROUGH
HPS

by
CAROL A DENNARD

The right of Carol A Dennard be identified as the author of this
work has been asserted by her in accordance with Section 78
of the Copyright, Designs and Patents Act 1988

The book cover picture is copyright to Carol A Dennard

This book is published by
Grosvenor House Publishing Ltd
28-30 High Street, Guildford, Surrey, GU1 3EL.
www.grosvenorhousepublishing.co.uk

This is a work of non-fiction based on the experiences and recollections
of the author and as such depicts real events from a personal point of
view. All the people inhabiting this book either live, breathe or have died
but, apart from some notable exceptions and those dear to my heart,
their names have been changed to protect their privacy and
that of others.

A CIP record for this book
is available from the British Library

ISBN 978-1-78148-879-9

For Robert and Sophie, my shining stars.

Contents

CHAPTER 1

Words

September 2010. My hands in hot soapy dishwater, I gaze out of the kitchen window, the evening to come holding the same prospects as the one that preceded it. An autumnal nip is in the air and the round of birthdays has taken place with Robert, now twenty one, and Sophie at eighteen, starting their new academic terms. There is no magic or pizzazz about the number fifty seven, the age that Roger and I have reached, but at least all is well after a few little awkward twists and turns in the road of life earlier in the year.

Seven years have passed since I gave up family law and, as I get the scouring pad out to do its business on the crock pot, I play a familiar dirge to long suffering Roger about whether I will ever achieve some of the goals I have set myself; finishing the collection of family anecdotes, sorting out the photographs accumulated over the last five years, gathering together the collection of goods I have foraged from Boot Sales to launch my exclusive retro empire.

'And then there's Frank,' I sigh. 'I feel so guilty, get so cross with myself when I don't give him the attention he deserves.' Dear old amiable Frank who, wrapped up in his car coat and cap, had come home with me from night school. Not literally of course because Frank is a man of pure fiction, born of my imagination but one who already had a following of well wishers. 'How's Frank?' friends would ask, all eagerly awaiting the day when they too could meet him in the pages of my book. They still do, because as I write this he's still with me, still condemned to play the seasoned observer as he languishes in his hospital bed trying to make sense of his shrunken world. And whilst not knowing it,

1

whilst not admitting to it, I too was trying to make sense of a changing world. It was easier to blame my struggle to commit his final fate to paper on all the mumsy things that I'm not necessarily a natural or good at, whereas I was finding it hard, as with the children growing up and leaving home and with Barney the cat being poorly, to let him, go.

But on that particular evening Roger, who underpins us all, played his usual tune of *It'll all get done in good time,* signalling an end to the discussion of that old perennial. So I twittered on about a feature on the Olympics in the news roundup we had just watched on T.V. His customary glass of wine had by now definitely slipped him into the warm waters of relaxation mode so he didn't respond much, it being easier for him to float along on the assumption that my chatter was a random stream of idle observation rather than draw on his long years' experience of living with me and recognise that my thought processes were swimming down an altogether different channel.

'What sort of person do you think they'll be looking for?' I asked when the last of the water was gurgling down the plughole.

'Don't know,' he shrugged, his powers of concentration lapping at the pages of the Radio Times.

'And what would Games Makers have to do?'

He should have taken notice of the way I was stripping my rubber gloves off. Instead he chose to leave the kitchen, leaving me no other option but to investigate a burgeoning idea on the computer. An hour of mouse clicking later I emerged from the study into the living room.

'We'll see what comes of that,' I said to he who was now anchored in his regular sofa position, his unblinking eyes staring fixedly at the telly with Barney and brother Busby contentedly curled up together on his lap. The only glimmer of intelligent life from the sofa man was a pained expression in response to the sporting defeat being played out on the screen.

'Do you think Seb Coe will want me?'

He looked up at me blankly, having learnt nothing from the occasion when, by showing more interest in a game of men

2

kicking a ball, he'd ended up as my support act in the briefest of appearances on the telly.

'I've put my name down to help out at the Olympics.' His reaction came in that infuriating half tilt of the head, the raising of one eyebrow and the half smile so characteristic of his clan which said he didn't believe me, but, okay, he'd play along with the tease.

'I've done it online.'

He laughed, his scepticism well founded because that night neither Robert nor Sophie were there to help me. Not that I would necessarily have asked for their help because, and it was probably unintentional on their part, I often felt a lack of empathy when I asked them to repeat or go a bit more slowly at explaining which icon to press. And to be fair, it was me who usually lost their temper because no-one could explain why the computer worked in the particular way it did. According to them, it wasn't something that needed to be understood. Anyway, that was by the by on the evening in question because after my bold statement I paused for effect, a pause that proved a bit too long for his comfort.

'You haven't?'

'I have!' I said smugly, flouncing back to the kitchen, my belligerent exterior belying the doubt in my mind that I had actually filled in the application form correctly, let alone sent it. Okay, I had initiated our T.V appearance by a computer communication but that had been a fluke, my representations to the BBC more akin to a rant by email rather than the punitive amount of questions, ticking boxes and selecting options I had just been subjected to. And even if I had done it right, I questioned my ability to play a useful role in what was already being trumpeted as the biggest peacetime mobilisation of civilians ever. I was certainly no stranger to mobilisations and as I made our night time cups of tea, a sense of unease came upon me as I recalled that mobilisations and me didn't mix.

Many years before, a brief spell in the Civil Service had had me closeted in a draughty old office with a spinster who sniffed constantly and stunk of mothballs. We were overseen by a retired

Army officer holed up in a similarly draughty office across the corridor. On his last marching legs or not, said officer would send my colleague into a pink cheeked dribbling frenzy of delight when he deigned to rattle our doorknob. Not that he rattled it often because Miss Mothballs and I were the sad people consigned to the last chance saloon of the Mobilisations Department. I'd already created havoc in Postings, the wrong Corporal Smith being uprooted at my whim, and I had exhibited an over zealousness in sending soldiers to further their education when I worked in Courses. I suspected that not all had found Miss Mothballs the easiest of people to get on with so a scatterbrain like me was probably manna from heaven to the commanding officer and an added bonus that, once installed in Mobs, we shuffled paper and filled in index cards quite amiably together. On occasions we even caught the same bus home and as it pulled away from her stop I'd watch her step briskly along the pavement to the house that she shared with her brother and his family. I say shared but I think the reality was that she occupied the two attic rooms and joined them downstairs on high days and holidays to fulfil the function of prissy old Aunt.

To this day I don't know what Miss M and I did or even what we were supposed to be doing. Perhaps it was all a ruse to keep us gainfully employed on something that didn't really exist? The days were mind bendingly boring, made bearable only by my leaving Miss M to her thermos at break time whilst I consorted with non Mobilised friends in the canteen. Miss Mothballs and the building are long gone but not the sense of relief at the lucky escape from the likes of her and me bringing the country to the brink of destruction if war had been declared and our index cards dealt from the pack. Such was my undistinguished career in the Civil Service; the career my late father had said would be a safe bet to continue in with a secure pension in bright lights to look forward to. As my sixties approached I began to think he had a point.

'You know what your dad used to say,' Roger shouted from the sofa. I didn't reply. I didn't need reminding, had already felt the ghostly presence of Dad's breath upon my neck when I'd been completing the Games Maker application form. Not that he would have had the remotest idea what the computer could do but it was the principle of the act I was committing that his spirit would object to. So, with Roger now calling out with a request for a biscuit, I bit my lip and wondered if the Games were just another diversion from getting Frank printed and out into the public domain? And had I done a disservice to the nation by putting my name forward to Mr Coe and his committee, little comfort coming from the fact that when my trembling finger had hovered over, then clicked, the SEND icon I had ignored the words falling from Dad's spectral lips, his longstanding advice to 'NEVER EVER VOLUNTEER!'

CHAPTER 2

Don't Ask

The days blew into weeks, frosted into months and we slid into another year with snow. A hot Easter came and went. I'd heard nothing from Mr. Coe and little hugs and kindly utterances of 'never mind' from Roger didn't help the dip in my morale when I thought I was such a numbskull that I couldn't even get a post as a volunteer. Then in early June 2011 an email blinked at me and set my heart racing.

'I've been offered an interview for the Games!' I stood in the living room and proclaimed. 'What shall I do?'

'Go to it, of course!' said Sophie, impatient with her elder for being so dithery. And if it hadn't been for her dogmatic encouragement I probably wouldn't have played with a few more drop down menus on the computer and got a date to attend a Selection Event with the Transport Team at London Excel. I thought it a bit odd because my stated preferences had been for Client Services, Arrivals and Departures or Accommodation List. I had envisaged being the friendly face welcoming athletes to the Olympic Village, the helpful hostess checking dignitaries into their hotel. In that kind of post I'd be able to partially fulfil the dream I'd once had of being an air hostess, welcoming passengers on board; a dream helped along by the 'air hostess' outfit I'd been given as a child, feeling the absolute bees knees as I went everywhere with my little blue hat with its shiny tin plane pin worn at a jaunty angle with matching blue bag.

A post in Client Services would fulfil a dream and also satisfy a grudge, a grudge long held since a summer holiday job I'd had as a teenager at a motel local to where we lived at the time. The motel mirrored the TV series Crossroads with its seventies décor, intrigue and in-fights. I was a chambermaid in the morning and a coffee bar assistant in the afternoon and constantly at the mercy of the glammed-up receptionists who considered themselves better than the rest of us menials put together. With the flick of a receptionist's false eyelash I was banned from making an entrance in my nylon overall via the grand sweeping staircase down into the presence of guests in reception. With the point of a painted nail at a room list we were told who was leaving and when others would be arriving and on occasion told to leave a particular room till last to enable a commercial traveller or visiting businessman to sleep off his soaring bar bill. The powdered-nosed receptionists inhabited a different world where they worked out bills in Kalamazoo for the men wearing suits and polished shoes whilst upstairs we cleaned nasal hair from the washbasins, picked up soggy towels left where they'd been dropped and, sometimes, urine soaked sheets from that aforementioned sleepy salesman.

The Motel was eventually razed to the ground to make way for an Industrial unit but reclining on the bed listening to Waggoner's Walk on Radio Two whilst we drank coffee with powdered milk will always live on in my memory as will the chambermaid giggles we had in the laundry cupboard after illicit squirts of a lady guest's perfume.

And a giggle was what I promised Sophie we would have on the day of our trip to Excel at London's Royal Victoria Dock.

'I'll just see how today goes,' I said, after parking the car. It was to be a familiar refrain throughout the experience, a refrain demonstrating self doubt that I could actually rise to the challenge mixed with a dogged determination not to give up on something once I've started it. 'It's an adventure just being here, isn't it? It's not what I expected.'

Actually I don't know what I expected, my only association with docks being the fact that I had had a grandfather and uncles who had spent all their working lives as Dockers down West. They were long dead but as we turned left and walked up a road bounded on both sides by modern apartment blocks I could well imagine their looks of utter amazement at how a dock could be regenerated.

'I can't believe it, can you, Sophie?' I had spotted up ahead of us an open plaza and steps to the exhibition and conference centre which is Excel.

'Stay calm,' she replied, long used to how I can become uncommonly enthusiastic about buildings. I followed her lead, making restrained comments about the hotels and number of restaurants housed in the converted dock buildings. 'When we go to meet Robert we'll have to get to the other side of the restaurants because I think the Docklands Light Railway runs parallel to them.'

'Fair enough.'

We went for a comfort stop in the toilets housed in the main Excel building. The queue was lengthy, putting paid to any thoughts of a quick cup of coffee and then we were back out into the sunshine.

'I bet all this lot have got interviews,' I muttered to Sophie as we followed a trail of grey haired men and women, suitably dressed in M&S's summer season colours, down the ramp and into the Games Makers hub by the waterfront.

I booked in. We sat in a circle of blue foam benches, the interviewees surreptitiously eyeing each other up. I was still treating it as all a bit of fun until a very earnest young man in a suit turned up. With beads of sweat breaking out on his brow he sat down and nervously twiddled with his tie. Others too began to look less composed and when a very flustered lady hobbled in with two walking sticks and reported on a marathon journey exacerbated by her worrying that she had missed her appointment slot, it dawned on me that I was waiting for a proper interview.

An interview! I hadn't been to one for donkey's years. My fellows were taking it seriously and yet I was dressed up for a summer BBQ in sleeveless maxi dress and gladiatorial style sandals. I was called up to the vetting desk and, thinking it a cool thing to do, left my handbag with Sophie. I returned, on the first occasion to root in my handbag for my authorisation letter, the second occasion for my driving licence photo card and, on the third, for my licence counterpart.

'Don't come back again,' Sophie hissed as my reappearances had the other candidates looking up enquiringly and the look she gave me said that I wasn't fooling her or anyone else by laughing at my own ineptitude.

'I won't. I'm going to see a film.'

The eyes of the tall man by the entrance to the film area commanded my attention, ordered me to stop before a word had passed his lips. My feet were rooted to the spot as he gazed at my name badge then looked deep into my eyes.

'Where are you going?' he asked.

'To the film?'

'And then?'

I was struck mute, having forgotten everything they had told me at the vetting desk.

'You will have to go to pod five. You will remember that won't you?

I nodded.

'Pod five,' he said escorting me to a blue foam bench in front of the widescreen.

Looking back, I view my encounter with him as a hypnotic preamble to the film that, bursting with colour, action, loud inspirational music and words personally directed at me from Lord Coe and Eddie Izzard, sent subliminal messages from the organisers to say that they needed, nay demanded, I join forces with them to make the Games great. I rose from the film feeling good, feeling part of something big and, trance like, followed the others through to I knew not where.

A man with a silver mane stood at the top of the stairs. 'Are you Carol for pod five?' he called down to me.

'I think so.'

'You can take any chair,' he said, pointing to one of two in the pod. It crossed my mind that this could all be part of the test but the chair offended my sense of Feng Shui. I took the other one so as to have a clear route to the Pod's exit and a view of what was going on outside. He seemed discomfited by this but quickly moved on to tell me he used to work for British Gas, gave an explanation as to how the interview process would work and landed me with his opening question.

'What is your favourite Olympic sport and why?'

I couldn't think of one sport let alone why I would like it. There was an awkward silence, his pen poised over the page of questions on his clipboard. I knew there was a word that covered the things that athletes do in a Stadium but it eluded me.

'Running?' I framed it more as a question. 'Um, um, the things you jump over.'

'Hurdles?' he prompted.

'Yes, hurdles.' A vision of about three sets of them and the Games Teacher in her Arran sweater looking very bored on our school's playing field flashed before me. He nodded, encouraging me to elaborate.

'And jumping. Long jump. Yes, long jump. You see I've always been tall and I've got long legs.' I slapped my thigh a`la pantomime and stretched my foot out. My blue plastic sandals, with cheap silver spikes in them, looked every inch the foolish impulse buy they had been. And foolish indeed was my body language which in other circumstances could have been misconstrued as a come on but his British Gas background didn't count for nothing and we progressed to other questions which proved equally as perplexing as the first.

'Can you think of an instance in life when things haven't gone according to plan and how did you deal with it?' he asked. I was tempted to bring the conversation bang up to date by saying that the interview itself wasn't turning out as I expected it but thought that might sound flippant. The seconds passed as I desperately tried to recall something. I took a sip of water and shuffled in my seat, inwardly cursing Lord Coe and his chums for persuading me to apply in the first place.

'Well, you just get on with things don't you?' It was a less than inspiring answer and I could tell from his face that inspiration was not the word his pen was getting ready to write so I rattled on about the fickleness of human nature. And I beefed up on those occasions when I'd had to deal with temperamental clients throwing hissy fits. I recounted the story of one such client who, in the hallowed corridors of the High Court in the Strand, had taken his jacket off and thrown it down on the ground and stamped on it in a classic gesture of protest at what his wife was alleging and claiming from him. And I explained the challenges of having your case suddenly switched from one Court where a charitable and sympathetic arbiter of justice was presiding into another one where you were growled at by a less benevolent one.

I saw him turn back to the front page and guessed he was about to pick up on the fact that I was drawing on episodes from my former life, a life some had said I had been foolish, while others called it brave, to turn my back on. I rallied and so as to show that I hadn't become a daytime couch potato or a lady who lunched her way through a comfortable existence I brought Frank into play.

'Frank?'

'He's fictional.' I smiled because Frank, for all his quiet ways, always manages to elbow his way into a conversation and I explained that, whilst not outstandingly handsome or heroic, it would be the very ordinariness and vulnerability of Frank that would reach out to people when he is finally introduced to the world. Hardly drawing breath, I waxed lyrical on the trials of a writer, the discipline you need, the dexterity, insight and confidence required to handle your characters and the organisational ability to bring the thousands of words scattered in a dozen files and scraps of paper into a coherent and believable story. By the end of my spiel I think Frank was as real to him as was the Pod and he would have drawn up another chair for him if we'd had one.

'But writing is a solitary existence,' he observed. Yes, I thought, it can bring you close to madness. 'So Carol, what makes a good team player? I'd like a short one or two sentence answer on this one please.' He smiled and for that I was grateful because underneath my cheery exterior I felt I had dug a big enough hole for me and Frank and all the people in Frank's story to fall into. I kept the answer short and dredged up what I considered were modern 'buzz words' to illustrate that Seb and Eddie would be missing out on a valuable team player if they turned their backs on me.

'Well, we're done now,' he said, mulling over the last page. 'I've got you down on this list as a driver.'

'Really?'

'You sound surprised.' He was too much of a gentleman to say there was a note of disappointment in my voice.

'No.' I wasn't brave enough to ask if there were any other roles in the Transport Team going spare because I still harboured the meeting and greeting idea even if it was only handing over car keys with flair or perhaps working in a transport nerve centre with a large map and board and moving plastic flags along in Churchillian War Bunker style.

'So you'd still like to be considered for the post?'

'Oh, yes. Actually you've reminded me that I once worked for a car hire firm.'

'You did?'

'In the summer of 1976. It was a sizzler that year.'

I took another sip of water and watched him working back through the form with his pen. If he'd asked I could have told him about my boss, Liz, whose claims to fame were that she had come up north to escape from Balham, had had the sweat glands in her armpits removed and was having a torrid romance with Ken the mechanic and car wash man who she referred to as her bit of rough. I knew not what had prompted her departure from Balham, why she thought her sweat glands were a problem and whether their removal came before or after Ken but decided it could make a good short story sometime. And if my fellow inhabitant of Pod five had shown the least bit of interest I could have told him of Lesley, a lackey under Liz like me, who, despite the blistering heat, invested heavily in self tanning creams and on one hot and sticky minibus journey to Manchester to collect cars the sun tan ran into her white blouse. It was an embarrassment the rest of us were too polite to mention. The white blouse came with the uniform and as my interviewer signed off the last page I wondered if it was worth discussing with him my phobia of having to wear a uniform. It had started at school and was reinforced by the blue, red and white toy soldier creation of the car hire company. The designer had heaped insult on injury with the addition of gold buttons and wide epaulettes and in my book should have done time for it.

'We're finished.'

'That's good. What happens next?'

'You'll get an email but don't worry if you don't hear from us for a while, there's another ninety thousand interviews to be done!'

'You'll be kept busy then?'

He laughed and reminded me to write my name and a comment on the white board in the other room because all the boards were going to be kept for posterity.

And that was that. Interview over. I can't remember what I wrote on the white board or even if I was capable at that point of doing joined up handwriting but I would guess it was something positive even though the words didn't reflect the way I felt. For, as always, I had no sooner stepped out of the Pod and shaken hands with my inquisitor than I was revisiting what had been said, what I could have said and what would have been better left unsaid.

'How did you get on?' asked Sophie, searching my flushed face for an answer.

'Don't ask! I just want to forget it,' I marched off from my most staunch supporter to join yet another queue for the toilets, a cruel reminder that the bladder needs emptying more often as you get older.

CHAPTER 3

I Have a Dream

Four months after the interview I received a letter welcoming me into the Games Makers fold and once the decorations for Christmas 2011 were safely tucked away I am invited to Wembley Arena.

'What do you think Orientation Training is?' I asked Rog as we performed the evening dishwashing ritual.

'Haven't a clue.'

'I've only ever heard of Orienteering.'

'That's cross country with a map.'

He busied himself emptying the contents of the pedal bin. I wiped over the worktops and thought about the girl who had had the nerve to join our school in the midst of our secondary education. She was tall and bronzed with long blonde hair and handsomely proportioned in the bust department; intelligent too, joining the cohort of those, unlike me, destined for university. And her athleticism was beyond parallel; one look at her bulbous calf muscles would have the other side's hockey team quivering in their school minibus seats. There was none to match her performance on the pitch or, on account of her well developed arm muscles, her fabulous serves on the tennis court. But it was on the Orienteering trips to Wales that she apparently excelled herself. It was only hearsay of course because neither I nor any of my right thinking friends would ever have contemplated a weekend away in a canoe and a bivouac led by the boys' school's games teacher who, to use one of my mother's expressions, had eyes too close together for comfort. 'The Amazonian' outperformed the girls, boys and man alike, the heroine of the hour, the sort much reviled by a crabby green eyed monster like me who gave her that nickname.

I stood gently squeezing the moisture from my J Cloth whilst Rog rooted in the cupboard under the sink for a new pedal bin bag and wondered what she looked like thirty five years on. I reckoned she'd be the sort to volunteer and would have answered all the sporty questions much more effectively than I had. They'd likely have her down as a team leader but I took solace from the fact that I'd got through the interview without a clenched calf muscle or tensed bicep to speak of and glad too that I had got through the checks on my driving record by AA Drive Tech.

Rog straightened up and did his usual puffing and sighing at not being able to open the bag. I snatched it away. He squirmed in distaste as I dampened my thumb and forefinger on my tongue and rubbed the bag between them to open it. 'I wish you wouldn't do that. It's so unhygienic.'

'But Wembley Arena is pretty big. Do you reckon they'll have us doing all sorts of exercises?'

'I think you're reading much more into this than you need to.'

'I always do, don't I?'

The second Saturday of February arrived. Above ground it was the coldest day of the winter with a forecast of snow later on. Below ground, as the train whooshed out of London Bridge Tube Station, I was regretting my decision to wear a thermal vest, thick woolly jumper, leggings, jeans and coat lined with synthetic fur. My rosy cheeks were mirrored in the face of a little boy who, restrained in a thick puffa jacket in a pushchair, was getting agitated with his gloves and hat. I smiled in sympathy at him, acknowledging his frustration that his mum and dad had taken their wool beanies off. A man in buttoned up crombie and trilby got on, his lady companion in floor length black coat and Cossack hat, clearly not the sort to be on their way to a Games Makers event. I smiled inwardly. I was being premature for a bit of Games Makers spotting as the train was going in completely the other direction to Wembley because I was heading for the 02 to buy some tickets. But where were the two uber large men in jeans and short sleeved football shirts, who were sitting directly opposite me going to?

One man was sitting with his hands on his knees, the other with his hands resting on his distended stomach. Their voices drowned out those of fellow travellers and yet I found it rather touching that the bigger of the two admitted that he had got up at five o'clock and had a shower because he'd been looking forward to this day all week and couldn't sleep. And, unlike his companion, he'd breakfasted well on a long list of foods. I found it less touching when he started excavating the wax in his ears and picking at the dandruff in his lifeless hair, my pedal bin bag opening technique paling into insignificance against his nibbling at his finger nail to get a taste of each. His finger pickings had whetted his appetite because he suspended mining operations to announce that he'd buy the chips when they got to West Ham. 'The burger as well, if you want.'

'Alright then, I'll buy the programme,' countered his bald companion whose bloated face was smeared with foundation that didn't cover or match his complexion. It must have been my early morning raising that put me in an even more emotional frame of mind than usual because I found this beefy bloke's use of makeup touching too; a device to hide whatever it was that had ravaged his skin.

'We'll be there any minute,' said the bald one.

'Bermondsey?' replied ear picker extraordinaire.

'Yeah and they won't be expecting to see us will they?'

'How many do you think there'll be there?'

'Dunno.' The makeup artist started limbering up. Maternal sympathy quickly turned to abject antipathy. I scrabbled in my bag for the handy little Tube map that I always carried. I focused on the Jubilee Line and there it was, Bermondsey. Bermondsey; it was the next stop.

'What the fuck?' shouted the one with the predilection for scoffing dry skin as the train juddered to a halt. The shock of it had me making eye contact with the bald one. 'No-one wants to sit with us,' he laughed. My neighbours had fled, were huddled further along the carriage, the young couple now paying due attention to their toddler in the pushchair.

'Why's that?'

'Cos of you I 'spect.'

His mate shrugged and flicked a piece of dandruff in my direction. The heat from my clothes was overwhelming but then the train woke up and as it hurtled along I maintained the staring into nothingness pose of the middle aged woman and got my feet in the right position to spring up and alight before the Bermondsey boys got on.

Adverts flickered past the carriage windows as the train rattled into the station, the pull of the train's brakes accentuated the risk of standing up before the train stopped, heightened my fear of tripping over the football fan's large trainers or toppling into one of them. In turn they craned their necks and peered past me to see who was waiting on the platform.

'There's no one there,' said the one with the face foundation. It was hard to tell if the tremor in his voice signified disappointment or relief. His mate got up, his hulk all but filling the space between the opened doors as he hung on to the overhead rail. I looked down the compartment where the couple were performing the delicate operation of getting the pushchair off the train. There was nothing for it but to sit tight until I reached my destination.

The doors closed. We sped out of the station. 'Too early for 'em, you think?' asked the hulk as he pulled up his jeans, scratched his arse, and pulled down his shirt.

'Could be.'

'I don't half need the toilet.'

'You'll have to wait.'

'I don't think I can.' He looked around the carriage.

'Sit down!'

And like a lamb the hulk did and, as if the previous conversation hadn't taken place, they compared notes as to what time each of them got up, what they had for breakfast and what they were going to do. The hulk wiped the back of his hand across his mouth as if he had just wolfed a burger down and I got off the train at North Greenwich whilst they discussed the sauce and who should pay for two cups of tea. That was the limit of their discourse, the extent of their aggression, the source of my unwarranted concern and judgmentalism at just past ten.

I achieved what I set out to do at the 02, the cold propelling me back like a bullet to the Jubilee Line. Twelve stops later I stood in West Hampstead, for no other reason than I had never been there before and I had plenty of time to kill. I walked up one side of the main street and down the other and, having gone with the preconceived idea that it was a fairly affluent area, was surprised at the number of charity shops. Bulked up in all my clothes and not wanting to steam my glasses up each and every time I went in to a shop, I fought off the temptation to add to my growing collection of retro cookware.

I resisted too the lure of joining the newspaper reading brigade who had now come out in force to occupy the establishments offering Eggs Benedict and Macchiato coffee. Instead I stepped into a caff, greeted by the smell of fry- ups and a man with coffee froth on his beard who muttered about the stream of cold air that came in every time someone opened the door. An old lady with a cut on her nose was huddled at a table near the counter. I assumed they were both regulars, as were most of the customers from the playful banter and requests for 'the usual' that I heard as I took a front of house seat near the plate glass window.

An omelette and chips and a steaming mug of builder's tea did me as I watched the theatre of street life; all manner of people, hunched against the weather, passed along the pavement, their rate of progress significantly quicker than the drivers of the Porsches and Mercedes inching by. I made up stories about where they were coming from, where they were going and a sad tale too about the old woman with the cut on her nose who hobbled to the cafe door, her scarf bandaged round her head in the way that Mum always said would calm a toothache down. And it was a good job the man who came and sat at the next table to me couldn't read the chapter of his life I'd invented on account of his beefy countenance and the weekend suitcase by his side. The 'past' he was running from, the 'future' he was travelling to was made all the more interesting by the after shave he'd doused himself in and the way he meticulously mopped his lips and frantically wiped the toast crumbs off his fingers with a white paper serviette. Without a shadow of a doubt, the meal was a preparation for something.

'Anything else?' The chirpy waitress asked as she took my empty plate away. 'Another cup of tea?'

'No thanks. I'd better be going.' In the narrow aisle I went into battle with my coat to get it back on. Whilst window gazing and weaving stories, the Saturday morning haven for mainly grey and shaven-headed men had filled up. To the mutters of the bearded man, I left. It was onwards and upwards to Wembley.

The train to Wembley was a different kettle of fish altogether, stuffed as it was with people talking about Games Makerey things that I personally thought ought to be kept private. Emerging from the station I stopped to draw breath, staggered by the crowds on the walkway to the Arena. I joined the masses, kept my own counsel whilst those around me struck up conversations mainly about the weather. Turning the corner, a random man stopped me.

'Do you want accommodation for the Games?'

'Possibly!'

'Take this then.' He pressed a leaflet into my hand and was gone.

'Let's see your ticket. Ok, North East Block.' A steward pointed towards a line of people which snaked up and down, round and round. I beheld a political ad of years gone, a vision of an interminable dole queue and yet we were all volunteers prepared to shuffle along like penguins as the cold pinched our faces. My mood descended into matte grey and apart from establishing that the young man in the woolly hat next to me came from the Midlands and his employers were prepared to pay for his accommodation in London for the duration, I switched off from all communication as did he when he tuned into his iPod. But others didn't, shrill icicles of conversation stabbed me in the back, all bluster and bravado that my frostbitten toes could only shuffle away from.

Inside, there were more stewards than you could shake a stick at, eager to make sure you had a Games Makers Workbook. It was all so in your face, as was the bizarre experience I had at the drinks outlet. It was an experience confusing enough to live through let alone relate except to say that I finally staggered into the Arena with a large free cup of coffee and two compensatory bars of my favourite chocolate and only began to feel faintly human again when settled in my allocated seat.

The enthusiasm that I had grudgingly picked up on outside was already replicated twenty fold. I made no overtures to anyone but listened and observed as other volunteers arrived with many appearing to already know each other. My ears pricked up even further at one woman's disclosure to the man at the end of my row that as a driver she was going to be based at Park Lane and knew all her dates. If she knew this then why didn't I? Was the Olympic Committee toying with my good nature, treating me as a mere reserve? Had I endured Arctic conditions only to sit on the sidelines and listen to others talk about their duties and shift patterns? And from what I could make out, volunteers had travelled from far and wide so come the day come the hour what did they know about parking and accommodation that I didn't?

To shut out the torment I bit into my first bar of chocolate and read through the leaflet the mystery man had given me. It wasn't the golden ticket to a comfortable discounted hotel room or details of a social network whereby Games Makers would be offered a bed for a night or fifteen. No, it was a camping company offering tents in the grounds of schools with full use of toilets and showers. I chuckled, thinking of me silhouetted against canvas as I struggled to get into a sleeping bag. I chortled at the thought of me at three o'clock in the morning tip toeing over the guy ropes of other tents with a torch to find a cracked toilet seat to sit on.

Whilst I sat contemplating the attractions or otherwise of sitting round a campfire with other jolly Games Makers, the Arena was filling up. It was rumoured that there were eight thousand, perhaps ten, packed in that afternoon and the buzz from the crowd and the evangelistic zeal demonstrated by those that orchestrated and took part in the event would have made the most ardent of revivalists green with envy.

The stage was set, with wide video screens suspended high above it and rousing music booming from the speakers. We held Games Makers Workbooks, our bibles, in our hands and the audience's emotions rippled and writhed with anticipation as to whether the man himself was going to come and walk among us.

It was a hard pill to swallow but we had to accept that Seb couldn't be with us in bodily form that day. He sent us a message via the wide screen, his mellow yet authoritative voice assuring us we were in his thoughts that he was with us in spirit. But we were not to feel abandoned for he had entrusted each and every one of us into the care of his silver haired disciple, the neat and perfectly formed Jonathan Edwards whose casual style and jumper put me in mind of Val Doonican. And just as Val Doonican could have persuaded Mum to do almost anything from his rocking chair, so was the calm and relaxed manner of Jonathan, speaking from his comfy sofa, enough to open up my heart to the message he had been sent to impart.

Truth be told, our Jonathan was preaching to the converted, the case for belief in the London 2012 workforce successfully playing host to the world was convincing enough in its own right but the thing with messages and beliefs is that you have to keep repeating them so that they become a way of life. Better still, embody them in a set of guidelines and with the right kind of nurture the believers will uphold the vision no matter what.

Nurture came in the shape of Eddie Izzard. He arrived to rapturous applause, as cool in real life as he was on the telly but when the camera zoomed in for a close up shot on the wide screen, his black T shirt was shown up to be a bit ragged round the neck and, to my mind, had been subjected to too much washing powder for whites as opposed to a colour safe one. Fashion faux pas or not, his opening quips were entertaining and, without question, his mission was to educate, inform, and to post the ambition of London's Organising Committee of the Olympic Games to the mast.

That ambition was for the London 2012 workforce to prove to the world what exceptional hosts we could be and to achieve that he urged us to follow our hosting actions. Three words (why is it always three little words?), I DO ACT, would see us through. With the backup of pre recorded scenarios and the waters of his comic style washing over us we repeated out loud the words he and Jonathan, his fellow disciple, so wanted to hear; **Inspirational** we shouted. **Distinctive, Open,** we bellowed, **Alert, Consistent** and

Part of a Team we roared. The message had struck home and he left to clapping and cheering and many would have followed him out into the street to whip up support for the cause.

We watched a presentation on the uniform, what it consisted of and how the colours had been chosen. As I recall, the red had something to do with London buses, Beefeaters and post boxes whilst purple was connected with royalty. A lady from the leading catering sponsor had a cosy sofa chat with Jonathan about the amount of food it was estimated would be needed at the Olympic Park. I had half a mind to ask her to come down and do some market research with the lady sitting to the left of me who, having grunted a hello at me when she first arrived, spent the first hour stuffing crisps and chocolate in her mouth like there was no tomorrow, splattered herself with cream from her muffin then fell through the back of her seat and spilt coffee everywhere.

Jonathan invited us to turn to our neighbour and introduce ourselves. Because of all her gobbling I shamefully ignored the lady to my left and turned to the young woman on my right. I shook hands with the stunning looking student who said her Games Makers role was as a runner, ferrying the results of Badminton matches to the press office.

'I've never got the hang of this Mexican waving,' I admitted in the break. 'And what with all my stuff,' I puffed. So we gave up trying to synchronise with the masses and took to chatting and my second bar of chocolate.

'If you're in your third year, I suppose you've got to do a dissertation?'

'Yes.' Her eyes lit up as she explained that she was shortly to fly out to the deep south of America to interview one of the last remaining leading white female champions of the black civil rights movement.

'I can remember when Martin Luther King was shot. I have a dream and all that.'

'It's going to be awesome but I've got to submit the paper earlier than I expected because the student accommodation and facilities of my university are needed for the Games.'

'They can't do that!'

'Apparently they can but I'm so privileged to be able to get the opportunity and the Olympics are going to be awesome too.'

'You're a credit, do you know that?' I'd embarrassed her, for that I felt sorry, but it had to be said.

There followed a toe curling and cringing dramatic piece in which two actors played the role of news readers reporting on an imaginary 'typical day' in the life of a Games Makers. The cameras panned in on the accreditation card hung on the back of Ms. Imaginary's door so that she wouldn't forget it because, lesson one for all of us, if she did she would be denied access. Luckily she remembered it and we followed her walking down the street smiling at everyone and, on the Tube, displaying a radiant friendliness that would, in normal circumstances, be a huge cause for concern amongst her fellow passengers. I have no recollection what her duties were when she got to her destination venue and was welcomed by an equally cheery band of Games Makers because I was having doubts, serious doubts that I could emulate her. It was easy to get carried away in the feverish atmosphere of the Arena, to marvel at the passion to learn and to serve of the young lady in the next seat, but would the message sustain me in the weeks and months ahead until the day when the wearing of my uniform would declare who I was and what I stood for?

As one would expect, the afternoon finished on a high note, in gospel mode with singing and clapping. Inspired and empowered we shuffled outside. Soft flurries of snow fell as I joined the slow moving ice floe of thousands making for the Station. We crowded onto the trains, brandishing our Workbooks (our 'bibles') at bewildered passengers.

By the time I got back to the car in Orpington it was snowing hard. I rang Rog who said he had the fire going.

'And I've got a riveting DVD in my Workbook to watch.'

'What?'

'No matter.'

'Just drive carefully and get home please.'

I was shattered, the prospect of the journey almost too much to bear. But bear it I had to and by the time the tyres made tracks in the snowy white blanket that lay across our garden and drive

I had come to a conclusion about the events I had replayed in my head. It hadn't been Jonathan's scripted calm words, Eddie's fun presentation, the Mexican waves or rousing closing songs that had impressed me. It was the humbling thought that, whilst my student neighbour was preparing to travel to the southern USA to meet a woman who had not been afraid to stand up for what she believed in, I fretted about wearing a red and purple uniform.

CHAPTER 4

Online Assessment

The snow came, the snow went and so did my intention to read every jot and tittle of the Workbook and watch the DVD that came with it. There seemed no point if, as I gathered from my Wembley eavesdropping, everyone else was already established whereas I was possibly sort of, maybe, part of something. It had been on a par with everyone talking about a party that I hadn't been invited to. I needn't have been so prickly because it wasn't long after Orientation that my Inbox flashed up with an email from HQ inviting me to complete an online driving assessment.

The assessment was in four sections, each section to be completed in one session but not necessarily all four sections at the same time. From their very description I sussed that two of them would be along the lines of the theory and hazard perception tests that the children had had to do for their Driving Tests. It was a far cry from when I'd had driving lessons in a Morris 1100 with a creepy instructor who flashed pictures from Health and Efficiency magazine at me as we headed out a few miles to find a decent set of traffic lights. It was a far cry too from my driving test when I was asked what I would do if I drove through water.

'Check the engine to see if it's wet,' I had innocently replied. 'Pillock' I was heard to say when I came away with a notice of failure and the Examiner's tip that hand signals worked wonders when you wanted to dry your nails. The second examiner had had no option but to pass me; the alternative was death because I was in such a temper. But nigh on forty years on, the spiky edges of that volatile temperament had been polished and smoothed, but not the fear of failure.

I invested in an up to date Theory Test DVD and played it on the computer much to the initial bewilderment of Richard the decorator who had the misfortune to be working in the living room at the time.

'Richard, what do you think the braking distance is if you are travelling at forty miles?' I shouted into him from the study.

'Did you call?' He ambled in with rather fetching speckles of paint in his hair.

'I need to know what the distances are for forty and sixty miles an hour.'

He obliged with the answer and I summarily dismissed him with the promise of a cup of tea.

'Richard, are you up the ladder?'

'No.'

'Can you come in here a minute please and tell me what you think this road sign means. I've never seen one like it before.'

He came up with the answer to that too. 'I've got the practice hazard tests to do now.' I waved my hands in that jittery jelly way that I find so irritating when young minor celebrities do it on the telly.

'What's that then?' At first I thought he was humouring me, but then I realised that even though he was in his thirties it was unlikely he would have done anything like this for his test.

'Well, you play the film and it's shot as if you are behind the wheel of a moving car and you have to click the mouse when you see a hazard.'

'I don't think I can help with that then.'

'No, you probably can't.' Not that I hadn't been turning it over in my mind to let a more capable soul, say Sophie, sort the whole kit and caboodle for me. It was unlikely she would agree to such a dishonourable thing anyway. But would it still be classed as cheating if I kept control of the keyboard and let Richard's eyes do the hazard spotting? No, it would be of no benefit to me whatsoever, the time delay between his telling me to click and me striking the key would be too great.

'I'll get back to work, then, shall I?'

'Uh hum. I'll be out in a minute.'

My hand shook, perspiration tickled my armpits. No flying bird or waving blade of grass in the hedgerow was immune from being perceived as a potential hazard, whereas I blindly disregarded tractors reversing across dual carriageways and the all too obvious brake lights of the vehicle in front. Richard's paper hanging brush swished all morning whilst I was busy watching for pedestrians emerging from behind parked cars and there was always a cyclist or a woman pushing a buggy on a deserted country road. The study air was blue with tuts and curses as I consistently got a low score. When I emerged at lunchtime, Richard had taken refuge in his van but I had no appetite for food or drink. I swore again, suddenly remembering what Sophie had once said that the test would only recognise two or three hazards per scene and would penalise you for guessing. I took a deep breath, closed the study door behind me and sat square on with my chin pointing at the computer. I was damned if I was going to be beaten by a machine.

Throughout the afternoon my scores began to rise; fifteen out of twenty, nineteen out of twenty then, Bingo, a full house and I hurried into the living room, waving my arms like an Olympian athlete.

'Richard, I did it!'

He was clearing up the dust sheets. 'I'll be off in a minute.'

'Oh I'm sorry. I've been neglecting you.'

After spending as much time as either of the children had done in preparation for their real live tests and having deprived Richard of refreshment you'd have thought I would have been eager to get back in and zip through all four sections of the assessment and submit it. Not a bit of it. Days came, weeks went. My Inbox took the strain of the reminders that the assessment deadline was approaching.

'I bet it won't take long and the longer you put it off the worse it will get,' said Rog after a slurp of wine, the taste made all the more special because it was a Friday evening.

'I know!'

'You've got all weekend. You could space them out, one tomorrow morning, one after lunch…'

'I know!'

I left it till the grey drizzly Sunday afternoon when Rog was out in the garden doing whatever it is that gardeners do on dark, damp days. The Driving History section was no problem with no onus that I could see for me to disclose the two long spent speeding convictions I had incurred in my driving career. The Theory test; came up with a pass. Hazard Perception? Let's put it this way, I got through. Then it came to crunch time, the fourth and final section and Roger, bringing with him a chilly aura and earthy smell, came into the study and looked over my shoulder.

'Nearly finished?'

'No. Look, can't you see I've got to answer all these questions.'

Question; after two hours driving should you stop at the nearest pub and down a glass of vodka? (Not a real question but you get the gist.) Please enter whether you agree or disagree, with ONE being you strongly disagree and TEN being you strongly agree.

'Standard Isometric tests, to test your aptitude and attitude. Just put the first thing that comes into your head, your first instincts are usually right. I'm going for a bath.'

At first I was bold, taking Roger's advice. I moderately to strongly disagreed that I wouldn't take a rest after two hours driving because, come on, I had driven much further than that in a stretch on our trips down West. And I strongly disagreed that after two hours I needed to shake my limbs. Who were these people? If everyone did that at the side of the A303 how many more precious hours would be added to the journey to Cornwall?

Then boldness left me just like the water I could hear draining out of Roger's bathtub, my muddled mind in a lather over the *would's* and *wouldn't's* and *coulds* and *couldn'ts*. And into the soapy mix was the dawning realisation that all the preceding questions had focused upon a magical two hour time frame. Even now as I recount the experience my head is beginning to pound, my face getting hot and flushed. I relive my state of indecision, the way my finger trembled over the mouse like a kestrel, waiting for the right moment to go in for the kill on the sliding scale that came up on the screen after every question. And indecision led to more uncertainty because I began to think that the blighters were switching and swapping the numbers so that sometimes number One became agree and number Ten morphed into disagrees.

Freshly scrubbed and munching on pre Sunday roast peanuts, a relaxed and docile Roger wandered in.

'Don't spend too much time thinking about the answers, Carol. There's no right or wrong answer.'

'Are you trying to be funny?'

'No. Simply trying to help'

'Well don't!'

I turned back to the screen. I was like a car out of control, the last few questions seen through watery eyes as I careered through ones and fives and twos and tens relating to my views on speed, road positioning and courtesy to others. I slammed the mouse down and pressed 'submit.'

By some wizardry my final scoring was translated into differently coloured boxes reaching up like skyscrapers. Each and everyone had crossed a line which I took to be the margin of safe and acceptable driving. The only perception that Lord Coe and his aides could possibly have of me was as of a road rage girl racer. There was a written analysis and commentary with suggestions on how to improve.

'I can't bear to read it.'

'It's not all that bad,' said Rog quietly. 'They are just giving you tips.'

I reverted to hot tempered teenage type, the one who blamed her mother for misplacing her licence then, without apology, left her aghast when she shot off in a blind fury for her second driving test. Hot tempered and angry at the world I clicked the exit button and the screen went blank.

CHAPTER 5

Dirk and the Boys

I had to eat humble pie in front of Roger when the invitation arrived for me to attend a Role Specific training day. Having got through to this stage I thought I'd better study my bible, the Workbook they had dished out at Orientation Training. It was split into three sections; My Orientation, My Role and My Memories. The sections were designed to mirror our progression through the training and held out the promise of additional handouts during the face to face training sessions. In a pocket at the back there was a Games Makers CD which contained our e-learning, a way of refreshing the training prior to the first shift. Clearly presented with sharp blocks of pink and blue colours, various icons flagged up training purpose, learning objectives, interesting facts, important information and boxes to make notes in regarding exercises we would be required to do. I read the book from cover to cover, anxious that I would be able to retain the information, troubled that I would be able to separate the do's and don'ts when it came to putting them into practice.

Then the emails started, referring time and again to skills modules with training anticipated to last from eight a.m. till six p.m. It sounded a bit more involved than what I had come to expect from overpriced courses in stuffy hotel meeting rooms in my former life. Back then it had been largely a matter of a speaker reading through the contents of his/her notes with a power point thingamajig overhead, augmented by filter coffee, and small talk with boffins and buffoons in the breaks with the prospect of a doze in the after lunch graveyard slot.

Such was the apprehension I felt about the training day, I felt compelled to consult with a friend who inhabits the world of 'getting people up to speed.' As is my usual wont, I left it till the night before the training day to make the call, applying a light yet business like touch to my concerns at what ten hours of training might consist of.

'They do like their acronyms,' I tittered over the phone, recalling Eddie Izzard's T shirt and stunning rendition of I DO ACT at the earlier Orientation day. 'I'd better not divulge it, Lynda, or the other ones I've picked up on in the Workbook like H.O.T because they relate to security.'

'A valid training technique.' I imagined Lynda at the end of the phone with her signature professional look on her face

'I've been mugging up the best I can. Sophie's been great, she's been helping me learn the alphabet in sign language.'

'A very useful tool, Carol, another one to add to the whole new skill set you look to be acquiring.'

'Am I?'

'Of course you are.'

'If only I'd been as conscientious about learning when I was at school !' I laughed. 'So what do you think they're likely to make us do?' Lynda came up with a number of tests that might be used.

'Isometric?'

'Exactly, Carol. You've got the idea.'

'Thought so. I had some of that in my online assessment.' Not that I would have known if Rog hadn't told me and I thought better of mentioning the paddy I had had over it.

'They may put you into groups to discuss particular scenarios.'

'That means I'll either come over all dumbstruck or rabbit on and appear as if I'm taking over.'

'You will have to achieve the right balance of participation because they might film the group to see who is coming out the natural leader.'

'You're joking!'

'It's a method of assessing those with potential.'

Lynda was patient and kind, her vocabulary of buzzwords impressive. In the course of an hour plus so many ideas, so many scenarios and possible role plays had been bandied about I felt that she and I could set up in business delivering our own training packages. But blue sky thinking, acronymic strategies and in house packages didn't make for a restful sleep.

Whilst Roger slept the sleep of the innocent I lay awake looking at the ceiling, racking my brains as to what the letters A.E.I. stood for in relation to the decision making model they advocated regarding the boundaries of responsibility. In relation to suspicious activity within my venue would I think to apply the triple A test of *Access, Appearance, Avoidance* when coming upon a suspicious character? Would I be asked questions on diversity and inclusion? How would I convince them that Hapless from Hastings could contribute towards delivering a safe and sustainable games? Rog's feet shuffled under the sheet, he turned over and pulled the duvet up round his shoulder. Not wanting to disturb him I kept rigid and still, because he was going to have to get up an hour earlier than usual to take me to the train station. For me, he had already put up with the debate on what to wear to the interview, a lengthy portrayal of what occurred at orientation training and my histrionics re the online assessment. As the first birdsong of the day made its welcome entrance through the open bedroom window, I realised that I had made a hurdle of everything so far in the process. Had I simply been a Peter crying wolf and was the Role Specific going to be the actual testing time? I turned my head. The bloodshot red digital numbers on the clock told me the alarm would soon be ringing and Act, Escalate and Inform would become as much a reality in our household as in any Olympic venue.

Despite the anguished night, I travelled up to London on the train, confident in the knowledge that my chat with Lynda had prepared me for anything. I alighted the DLR at Custom House, went over the bridge and along the walkway past the main doors into Excel, then down the ramp. The doors to Fleet Depot on my left were wide open, the waters to my right lapping gently against the dock.

Presenting for registration it was clear that there had been some re-jigging of the premises. Where once there had been blue foam sofas in the waiting area for interviews, these were now replaced by an altogether more business like row of desks and computers.

The room where once I had been held spellbound by Eddie was blocked off by a plasterboard wall and door, behind which the admin staff worked. I was directed to the right and up some steps. Where once the pods and white board on which I had written my name had been there was one long room where row upon row of chairs were set up.

The main block of seating was already quite full and so that I could at least see the speaker's lips move and make out what was being said, I made my way towards the front row of the second block. After our trips to Disney where we found the Americans maniacal over filling seats up in strict rotation, I could see no point in leaving a seat between myself and the only person in that row and, in my opinion, a man with glasses on a chain round his neck, light chinos and rubber clogs is someone of interest. Age? Certainly in his fifties and if the tummy straining at the buttons of his open necked short sleeved shirt was anything to go by, quite possibly having tipped over into his sixties. It wasn't long before Robin and I were soon joined by Merv who left a respectable gap of one seat between me and him and was dressed in striped polo shirt tucked into the middle age expanding waistband of his jeans. What a contrast; Robin cool and confident, Merv cocky and excitably chattering on about his journey and nailing his intention to get away promptly later on to meet his son for a drink.

As the ranks swelled behind us I got the first inkling that, along with the three of us, very few of the volunteers had actually opted to become drivers at Fleet Depot Excel.

'It reminds me,' I said, chuckling and looking from side to side at Robin and Merv, 'of what my father used to say.'

'What was that?' asked Merv, looking at his sports watch.

'In the Army they'd ask you what you were good at. You might be good at cooking but, perversely, instead of putting you in the Catering Corps they'd put you into the Signals or vice versa.'

'I think your father was right,' said Robin. 'I thought I was going to be one of the selected few involved in handing out the medals at the ceremonies. I have all the knowledge and background for it.' From his sullen face I surmised it had taken some while for him to get over that particular rejection.

'And as much as I'm an experienced driver, there's any number of other duties I'd be good at,' countered Merv, his explanation as to why this should be so interrupted by the arrival of the first enthusiastic speaker who introduced the main personnel who made up the management structure at the Depot. Then there was information on who made up the Olympic family and how their transport needs would be catered for. The number of cars allocated to the individual delegations was preordained by the governing body. The T1 drivers, driving the BMW five series, would be allocated to one specific client throughout. By a show of hands the T2's made up the majority and would be assigned to delegates associated with their specific sport. The T3's would operate on a pre booking, first come first served basis across the board of the 'family'. Poor Robin confided that, as well as wanting to be a medal presenter, he had harboured aspirations of being a T1 but had ended up a T2 like me whereas Merv boasted that he was of a more flexible disposition and could well handle his duties as a come hither, go anywhere T3.

We had a talk on guest protocol, the speaker identifying the rear seat behind the front passenger as being the seat of honour and that we should be polite and respectful and not go in for inane chatter and intrusive questions of our clients. There would be some hope of that with Merv because, along with his incessant fidgeting, he had a whispered quip or comment to make on everything from the thorny issue of what to do if presented with a gift of a Cartier watch from a client to the matter of dealing with questions from the Press. Merv had a view on everything but fell quiet when it came to security. The proposed scale of the security operation gave me great comfort because a terrorist attack had been put forward by members of family and friends as a reason against me continuing as a volunteer. Merv took a serious interest in how tight the restrictions were going to be on access to prescribed places, even down to the finest detail that we were weren't to fill our water bottles up before going through the Vehicle Screening Area but should wait to quench our thirst till we were in the venue. I could have taken his sober countenance as a sign of malice intent but for the fact that he didn't fit the triple

A test that I had been repeating to myself at three a.m. that morning. The day wasn't turning out as Lynda and I had prepared for. Indeed, nothing could have prepared me for the bombardment of information or for the showering of encouragement and gratitude heaped upon us for being such a fine bunch of people for volunteering. The responsibility rested on our shoulders to get our technical delegate to the right place at the right time and, in between, to smile and oblige without question if, after their sporting duties, they wanted to go on a little shopping spree to Harrods or visit a historical site. We were entrusted with keeping them happy but had to obey the laws of the land and never ever put our hand in our pocket to pay parking charges. From the murmurs in the audience it was clear that the proposition that we were totally at the technical delegate's disposal came as a surprise. Equally, it seemed that the possibility of having to transport children hadn't crossed everyone's minds, including mine.

'My God, do we have to take children in the car? I don't want to have to deal with children and car seats,' muttered Robin.

'What if they are travel sick?' I whispered. 'I don't do sick.'

'Nor do I,' Robin added with vehemence. 'It would have to be either me or them being picked up by another driver.'

'They won't have time to be sick when I drive them,' said Merv, returning to fidget and squirm as much as a child would do when it wanted the toilet.

'Ok,' said the speaker cheerily. 'Before we all have a well earned break, here's a little test for you all. I want you to turn to your neighbour and spell out your name in sign language.' Much merriment broke out in the room.

'Seeing as there's just the three of us, I'll go first shall I?' suggested Merv.

'But we know your name,' said Robin. It put Merv off his stride because he asked us to wait a moment while he turned away to have a quick practice and I, wanting to do Sophie's tuition justice, frantically thought through the letters of my name in my head.

Left to his hand puppetry and with the room humming with noise which clearly defeated the whole object of the exercise,

Merv didn't pick up on Robin's avowed intent not to play the current game.

'I'm not bothering with all that. How many hearing impaired delegates are we likely to have? And if we do they will have assistants or someone else with them to help out.' Robin's words made perfect sense but I was torn between the reasonableness and logic of his argument, the fact that as conscientious Games Makers we were meant to have leant the contents of the Workbook and, ridiculous as it sounds, I felt a bit sorry for Merv earnestly trying his best. I was on the verge of a diplomatic counter argument that we might have occasion to meet a hard of hearing member of the public requiring assistance when Merv turned towards me. Like a child learning to read I spelt each letter of his name out. Then he eagerly looked at me, waiting to spell-check my efforts but with Robin looking on I bottled out, feigned a sneeze coming on and reached for a tissue in my bag. When I surfaced Robin was casually making his way to the canteen where the coffees were being served and Merv was nowhere in sight.

Robin didn't do children and I wasn't prepared to do vomit and, after coffee, Merv declared that he didn't do Sat Navs.

'They can't make you use them, you know,' he said, whilst we were lining up on our way out of the rear exit doors to the car park to familiarise ourselves with the cars. A cordon of smiling staff ushered us across a service road under Excel into a small, gloomy, cold car park area where twelve or so BMW's were parked, some with their doors open, some throbbing, some still. Where Merv wandered off to I couldn't tell for I was lumped in with a group of three other women to undertake some instruction given by our vehicle buddies, a man and a woman in high visibility jackets. It was at that point that I began to consider Lynda's proposition of the night before, that there might be cameras trained on us to establish the alpha person in our groups.

I wouldn't be able to recognise two of the women from Adam now, all three of us quiet and pasty faced in the gloom as if going to our own executions. The fourth, Isabella, made up for our sobriety. Tall, long faced and decidedly plumy mouthed she twittered on as our vehicle buddies walked and talked us round the car.

'How do we change the tyre if it blows out?' she asked.

'It won't.' said the man.

'It might,' she came back at him.

'It should run for fifty miles before it needs changing.'

'And am I responsible for checking the water and oil?'

'No. A warning light would come on if there was a problem but there won't be.'

'How can you be sure of that?'

Her third degree became frankly irritating especially as she kept either pushing in front or whizzing ahead to shout out another question before the poor buddies had had time to answer the preceding one. By the looks on the other women's faces they were as cheesed off with Isabella as I was so, when invited to sit in the car to have some instructions on the controls, the three of us scrambled to get in the back seat, all developing an interest in the interior furnishings. In the front Isabella fiddled frantically with any button she could get her mitts on and I would have given anything for her to press an ejector button. Not for the first time that day was I going to wish there was one and be happy to carry the can for activating it. But worse could have happened if it hadn't been for the quick thinking buddy who saw Isabella reaching up to press something in the ceiling and gently pushed her outstretched hand down.

'And don't, don't, don't ever touch this button here because if you do the SOS signal will activate the emergency services and you could end up with a helicopter hovering over you and an armed response unit surrounding the car.'

'But what if it is an emergency?' Isabella demanded. 'A client having a heart attack, or a potential kidnap?' I had to hand it to the man, he dealt with Isabella very well, and with grace shunted us over to another car where an eager beaver gave us some instruction in the use of the Sat Nav. It was complete gobbledegook and Isabella took over the handling of the controls so I was no wiser than I was when I first entered the car park save to make a mental note to avoid her like the plague.

Seeing the cars acted as a focus, brought it home what we would be doing. Back in the briefing room, questions were fired which showed that many had come along with a different vision of what we were expected to do. Most, including me, had thought we'd be transporting athletes, prepared as we were for silent journeys as the sportsmen and women retreated into their hoodies and dug deep into their zones. That's not to say that there had been any misrepresentation of what our duties were but technical delegates were viewed as less exciting. The presenters were at pains to point out that we had a very important role, that getting the delegate to a specified place at an appointed hour could mean the difference between the starting gun being fired on time or not. That apart, the thought of a delegate swanning round posh shops and restaurants courtesy of the Olympic budget wasn't sitting that comfortably and our hosts endeavoured to assuage the whiff of dissent in the air by saying that the precedent for such hospitality had been set at previous Games and we were obliged to provide what the governing body asked for. There was nothing else they could say except to announce that we should collect our lunches from the canteen. Ah, food, always my saviour in times of trouble.

When Sophie and I had travelled up for the interview the year before I hadn't taken in the geographical bearings or surroundings of Excel so, with tucker bag in hand, I thought I ought to work out where I was. Cooped up inside all morning, the sun made a sudden blistering attack on my eyes as I stepped out onto the concrete promenade. Scores of other volunteers had had the same idea and some were sitting on the stone benches, others on the ground, their backs up against Excel's walls. I leant up against the railings, the sun's rays on the water almost unbearably bright. My eye followed the line of the white bridge that spanned the water, then panned right, taking in the tall black cranes left from the days when the place was a working dock. Behind the cranes flats and houses had been built replacing what I guessed had once been warehouses and depots for the goods offloaded from the boats. Following round, the sharp lines of the banking giants of Canary Wharf came into view, their glass windows glinting against the backdrop of a blue June sky.

'It's a fine sight isn't it?' I turned to find Robin at my elbow.

'Yes, I can hardly believe I'm in London.'

'Can you see the Gondola? It stretches from this side across to the Dome.'

'Where?' I peered into the distance. 'I can't see anything.' He gestured to a point some way in the distance from us and I followed his finger back across the sky line dominated by the financial buildings. A string of incongruous little pods were suspended from wires in the air stretching across the water.

'They're getting it ready for opening just before the Games start. And behind us in the other direction, there's City Airport.'

'Incredible. I never dreamt this was all here. What vision some people have. '

'Where was it you said you came from again?' asked Robin.

'Hastings.'

'Mm, I see. You'll excuse me please.'

I ate my lunch on a concrete bench in the company of a man whose name card said he was Will. With long flowing white hair and a rocking socking band on his T shirt, I felt a novice in the presence of wisdom when he told me he'd been a Games Makers interviewer and, whilst under a strict obligation not to disclose names or pack drill, had been blown away by the high calibre of applicants. 'It was humbling I can tell you. And have you found that once you start doing voluntary work you go on to do it time and time again?'

'First time,' I said lamely, forgetting to mention that, with the idealism of youth, I had once believed I could change the world on soup kitchen rounds and a few chats with hostel dwellers tied into a routine of three nights in the warm and, two nights out in the cold.

Lunch over and back in our seats, there were still murmurings of concern over our duties which the arrival of a presenter dressed in black polo shirt with yellow logo and black trousers did little to calm. As if on cue, his introductory words were followed by the sound of a cavalcade of feet and a long trail of men dressed in black trooping through to exit into the car park. They came and went in a flash but we knew they were there, their presence quelling all hints of rebellion, our speaker asserting his authority to speak to us on matters of utmost importance to T1, T2 and T3's.

The presenter was the head man of a vehicle training organisation, his remit to deliver a refresher on road safety. Boy did he have the Tigger bounce and patter to make an audience respond to his demands. Even I, not one for audience participation, was on the brink of answering a question on braking speeds but, in a complete *volte face* from the attitude he displayed towards the sign language, Robin shouted out before me whilst I sat glowing with pride that I had learnt something from my online assessment. Merv, by comparison, wriggled impatiently throughout the whole presentation, snorting derisively during the tongue twisters that made up the Driver Matrix. I thought *Fake space to Make space to Take space* was a bit beyond my capabilities especially if I had to get to grips with a new car and I became too analytical with *Slow to Know to Go* which I took as either summing up my life thus far or providing me with scope for life changes post the Olympics.

A comfort break was suggested.

'That's considerate,' I said. It was much needed, my apprehension building as I tried to work out how 'getting to know the cars' was to be achieved.

'The Assessors will be waiting for you,' one of the Managers said ten minutes later as he ushered us out through the rear exit.

'Assessors?' exclaimed Robin. 'They kept that quiet.'

'The men in black shirts?' I ventured, now having a vague recollection of an email mentioning something about an In Car Assessment.

'Mm. It puts a different perspective on it, doesn't it?'

Merv's perspective was to get all hot under the collar about having to be assessed but as I pointed out to him they were hardly going to let us out without some kind of evaluation. 'Suppose not,' he grumbled as we were herded out into the main part of the car park. It was huge, cavernous and the clunk of car and boot doors and sound of engines revving gave it the feel of a boy racers' evening meet. And any boy racer would be sure to be pleased with driving a car with a distinctive burst of colour and emblem on the side of it. The livery varied, the main blocks of colour being in pink, orange, green, purple or blue with a London 2012 logo complimenting it. I was to become particularly fond of the Tourer car that I was often allocated because it was larger than the saloon and the light blue livery against the dark blue of the car was, if logos can conceivably ever be classy, classier than the others.

Earlier that day I had lost Merv and Robin in the whirlwind of Isabella. Now, in a garage of candy coloured cars, I simply misplaced Robin who I suspected might have strayed off the path deliberately. I put it down to his reserve with Merv but it could have been me, the country hick who had been enthralled by a plane reaching for the sky from City Airport. Robin was lost to us but Richard took his place, his notable features a large rubbery bottom lip and a very long white hair sticking out from his eyebrow like an antennae. He was matched up with Merv and me by a Supervisor who was allocating groups to the Assessors.

'You can take this set of three,' the Supervisor called out to a tall rangy man who hovered in the aisle between two sets of cars. He bore the expression of someone returning to a car park who couldn't recollect where his car was parked. Although dressed in black, it appeared a more hastily put together ensemble, not worn with the panache of Tigger the head trainer, nor do I recall it bearing the proud logo of corporate identity. Our Assessor, peering over the top of his glasses, shyly came towards us. He jotted down our details on his board, a board which looked worryingly similar to the board my Driving Examiners had used to bang on the dashboard as a signal to do an emergency stop way back in the days of real driving, the days of double declutching and pulling the choke out.

'Sorry,' I said. 'I didn't catch your name?'

'Dirk,' he replied, looking anxiously at his watch. 'We'd better get going. Can you please put your bags in the boot?' He walked us round to show the boot where the first aid kit and safety triangle was stored and Merv, to give him his due, took my bag and stowed it safely away. The three of us waited for the next instruction from the unassuming Dirk who checked his watch again and appeared uncomfortable in the presence of Merv who had ants in his pants to get going.

'Whoever wants to go first ought to sit in the front passenger seat and we'll change over after I've driven out of the car park.'

Merv squeezed past me, opened the rear door and held it ajar so I could slide in next to Richard. I scooted round and asserted title to the front passenger seat. It was an act of unprecedented boldness on my part. Was it the Isabella influence, the suspicion of watching cameras? No. It was an act of self preservation. I wanted to observe how Dirk drove the car. Would it be hands in the ten to two position on the wheel and gear in neutral and handbrake on at traffic lights as I had been taught long ago? Or would he adopt the more modern approach that the children had been taught, of keeping the car in gear with foot on brake so that you can make a speedy exit and thereby keep the traffic moving? Whether it was Machiavellian or simply sad, I knew that if I pandered to Merv's clear desire to be the first to drive then it was more than likely that I would succumb to an attack of nerves in the back or lunge at Richard to pluck out his antennae.

Dirk drove through the rabbit warren of the car park. Apart from the section closest to the Depot room where the clutch of cars was waiting for us, the rest of the car park was empty. A vast expanse of parking bays and sparse artificial light made the place more sinister; a cinematic reel played in my head of gangland hit men suddenly appearing from behind the concrete columns. We'd be sitting targets, even the Germanic suspension would find it hard to cope with the dozens of ramps we had to bump over on the long journey out into daylight. And out in the daylight of Seagull Lane Dirk and I swapped places and I did all the things that my creepy former driving instructor had taught me to do for the Examiner; I over exaggerated checking my sitting position, the rear view mirror and the wing mirrors.

'Can you sit back, please,' I asked Merv who was leaning through the gap between Dirk and me to see what the delay in getting started was. Oh for a fly swatter to have swished him back because if he appeared in that gap once that day to pester the driver, he appeared in it a hundred times.

'Well executed.' Dirk's compliment came after I had negotiated my first roundabout.

'Don't hesitate,' he advised as I lurched through an amber light.

'Pay attention to the spoken word and visuals of the Sat Nav,' he warned as I made to take a left hand turn down an unmarked road in Greenwich.

'Didn't I?' I asked.

'No. You were being told to prepare for a turn that is a quarter of a mile away.'

'Where does the signal come from?' asked Richard, his white antennae strikingly more noticeable in the rear view mirror.

'Munich,' replied Dirk and, hackneyed as it was, this gave rise to us naming the device Helga.

In a car park that I can still visualise but can't place on the map, we decided to change over. There was no consultation process; Merv was in the driving seat before Dirk had completed my assessment tick boxes. And, as anticipated from our conversation earlier in the day, Merv displayed a less conciliatory attitude to our technological host. 'I haven't got one, I don't need one and I'm not going to learn how to use one,' he said as he blasted through a gap meant for pedestrian access and bounced off the kerb cutting across the flow of traffic. 'Where are we heading again?' he asked with juvenile glee as he revved at the traffic lights.

'Woolwich, the Royal Artillery Barracks.' Dirk double checked the itinerary.

'No problems.' Merv fidgeted in the seat. 'Are you alright in the back?' His eyes were devilish in the mirror. They told me he had, in the mists of time, been the sort of teenager who must have loved making his girl passengers whinny and squeal with his driving antics. But it wasn't all about driving that day. It was about effective visual, listening and communication skills. We had Helga the Sat Nav, Dirk had a two way radio linked with the schedulers at Excel and Richard had his swish Smartphone. And we were, after all, reasonably intelligent and switched on people. How else had it come to pass that we had been selected to help out at the greatest showcasing event for Britain for many a year? Perhaps we were a little too puffed up with pride and self satisfaction for our own good?

Mid afternoon sun lasered through the car windows. The air conditioning gave no respite as Merv's foot teased and taunted the brake pedal whilst he bad mouthed the car on account of the personal torment and confusion he confessed over why he had been given a driving role. Richard said nothing, preoccupied as he was with his phone.

Turn left in three hundred and fifty yards.

'Listen to the Sat Nav instruction,' said Dirk.

Prepare to turn left in one hundred yards.

'You've got to turn left, Merv.' Dirk, pointed his pen leftwards. 'Left?'

'Yes. NOW !' I'd say that Dirk, being such a nice chap and all, raised his voice in panic rather than in anger. And If Merv was one for having females squealing in the back, he got one that day. I let out a strangulated *ooo* and grabbed at my door as Merv did a Starsky and Hutch turn.

'Sorry about that,' said Merv, though his eyes told a different story.

'Be aware of speed limits in built up areas,' advised Dirk moments later.

'I'm on the button,' replied Merv not even giving the Speedo a glance.

'And be aware of your proximity to parked cars.'

'I'm miles away.'

We bounded down a hill.

'At the traffic lights please turn left.'

Merv turned left, right and left again till we ended up in a lane going to nowhere. 'This'll do us, won't it?' he said, with a confidence one could only marvel at.

'A convenient time to change over drivers, shall we?' replied Dirk, who turned round and appealed over the top of his glasses to Richard.

So it ended up with Merv and me in the back. He was easy to talk to and we chatted about families and cars, even motorbikes I recall. I put his perspiration down to anxiety and nervousness, his antipathy to operating the Sat Nav more to do with male ego in not wanting to look a fool.

Richard was altogether calmer and quieter than Merv, with no aggressive roaring up to or zooming away from traffic lights as Merv had done. Indeed with the heat in the car and Merv in full flow relating some personal encounter, the constant stop starting at traffic lights had a mildly soporific effect on me. The wakeup call came when the car took a sharp turn left. I looked through the window at the notice board and quietly confided to Merv that I thought we were in the queue for the Woolwich Ferry.

'Woolwich Ferry?' Merv shouted, craning his neck to get a look at where we were. 'Were we supposed to come this way?'

'It's no matter,' said Dirk the forgiving. 'It's an alternative route.'

'Is it?' Merv made eyes at me as if to say he doubted it. 'Where are we off to again?'

'Lee Valley.'

Merv shrugged.

'Well this is a bit of an adventure isn't it?' I turned to gaze out of the window with no real idea as to where the ferry went to and even less where we were going.

With the ferry chugging into its mooring at three forty five on a hot Friday afternoon I felt a real ache to catch a train back home. I wanted out. I nearly got it because Richard drove off the ferry, tried to overtake an ambulance and narrowly missed a police car coming the other way. Merv shuffled excitedly in his seat, Dirk quietly mentioned the desirability of taking into account other road users and I gave in to the notion that if the end were to come, I could only ask for it to be quick and painless and I hoped Roger and the children knew how much I loved them. It was all I had to keep me going as I watched the houses, industrial units and then open countryside flicker by.

'We've just passed a sign for Cambridge, Carol,' whispered Merv.

'Cambridge? That can't be right can it?'

'Apparently it is.' He wagged his finger in the direction of Dirk. My thoughts raced back to when Sophie and her then boyfriend had taken a trip into the wilds of Kent one dark December night and she had phoned to say that they had been chatting so much that they had only just realised that the Sat Nav had taken them on the road to Cambridge. I had not been best pleased then, had found it hard to see the funny side till Sophie was back in our care and now the same kind of feeling was beginning to take hold of me. For even though I didn't know exactly where we were, I knew that more and more mileage was being put between me and home as Richard rung the changes between lanes.

'You should always maintain a respectable distance, Richard,' said Dirk.

'Pardon?'

'Haven't you heard the saying that only a fool ignores the two minute rule?'

'What?'

I found Dirk's kindly explanation as to how the two second rule worked interesting but it didn't go down well with Richard. His rubbery lip quivered and he wildly swerved into the outer lane and opened up the throttle. His tarmac guzzling was short lived, the traffic build up acting as a brake on his heavy accelerator foot. When forced to slow down he leant his head up against the window in sullen resignation whilst a few lunatic drivers wove in and out of the lanes ahead of us. We inched along, Merv getting more and more agitated by the minute. 'Is it really necessary for us to go all the way to Lee Valley, Dirk?' he asked.

'It's on our itinerary.' Dirk tapped his board.

'But even so, it's going to take hours to get there.'

'It seems madness to me,' said a petulant Richard.

Parents with experience of car journeys with fractious children would readily identify with the two boys getting eggier and I too wasn't exactly blameless in adding my wet, whiny voice to the chorus of that we ought to consider pulling off of the motorway. Dirk consulted his clipboard whilst Richard eased himself across the carriageway and into the inner lane, ready to strike when the next exit sign came into view. Not that Richard actually made the decision because Dirk did vaguely, kind of, in a roundabout way, give the impression that, whilst not being precise about it, it might be or could be or there again be a sensible thing for a breather to be taken. A stop at a drive thru to get ice creams and a milk shake always did the trick on family trips but in this instance I had to make do with a drive along the road to an industrial estate and then a bumper ride up onto a gravel verge, the car finally coming to a rest at an angle, its wheels straddling the concrete kerb edging.

'Why did you choose to stop here?' Dirk demanded of Richard.

'Where else could I go?'

'You could have grounded the car. That's not the way to treat it.'

Richard leant up against the window in another of his sulks. Dirk started playing with the controls on the two way radio. Merv bobbed his head through the gap in the seats clearly itching to get his hands on the device. 'Sit back,' I said, in much the way I used to do with the kids. Dirk radioed in to the Schedulers. It was painful to listen to his long pauses and intermittent sighs as he explained that there were traffic hold ups on the road to Lee Valley and asked for clearance to abandon our quest and proceed back to Excel. 'Over,' he said with little conviction. You could have heard a pin drop as we waited for the answer.

Weeks after the event, when our escapade had become a piece of Fleet Depot Excel folklore, the Schedulers maintained they had called all cars making their way to Lee Valley to turn back at an early juncture because of huge traffic problems caused by an accident on the M25 the previous day. It begged the question why we had been sent that way in the first place but did explain why our Scheduler gave consent to our return. However, what it didn't explain was why a blanket authority wasn't given to return by an alternative route or was that because, in the translation of Dirk's imprecise ramblings, the Scheduler herself got lost as to where we were and what we wanted to do. And Merv and Richard were not happy bunnies, both maintaining that Dirk hadn't come over forceful enough with her.

'Start it up, Richard, and take us back a different route,' commanded Merv.

'Didn't you say we could get back through Chingford, Dirk?' Richard's hand hovered over the ignition button.

Dirk shifted uncomfortably in his seat, his whole demeanour that of someone who really didn't want to be where they were at that very moment. It was hard to imagine where in fact Dirk would ever feel at ease for if someone had asked me what Dirk did for a living, a driving instructor would have been way down the list. It might have been that he was more at ease on a one to one basis with a young adult than with three mature people each with their own views and opinions but that didn't help the current situation.

It didn't help the situation either that Dirk elicited in me the same kind of pappy patronising feeling once engendered by the door to door salesman who I used to buy household products from. It wasn't that my sweeping brush salesman was good looking or was full of hard sell patter. I fell for the woebegone look, the wistful references to his artwork, the apology that fell from his lips for having disturbed me when he came to collect the catalogue. I accepted the apology as a gift, seeing it as an artwork in itself, a representation to those who understood him that he was sorry that he had to make ends meet by selling products of questionable and negligible labour saving quality. His powers of persuasion were a mystery and yet he managed to justify my purchase of metal rings to keep fried eggs perfectly round and several bottles of clear odourless liquid which had the ability to do anything I required of it.

The three of us sat holding our breath, like kids waiting on the decision whether they can have an ice cream or not.

'Carol can take the wheel,' said Dirk. Richard swung round and looked at me as if I'd done something wrong and Merv, after recovering from the obvious shock, asked if I really wanted to because the traffic would now be at its worst.

'So?'

'And you will have driven the most.'

'She didn't get much of a chance before,' said Dirk.

'So, which way?' I asked Dirk, after Richard and I had switched over seats.

'We will return by the Olympic route.'

'Aw come on,' complained Merv.

Routine paranoia set in as I eased the car off the kerb, worried that I might grate the undercarriage on the kerb. Should I take Dirk's directive to drive as a compliment, mine being the safest and surest pair of hands to get all four of us back to base? Or was it that he wanted to test my driving skills further? If so, would a long stretch of driving relax me into my usual bad habits or make me so tense that I would make silly mistakes for him to record on the driver assessment form. And why had he made me, all fingers and thumbs, set Helga when he had let Merv get away with a stubborn refusal to do it? With an anxious Dirk, two big boys smarting from his decision in the back and a big burly lorry and driver from the estate on my tail I headed back to the roundabout. Going home from work traffic was flowing thick and fast.

Helga said I should leave the roundabout at the second exit from whence we had come. What was I to do? If either of the boys was behind the wheel it was a fair bet they would take the first exit and turn left into local traffic. And if I didn't do the same would they play up in the back? I stole a glance at Dirk, his expression that of the sweeping brush man when, with rain drenched shoulders, he had stood at my door explaining the delay in delivery of my order of a handy zip up plastic bag for unused Christmas wrapping paper. And I remembered how I felt when the man suddenly stopped calling. 'Do you think he's ill?' I asked Rog. 'He never looks what you'd call healthy does he?' I imagined him nursing a consumptive cough in a garret. The cynical might say he'd made enough money out of women like me to retire. The romantic optimist might conclude he had managed to get his paintings exhibited at the Royal Academy. So with such a track record how could I possibly override Dirk's instructions, how could I be responsible for etching further worry lines into his forehead by making him deal with calls from the Schedulers demanding an explanation why we had veered off course? I did the decent thing, turned right and joined the queue to merge with the slow moving river of traffic heading back to London.

'I said it would be like this, didn't I?' grumbled Merv. And the grumbling and grizzling from the boys made my head swim as

I silently heaped blame on myself that this was the inevitable result of my being just a bit too clever in jumping into the driver's seat all those hours before. The chain of events might have been avoided if Merv had assumed his divine right to take the wheel at the start because if he'd carried on the way he had been driving, Dirk might have booted him out, the journey on the Woolwich ferry might never have been an issue, and we might have been long gone to Lee Valley and back before the traffic built up.

The traffic thinned and the back seat passengers, having played themselves out, settled down. Richard, bless him, got on with some emails and I did suggest to Merv that he might like to occupy himself with my copy of the Fleet Drivers Route Book which I'd left in the back, my prize possession from the bag of goodies we had been given earlier. He declined and all but pressed his nose against the glass, his mood indicative of late Friday afternoon lethargy and the sad fact that we had run out of things to say to each other. Helga was quiet too, the mantle of responsibility falling on me to get us back safely as the traffic speeded up then fell back to an average of five miles an hour. The only sound in our vehicle was the occasional crackle of the radio with various call signs being bandied about. I don't know how many messages Dirk and I missed before Merv, roused from his daydreams, hollered at Dirk that the control was trying to raise us.

'Can you please state your position?'

'We are on the A12. Traffic is moving slowly, over.'

'Tell her how slow, Dirk,' shouted Merv.

Helga brightened up and said I should prepare to turn left. I wasn't going anywhere fast but it did put a spring in my right foot as I drove off of the motorway.

'Watch out, Carol, you might break into fourth gear.' Merv thought he was being funny. It was lost on me. Of all the journeys I have ever made, it is one that will long live in my memory as one of the worst. I pulled up behind a Jaguar at a roundabout. As it pulled away it broke down before our eyes. Next up, ambulance, its lights flashing and sirens going, nearly ran us off the road in its rush to get past. The boys got more fractious as we edged closer to London, as signs for places that I recognised started appearing.

'I won't be able to stand the engine cutting out all the time,' said Merv.

'Its energy efficient,' said Dirk.

'If it's as hot as this during the Olympics we'll all suffocate,' said Richard.

'I'm not too sure about these controls,' dithered Dirk.

'Come on, Carol, I should be in the bar sipping a cool beer by now.'

The thought of a cool beer was torture. As a distraction I looked out for street names that I recognised from our trips up to see Robert and, passing a empty building with smashed windows and a mattress leaning up against a filing cabinet, I made up stories about who might have once worked there, who might still use it as a shelter against the heat of a London summer, the cold of a London winter. And intermittently Merv called to Dirk to answer the radio and sometimes he imparted good news of a break in the traffic and other times he didn't.

'It's gone past seven o'clock now, Dirk.'

'This is the worst it will ever be, Carol,' he replied. 'There'll be Games Lanes for you all to zip down.'

'Thanks Dirk,' I said, trying to put a brave face on it as the radio crackled once more with the last sad little message from the scheduler.

'We're still here for you, OVER.'

CHAPTER 6

Travel

Role Specific training had been a bruising experience and the relieved looks on the faces of the welcoming committee back at the depot showed that they too had found the long, hot afternoon and early evening challenging. Merv was very agitated and prepared to dob Dirk in it for the whole sorry debacle. I also took it that he was narked that I hadn't taken his desire to meet up with his son for a drink very seriously. In other words, I hadn't employed either feminine wiles or bully boy tactics to snake my way between the lanes of crawling traffic. Limping home as we had, as Dirk had wished it, wasn't Merv's style at all.

'I shouldn't give it another thought,' said Rog, his eyes drooping later that evening after I had related the saga to him.

'He made it clear that he didn't want to be with us. He said he wanted fresh air and was going to walk to Canning Town!'

'I'd be the same after a long journey in a hot car.'

'What about his face being a picture when he got on the train at Canning Town and ran slap bang into us because our train had been delayed.'

'He wasn't expecting you,' he yawned.

'So why did he then get off the train?'

'You probably won't see either of them again.'

'And what about poor Dirk? They wouldn't get rid of Dirk would they? It wasn't his fault.'

'I expect Dirk can look after himself. Do you want to put the news on?'

I never saw Dirk or Merv again. I saw Richard beetling into the car park one day. He couldn't have picked me up on his antennae for there wasn't a hint of recognition and I couldn't be fussed to go over and make a fool of myself in reminding him of how and why I knew him.

But where was I after that baptism by fire, how did I feel now that I had a Fleet Drivers Route Book to acquaint myself with? I was mentally in a place that I frequently inhabit with Frank. Remember Frank? Frank, my imaginary soul mate who's had to endure all sorts of privations and distress for the last few years whilst I painfully excise and extract his story from him. There had been a time, about fifteen months and eight days before the start of training, when I had actually got Frank's fictional neighbours to collect him from the hospital and, after the type of journey I would not have wanted to put any Olympic guests through, they transported him back to his bungalow. I imagined my readers on the edge of their seats as they read the last line; I saw the book signings and the press interviews hailing me as a fresh raw talent; and then, and then?

My look in the crystal ball of literary fame was very fleeting because when I re-read the penultimate line, where Frank is teetering on the brink of an ultimately life changing decision, I realised he and I had to address some emotional development and continuity issues. It meant that, as much as I hated doing it, I had to tuck him back up in his hospital bed and start the process of redrafting. It was back to page one with a red biro; page one, where Frank and his fellow patient, George, indulge in some chummy banter whilst they await the arrival of Frank's important visitor. There was reluctance on Frank's part to go back to the Ward but nothing compared to the negative self doubt and apprehension on mine that I would ever see Frank fully recovered and released out into the future I had planned for him.

'I'm going to be the laughing stock of our friends if I take much longer over Frank,' I grizzled over breakfast one morning.

'Some people take years and years to write a book.' My dear husband is always well meaning.

'But I don't want to be some people!'

'Well, what's going to happen if you carry on with the Olympics?' he said, getting up from his chair. 'And have you replied to those emails yet?' I shook my head. He departed upstairs to clean his teeth, leaving me with the problems I'd been pondering over in the previous few days.

Problem one; even though Frank would be with me in my thoughts and I'd no doubt be reaching occasionally for a scrap of paper to jot an idea down about him, was it right to abandon him during my six week roster period? Not that I would be performing duties day in day out for six weeks. My commitment was for fifteen days, though the timing of the shifts, either six a.m. to four p.m., or two p.m. to midnight, would inevitably impact on preceding and succeeding days. Frank and I had been through so much together and at such a critical point in his development was it right to be going off seeking new adventures, perhaps bringing new characters back with me to the Den where Frank and I spent so many precious hours?

Problem two; I had been avoiding dealing with the emails Roger had been referring to which related to an appointment to collect my uniform from the uniform distribution centre (UDAC) and an invitation to attend a Venue Specific training day at FDX (Fleet Depot Excel). The training was on a Sunday and with planned engineering works on the line it would be impossible to get there by train for the eight a.m. start.

The emails had highlighted problem three which was the all encompassing problem of how I was going to get myself to the Depot on shift days. The process was hotting up and I was moving ever nearer to a point when it would be wrong to back out.

I had looked into the possibility of joining the 'working up in town' brigade but the first daily, and very expensive, train from Hastings left just after 5 a.m. with the last train back from London at 11.45 p.m. What about an early morning drive to Orpington, take a chance on getting into the Station car park and hop on a train from there? The train times were only marginally better, holding with them the prospect of crowds of commuters, much elbow shoving and grab a seat women with grating voices to London Bridge. And would luck have it that I would meet up with the dandruff ear wax chomper and his matte powder finish mate from before on the Jubilee line or end up with my nose pressed into someone's smelly armpit on the train to Custom House?

I studied underground and overland routes, soon realising that to get into London from other stations could mean a quintathlon journey of train, tube, bus, walk, tube. Could I stay with Robert in Bow? It was not a runner; he said he had other flatmates to consider (was I that rowdy!) and Mother would be unable to resist picking up his socks from the floor. Should I have taken his announcement of a proposed move from Bow to another location immediately prior to the Games as another hint? And along in Tower Hamlets a friend of a friend had kindly secured me some parking permits but it meant I would have to take my delegates on a detour everyday so I could change the permits over after five hours to prevent a penalty notice.

'Do you know how big Tower Hamlets is, Mum?' Robert asked when I'd ventured to discuss this possibility. 'It's the largest borough in London.'

'Well it can't be that far. That's what we've always said about catching the tube. Most things are within walking distance.'

'I don't think you realise, Mother dearest, do you, how vast London is?'

'No, I don't think I do.'

Nor did I realise that my dearest husband's long time association with a benevolent organisation was going to count for naught when it was revealed that they were intending to charge fifty pounds a night B and B to fraternity fellows attending the Games. I wasn't expecting something for nothing but as a volunteer I had thought some grace would be given particularly as all I wanted was a bit of cupboard space in which to curl up in my sleeping bag. As for breakfast, I was happy to pick up breakfast in a caff, any caff similar to the one in West Hampstead that had its own legion of Phil Mitchell look-a -likes and a grumpy man complaining about the door being opened or whatever else there would be to complain about in the sizzling summer everyone was hoping for.

Have sleeping bag, have sleep? I gave the camping website another whirl but all the previous objections I had had to it still existed and, even if the summer was to end up as one of continuous balm, I knew I wouldn't be able to get out of my mind the brutal cold that nipped at my cheeks and fingers on that February day at Wembley. Hotels? Cometh the Games, it was predicted that all would be occupied and, if not, the rates highly inflated.

Yes I had explored every option, had even found a website offering bed and breakfast accommodation in a Moroccan style room in a fashionable part of the East End, but as Roger came down the stairs after brushing his teeth and putting his tie on that morning I wasn't sure he would be up for me having that much fun.

'Do you think it's worth me carrying on with this Games Makers thing or not.' I sighed as he went into the Study to pick up his briefcase.

'It's entirely up to you.' I could tell he was already slipping into office mode as he tied up his shoe laces.

'But...'

He made his escape through the front door, his footsteps crunching across the pea beach drive on his way to the car. From the doorway I watched him perform his usual routine; unlock car, open the back passenger door, place briefcase in the foot well behind the driver's seat, close back door, open driver's door. He paused, leant his arm on the driver's door and looked over at me. 'No-one would think any the less of you if you backed out of being a Games Makers you know. At least you've tried.' He waited for a response that didn't arrive. 'Okay then, I'll be back usual time.'

BACK OUT? TRIED? TRIED! I slammed the front door shut in a flash of temper inherited from my father. My husband and late father were poles apart in many respects, except in one; the belief in having my best interests at heart, that belief shown in ways that sometimes I found difficult to fathom.

The flash of temper summoned up Dad's spirit that morning and so he came purposefully holding a clutch of school reports in his hand.

'Do you know what it says in here?' he asked, that dark look across his face which could, at one and the same time, scare and enrage me.

'No,' I lied, having opened and resealed it as any reasonable child would do.

'Carol is a cheerful girl but, BUT, BUT she could try harder.' I had never been allowed to forget it. 'Do you know what I used to say to the squaddies on the parade ground when I was a Sergeant Major?'

'You could hear your father's voice all over Aldershot.' The spirit of Mum interjected, her head shaking from side to side at the memory.

'Do you know?'

'No, but I expect you're going to tell me.'

'When I say jump, you jump and you don't come down till I tell you to.'

'Bulldog, that's what they used to call him, Carol. They wouldn't answer back to him.'

'Try harder. That's what you've got to do, or else!'

'Else what?' Else the whistling would start, his whistling which signified that he was cross, up the pole with the rest of us, or was it with himself?

Father and husband would come at things from different angles and that morning, with Dad's spirit an all pervasive force in a house he had never lived to see, Roger's words had prompted an 'else what' moment. I had a choice to make. Give up on an opportunity that wouldn't come round again in my lifetime or seek to find another way round the question of travel and not let my feet touch the ground till I had exhausted every possibility.

I checked and double checked all the various avenues and permutations of trains, hotels etc that I had explored before. The result was much the same. I was going nowhere, nowhere that is until I alighted on the postscript to an email received from a friend some time before. One day, when I have grown fat on the proceeds of receiving royalties, I will tell this friend how it came about that by the end of that morning I had devised a new board game called Parky Malarkey (still waiting arrival at all good toyshops and catalogue retail outlets).

Whereas in possibly the most famous board game of all time the aim is to buy up real estate and make as much money as one can, in Parky Malarkey the aim is to move your piece around the board to find and book a safe parking space at a reasonable price within easy access to your destination. I spent many hours on a parking website comparing the relative merits of spaces and with practice I became adept at identifying the difference between a navigable tarmac space and a hard brick standing that one could only reverse into. I got so cocky about it that I felt that my intimate knowledge of parking spaces would count as another plus point to add to my C.V along with the qualification that a certain leading sponsor of the Olympics was offering to give volunteers.

The pieces to move round the board would obviously be cars but of differing sizes because some spaces were only on offer to small cars and a picture of the space, sometimes a square of concrete with posts on each corner which looked the same whichever way you rotated it, showed it would not be suitable for an estate or four by four vehicle.

The squares around the edge would denote areas of London, though I found from my research that owners of car parking spaces in certain areas, Mayfair and Pall Mall for example, didn't go in so much for renting them out. In that case I'd have to decide whether to make their squares on the boards smaller and, as always, allow them to charge a higher fee. It obviously depended on what you would be looking for and moving my little red car round the board my intent was to land on a space in Canning Town, Canary Wharf or, so I thought at the time, the Isle of Dogs. Playing the game one could pick up *Nearby Cards* which would either state or ask you to list the most accessible Underground and Docklands Light Railway Stations to the space. There would be Street view cards showing a hard standing with a wheelie bin next to it, a row of cars next to a block of flats or a view afforded of a wire fence guarding some vans on an Industrial estate, all factors upon which to base your decision whether to proceed or stick until something better came along. I thought bonus points could be awarded depending on the facilities on offer. There was a whole host to steer your way through; a gated complex, 24/7 access, lighted CCTV cameras, security Patrols, security fob key provided, an endless array of accoutrements to keep your vehicle feeling safe and secure. However, points would be deducted if a counter landed on a bad review square, reviews which said communication with the owner was nonexistent or a vehicle had been vandalised whilst parked.

In order to start the game off you'd have to do as I had done. I registered with Overdrive Inc's site with a username then wrote a message stating my requirements. I explained that my shifts meant I would be parking at unsocial hours but I was a quiet soul, fully housetrained and would freewheel the car in and out of the space if it would keep the neighbours and owner happy. I clicked Send and off went my plea to the owner. I waited, excited when an email arrived telling me that I had to click on the link because I had a message waiting, a booking awaiting confirmation. But, as can happen, the vagaries of life, the fickleness of folk, had me returning to the start more than once.

Maxi boy apologised because he'd moved and had forgotten to take his space off the market. I'm sure he was a nice enough guy but thinking about it afterwards, I concluded I might have been naïve to turn up in a quiet back street at five thirty in the morning to pick up a security fob from someone called Maxi boy. It made me think whether I ought to have, at the very least, either a set of cards giving descriptions of the owners, a generic set of tall, small, fat or thin pieces on the board or did the appearance or designated name of the owner really not matter?

Fast Buck Francis had the ideal spot for me but he wrote to explain that market forces dictated that he had to increase his charge tenfold but he'd do me a good deal if I rented out his luxury apartment at the same time. I refrained from using bad language or raging against the forces of capitalism and simply communicated that I was shocked and disappointed and not prepared to pay those prices. I was all set for becoming mates with Glitzy Ritzy but she then bought a car of her own and there was no room for me. My relationships with Maxi, Francis and Ritzy were never meant to be and though frustrated with the backward steps I had to take at the time of the Dear John messages, the dice fell in my favour when Kreety K said a space was available for the duration of the Games.

And that was that; I'd won the game but felt guilty for doing so. I'd cheated. I'd sold my soul to the likes of Overdrive Inc. I'd not held fast to Seb's vision of environmentally friendly and sustainable games, but I'd tried.

CHAPTER 7

In the Quartermaster's Store

Midway between the two training sessions I was summoned to collect my uniform, the uniform that had been modelled at Wembley. At least some inspired person had chosen colours other than red white or blue but to me it wasn't haute couture and looked a cross between that of a leading supermarket chain and a major fast food outlet. In short, I wasn't crazy about it but I was never enamoured about my school, Brownie, Girl Guide or car hire toy town get up so I guess I'm not a uniform person full stop but it was part of the deal so I had to put up with it.

On a sunny Saturday in June Roger and I made our way to UDAC, the uniform distribution centre housed in an industrial unit in East London. We were early and Rog wasn't allowed in so we went in search of toilets in West Ham. It was a bad move, even the lovely café opposite the Station would only oblige with drinks and a tempting selection of food. Perhaps the owner had had rather too many football supporters needing his facilities. I could only admire his pluck in refusing the use of them to the likes of the man I'd sat opposite on the Tube a few weeks before who'd been busting for a pee. A vision of that man haunted me as I bid a swift goodbye to Rog who headed off to Canning Town and I hurried back to UDAC

I stood in the reception area queue in the warehouse. Whilst volunteers struck up conversations with each other I had 'rats big as alley cats and snakes, big as garden rakes' on my mind, these the words of The Quartermaster's Store song that I remembered from childhood days. I was thinking about Dad and what he would have thought of the place, whether it would have lived up to his military expectations. I smiled to myself recalling how Mum used to trill the bit in the song about 'eyes being dim and unable to see' when Dad was choosing to ignore something she'd said. And were the volunteers going to be treated in the same way as the soldiers had been in his day? Summoned to pick up their uniform, one look from the QM would decide whether they would be issued with large or small. There was nothing in between.

I was beckoned to the row of desks by a smiling young man who started the process off by zapping my email authorisation with a hand held scanner.

'How are you today?' he asked, brimming sunshine and light.

'Fine, very well thank you. Isn't it a beautiful morning?' I couldn't help but be as upbeat as him.

'It is.' SNAP. He took a photo of me before I had time to blink and then directed me to carry on down the hall, bear left and follow the painted line all the way round to the next desk. I took the lengthy walk alone but, fired up with his enthusiasm; it would not have been out of place if a group of volunteers making that journey together had broken into a chorus of American military chanting to accompany their steps.

The line curled round into another area and in the vein of a General Kitchener poster a sign commanded us to *Stay behind the line until called*. I did. I heard my name. I approached the desk. I marvelled at how they knew who I was, that the lady held a photo of me aloft, the one snapped only a minutes before.

'Take the line to Accreditation,' the lady said.

I took the line.

'A driver?' asked the lady at Accreditation.

'Yes,'

'I am processing your access codes. Do you know London well?"

'No, not really, but I'll be fine.'

'You may get to drive someone famous, like Usain Bolt.'

'Yes.' I smiled, toying with the idea as to whether I should mention what a coincidence it was that the only two stars I ever met were indeed in the days when I was employed as a driver.

She did look to be of an age to remember them but as she tapped her computer keys I didn't trouble her with the useless fact that a completely unassuming Ronnie Carroll walked into the car hire firm's office in the corner of the bus station and ordered a car. It was a modest vehicle as I recall and he looked a bit below par but during our next weekly phone call it was a delight to hear Mum's sing song 'you never did' when I told her I had met one of her crooner heart-throbs. And I let the moment pass to tell the woman how, despite my having to wear a silly Toy town uniform, I had been gratified with a wink from Malcolm MacDonald, Newcastle United football stud as he drove past me in his red Ferrari in 1976. Such silly memories I held on to as she handed me a sheet of paper and told me to proceed to the collection point.

As I followed the line, I reflected on the thought that past workplaces, the Motel, the Ministry of Defence building and the bus station which once echoed with the sound of Ronnie Carroll's feet were all gone and the venues for my future duties were untried and untested. Could it be any more exciting than that as I took a ticket from the dispenser? I was number three hundred and fifty seven in the shoe queue and the bell was bleeping for number three hundred. It gave me time to read my Games Makers pocket guide.

The bell went. My number flashed up on the screen.

'What size?' the man asked directing me to a chair.

'Eight.' I slipped my feet out of my sling back sandals, embarrassed as always at the sight of them. It was the price paid for wanting to be fashionable, the toll exacted for being made to feel like a freak at fifteen when asking for an unfashionable size, thereafter risking bloodied heels, corns and calluses by squeezing my toes into the best shoes that nine pounds, nineteen shillings and sixpence of hard earned money could buy in Freeman Hardy and Willis.

'Eight?' he repeated loudly. 'Are you sure?' I tucked my feet under the chair, fearful he would arouse other people's attention to look at them. I had suffered for my pride and conceit having spent many years, come rain or heat wave, wearing socks in other people's presence to conceal their ugliness.

'Put these socks on,' he said. 'You can't possibly try them on without.' I felt more like stuffing the socks in my mouth to mask the scream of terror at the thought that I was going to heap misery on my gnarled but loyal feet by shoving them into a pair of the grotesque grey trainers with red laces stacked on the floor close by.

'Stand up and let me feel where your toes are,' he ordered after I had brought myself to the point of putting the slippers from Hades on. I felt like a six year old.

'No, you can't have those. Try eight and half.' He went off like a whippet to fetch another pair and I was plunged into utter despair when, after I tried those on, he chose to wrest a pair of nines from another gentleman. It was then that I understood how Robert must have felt when, at coming up three years old, he had been seized by panic at the thought of the tall foreboding woman dressed in black in the local shoe shop coming towards him with her shoe measuring contraption. Screaming and kicking he had taken refuge under one of the chairs, refusing to come out till Mum and I, our faces as red as beetroots, had promised that we wouldn't let the Mrs. Danvers lookalike move any closer to him and that we would leave the shop. I had no such option as the man hurried back with the nines.

'I'm still not sure,' he said, tilting his head as he squeezed the grey mesh upper onto my delicate nail less big toe underneath.

'No, they're fine, perfect.' I wrenched them off, stood up straight and tall and pulled my shoulders back. 'I'm not going any bigger.' I was determined to put a stop to his nonsense, to avoid his turning me into a walking talking accident hotspot with my foot flailing inside the grey monstrosities as I tried to work the pedals in those sassy new cars. He didn't argue, just marked my piece of paper with a nine in the box marked shoes and despatched me to a row of chairs lined up against a wall.

'Shuffle up ladies, keep moving along, keep the line going,' a volunteer in full regalia and even fuller voice shouted and we shuffled from chair to chair until one by one we were ferried into a row of individual changing cubicles and told to take our coats etc off and wait for our dresser to come. There were two rows of cubicles facing each other and between them hung rails of shirts, jackets and trousers. Even though it was only a matter of minutes it was strange standing there waiting to be seen, knowing that someone was in the next door cubicle and the next and the next, all waiting too. This was high volume fitting and equipping and I felt a cross between an army cadet and a prisoner in solitary confinement in Cell Block H.

A measuring tape draped round her neck, my allocated dresser eyed me up and down over her glasses. She scribbled some figures down, told me to take my things off ready for the fitting and pulled the curtain. It was disconcerting to say the least, as was the picture of Mr. Pantling, long lugubrious Jack, who popped into my head. He was full of old nonsense, as befitted the lunchtime crowd who used to gather in the lounge bar of Dad's Sunday local. Dad would open the door and we'd follow on to a chorus of 'There ee' be. What's on then, Dick?' Dad would come out with some old rubbish and gesture to the window seats for us to sit down whilst he joined the gathering at the bar. Later Jack would send a drink over and Mum would say she didn't know whether she wanted to drink it as it came from him.

'Go on, drink it,' encouraged Dad and he'd wink at me. 'Watch Jack, Carol. See the way he stares at people? He's sizing them up, always on the lookout for new clients.'

'Honestly, Carol, don't listen to your father.' But she couldn't help but laugh and I guess they both had the last laugh on our friendly funeral director because he never got the final measure of them.

'You're very slight, aren't you?' my dresser said looking at the fit of the trousers and shirt she had made me put on.

'I think it's the cut of them.'

'Comfortable?'

'Very.'

The jacket proved more problematical, the debate over the correct size turning into a three way contest.

'You see you're slight at the top as well, aren't you?' the dresser said, exchanging the medium jacket I had just tried on for a small and passing the former into the woman in the cubicle next door.

'You can always pull the cuffs up.' I heard the dresser say to my neighbour and we had a bit of banter together through the cubicle about how those words were reminiscent of school outfitters at the beginning of a new school year. Then the dresser bobbed back to me. 'How are you getting on?' she asked.

'It's not very long.' I stretched my arms out then folded them back in and hunched my shoulders round. 'And it's what my late mother in law would call 'clippie' at the back.'

'You can always pull the cuffs down,' my dresser said, eliciting laughter from the other side. It might have been all a bit of a laugh but beneath it the dresser obviously wasn't working from the same brief as the shoe man had been because she couldn't be persuaded to let me retry the larger size. 'You're a Driver so it's not as if you'll be standing out in the rain for hours on end at Horse Guards Parade is it?'

'No,' I said lamely, wishing some of the assertiveness I had shown in the closing stages of my relationship with the shoe man would return.

'Now if you'd both step forward with your sheets I'll sign them off and then you can go to despatch.'

Piece of paper in hand, I stepped forward as did the mystery volunteer next door. We turned our heads. I looked down. She looked up. At half my height and twice my girth, she explained she was destined for a role in the great outdoors so a tent of a jacket would do her.

'And I'll be sitting down most of the time,' I agreed, barely able to contain my admiration for the sense of humour who marked our sheets with the required sizes. I followed the line to despatch. Imagine the service counter in the largest Argos you have ever been in, then double it, even treble it. I stood lost for words as it stretched away from me. Behind it was a long row of pigeon holes filled with plastic wrapped goods. A man beckoned me to the start and his words were equally lost to me as I gazed into the huge warehouse behind with shelves stacked high with boxes.

'Are you alright, madam?'

'Yes, just staggered by all of this.' I let him check my accreditation and he stamped my sheet and handed it back to me.

'There's your bag and I'll pop your water bottle in. Proceed along the counter, stopping at each collection point.' I did as I was told, my mouth open wide enough to catch flies as I marvelled at the military precision with which at each marker I was asked to produce my sheet and was handed the required parts of uniform before proceeding to the next; two pairs of trousers here, two tops there, a jacket (small) my big trainers in a big box, a brolly, a shoulder bag, two pairs of socks and a baseball style cap.

'Could I put my pocket guide in the bag as well?' I asked, the regimented discipline of the whole operation having so quickly entered my psyche.

'You could do that, yes, but it will all have to be emptied out again at the till.'

'Till?'

'Don't worry. You're not going to be asked to pay for everything. That's all been taken care of.'

'It wouldn't matter if I had to.' I wasn't exactly lying through my teeth because, even though it would have taken a fair few bottles of wine to make me part with any money for the trainers and the hat (and possibly the socks, perhaps also the jacket and, um, the tops). I was so overawed by the sheer magnitude of how much merchandise had been provided by the corporate sponsors, how organised and efficient the whole operation was, that I would have gladly made a contribution to it. 'With all this to carry I feel like shouting Crackerjack.'

My recollection of Eammon Andrews and the Crackerjack programme was not exactly lost on the man but the look on his face did make me momentarily wonder if he had the power to forfeit my goods on the grounds that a woman of a certain age, who feels tempted to shout Crackerjack in a warehouse in East London, was unsuitable to discharge Games Makers duties with the sense of decorum LOCOG demanded. Had I blown it before even having a chance to parade about our house in full military dress?

'The tills are that way, Madam. There shouldn't be much of a wait. Have a good day.'

The young woman at the till was as happy and smiley as the young man who had snapped a mug shot of me earlier. She emptied everything out and zapped it with her scanner but when she was putting the things back into my bag I noticed a red watch had been added to the collection.

'How did that get there? I don't remember picking that up.' It was my defence in mitigation for being so awestruck in Despatch.

'That's our little thank you gift to you.'

I was like a kid at Christmas, not showering her with kisses exactly but showering her with gratitude. 'I do have two watches but don't wear them and I had been thinking of buying a watch just for the Olympics and it would have been in a neutral colour so as not to be too obvious but red, oh how I love red but haven't the nerve to wear it but how well it would go with the red in the uniform, even the red laces on the trainers. They've thought of everything haven't they?'

'Yes, they have. Don't forget to pick up your Oyster Card on the way out will you? The office is through there.'

Out in the sunshine Roger was leaning against a wall with the rest of the civvies. I felt a bit sorry for them, no inkling of the experience.

'I can't believe the organisation of it,' I said to him. 'It's something else. Dad would have been proud of it.'

And there were watches, big as sasquatches,
At the store! At the Quartermasters' store!

CHAPTER 8

Triton 29

A s much as I have an aversion to wearing uniforms, a brand
spanking new Games Makers one hanging in my wardrobe
awaiting the start of the Games, gave me an incentive to get up
and leave home at six a.m. one Sunday morning to attend a Venue
Specific training day. It wasn't quite such an early start as I would
have on the morning shifts come Games time but I decided to treat
it as a dummy run for the real thing.

I love the serene calm of early mornings, to drive on the edge
of the day that is just beginning. It matches my equal love of the
dark of night when I feel l could put my foot down and drive and
drive and happily motor into an unplanned destination as the
dawn is breaking. I can ride those rising suns and floating moons;
it's the bits in between that I sometimes find tricky to navigate.

There was hardly any traffic on the A21 and not an enthusiastic
dog walker in sight as I drove through Whatlington, Hurst Green
and Flimwell. Dipping into the valley after the Weald a magical
mist hovered above the fields which made me think of Stan and
a batch of early mornings in my teenage days.

Not that where we lived was shrouded in magic. There was
no pavement shielding our house from the main road so in winter
you were splattered with rain from lorries thundering by and in
the summer the air was filled with petrol fumes and tourist chatter
from the open windows of cars edging bumper to bumper past us.

It was commonly agreed that we took our life in our hands
when we set foot outside the gate but at six of a summer's morning
traffic was virtually non-existent apart from a few holidaymakers
eager to make it to the coast for the first surfing lesson. Without

fear of mishap I'd stand at the gate and look up towards the town, waiting for the first glimpse of Stan.

'You've got to watch that Stan,' Dad always warned. Mum was more obliging. 'He's alright. We have a yarn and a laugh together,' she'd say because, despite his long Viking straw blonde locks and raffish reputation, she had a soft spot for his cheeky chat. And I guess I liked him because he was a bit wild, as wild as a chunky, bandy as a coot and ruddy faced milkman cum fruit and veg man driving down the road on his milk float at five miles an hour, can be.

Stan and me, having a ciggie and a chat, each mindful of the other's fragile state if a skinful of cider had been had the night before. We'd proceed at a snail's pace past the local Pub and the mobile home park where man-eating Irish Terry lived. Then the milk and cheese factory would come into view with steam rising from its chimney, whilst on the ground huge tethered bulls chewed cud in the pasture around it. With the bottles clinking and chinking in the back I'd look out across the fields and when we reached the roadside turreted cottage he'd ask, 'You be working tomorrow?' and I'd give him his answer as he steered the float across the road to bring it round in front of the main entrance to the Motel.

'Thanks, Stan.' I'd hop off the float.

'What does she think she's a doing of?'

I'd look in the direction of the plate glass window through which the Motel receptionist would be motioning to me, a lowly chambermaid, to go round to the side entrance via the coffee bar.

'I think she fancies you, Stan.'

'What's on?' He pulled his hair back behind his ears. 'You trying to get me into trouble?'

'Wouldn't take much!'

'Get on wi 'ee. I like a bit of meat on the bones!' He'd trundle round to the kitchens to make his delivery before wending his way back. He was alright was Stan; he never lunged, took liberties or caused me any grief though others told of a different side to his character but that's another story for someone else to tell.

Whilst my heart never skipped a beat for Stan, fast forward it nigh on forty years and that training day morning my heart was fluttering. It always does when I first catch sight of the London skyline but this time it was going like the clappers. I was nervous, but not about whom I was going to meet at training. I was even up for seeing Merv and Richard's antennae again if that was what the fates determined. After all was said and done, it was Merv who had, to borrow one of Stan's expressions, been a right pillock and though I hadn't driven at a speed that suited everyone's taste, I'd acquitted myself well on a hell hot day and delivered us back to the depot safe and sound. No, the nervousness was caused because another trip into unknown territory was awaiting me.

I'd booked Kreety K's space for the duration of the Games and Roger and I had driven to KK's to suss it out on the day I had collected my uniform. However, the space wasn't available for the Sunday in question and so I had to search Overdrive Inc's website to find an alternative. The alternative space was owned by Triton 29 and I looked upon the proposed use of his drive as a test run of Overdrive in operation and, whilst from the map, Triton's space was on the other side of the DLR, it looked to be no greater distance from Excel than Kreetys.

I flew past the Holiday Inn in Canning Town, realised I'd overshot the turning, double backed and entered Newham. There were no milk floats to be seen. There were definitely no tethered bulls though there may have been some of the muscled gym work out kind behind the net curtains and blinds of the matchbox houses. And there wasn't a twee turreted cottage in sight either.

There was a parade of shops, some boarded up for good, whilst other traders were dormant behind heavy metal shutters. Suddenly conscious of the tinny noise of my car, I kerb crawled along the street and turned into the parking area that the AA Route planner had determined as my destination from the postcode details.

The parking area was marked out into a number of parking bays though there were only a few cars to speak of. This was not what I had been expecting and to add insult to injury, there wasn't a pigeon, stray cat or urban fox there to greet me. Not for the first time during the Games time experience did I feel alone in an alien environment. I switched off the engine and looked around, unnerved that the run of house numbers indicated that the house where Triton 29 allegedly had his rental space was out of sight and only accessible by a path. By my estimation, the only way Triton 29 could watch over my car from his window (as he alleged on the website) would be through an exceptionally long periscope or CCTV camera. Triton's last cheery email message had been, 'Come when you like.' Would he be so cheery if I walked along the path and knocked on his door to complain about the misrepresentation and check if there was a particular space I had to park in. If I failed to take that walk, was the vision of clamped wheels and glued notices slapped across my windscreen just a product of my fertile imagination or a premonition of what might await me after a day of training?

I had a number of options; leave the car to an indeterminate fate; zoom over to Tower Hamlets, hopefully find the right parking zone and play five hour Russian roulette with the traffic wardens by using the parking permits that the friend of a friend had obtained for me; or accept defeat, turn tail and go home. The fourth option was to ring Roger with the suggestion that he should do the gallant thing and spring out of bed, catch the train, bus, train and tube and, wheel clamping and glued windscreen permitting in the interim, collect the car and I'd make my way back by tube, train, bus and train later in the day.

Time was ticking against me while the car's engine cooled down. What I wouldn't have done for one of Stan the milkman's roll ups. Instead I drew deep and hard on the last of my packet of extra strong mints. The vapours led me to the conclusion that I would have to rouse Triton 29 and be done with the consequences even if he turned out to be a half asleep gorilla of a man wielding an axe at me. It wasn't the ten measly pounds I'd paid that bugged me. It was the fact that I'd been duped by Overdrive Inc into thinking that a person called Triton 29 would take my car into his care and protection and stand guard over it. What fool me? Minty courage left as quickly as it had come and I decided I couldn't face a brusque and bristly man at 7.35 a.m. There was nothing for it but to leave the car where it was and hope and pray that I hadn't parked in the space of a stroppy householder who had a personal vendetta against him at number twenty nine and would be waiting for me on my return. I pulled the parking pass out of my bag to put in the wind screen. I looked at the pass, and then compared it to the directions I had taken from the Internet. I was in the wrong road.

Fortunately, the map I had downloaded as part of the route planner's directions extended to surrounding streets and, lo and behold, the address I was after was only a street away. What if he was standing on his threshold patiently waiting for me, the unimaginatively codenamed *carold*, at that very moment? I wondered if he looked anything like the representative figure I would mould him into for my Parkey Malarkey board game. I reversed the car, guiltily pulled away and slunk round to the right road and the right address. Triton wasn't waiting for me but immediately outside his front door a parking space with tufts of grass coming through the breaking concrete was empty and waiting for me.

I looked in my rear view window and saw I was in the sight lines of a topless young man in jogging bottoms who was smoking a cigarette and pacing up and down like a caged lion in his front yard across the street. I shivered at the thought of the nippy morning air striking against his anaemic bare skin as I put the parking permit in the windscreen. I got out of the car. Aware of the young man's sly glances at me, I made a feeble attempt to rattle Triton's letterbox. Silence seeped through the gaps in the semi closed Venetian window blinds. There's nothing more I can do, I told myself as I gathered my things together and, for the benefit of the troubled man in bare buff, made a great play of locking the car door before walking purposefully down the street. At the end of the road I took some bearings, the two beaten up telephone boxes on the opposing corner would be my markers for later. I glanced over my shoulder at my little red car. It was a good servant and bore the dents and scrapes of youthful living and music festivals with good grace. I bit my lip, turned and headed for the bridge over the DLR and onwards to Excel.

By the time I arrived at FDX the place was already filling quite nicely though proceedings were delayed a while to let those having trouble with transport arrive. I took up a seat on an empty table. It formed a T shape with another table where two men and a woman looked to be in conversation. I didn't intrude, merely reciprocated a smile from one of the men.

I felt someone brush across the back of my seat. I turned and looked up at a tall man wearing glasses and a cap.

'Is this taken?' he asked, pointing to the seat next to me.

'No. Please have it. '

'Can you believe that, today of all days, the trains are all up the chute?' He settled in his chair, took his cap off and bared his suntanned balding head.

'Have you travelled far?'

'From Bexleyheath. And you?'

'I drove, from Hastings.'

'Hastings? Bloody hell! Where have you left the car?'

I explained about Overdrive Inc.

'If my journey from Bexleyheath is going to be anything like today's I'll have to remember that for future use.'

'Please don't. I'm probably being unfair but I'm a bit concerned that my car's going to be there when I get back! '

'Christ, you're very calm.'

'There's not much I can do about it.'

And that was the strangest thing about the Games Makers experience because for the first time ever I was able to completely shut off from what was happening on the domestic front. When I worked I was thinking of what had to be sorted out at home and at home my mind would be running through what had to be done at the office but in the Games Makers environment all I did was think about what I was currently doing with a few daydreams thrown in to add colour.

John, all legs and arms and age spots, greeted the lady and fellow who fetched up in the chairs opposite us and I took it that he had met them before because he knew the lady hailed from up north and displayed an easy camaraderie with Sam whose moon of a face, ready smile and quiet Filipino way was as engaging as John's wry observations on the people now piling in.

'Can you believe that this lady has driven up from Hastings?' John said by way of introduction. Sam nodded. 'Can you believe that someone would even admit to coming from Hastings?' John's laugh was infectious, Sam's grin widened and the remark set the seal on the banter and good humoured insult trading reminiscent of the kind I have with cousin Brian.

Whilst John took significant slurps of coffee (caffeinated with three sugars) from his polystyrene cup, the training started with a focus on our roles as T2 drivers; how a typical day would work and the importance of knowing our clients and our routes. As on the previous training day, they indicated that drivers would be allocated to a particular car, that you would be driving the same delegates and thus be able to build up a relationship with them. At shift changes the rapport between driver and client would be such that everyone would know what the client's requirements were for the next day and the prospect of becoming real buddies wasn't beyond the realms of possibility. I envisaged busy days ferrying my very own delegates to and from their Park Lane Hotel to the Olympic Park then waiting in the car under a streetlight for them to turn out of a restaurant in Mayfair.

Tommy the Beard, one of the managers, suggested an open forum for questions.

'Can we accept gifts?' A man asked

'The answer is no, unless it's of minimal value, a souvenir badge for example.'

'Why can't we have five series cars like the T1's?' an aggrieved voice rang out. 'Especially if we have to transport more than one person at a time!'

'Yeah, and what about if your passengers want to go to different destinations?' someone else jumped in.

'Use diplomacy and tact,' advised Tommy. 'But in the end it's for them to sort it out.'

From the far end another man's voice entered the fray. 'Shouldn't you spare a moment for the T3's?' The voice had a certain gravitas about it which stilled the ripples of chatter that had started breaking out about how to deal with warring delegates. 'For the T3's may very well feel inferior because they are, after all,' he paused, 'a glorified taxi service.'

John let out one of his loud laughs and looked at Sam. 'Bloody hell, who said that?'

Sam craned his neck. 'That man over there with the dark hat.' I have since put it down to tiredness but I found the predominately male angst about the cars, even if tongue in cheek, and the comments about the T3's, childish. Fatigue also played a part in my getting irritated with the predominantly female concerns that were batted across the room.

'I caught the five thirty two this morning but what about the early shifts?'

'Have you tried the East Coast mainline?'

'No, but my friend tried the.....'

'Okay, okay,' shouted Tommy the Beard. 'We haven't time to discuss individual transport problems.'

'Thank goodness,' I whispered to John.

'You can raise anything like that in the break and after the break you will all be going out in the cars again for some further practice.' The news caused a brief ripple of excitement and then he brought us slap bang back into the grown up world by explaining all the security measures that would be in place for the Games.

We were told of the plans to draft in more military than you could shake a stick at and that we would be getting a taste of things to come that very day because the car park at Excel was already in lockdown with all cars, drivers and passengers subject to searches and screening. I don't recall the words *'terrorist attacks'* being used in any of the literature or by anyone in authority. Reference was only ever made to the threat from people who might be intent on disrupting the Games. There was a need for vigilance, the need to know when to act, escalate or inform.

'And if they are using the dogs today, stay in the car,' Tommy warned and the thought of unseen people in unseen places plotting to mount some kind of aggressive strike was made all the more real. 'Any questions?' Tommy paused. 'Yes, you, Sir.' He nodded to the gathering nearest him.

'It's him again,' said Sam.

I could only hear a mumble but Tommy's responsive face was something to behold.

'Did everyone get that?' Tommy called out.

'No.' There was a roar of voices from our end, John's included.

'The gentleman here,' Tommy pointed into the crowd, 'wants to know whether the screening measures will involve rectal examinations?'

'Bloody hell,' said John as the question was passed down the line to those who still hadn't heard what was being said. 'Avoid getting into a car with that man with the hat.'

At that stage it was obvious Tommy had taken the briefing as far as he could and that a toilet break was becoming an issue for some restless audience members. He clapped his hands to bring us to order. 'You'll see that there is a plastic wallet containing a key on each of the tables,' he announced. 'Get into groups of four and we'll get you out learning those routes. Have you all brought your route books?'

'I hope it's not going to turn out like last time. We didn't get back till half past seven.' I confessed unthinkingly

'Bloody hell, that was you, was it? Did you hear that Sam?'

'I can laugh now but I didn't at the time.'

'Where's a wallet for us?' our lady of the table demanded.

'Yes, where is it? 'echoed John.

'Someone must have had it.'

I didn't like her tone and it was the combination of her harsh schoolmarm presence which would reduce me to a quivering wreck in no time and the naughty schoolboy manner of John who would make me laugh and irritate schoolmarm further, that influenced my decision to avoid spending the day with them. Under cover of John calling out to Tommy about the missing plastic wallet, I slid my chair away from him and pulled up closer to the three on the adjoining table. What was that saying about devils you know and devils you don't?

Finding a woman suddenly at his elbow proved unsettling to my new male neighbour who, catching wind of my presence, grabbed at the plastic wallet. This was a foretaste of how possessive we T2's were to become over the contents of a plastic wallet which held the key and all the documents relating to your allocated car. And this particular man, who had a disposition to powder blue smock tops, was someone who had to have everything planned for, recorded and ticked down to the last detail so his response was appropriate to the level of threat he perceived that day.

'Hello, I'm Carol,' I said brightly.

'I'm Graham,' he said, pinning the wallet to the table with both hands.

'And I'm Costos.'

A hand was held out to me by a smiling man, his olive skin and brown eyes warm and inviting. The slender lady of the trio, with fly away hair and a perfect complement to nautical Graham in her rainbow coloured anorak, didn't say a word.

'And you are?' I ventured.

'Judy.'

'Judy,' I repeated. 'Sorry if I forget all your names.' It was such a lame thing to say but the men agreed it was a common problem as Tommy began reminding everyone to get into fours.

'That's lucky, isn't it?' I said innocently, not having the courage to look back to see what was happening with the three I had discarded.

'Good,' beamed Costos.

We trooped out into the gloomy car park, Graham holding the wallet to his chest, and Judy, her arms crossed, showing complete disinterest in listening to Costos's animated chatter. Standing before our beast of a BMW, Costos greedily eyed the key in Graham's hand and nailed his colours to the mast by saying that he would be happy to be the first to drive. Graham, putting his glasses on, surprised me by saying that it was fine by him. It was fine by me too. Judy shrugged and plunged her hands deep into her anorak pockets whilst Graham said that we had to check the car thoroughly and complete all necessary forms before Costos could take the wheel. And I accept that ordinarily it wouldn't need four grown adults to do all the checks we were required to do on the car but it would have made for good teamwork if two could have jointly located the warning triangle and first aid kit in the boot whilst the other two checked for chips or cracks in the windscreen. But Judy was having none of it and went and sat in the back of the car. As always, I felt torn between two camps. Should I hang round like a lemon with the boys inspecting the roadworthiness of the tyres or sit in with Judy who might be feeling left out or unwell.

'It's quite roomy in the back, isn't it,' I said, as I got in beside Judy. She shrugged. I was undeterred. 'The men are having one last look round the car. It is a to do isn't it?'

'I'm not going to be the last one to drive.' Her gaze was fixed on the concrete pillar by the side. 'I don't like parking.'

The men got in, a fresh fabric conditioner ocean smell permeating the car from Graham's smock. Judy sighed and tutted and shrank further and further into her anorak as the men fiddled with the switches, knobs and controls on the dashboard. Costos told Graham what the mileage was and how much diesel was in the tank. Graham wrote it down and read out the locations we had to drive to. 'Any preferences for how we organise who drives when?' he asked.

'We'll do it clockwise,' said Judy.

'How will that work?' I asked.

'Costos drives first then Graham takes over and I move into the front and so on.' It wasn't so much the circular movement that she made with her hand that I flinched from, it was the tone of condescension in her voice but I guessed I'd asked for it.

'And we'll have two venues per person. That's fair isn't it?' said Costos.

Using the two way radio, Graham called the dispatchers to say that *Charlie One Two Three was setting out from Excel, destination Greenwich, Over.* And we had the obligatory *Roger* and *Over and Out* and then Costos drove at the obligatory five miles an hour through the car park, over a succession of vicious speed humps, and out into the bright daylight.

Judy, slumped down in her anorak resumed her window gazing and made the occasional comment as Costos confidently drove us to North Greenwich Arena and Greenwich Park. This was of course a couple of months before the Games so some venues as such weren't in operation, indeed a few were still under construction or hadn't been converted to an operational facility and no access was permitted. It meant you had to get onto Helga's wavelength and use your imagination as to what, where and how we were going to manage when we were working.

It came as some relief when the clockwise plan was put into effect and Judy moved to the front passenger seat and Costos joined me in the back. We chatted away in the sure knowledge that we were in Graham's safe driving hands, Costos explaining that he had been inspired to become a volunteer as far back as the Athens Olympics where the enthusiasm of the volunteers had been infectious. Travelling the tin pot sixty miles from Hastings everyday was put into perspective by the fact that here was a man who I guessed was Greek but lived in Spain and was actively looking for a house swap with anyone in London for the duration of the Games. And Graham, coming from down West, had already sacrificed a lot of his time because he had been an interviewer. He told us that the interviews had been conducted on the basis of the applicants not having to prove why they were suitable but more on the basis of the interview questions determining if there was anything about the applicant that would make them unsuitable. I wasn't sure whether that could be taken as a confidence boost or not.

Anyway, there we all were and I was happy to sit and hear about Costos's life, and, with unprecedented familiarity, I told him about Frank.

'The trouble is trying to find a publisher, Carol. They have hundreds of submissions and the majority end up on the slush pile.' He sounded as if he had had firsthand experience and so we lapsed into the roles of him being the guide pointing at familiar landmarks in the City and me the old lady taken out for an afternoon ride, making frequent ooh and aahs at the large number of people soaking up the Sunday near St Paul's.

Judy needed for the toilet. I suggested that at the next location, a hotel, we could park up and ward off any traffic wardens so that she could pop in and use the facilities. 'At least in a five star hotel they'll be clean and have nice soap to use.' My words were a sop to the indifference she had shown to me in the back seat and if it had been anyone else I would have done the girly thing and tripped in with her but Graham also needed the loo and felt confident enough to leave the recording of mileage and time of arrival at the hotel to Costos and me.

I moved into the front passenger seat, Costos shuffled along into my vacated place. 'I've set the Sat Nav and radioed into control,' he told Judy who, refreshed and surprisingly cheery, installed herself into the driver's seat with Graham and his tumble dried fragrance directly behind her. I was happy to be the silent companion, thinking she might appreciate this whilst she reacquainted herself with the dynamics of the car, and the men, bonding beautifully in the back, were equally respectful and talked in low voices. Helga was mouthing on as was her wont and I must admit I wasn't paying much attention. All was set fair but a spat was inevitable, riding as it did on Judy's frankly bullish approach to driving, a bewildering array of one way streets, meandering tourists and the fact that no-one had ever heard of our next destination. Oh, and there was the explosive mix of the constant battle that rages within me that I must be inferior and quite clearly wrong on all matters until someone riles me. And so it came to pass that at some place that I have since expunged from my memory Judy violently swung the car to turn left, the wheels touched the kerb and I jolted forward as she revved away. Costos leant over and pointed out that he didn't think we should be but we were now heading over a bridge.

Judy blamed Helga saying Helga should have known that the pavement had been raised making it impossible to take a left turn. With the benefit of experience I would now hazard a guess that Judy had misconstrued one of Helga's *bear left* or *half turn left* instructions and had actually missed the correct turning to begin with and the men were too polite to say it. Giving Judy the benefit of the doubt and forgiving Helga for not being programmed to be as streetwise as she could have been was the best all of us could do, thankful as we were that we hadn't headed smack into a one way flow of traffic.

'Reset the Sat Nav,' Judy snapped.

'What now?'

'Now !'

'It'll reset itself,' said Costos.

I could feel my palpitations starting.

'Reset it,' she shouted over Helga who had woken up to the seriousness of the situation.

'Can't you pull over somewhere once we're across the bridge so that we can do it?'

'No! Why should I?'

'I can't set it just like that.'

'You're going to have to do it when you're driving on your own.'

'But I wouldn't reset it when driving along.'

'I'm driving, you're not, so set it.'

'I can't see the point whilst you're driving along?'

'Are you stupid?'

The end of the bridge and road signs for onward journeys came into view. Costos leant forward. 'Wouldn't it be better pulling over into a side street so we can work out where we are?' To this day I don't know where it was we ended up. She parked half on a kerb, huffing and puffing about the yellow lines, conveniently forgetting that we had gone out on a limb for her when she went to the toilet at the Hotel. I couldn't bear to look at her. She shuffled about in her seat whist the men looked at the destination sheet and concluded we ought to scrub the one we were heading for and carry on to the next one.

'The Sat Nav needs setting and you obviously need the practice,' Madame said.

I could have said stuff it, you do it yourself, but I knew she was right.

'You'll have to be patient with me,' I said, trying to make sense of the screen. Patience wasn't an option with her as she sighed and groaned in frustration at how long I was taking even though Costos was using his schoolteacher skills to coax me through it.

'I might as well...' Judy's freckled hand hovered over the navigational control.

'No,' I hissed. 'You wanted me to do it so I'll do it but you'll have to wait!'

A deathly hush descended on the car.

'There!' I said as I pushed the Start Guidance button, concerned that the smell of my anxiety induced perspiration would not go unnoticed.

'Call the Dispatchers and tell them what we are doing,' she commanded as she bounced the car off the pavement. Costos touched my arm. I turned round and with a smile of encouragement he handed me the two way radio.

I pressed the button on the side of the walkie talkie and, without drawing breath, gabbled the whole sorry tale of our not finding one of the locations so we were going onto the next. There was no response. Costos said I had forgotten to give the call sign. I tried again but nothing happened. Graham said I should go more slowly and say OVER more clearly at the end of the message. I tried again and again.

'They must be busy,' I said.

'Are you sure you're pressing the right button?' Madame asked.

'Not the green one,' added Costos. And of course I had been pressing the wrong one and I wondered if the dispatcher who finally acknowledged my message caught the catch of emotion in my voice.

I could have made light of it, regaled my co passengers with tales of my time at the jam factory. I could have asked them to imagine me in long blue overalls, a white mesh hat on my head and my feet suffering the slings and arrows of chilblains from wearing wellington boots on cold wet floors. Judy would probably have believed how, for all my education, it had taken me ages to learn what alarm bells to ring, which buttons to press, which switches to hit when my inattention to the controls resulted in too many jam jars whizzing along the belt at dangerously high speeds. Would Costos laugh at how my day dreaming interfered with keeping a sharp eye and an alert ear whilst operating the hopper so much that, without fail, the whole line would be brought to a halt because I'd let all the jars through without lids on. And manual dexterity wasn't my thing either, my output of boxed jars far below that of fellow workers whose lives had revolved around jam and marmalade day in, day out for years. Yet the permanent staff put up with us transients, knowing full well that we were unlikely to hack it for long. Surprisingly I wasn't the most kack handed; Leon the artist, small, beer bellied with ginger beard and tinted specs was the worst. Very few could understand his caustic wit, none less so than Chuck the Supervisor who strutted round like the cock of the north, the idol of the young girls foolish to fall for the swagger he cut in his long white overall and mesh cap. Chuck and his second in command, the efficient and sour Vicky, would decamp to their Citadel looking down on us on the factory floor, presumably wondering whatever the management must have been thinking of in employing us misfits whose idea of sluicing the deck was to cause a major flood. Yet for all the times Vicky and Chuck questioned my ability to check the temperature controls on number one tank there was a comforting regularity to it all. They passed through their lives, they passed through mine; Christmas marked by the gift of hampers of jams and pickles, New Year canteen gossip revolved round the secretary with the big hair who pranced about like lady muck all year but draped herself across every mesh less male operative at the annual party. Then I left, never knowing the ending to the scandal of the girl from the factory floor with the Manager who seduced her with the promise of his fast arriving pension built on the proceeds of jellied fruits and preserves. But they knew who they were and what they were doing and I knew where I was with everyone but not so with the likes of Judy who was now back on the right course heading for our next destination.

I remained on the edges of the conversation, spawned by the walkie talkie business, as to whether Zulu, Zebra or Zero represented Z in the phonetic Alphabet. I acknowledged Graham's potted history of the East End and his knowledge of the antics of the Krays which culminated in him pointing in the direction of the Pub where the brothers committed their infamous murder. If I had felt comfortable with Madame I would have told them of my intention to look deeper into the story Dad had told me that he used to have an uncle with a pub in Whitechapel between the wars. As it was, I left it and Judy to her own devices with Helga, and Graham acted as co-pilot from the back.

In the middle of Stratford High Street Helga announced that we had reached our destination. As we idled at traffic lights the men confessed to being hungry.

'Where shall I stop to eat?' Judy asked.

'Go where you like,' I replied as the men discussed what fillings they had in their sandwiches which were stowed away in the boot.

'But where, where?' she floundered as the traffic lights changed. 'Shall I go right or left?'

I was hungry too so it would profit me none for her to take off in an unknown direction and precipitate another fiasco with Helga and the walkie talkie. 'Go over there,' I said, pointing to a supermarket car park. 'Then if anyone wants more food or the toilet, it's all on hand.'

'Where shall I park?'

'There's a space,' said Graham but she overshot it and another was snaffled up by another car because she prevaricated over the length of ours. We circled round a couple of times, several spaces rejected for all sorts of reasons and then Costos became troubled that we'd have to pay.

'I'm sure we can rustle up the fee between us.' Overcome with heat and tiredness I think my sarcasm showed. 'Anyway, it's only pennies so I don't mind paying but my bag is in the boot with the packed lunches.' But no, she didn't want to hang about in the car park waiting for a suitable space so we finally ended up in a residential street and ate our lunch perched on a low level wall.

We changed drivers to yours truly and Costos jumped in to set the navigation and did all the *Charlie's* and *Rogers*. As I drove along Judy suggested we stop somewhere for a coffee.

'We could have done that at the supermarket!'

'No. I meant let's hole up somewhere for the afternoon at a coffee shop and we can put whatever we like on the forms because no-one would ever know.'

The thought was unbearable to me, unpalatable for Costos and a definite non runner with Graham. When we arrived at my first destination she put it forward again. Our eyes met in the rear view mirror. 'If you want I could deposit you somewhere and we'll pick you up on the way back.'

'That defeats the object, surely, doesn't it?'

Not in my book it didn't.

Driving along Hartmann Road, the approach road to City Airport, my second destination, one of our fleet cars coming from the other direction stopped and waved us down. I pulled up alongside him and opened the window.

'I should turn around now and forget about the Terminal.'

'Why?'

'They aren't happy with all of our cars going down there. They've had a go at me because I'm clearly not dropping off or picking up anyone.'

I took his advice and pulled over into a dead end and turned the car round ready to head back to Excel.

'It's my turn I believe,' said Costos, pressing the door handle to get out.

'It's hardly worth changing over now,' said Judy. She was right but I capitulated to Costos whose eyes were full of longing, excitement and determination to drive again and it wasn't worth Judy arguing against his point that, by strict rotational rights, he was entitled to drive to the ninth and last destination on the list. And on the short journey back it wasn't worth Graham questioning Judy's figures on the height and weight limit of a wheelchair assisted vehicle because Judy was going to be a WAV and knew all there was to know.

On our way back into Excel we had our first taste of the security measures that Tommy had mentioned earlier that morning. A Vehicle Screening Area, a large tented building, had been erected between Excel and Custom House Station. A soldier waved us across the gravel towards the tent and once inside Costos came to a stop at the precise spot indicated by another soldier. Costos wound his window down. The soldier peered in at us. 'Let me have the key, Sir. All of you stay in the car and wait until the dogs have cleared.' It was all very friendly and they were on our side, were there for our protection but with a group of soldiers gathered round and bonny spaniels jumping up and sniffing the car it was enough to make me feel that I must be guilty of something.

'I shouldn't have given him the key,' Costos fretted. 'I must remember not to give them my key.'

'It's not for real,' sighed Judy.

Costos parked the car in the car park, he and Graham filled in all the forms and I verified the petrol consumption and their signings off whilst Judy zipped up her anorak.

'Coffee anyone?' asked Costos. 'Next time we're here it will be for the real thing,' Judy's desire for coffee vanished into thin air just as she did.

I carried a bellyful of coffee and Costo's 'Good luck everyone' with me as I left Excel and the Dock with its contemporary apartment blocks and restaurants. I crossed the footbridge into the streets of Newham with its more traditional housing. The newsagent was open, a few young boys were kicking a football and a couple of teenagers were mooching about puffing at their fags. There were still no signs of life from Triton's house but my car was as I had left it and a van was parked next to it in the neighbouring property's space.

'Afternoon,' said the neighbour.

'Afternoon,' I replied. There was nothing more to be said and I got in and drove away.

As the car ate up the A2 I nibbled at the day. I gave myself a pat on the back for taking a gamble on Overdrive Inc and yet it felt odd, impolite, that I had used Triton's drive but hadn't met him in person. Was that how things worked in the city? Was I being a plain country hick in thinking it should work in any other way? And why had I been so sniffy about Newham, the housing no different to places that some of my relatives lived in. And why had I dodged the issue of going out in a car with the schoolmarm woman and John. Why had Helga made me feel inadequate? If I didn't get to grips with my phobia of gadgetry and study the Route Book before the first shift would I end up on a collision course? The signposts for the M25 loomed, as did the question, and what of Judy?

When I picked the afternoon apart, Judy had done little else than nestle into her anorak and negotiate some impulsive switching of lanes. She hadn't taken part in checking the car or doing any of the paperwork either going out or coming back. She hadn't actually set the Sat Nav or operated the walkie talkie. Apart from the clockwise thing and the suggestion we skulk off somewhere for a coffee, she had been generally negative and hadn't come up with any ideas, taken part in any collective decisions or reversed or parked the car. So why, oh why had I allowed her to make me feel dumb? Why oh why was I probably going to let Judy dominate the conversation when I got home? As the car merged with the traffic on the A21 I had a sneaky feeling that the Games were going to reveal more about me than perhaps I wanted to know.

CHAPTER 9

Give 'Em Plenty

I walked into Robert's bedroom. It was all so familiar, from the broken skateboards hanging on the walls, his own particular brand of trophy from years of heart (my heart) stopping tricks and injuries, to the photos, books and CD's that filled the shelves. And on the top shelf, guardian of the memorabilia of ski trips, holidays and party going, Sooty leant out of an engraved pewter tankard to see who the intruder was in his master's domain, the master now following a life in London. The time had long past when I used to peek in to see how many pairs of socks had been left strewn on the floor and the two pairs of Doctor Marten boots now neatly stored in the shoe rack were depressing in their orderliness.

My presence in the room, where once a mix of Dylan, Bob Marley, Frank Sinatra and Bowie used to blast out, wasn't to assuage a middle aged maudlin appetite for what had gone before but to look ahead in a positive way; to check that I had everything ready for the next day.

The trousers, top and jacket of my uniform were on a coat hanger hanging on the front of Robert's cupboard. A separate hanger held my clean underwear. On the floor beneath it were the trainers which had become the object of my bile. Into one shoe I had tucked my pair of grey socks and red Swatch watch. During training Seb's mates had suggested that the accreditation card should be hung on or near the front door but I decided I couldn't take the risk of overlooking it so it was jutting out of the other trainer. Downstairs by the front door my Games Makers bag, resting on my Fleet Drivers Route Book, was packed with my umbrella, hat, tissues, lipstick, purse, pen, paper, mobile phone, comb, Fleet Drivers Handbook, Games Makers Pocket Guide and, just in case I needed to check up on the credentials of a Games Makers wearing non regulation socks, the Accreditation guide. These were the essentials and my very existence would depend on them. I also had my civvies basket packed next to it. It contained my Overdrive Inc Permit, my make up bag for those last minute touches, blood pressure tablets, a bottle of water for the taking of the aforementioned tablets and a banana and cereal bar for my journey. All was ready. Even the car was full up with petrol and a selection of melodic CD's was handily placed on the passenger seat.

I took the few steps back to our bedroom, set the alarm clock and slid under the duvet, willing myself to go to sleep. There was nothing to stop me, my state of preparedness for my first shift second to none. The washing basket was empty, all the ironing had been done and the fridge was full. I couldn't remember ever being so organised. Or had I been? All I could remember about the long gone days when I was in respectable paid employment was rushing about like a hamster on a wheel. At work I'd be thinking about whether the children had got back from school okay and at home I'd be thinking about what needed to be done on Mrs So and So's file and in the cross over between I had often been short tempered and bossy. But perhaps I had been more organised than I had given myself credit for or was it more that I had taken heed of Seb Coe who didn't want bossy short tempered people with their minds elsewhere to act as hosts.

Seb had laid it down in the Games Makers Workbook that before the Games he wanted us to sort out personal admin tasks such as the payment of bills, purchase of birthday cards and so on ahead of the event. He also advised to ensure all health checks were up to date and that we ate healthily and did regular exercise. He encouraged us to build 'me time' into our daily lives, to enjoy being with family and friends, to spend time with happy, positive people. And he'd even said that on the night before the Games we were to wind down, take a warm bath, read a book and go to sleep in a cool well ventilated bedroom. At nine minutes past ten on the evening before my first shift I turned off the light knowing that Seb had also prescribed that if it was difficult to sleep, then prepare a *'do it'* list.

I had done everything and yet I had a growing sense of unease, of doubt, the same feelings I used to have the night before an exam. Eddie Izzard's personable qualities came to mind but had he done enough to help me remember what I DO ACT stood for? And what about the HOT for spotting suspect items. Just as I used to try and second guess what exam questions might come up, I considered the type of scenario when A. E. I. might be applicable. I imagined my finger hovering over the SOS button set into the ceiling of my Games Makers vehicle, the button we were told on the training day never to press unless we wanted to be surrounded by an armed response unit and hear the rotor blades of a police helicopter circling above. The SOS button was the sort you are forbidden to touch but oh so want to, and I recalled Isabella and how if I had had to spend much more time with her an ejector seat would have come in handy. I tossed and turned, wondering how I could turn the colloquial phrase of *this is doing my head in* into a suitable catchy acronym to make it into a bedtime nursery rhyme.

The alarm went off at three a.m. I woke up with a start. 'Take care,' said a sleepy Roger, turning his back to me as I got out of bed and made for the bathroom. Robert's bedroom may be in desperate need of redecorating but it proved cosy and comforting as I donned my uniform. Perhaps that's why he has insisted it should be kept as it is. Old habits die hard so I stood in the dim rays of the landing nightlight, my head inclined, momentarily listening at Sophie's door. I couldn't hear any canned laughter from a late night TV show that had run on after she'd fallen asleep or any murmurs of slumber from her. Comfortable in her own skin, sure of where she was in the world, she was sleeping the sleep of the content, happy that the homestead was to be left in her tender, efficient care.

I crept about, mindful not to wake Busby who still had to adjust to not sharing the basket with his brother Barney. A living Barney would have created a fuss, incited Busby to jump down and join him scratching at the kitchen door. As it was the only disturbance Barney, buried near his favourite waiting spot in the garden, would have felt that early morning would have been the earth's tremor in his bones as I switched on the car's ignition.

To begin with there weren't many cars on the road. I was out on the highway with the big boys, the truckers with their double, triple headlights, thundering along to or from their supermarket drops. And there was quite a community of lorries parked up in lay-bys, the curtains pulled across the sleeping berths in their cabs. How cosy, I thought, momentarily ignoring the likelihood of their cabs filled with the smell of fetid breath and stale farts.

BBC Radio's World Service was a comfort on that day, as on the rest, though it's to my shame that I can remember few salient facts from the journalistic items I listened to. Carefully researched and beautifully delivered reports of epidemics, pandemics, murders, mayhem, political skulduggery and catastrophes of global proportions were carried through the airwaves to me but like the majority of information I ever had to cram into my head and regurgitate, they shot through leaving little trace.

I motored at an average speed, past the road going to Westerham, the exit for Gatwick, the turn off for Bromley and the next to Lewisham, South and Central London. This was a cinch. The male newsreader with the fantastic deep commanding voice told me the time. 'You've got it wrong,' I told him, seeing how easy it could be for truckers and the like to fall into the habit of conversing with the radio. He repeated the time again. My foot instinctively depressed the accelerator down. Had I set the alarm clock wrong? Had Sophie altered the clock in the car? 'You old devil you,' I teased and eased up on the pedal when I cottoned on that my man of the World was on GMT so there would always be an hour's difference between us.

Turning off the M25, following the signs for Central London, I kept to sixty miles an hour then dropped to the mandatory fifty as I passed mile after mile of traditional 1930/1940's semis set back from the road. I wasn't prepared for the traffic building up so quickly after leaving the motorway. I switched the radio off because the jabber, albeit of international significance, was making me anxious. I complied with the arrows directing the traffic over into the middle lane, and slowed to the sedentary pace of the vehicles in front.

As one person's day ends another's begins. That's how it was for the men in yellow wet weather gear who were collecting up the road cones segregating the moving cars from the outer lane. The outer lane itself was monopolised by a Highway lorry with flashing lights, an extendable ladder and other gadgets worthy of a Tonka toy. The weary men were on the last lap before going home for their breakfasts and to tell their families, friends and neighbours they'd been involved in making a little bit of history.

Whilst the general public of London slept and the newspaper presses rolled forewarning of a gridlocked metropolis, the unsung workers were out painting the words Olympic Lane and drawing five rings on designated lanes of tarmac. There wasn't only painting to be done. Gangs had to go out to put up notices specifying that the Lanes were only to be used by official Games vehicles and there were others employed to connect up LED displays to flash if the Olympic Lanes were in operation or not. Last but not least, someone had to put up signs warning cars to avoid driving in London. Apart from all the training that the athletes underwent, the meetings and conferences that the big bugs at international and national level had to attend to and the briefings given to the volunteers, there were thousands of ordinary people employed to implement the plans to keep London moving and make it a safe and secure place to be in during the summer of 2012. Laudable as it would have been, I didn't break into a rendition of Land of Hope and Glory. All I wanted to do was to start my shift on time but the clock was ticking and I hadn't even reached the point where the signs say to stay in lane for the Blackwall Tunnel. I couldn't contemplate being late because this was going to be the day when I would become a cog in the wheel of a sixty six day operation involving five thousand vehicles and eight thousand and seven hundred volunteers all primed to deliver a service to over nine thousand clients across fifty five competition and non competition venues.

I arrived early at my parking place. I turned into the Avenue. Three storey sandstone coloured brick houses with integral garages and two parking spaces a piece faced each other. There was a central island with sapling trees dividing them. I reversed up into one of the two parking spaces, leaving enough of a gap between the car and the garage so I could put my basket in the boot. I wasn't going to bother to ring the doorbell. That wasn't because there were no curtains pulled across, any interior lights on, or that the streetlight exposed a glinting array of empty bottles and glasses in the first floor windowsill. No, I had learnt from the Triton 29 experience and was confident that I had got the right address and had done everything I could conceivably do in the days prior to my arrival to ensure that if the car was clamped or towed away in my absence I had a body of evidence to show honest intent on my part. I'd sent an email message to Kreety K to confirm my estimated time of arrival. I'd rung KK's mobile to say I might be earlier than originally suggested but couldn't get through which wasn't much of a surprise in view of a hostile review from a Mr Grumpy on the Overdrive Inc's website which I'd chosen to ignore at the time of booking. I'd even gone the whole hog and sent a letter by special next day delivery enclosing my part of the Rental Agreement that Overdrive Inc advised hirers to get the owners to sign. I'd had no response but I had the receipt for my money in my bag and I displayed my authority to park in the windscreen.

I strode towards the prom of the Dock, inhaled the scent of a burgeoning new day and delighted in the sight of the early morning sun playing on the water. It was by virtue of the expanse of water between me and Excel on the other side that had me thinking which route I should take. In preparation for this moment I had previously paid a website visit to the area and indeed had factored in the time it would take me to get from the parking space to Excel. However, I was equally open to changing my view if the reality on the ground didn't correspond with the impression of the place in my mind. I looked to my right and a short walk past one of the huge grey and defunct cranes would lead me to a bridge and once across it I would virtually be tipped into to the lap of the Depot. At one of the training sessions a question mark had been raised as to whether the bridge was going to be open early and late enough for us to use at the beginning and end of shifts and so there was a possibility that I'd have to turn back if access to the bridge was closed. Of course that wasn't the real reason for rejecting the route because, fearful of heights, there was no way I could contemplate crossing the bridge on my own. The alternative was to turn left and exchange the fear I have for bridges for the equally irrational one I have for dominating metal structures such as the row of cranes which have been left as a powerful symbol of what the Docklands once stood for. Originating from a family of Dockers I ought to feel a passing affinity with the hard life and times of those who once worked loading and unloading the ships that tied up to jetties. The other possibility was to walk back through the houses along the road I had driven down and face fast oncoming traffic.

I took a deep breath and turned left. Despite the giddy feeling that might be induced by the towering cranes, I relished the prospect of a walk round the dock. I walked on past the butt end of avenues identical to the one I had just parked in. A couple of joggers lost in their own mind zones with their earpieces in overtook me. What sort of breakfast would a jogger go home to; juice from a juicer, coffee from an espresso machine, bagels, muffins, and a pot of Greek yogurt? I wondered what all those fashionable cafes in West Hampstead that I forsook on Orientation day would have on their early morning menus. Would the café I went to on that cold inhospitable day months before still be teeming with burly men having double eggs and quadruple pork sausages for breakfast? The thought made my mouth water whilst underfoot the large flag stones gave way to cobbles and a narrow strip of brick as the walkway curved round in front of an apartment block. A few apartments showed signs of life. Was that someone ironing on the third floor? Who was that sleepy head stumbling towards the open plan kitchen? What did the day hold for them? I took the bend past a large wooden hut advertising Wakeboarding sessions and then a Thai restaurant tucked in the corner. Out of the bend I walked on past a construction site in the lee of a futuristic building, The Crystal, on my left and to my right the Emirates Gondola station was still having work done to it.

It was five thirty a.m. and I had thirty minutes to go before my shift started. I sat on a bench, peering across the water that separated me and the mystery ironer on the third floor of the apartment. A construction worker came and sat next to me. Steam rising from his cup of coffee, he balanced a newspaper on his lap. A chill breeze swept past and a shiver ran through me. This is silly I said to myself, why sit here when I could be somewhere warm and friendly with a hot breakfast inside me?

I strode past the apartment blocks, convenience stores and hotels of Western Gateway then turned right, then left to walk along the short stretch of prom which would lead me past the walkway to Excel side of the bridge and into FDX. Much had changed since my selection event and training days. Mesh fencing and a gate had been erected and the two young ladies who had been slightly ahead of me were in conversation with a soldier. I stopped and stood back to wait my turn, observing that both women, dressed in full Games Makers uniform were each carrying something that I hadn't been issued with; a square black bag. Why? And why was the question on a second soldier's lips when called over by the first. I only caught snatches of the conversation but the why had been prompted by the lady who wore a hajib, with soldier one asking number two whether there was a female soldier on hand to conduct the security checks. The lady said she would let them proceed and I watched on in high praise for how sensitive they were in making sure that they eliminated any risk of touching her when using the detector wand and when searching her bag. I hadn't even started my shift but had already learnt a valuable lesson in being aware and respectful of the traditions of others.

The welcome was warm and the greetings friendly as I stepped into reception, had my accreditation swiped and was handed a voucher and a black thermos cool bag. It was the black thermos bag that sealed the fact that I had arrived, that I was part of the team, that my hand luggage matched the ones that the two ladies at security had had. Directed round to the other side of the partition and a further row of desks I found more jolly people who wanted to check me in and give me my very own plastic wallet and a box containing a radio. A bell rang faintly in my head but I was too excited to stop to think why. 'Charlie Bravo, Zulu X ray,' I said and laughed. The Dispatcher looked at me quizzically, then at her watch. 'It's six o'clock,' she said. 'The kitchen should be open. Pick up your hot enhancement and take a seat at one of the tables colour coded yellow.'

If I'd had sense I would have found a seat first, checked out my documents and then done the eating thing. But when I got up the few stairs to the main area where we'd had the training and saw line after line of tables and chairs and a bunch of strangers I sought sanctuary, as I have always done, in the room where the cooking smells came from. I was stopped at the entrance by an inexpressive young man dressed all in black with an apron and a hat, the shape of which reminded me of those worn by the American matelots in the film South Pacific.

'Been here before?' he asked, with little of the excitement I had encountered so far that morning.

'No.' I lowered my voice. 'It's my first day.'

He looked me up and down. "Have you got your meal voucher?'

'Yes.'

Have you got a cool bag?'

'I have,' I said, extracting it from underneath my plastic wallet.

'You'll need one of these.' He handed me a blue frozen chill pack and ushered me into the room where we had collected our training day refreshments but now it was kitted out with catering display stands and server units. He stood by my side at the refrigerated drinks cabinet. He opened the door. 'You can take one bottle of drink.' I took out a bottle of fizz. He closed the door. Waiting on his every word I followed in his footsteps to the chilled food cabinet. 'And you can have one piece of fruit, one cereal bar and either a sandwich, prepared salad or baguette.' I smiled to myself, accepting it would be pointless to bring Dad into the conversation who, a devotee of the Army Catering Corps way of doing things, worked on the philosophy of *Give 'em plenty, give 'em plenty, one each, that's enough!*

'Lovely, thank you,' I said conscious of his eyes upon me as I moved closer to the counter to prevaricate between an egg mayonnaise (would it go Yuk in the boot of the car?) or a cheese and salad baguette.

'Over here, over here!' I looked up. A woman was waving a spatula and calling to me from behind the hot food counter. With no time to make use of my cool bag, I grabbed a honey oat bar and a banana.

'Do you want a bacon bap or a vegetarian option of scrambled egg and mushrooms?'

I opted for the bacon, resisted the offer of tomato sauce and turned to see the solemn lad explaining the one each rule to another fresh faced draftee. Calling him solemn is a tad unfair but let's say I wouldn't have him down as a natural bon viveur. Earnest is more the mark. Earnest is as earnest does for being part of the Transport Operation was as much a new experience for him as for everyone. Over the course of time there was the occasional flicker of a smile, a trace of humour from him when I had cause to trade a lukewarm warm ice pack in for a shiny cold one but he wasn't relaxed about his job. The fact that it was a paid job might have been the root cause of his solemnity, particularly when he and his colleagues came in for stick regarding the catering facilities. Okay the food was sameish, the roulette of daily life meant sometimes you didn't get what you asked for and sometimes were offered what you didn't want but I found it no less palatable than Dad's stories of marching on a diet of bully beef and carrots.

At six fifteen I came out of the kitchen. I stood still to get my bearings. I was going to keep my promise to myself that I would not get flustered by anything or anyone during my time as a Driver. Doubt, uncertainty and lack of confidence in my abilities had stalked me for far too long. I was determined not to be intimidated by the whiteness of the walls, the rows of white tables and chairs, and the animated chatter of the other Drivers who looked as if they'd been around for weeks. I was as good as anyone else in that room.

Laden as I was with my jacket, bag, Fleet Drivers Route Book, plastic wallet, radio, black cool bag, baguette, bottle of fizz, cereal

bar, banana, bacon bap, serviette and plastic cutlery, it was a
re-run of how I felt when I went to collect my uniform but to
shout Crackerjack catchphrase at the earnest young man would
have been tantamount to cruelty.

'Are you alright there?' The young woman had a lovely Irish
lilt in her voice.

'Yes, fine.'

'We've met before haven't we?'

'Mm, we have.' I spared her the detail that last time she had
been slumped in a chair waiting for Dirk, Merv, Richard and
me to return after our driving assessment. And whilst I would
have liked to know if she had listened to Merv's complaints
and whether Dirk had been kept on, it was easier simply to
exchange pleasantries about my journey, the weather and how
excited everyone appeared to be. She assured me I was early and
had plenty of time to get settled in and when she walked off
I marvelled at how young and obviously capable she was to have
been appointed as Manager and, my arms aching, I made for the
nearest table that had a coloured sheet of paper on it.

'Been out yet?' asked a man between slurps of coffee as he took
up a seat opposite me. Hardly, I thought, considering what time it
was and all the clutter I had spread about me but I soon established
that he was actually asking whether I had, like him, started two
days previously and had I been out driving.

'No, it's my first shift. Have you?'

'Oh, yes!' His affirmation came in a voice which was the
dead spit of the bulldog in a T.V commercial for insurance. A man
then a woman, then another man arrived and whilst it might not
have been their intention to exclude me, the very nature and tone
of their conversation served to make me feel like an outsider, like
I'd taken up someone else's usual place.

'Where did you get to yesterday?' A asked B.

The name of a Hotel was mentioned and B nodded knowledge-
ably like his namesake in the advert. C asked B what route he'd
taken to get there. B said the traffic lights at the interchange hadn't
been in operation so he'd taken an immediate left up another
street and then right at another. Personally I got lost in his so ons

and so forth's but he sounded pretty clued up to me though A, aided and abetted by C, got his Route Book out to double check that B had driven the best route. I gulped, my throat feeling dry and restricted as I time travelled back to the way I felt when fellow classmates started discussing the answers they had given to exam questions.

'Does anyone on this table need help with how to operate their radios?' I welcomed the intervention from a lady who had suddenly appeared and was standing at the head of the table. 'I'm Kay by the way.' Her smile was wide, her eyes bright and twinkly, her whole demeanour bursting with high octane enthusiasm.

'Excuse me, I'll be back,' I said to my new associates whose knitted frowns were equally reminiscent of classmates who had twigged that I had put a different and incorrect answer down to theirs. I told myself that this was only the first day, only the first hour so what did it matter if I was following Kay like a naughty schoolchild withdrawn from class. Thankfully I wasn't the only radio misfit and three of us gathered in a circle to listen to her. She had barely drawn breath when the circle was broken by a woman brandishing a box.

'What's this?' the woman in a right old fluster demanded.

'A radio,' replied Kay.

'Why do I need a radio?' The woman's lips twitched, her pale eyes flitted nervously about. The bell that had tinkled in my head earlier started up again, its increase in volume coinciding with the thought that the woman, albeit quite ordinary to the naked eye, was dangerous; the sort who can easily create dissension, unsettle and destabilise those of a nervous disposition by spreading tales of woe and imminent disaster. Fortunately Kay displayed no signs of being of a nervous disposition and was trained in effective customer care skills.

'To keep in communication with us.'

'But why?'

'All T3's have them.'

'But I'm not a T3!'

Clang went the bell in my head. 'Nor am I. I'm a T2!'

First day, one hour in; wrong wallet, wrong table, no radio required.

CHAPTER 10

The Comeuppance Car

Put into context, the radio debacle was nothing more than a boo boo, a silly slip up on the part of the eager Dispatcher who had married the lists and paperwork up incorrectly. Who could blame him because in the early morning disorientation and excitement of the first operational week at Excel who but a saint wouldn't do the same?

Of course, I attributed some fault to myself because I had compounded the error in not checking the slip of paper the reception person had given me and, after the banter with the Dispatcher, had made straight to the kitchen without checking my file which had a little sticker on it sayingT3. Neither had I queried the fact that I had been given a radio even though on the training day we had been told that T3's alone would use them. No real harm had been done and I would have no doubt coped had I ended up having to go out on the road as per colleagues A, B and C. What it did do though was highlight the difference between theory and practice, the gulf between Workbook, Handbook, Pocket guide and umpteen Power Point training presentations and daily reality. It was the same as the mindset and skill required in my former life to apply what I had regurgitated in exams to Mr. and Mrs. Blogs sitting in my office whilst I ground through their interminable house purchase papers. Trying to sound enthusiastic about the likes of Mr and Mrs Blogs' rights of way, way leaves and easements had on occasion proved a feat of endurance for me but I'd got there in the end. I had got there in the end though not without some self recrimination when I'd made a silly boob or been outfoxed by sharper minds. As I stood waiting for the Dispatchers to sort out a fresh set of papers I hoped to God my brain would kick into gear. Or did I? An ounce of common sense is worth a pound of brains, Dad was fond of saying so I wondered what he'd think of the organisational faux pas so far.

'It's nothing personal,' I said to my bulldog buddy as I gathered my bag and bits and bobs up from the table. 'I'm going over on that table to be with the T2's.'

'T2's?' He frowned, his right index finger wiggling its way into his ear.

'I'm a T2. Things got muddled.'

He looked in turn at A, B and C but they kept their heads down as if waiting to tell him that they knew all along that I shouldn't have been there in the first place. 'Nice to meet you. I'll see you around no doubt.' With that I decamped a few tables down.

'Is this the T2 table?' I asked of a man sitting back in his chair all very relaxed with his clasped hands resting on his chest.

'It is.' He smiled and pushed his glasses back over his nose.

'Can I sit anywhere?'

'Anywhere you like.'

'I'm Carol.' I walked round to the other side and took a seat opposite him.

'I'm Chris though I probably won't remember yours because I'm rubbish at names.'

We fell into conversation, covering the usual ground of where we had come from, how we had travelled up that day.

'That's handy,' he said of my parking space. 'You've only got to walk over the bridge to get here.'

'No way, I don't do bridges.'

'Well this is the life isn't it?' He looked about at the steady trickle of people who looked as bewildered as I had done earlier. 'I've hit sixty and only retired a couple of weeks ago and now I'm here.'

'I need to sit down!' The lady who had precipitated my move plonked her bag on the table and her backside on the chair next to Chris. 'I'm Chris,' he said. She gave him the once over and with an equally puzzled expression on her face looked over at me.

'And after all that palaver, I'm Carol.'

'Pardon?'

'The mix up just now with the radios? 'Hilda is it?' I gestured to her accreditation card hanging by her midriff.

'What?' Her eyes flickered, her mouth twitched.

'Your name, it's Hilda?'

'Hilda? No, I'm Gillian. I don't know why it says that.'

There was no time for further investigation because Tommy the Beard, one of the Depot Service Managers who had been instructive at training, arrived as did a couple of other volunteer Greenhorns. Tommy told us that we would have daily briefings before we hit the streets and on return there would be a shift debrief and handover of documents and car. I drew parallels with T.V cops and fly on the wall documentaries for we were to be out there in the thick of the action with the best of cops, servicemen and those who kept the wheels of the nation turning. It just shows you what a uniform, a hot enhancement and a group talk can do.

Over and above my flights of fantasy I was encouraged by the fact that the Tommy was being asked questions which revisited ground we had covered in the training days, proving that others in my company hadn't retained all the information and were as uncertain as I was about various aspects of what we were required to do. I also felt vindicated when an older gentleman slipped into the seat the other side of Gillian. She didn't give a first, let alone a second, glance at his lovely open face, cherry cheeks and white slicks of hair either side of his balding pate.

'I got on the wrong table and they're not so friendly back there,' he confided across the table to me.

'I did the same.' I smiled and nodded in understanding.

Tommy answered questions and reiterated that regardless of our role, we had to observe the Highway Code, all speed limits and parking regulations. Gillian kept looking from person to person as he explained that the congestion charge was not our concern but it would be on our own heads if we were caught speeding or for any other traffic contravention. He warned of the cameras in the Blackwall and Limehouse tunnels and the Olympic Lanes didn't give us carte blanche to play at being Mr Toad and toot toot at other road users as we sped past. I hoped Merv, a dead ringer for that role, had been given the same talking to. Car parking fees were also our responsibility but if parking charges were incurred as a result of a client's specific request to go somewhere other than between venue and hotel then they would have to pay them. I could see potential difficulties on that one if you found yourself battling with a language barrier or playing piggy in the middle between awkward delegates when under pressure to scoot into a fifty pound an hour car park to escape a traffic warden. And Tommy was at pains to explain that the cars were not to be left unattended except in designated controlled parking areas. They knew who we were and, when the tracking devices went in, where we were supposed to be. A car left unoccupied in a place it wasn't supposed to be could result in serious and dramatic consequences; it might even be blown up! Understandably that possibility caused a lot of twittering and then, out of the blue and without reference to anything that had previously been said, Gillian piped up. 'Is this is a mobile phone?' Tommy, a little taken aback, replied that it was.

'Will someone show me how to use it?'

'Of course.'

'And what's this?'

'Bluetooth. I'll explain about the connection in a moment. You put it in your ear.'

'I am NOT having that thing in my ear!' The look of outrage and indignation on her face was priceless and I laughed. I couldn't help it, but should have known that the comeuppance car for laughing at Gillian had started its engine and was steering its way towards me.

'And this?'

'It's the charger.'

'I don't know anything about any of this!'

Poor Tommy. He was momentarily lost for words then tried to pacify her by saying she might like to stay back whilst the rest of us got ready to go out in the cars to get to know the routes.

'No clients?' someone asked.

'No, but you will each have your own car.'

If I had thought about it sensibly, it was obvious this was how they had planned it. I took the news with a mixture of disappointment and relief; disappointed because I had, over the preceding days, been mentally gearing myself up for the first day being IT and yet relieved because I hadn't been out in the car on my own.

'There's a fleet of Automatics out in the car park waiting for you.' Tommy announced with 'let's get to it' enthusiasm.

'Automatic?' cried Gillian.

'That's what the sponsor has supplied.'

'I can't drive an Automatic!'

Tommy's shoulders fell. A note of impatience came into his voice. 'Is there anyone else here who hasn't driven an automatic?' Gillian's eyes flitted round and alighted on me.

'I haven't driven one for years,' I confessed. 'It was a Ford Granada and a bit jumpsy in reverse as I recall.' The comeuppance car had arrived to collect me.

CHAPTER 11

Call him what you will

It is no exaggeration to say that the gloom of the car park at Excel stretched out as far as my eyes could see yet in the foreground line after line of saloons, estates and hybrids in differing colours, logos screaming from their sides and individual call signs shouting from their windscreens, demanded your attention. T3 cars were parked in the section to the left, the T2 cars to the right but altogether they only took up a small proportion of parking available. Beyond the area reserved for the Olympic cars there were hundreds of empty parking bays and areas were roped off with swags of orange tape to mark out the route to the outside world. The walkways were soundless, the bells of the lifts up into the venue building were silent. Evidence of life was found in the clunk of a car door, the sound of an engine ticking over or the beam of headlights. I took comfort from those but more sinister, less easy to pinpoint from whence they came, were the whirr of motorised buggies and indistinct voices of soldiers and security personnel who would appear and disappear out of and into the shadows on a whim.

On shift day one I didn't have Costos or Graham to take on the tasks of vehicle checking and all the stuff that they had voluntarily taken on doing, leaving the women to sit and have a non natter in the back. It was all down to me to inspect the car, fill in the check out list and driver details, acclimatise myself to the controls and adjust the seat if I wanted to. Not that I was a regular seat adjuster but one notable occasion was when I didn't fancy a new career as a contortionist after taking possession of the car from a very short person.

My checks on the car completed, I waited for a Dispatcher to come along and refresh my memory on the Sat Nav. Refreshing wasn't quite the word to use considering that training day one had been a botched affair and training day two with Madame Judy yelling at me had proved the stuff of nightmares. If I had some one-to-one training with a Dispatcher specifically sent out to provide instruction, I felt certain that I'd be able to establish a working relationship with Helga.

'Please treat me as if I know absolutely nothing about the Sat Nav, Pauline, and I'd appreciate it if you can do it using words of one syllable.' The brief was plain enough but Pauline, being the lovely, kind soul that she was, either didn't comprehend that I was serious about going back to basics or else felt awkward at my suggestion she talk to me as if I was in Nursery. Nor did Pauline know that my nods of apparent comprehension were unreliable, that I can make a good play of appearing to be listening and assimilating.

'Sorry, Pauline, I'm jumping ahead but I need a split screen, the map to the left with a viewing platform of 125 yards and directional arrows, road names and distance to the right and, especially when driving through the City, I don't want to stick to a one dimensional landscape. I'd like a vista of the landmarks and buildings ahead.'

The split screen was the only positive memory of the Sat Nav that I had from the previous training days. I had been impressed by it, Dirk had recommended it and Judy, flicking her fly away hair, had denounced it as a complete nonsense and so, on all three counts, a split screen commended itself to me.

Looking at it from Pauline's point of view she could be forgiven for thinking that my request showed a better understanding of the workings of the Sat Nav than my request for Kindergarten language had led her to believe. For all she knew I might have been nodding profusely in complete understanding of her explanation of how Helga worked, had taken on board that the Dors system was not fully operational and, if needs be, we would have to rely on putting in the postcode and address of my destination. She had witnessed with her own eyes the fact that

I was writing notes though even as my pen scribbled I was finding them incomprehensible.

She too might have had similar experiences as I had in the past of coming across people who say they know nothing about cooking and end up on an absolute beginners cookery course displaying Michelin star skills, or of people who attend a beginners course in watercolours and turn out sketching, painting and framing Notre Dame cathedral in the time it takes others (me!) to colour wash the sky in. From Pauline's perspective I had intimated that I knew the screen could be changed and even used the correct, or pretty damned near, lingo. What she didn't know was that, like my father before me, I can be pretty good at bullshitting.

It may have been all or any of those factors that influenced Pauline to call over to Donna, another Dispatcher, to come over. From then on the focus changed and all the basic instruction I needed was swept away in the conflab between the two women on how best to adjust the settings to a split screen.

'It doesn't matter, honestly,' I said. 'Remind me, is it the middle button I press for start?'

'There, we did it for you,' said Pauline, clearly chuffed to bits. 'We'd better get on. Are you going out now?'

'No. I've got a secret assignation,' I laughed.

'Oh.' She raised her eyebrow.

I waited in the car, looking over the notes I had made; *Navigation, split screen to right. Left London Hotels. Press I Bring to /11 but don't enter 2. Enter calculate new route pressing 2 to get to map.*

I looked at the controls on the dashboard, too afraid to twiddle with anything. I watched other cars, headlights on, drive slowly past. I got out. Further down I could see other drivers doing their vehicle inspections and in the glare of an interior car light a driver and Pauline had their heads bowed as if in homage to the Sat Nav. Another car sidled past, a fellow comrade raising his hand to me. I felt conspicuous, began to think I had been stood up, had misheard or misinterpreted Tommy's last words to me. I gathered my things together and with a heavy heart locked the car. I gave it one last look and headed back towards the Depot, my smile a shield against the querulous looks of a fresh batch of drivers let out to go to their cars.

It was a smile that easily slipped back into a juvenile pout of disappointment and I blush to think that this was the face that first presented itself to my man who burst out through the Depot door and swaggered towards me.

'Are you Carol?'

I stopped in my tracks. My smile returned. 'Yes.'

'Excellent.' He proffered his hand.

Alan Fisher, a dear departed writing guru of my acquaintance, once said that if you want to give a male character a strong presence, you give him a one syllable name that has a slightly dangerous edge to it. He maintained that Sam, Tom or Bert didn't cut it but mean and moody Max always worked, as would masterful Todd and a smooth yet powerful Jet exudes a special magnetism.

Alan also maintained that you could fashion men with punchy, sit up and take notice names to have vague, unhappy pasts and ill defined or precarious ways of making money to fund their complicated lifestyles. In Alan's fictional world, Max wouldn't ride a moped to a job at the pickle factory along with his thermos carrying mate, Kenneth. He posed the question; does a name define us or do we grow into that name? Is it hard to imagine the sex appeal of a Cecil?

What was the appeal of the man dressed in mesmeric black who wanted to shake my hand? What imagination did one need to find some allure in his dark eyes and a complexion that would toast so easily under a Grecian sun? My hand in his, I didn't catch his full name but it didn't matter because he had thought of everything.

'It's a bit of a mouthful I know so why don't you call me Jet.'

'Jet!'

Alan had never spoken much about the desired build of an idealised fictional hero. I was glad I didn't have to hold Jet up to a preconceived model because he was too short and stocky for my taste. And if he'd asked for a word from the wise I'd have told him that constantly tugging his polo shirt away from his middle and pulling at his jeans is no substitute for watching the calories. I wondered what Alan would have thought of my less than fictional Jet who, with a clipboard held fast to his strong chest, introduced himself as the Instructor charged with the task of making me fall for an automatic transmission. Dirk wouldn't have been able to make me fall for anything, except onto a sword on account of the heat and traffic on my first training day or possibly to engineer a bank robbery on his behalf so as to release him from a career I don't think he had voluntarily chosen. Jet on the other hand oozed confidence as he turned me round and guided me back to the car. 'Carol, you're going to love it. I promise you, you're going to love driving this car.'

I didn't have the heart to burst the bubble of his enthusiasm and remind him that it was only a car, a few bits of metal bolted together with some rubber tyres, and yet enthusiasm is too mealy-mouthed a word to ascribe to him. Passion is more appropriate. Yes, he was passionate about the gearbox and in his belief that with his encouragement I would never look back at a manual transmission again. We came to a halt at the bonnet. He looked into my eyes. 'Trust me,' he said.

'I do.'

'I'll drive first, Carol and we'll talk. Is that a good plan?' His tone, the inflection on my name, he made it sound as if we had known each other for years, as if we were merely picking up where we had left off. But did he feel a degree of resistance in me as he steered me round to the passenger side, the fire he had stoked in my belly urging me on to get behind the wheel immediately and drive, drive, drive.

'I've done all the checks,' I said proudly when we were seated.

'Good.' He leant over towards me. 'We only need to concentrate on one thing and one thing only then, don't we?'

'We do.'

'Shall we go then, Carol?'

'Yes, let's go.' He slid the car out of the bay and we glided along, as much as one can glide at the obligatory five miles an hour through a landscape of speed humps. He turned and looked at me as we approached our first one.

'Think about your passengers, Carol. The passengers in the back will feel the bump more than you will in the front and your aim is to give them the most comfortable ride possible.'

I held my breath till we were down the other side.

'Now what did you think about that?'

'I didn't feel a thing.'

'I told you, didn't I?' He explained the controls as he drove. 'It's magic, isn't it?' And I said that magic only worked if you believed in it. 'Tell me what makes you say that.' So I did, reliving my backward kangaroo jump in the Ford Granada and a more recent experience of driving a Range Rover and breaking into a cold sweat when releasing the brake on a hill start.

'Don't be scared of it, Carol. You are the one in control, always.'

He asked me where I came from, what did I do, was I married, did I have children? That was the way of him throughout, genuinely interested and intent on having a proper conversation. The conversation really did take off when I found out he was in the business of selling cars and he found out I was going to have to change our car soon. In another time and place, other than cruising up the A12, we'd have been spitting into the palms of our right hands and shaking on a deal. As it was, he switched over into an Olympic lane.

'These are going to make your life so easy, Carol.'

'That's what Dirk said.'

'Dirk?'

I explained who Dirk was. He hadn't met him and it disturbed me when I thought of Merv's character assassination job on him. But it didn't disturb so much as to stop me raising a query about the necessity of indicating at traffic lights when the traffic could only go one way. It had been an 'issue' that rankled me with Dirk but Jet took a different view and came out in my favour.

'Ther'll be a bit of under taking in this lane, Carol, because I'm sticking to the speed limit but don't be bullied by other drivers.'

'That's what my daughter always says,' I said proudly, knowing she'd be cringing in embarrassment at me if she could hear me singing her and Robert's praises and witness me fawning as I was.

Yet it was a curious thing that, even though the Olympic lanes weren't in operation, very few cars were venturing into them. We came off the A12 at the Lea Interchange and he turned into a large open air car park which was being transformed into a transport hub. It was a hive of activity with lorries and dumper trucks coming and going and any number of workmen directing said lorries and dumper trucks and moving red cones about.

'Your turn to drive, Carol. Keep to this area where there's little activity but always mind the workforce.'

Confidence is supposed to engender confidence. I'm not so sure it does with me because, after the initial burst of high octane adrenalin in the car park, I was nervous, more so than I had been with Dirk, even with hyper Merv and huffy Richard in the back. Good old reliable Dirk hadn't said much. He had been disconnected, in a world of his own and I had taken advantage of his vulnerability and felt in control. It was different with Jet. Jet was very present, made me all fingers and thumbs.

'The art of automatic driving, Carol, is to forget about your left leg. You don't need it. Keep it away from the pedals. Come on move it away, bring the knee up.' It was alright for him, he had short plump legs. If I brought my leg up much further I wouldn't be able to see the gear stick thingy to put it into Drive or Reverse. 'When you're ready, Carol' He looked at his sheet of paper and the car manufacturer might say it's impossible but the car stuttered as I sheepishly moved my right foot from one pedal to another. The trouble was it felt like a dodgem car.

'Remember what I said about minding the workforce,' Jet said, as I narrowly missed two men in hard hats and fluorescent aprons. 'And watch out for the buses.'

'Why are so many of them turning round?'

'I've driven buses.'

'And where is that lorry going to?'

'I've driven lorries.'

'What about one of these?' I asked, feeling under attack as a dumper truck came bouncing towards me.

'Yes and dumper trucks.' And concrete mixer lorries, fire engines and ambulances. You name it he'd driven it, the roll call of vehicles that had come under his command tripping off his tongue as I made myself giddy going round in circles.

'Any workforce in the way that I can take out?' I joked when he insisted I show him that I could go into reverse.

'Nice, nice, very smooth. Let's head back to the Lea Interchange.' And I got a 'well executed' when I merged with the traffic on the southbound carriageway of the A12. And also fair praise when I overtook a breakdown vehicle. He had driven one of those as well and I laughed but pride comes before a fall and Jet didn't have much of a sense of humour. There I was thinking I was competent enough to give the Olympic Lane a test drive when he leant over slightly and, as if trying to prevent someone in the back from hearing, murmured,. 'Watch your speed, Carol. You don't want to have got to this stage and end up with a speeding ticket, do you?'

'No, I don't, do I?' I simpered, my immediate thought being that I should change down gear but couldn't. I considered the best option to be to maintain the same speed till I could work out what to do. Suddenly realising that I needed to take the next exit otherwise we'd end up whooshing into the Blackwall tunnel. I floundered, braked, switched over into the inside lane then veered off onto the slip road. Brought to a breathtaking stop at traffic lights I apologised. Jet tugged and loosened his polo shirt away from his armpits.

'It's that left leg of yours, Carol.'

'It's bad enough wearing these huge trainers but to then have all this business keeping my left leg out of the way. I feel, I feel, so inelegant!' Inelegant!

'Oh, aren't you sweet, Carol.'

Sweet, sweet! Who on God's earth and over the age of six wants to be thought of as sweet? I felt less than sweet negotiating the next roundabout with five exits and a strange contraption of a vehicle passing by which, you guessed it, Jet was quick to identify as being similar to one he had driven when he was in the Army.

'My brother was in the Army. He used to drive three ton trucks. In fact I used to have to go to school in a three tonner.' I smiled, sweetly of course, and wondered if 'sweet' was a word he would use on the assessment form he was filling in. Trying to regain some dignity by way of adult conversation I asked him what he'd be doing once the Games started.

'I will be at home, on holiday.' And the description he gave of his home country, sunshine glistening on lapping deep blue coastal waters, high rugged mountain ranges inland and warm and friendly people was a world away from the soldiers directing us into the screening area, marking our arrival back to base.

'You enjoyed it?' Jet asked as, after negotiating the speed humps, keeping well within the speed limit and reversing into a marked bay, I switched the engine off.

'Yes.'

'I told you you'd love it.'

'You did.'

And if you tell yourself something often enough they say you'll begin to believe it.

CHAPTER 12

Hotting Up

Jet left me in the car park to fill in my forms. I couldn't put my hand on my heart and say I had loved the driving experience. It hadn't been a case of a 'you might enjoy this' or 'you'll probably like this'. He took a commanding 'you will love it' approach and whilst my version of events betrays an air of mockery, I did find Jet's unbridled enthusiasm refreshing. It was just that I don't respond well to that kind of encouragement. However, his influence has had what the organisers of the Games love to call 'a lasting legacy'. I didn't notice it immediately but as time has progressed I often catch myself doing a Jet, from telling the gas man that he'll simply adore his new car to telling others that they have the power within themselves to accomplish things. And stranger than that, arrogant as it may be, I'm most times convinced that they will do as I say and I feel better for my telling them so.

I went back into the Depot and, Jet having obviously vouched for my roadworthiness, was given the all clear to spend the rest of the morning and the best part of the afternoon getting to know the car on my own. The day was turning out to be nothing like I had envisaged but if I'd checked my emails properly beforehand I would have had warning of it. I didn't, I hadn't but I still had the meeting with Robert and Hannah to look forward to.

I'd been up since three a.m., driven to my parking space, had a ten minute walk to Excel, a bacon butty, a real live briefing, a second driving experience to bring a high colour to my cheeks and the hands on the clock had only dragged themselves round to ten o'clock. In most offices it would be too early for a coffee break but I felt I deserved one.

All the lads and lasses who had been on my table at the beginning of the day were nowhere to be seen except for Gillian who was loitering by the drinks station which was a completely separate entity from the canteen/kitchen and located halfway down the room. Her lips quivered as I approached, as if she was rehearsing what she was going to say and yet she said nothing. My tone light, my smile underplayed so as not to overawe her, I asked how she was getting on.

'I wish someone would tell me.'

'Are you on your way in or on your way out?' My intentions were honourable, my purpose to bring some clarity to her state of confusion.

'Out where?'

'To the venues on the schedule. They look to be all over the place.' Our conversation soon proved the same and even when Kay the Dispatcher, who had been dishing out the radios earlier, came over it took a fair few minutes before she could unravel what Gillian's problems were. Admittedly I had only made Gillian's acquaintance that morning so we weren't bosom buddies but I certainly saw a different side to her when she finally cottoned on to the fact that we didn't have any clients to speak of. She had had lucid moments during the briefing though where her head had been in between times was anybody's guess but at that moment she got in what a former secretary of mine would call 'a right old snit', every tic in her face and twitch of her body denoting her displeasure. I backed away discreetly, made myself a coffee and wandered off to look at the map on the board which showed the main areas of the country, indeed the world, where we drivers had been culled from.

A comfort break later, I was back at the exit desk having my accreditation scanned.

'Going out in the car on your own?' the Dispatcher asked. 'Anywhere nice?'

'I hope so. Lee Valley.'

'The Water Sports Arena? It's a bit of a trek.'

'Don't remind me. We were supposed to go there on the training day but it became one of those so near and yet so far trips and I'm intending to get back on time today.'

'Were you one of the ones in the missing car?'

'I wouldn't call it *missing*.'

'We kept calling and calling.'

'An accident caused mayhem.' I applied a broad brush to the journey with the acoustically challenged Dirk and the man boys in the back.

'You shouldn't have any problems today but if anything does go wrong give us a call.'

The cool air of the car park stroked my face, flushed as it was from the notoriety that had latched on to me even before I had set off on my first solo mission. I walked with steadfast purpose towards my car, brought to a halt within inches of its bumper by the sight of a car crawling by. I did a double take. It was Gillian. I stood open mouthed like a person caught on a T.V programme of staged mishaps. She turned right. I fixated on her tail lights to the end of the row and then she turned left. 'She's gone the wrong way,' I said out loud. But had she? Which was the right way? Which way was I supposed to go?

'Are you alright?'

I turned. A petite lady appeared from behind a neighbouring vehicle. I had never seen her before, not on training days or earlier in the car park and with her trim figure, attractive face and general confident bearing, she was someone you'd remember. I immediately went into Games Makers Workbook / Online Training security mode, my brain working at a speed that my friend and training coach, Lynda, would have been proud of.

HOT! Had she been HIDING, lying in wait? There were pillars and dark corners a plenty in that car park and she was small and nimble enough to be able to secrete herself in a hundred different places. Her physique was ideal for burrowing her way between the vehicles only to pop up to confront drivers in those sensitive psyching up moments before they became fully operational Games Makers. Her bright eyes and engaging countenance was ideal for putting someone off the scent of suspicion. But I wasn't just someone.

Was she OBVIOUS? Well she was at that moment but she wasn't wearing a single item of standard issue uniform. Dressed in casual T shirt and trainers her only concession to some kind of official wardrobe was a high visibility tabard. I was as sceptical of that as of anything because it swamped her and she could easily have used her feminine wiles to purloin it from one of the workmen working outside on the perimeter fencing. It wasn't beyond the realms of possibility either that being so spry she'd be dextrous enough to hang inside the jacket on a hook near the fire bucket and no-one would be any the wiser.

Was she TYPICAL? There wasn't a grey hair to be seen amongst her beautifully cut and easy to manage hair. There wasn't an age spot on her moisturised hands or a plastic wallet held by her manicured fingers. Was it possible that the organisers had split the training days into age specific? I'd heard no hint of that and it would surely have flown in the face of the Workbook ethic on being non discriminatory. Or perhaps a younger element had been at my training days and I had been ageist, glossed over their existence, made a beeline only for those of a similar age or older than me?

'What are you up to?' I asked, without thinking through a strategy to flush out the credentials and intentions of the interloper.

'Are you sure you're alright? You look confused.'

I bristled at this one clever lady employing the art of deflection.

'Are you lurking here on your own?' The words spilled out, the training video bods seriously underestimating the pique a big and ungainly security conscious Games Maker could feel at being accused of doolallyiness by someone so bright and sparky. Scissor sharp, she looked up at me and repeated the word *lurking* as if it was a joke. In my book she had overstepped the mark, was impertinent in her boldness. It hurt me to fashion a smile but I did because it gave me a breathing space whilst I mentally ran through the Act, Escalate Inform jingle to help me decide whether this woman's demeanour and presence was reportable?

'Here she is,' I said loudly when one of the management team came threading her way through the sleeping cars. 'Maureen, I'm glad you're here. I need to talk to you about Helga.'

'Helga?' Maureen's frown was deep set, giving me hope that she had correctly read the SOS plea in my eyes. I explained the nickname which now seemed childish and trite.

'And Pauline said something about not pressing number 2 to override the previous instruction. I wrote it down somewhere but I might have got it wrong. I'd appreciate your help.' The mystery woman laughed, the laugh serving to reinforce what was already writ large across her delicate features, namely that I was utterly bonkers.

'If you don't mind waiting,' said Maureen.' I'll help Carol first so that she can get on her way.'

'No problem. I'm quite getting used to this high vis.' She did a twirl and, like friends I have who'd look stunning wearing a dustbin bag, immediately turned the tabard into a must have fashion item. 'I'll go back inside the Depot for a mo. Good luck.' I didn't know if the good luck was aimed at me or at Maureen. Feeling stupid about my earlier challenges, I returned the compliment though it struck me that she probably wasn't the sort to rely on a throwaway sentiment. She was a lady who knew want she wanted, where she was going and how to get there.

'Do you still want some help, Carol?' asked Maureen.

'No. No thanks. I was just... well it seemed... no... I'll see if I can work it out for myself.'

'If you have any problems, we'll be here for you.'

I did have problems, real problems, because I couldn't get Helga to respond nor get the wing mirrors to adjust to how I wanted them but on two counts I needed to get out into fresh air and daylight. Count one; I recalled from training that some drivers had waited till they got outside to pick up a signal hence the number of cars I'd seen pulled up in the shadow of the car park in Seagull Lane. Count two was I didn't want to still be sitting in the car twiddling with the controls when the others came back. I took a deep breath and started the car up.

All I had to do now was to remember how to drive.

CHAPTER 13

Cruising Down the High Road

In the movies things happen in cold, ill lit car parks; threats are made, scores are settled and a pack of hungry and bloodthirsty hybrid animals left to roam the concrete levels after a cataclysmic event have not proved beyond the bounds of an imaginative scriptwriter. Such thoughts filled my head as I proceeded at a stately pace, heeding Jet's advice to take the speed bumps '*slow and gently*'. I didn't spot any abandoned cars with their doors left open or an accreditation card and mobile phone left lying in a pool of blood but I was glad, so glad, to leave the grey emptiness of the place and nose the car out into the sunlight.

I turned left and watched Helga's screen show that I was driving along Seagull Lane with the car park to my left and the track of the Docklands Light Railway to my right. So far so good and then I correctly turned right at the traffic lights on the junction with Western Gateway but at the next set of lights the command to carry straight on put me in a dilemma. What did 'straight on' mean? With Dirk it had been slightly right, with Jet slightly left. I did a Jet and two roundabouts and four sets of traffic lights later I was on the A12 and giving nodding acknowledgment to the Devas Street turning which led down to Robert's former abode.

As the security blanket of the city and built-up residential areas fell away and the car started eating up miles on the M11, my stomach began to gurgle, an indicator of my hunger and apprehension, both aggravated by Helga keeping quiet. A pang of nostalgia hit when the signpost to Chingford loomed into view.

'Ah, Dirk and the boys,' I sighed, applying a tincture of rosy glow to my recollection of when we had turned off there. Dirk and Jet alike drove the streets of Chingford but Helga was silent on the subject of joining them. The silence was unnerving. I could have put the radio on but didn't want to unwittingly press something I shouldn't. It was an apprehension of levers, knobs and thingamajigs that lasted throughout the duration of the Games, so much so that if a previous driver had left the radio on I couldn't switch it off, my master plan being that, in the presence of a client, I would either feign deafness or else a mumbling affliction to disguise it. With no radio or urgent desire to break into song, I summoned up the ghost of Merv, imagined him clapping and whooping in the back as I warned the car that I was going to 'see what you Beamers made of' and sped ever further away from the metropolis.

Helga perked up as we approached Junction Six. She flashed impatient green arrows at me to exit and join the anti-clockwise ring of the M25. Flanked by fields and trees the car was enjoying its run and on an ordinary day I would probably have lapsed into a customary daydream only to be jolted out of it by a sign for an unplanned for destination flashing past. That just wasn't going to happen with Helga because she piped up with timely advice to leave the orbital at Junction Twenty Six and head for Waltham Cross.

Roundabout after roundabout followed. I took the exits that she told me to. 'Continue forward,' she said at a set of traffic lights. 'You will have reached your destination in three hundred yards.' Straight ahead of me was a new development of detached and semi detached houses. The lights changed. Banking on white water sports not taking place in freshly laid drives and front gardens, I turned left. A short way down the road 2012 banners billowed outside an entranceway. I crossed the carriageway to join vans and lorries shunting back and forth and slid into the only space available. Holding one hand to his hard hat a man came rushing up to me. I wound the window down.

'I'm not stopping but is this Lee Valley White Water centre?'
'It will be.'

'Ok, I'll just reset my Sat Nav and I'll be off.' But no matter what I did Helga stubbornly stuck to showing the chequered flag for the destination I was currently at on the housing development and I wasn't au fait enough with the controls to override her. I decided it was best to get to the flag and the development might have a pleasant communal green where I could eat the food which would have by now sucked the moisture out of the ice pack and be sweating nicely in the boot.

Back at the traffic lights I turned left. Crawling along, with houses on my right, a verdant bank falling away from the left hand kerb, Helga become more vocal and excited with every foot we took. I stopped at a dead end, opposite the side elevation of the last house on that stretch of road. I had a problem; Helga's flag on the map was sited at a point straight ahead in the middle of a field behind a fence. I reversed and did a U turn. My powers of concentration had been such that I hadn't noticed a London 2012 car parked on the opposite corner, at the mouth of the housing estate proper. I wondered if the owners of the adjacent house were going to get heartily sick of a succession of cars circling like crows for a prey that as yet didn't exist.

I pulled up behind the other car, got out and had a much needed stretch.

'It's good here, isn't it?' called the man leaning up against THE car.

'It's certainly not what I was expecting,' I replied, as he came towards me. He was six foot four or more, big with it and had long dreadlocked hair tied back in a pony tail.

'What have you got?' He drew heavily on his cigarette as he went round the back of my car. 'Ah,' he exhaled, 'a three series.'

'What's yours then?' I asked, trying to deflect attention from mine just in case he was thinking of running his nicotine fingers through the grime that had begun to form from the journey or start the nonsense of kicking the tyres that, for some unearthly reason, certain men examining vehicles do. 'I like the colour.' It was propped half way on half way off the kerb, a position I knew Dirk would have disapproved of.

'Five series.'

'It doesn't look dissimilar to mine.'

'Has yours got cream leather seats and other features?'

'No. Does that mean that you are a T1?'

'I am.'

'So why are you here?'

'My client hasn't flown in yet.'

'Not parachuting into that field, then?'

'Hardly. He's the...'

I wouldn't divulge it anyway so it's no great shakes that I can't actually remember the name, though I recall that as Roll Up Ronald puffed merrily away I was mighty impressed with the credentials of the much anticipated X of Y. It wasn't for me to mention it but I did wonder if the X of Y smoked. There were notices in the cars forbidding smoking but we had been told that in many countries the smoking laws were more relaxed or nonexistent and we were to politely advise clients to extinguish their cigarettes if they dared to light up. It crossed my mind whether Roll up Ronald had been matched with X because of their mutual liking for cigarettes. Or was the long exaggerated inhalation of this T1 symptomatic of his last days of smoking before his duties? It wasn't my problem until, having decided to forego eating my lunch on a Housing Estate pavement, I got back into the car. He poked his head through the window, ostensibly to double check Helga understood my command to go henceforth to my next destination but I could tell he was checking out the range of my three series dashboard controls. Yes, checking out my controls and overpowering me with nicotine smells in the process. I bid him a hasty farewell.

My journey along the Great Cambridge Road was taken up with considering my options should I ever have to pick up a client who smelt of smoke or anything else that offended my nostrils. Should I carry a car freshener with me at all times? Would ocean breeze or vanilla scented be best? Was I allowed to customise my car in this way? Would security allow a pungent pine tree to dangle from my rear view mirror? As the A10 receded and signs for the A406 appeared I realised I was taking it a bit far, was on the slippery slope to inventing a worry for worry's sake when there were more pressing things to get het up about other than the personal hygiene habits of clients.

One pressing thing was called the North Circular, a road where fast and aggressive drivers who knew where they were going tried to browbeat me as I headed falteringly down the main carriageway, hemmed in by lorries and concrete retaining walls. It was a road overseen by lines of houses and crisscrossed by flyovers and slip roads leading to traffic lights and roundabouts that led me close to where I wanted to be then further away and round in a circle again. Going round in circles? I didn't find it funny.

I was heading for Wembley Arena, close neighbour to Wembley Stadium with its unmistakable roof dominating the skyline. If I made it to the Stadium it would be a mere hop, skip and a jump to the Arena where my cold bones had been warmed by the evangelical zeal of orientation training, which now seemed a very long time ago. I was tired and fraught, and the signs for and sight of the Stadium roof itself became a mirage, one minute there, the next minute gone. I kept making the mistake of taking Helga literally, bearing immediately left down Dog Lane instead of holding my nerve and bearing left further on. I was cross with myself for prematurely branching off, loathed the traffic lights, took a dislike to the shoppers at the parades of shops, rubbished the houses bounding the roads as I went up and over the flyover, down and up and over, then down, and back again and over and down and back to Dog Lane, Neasden Lane, Blackbird Hill, Forty Avenue and so on and so forth until eventually I limped into Engineers Way, my destination proving to be another uninspiring dusty site. It would only take one happy snapper from a national newspaper whose editorial comment was critical of the Games to come out of a leading DIY retailer and catch me sitting on the kerb by the car in the retail park for the following day's headline to read *Is this the real face of volunteer Britain? A kerb welcome to the world. British taxpayers fund the baguettes.* But I didn't care a damn. My armpits were sticky and aglow; I was delusional and ravenous. I tore into my baguette and took belch inducing gulps of fizzy drink and didn't give a monkey's as to whether I would later fill the car with noxious smells. I was human after all.

124

Time; it is one of my obsessions, one of the things I have difficulty coping with. It was way past two o'clock, the shift ended at four. Afterwards I was meeting up with Robert and Hannah at Custom House Station. From looking at the map I guessed Helga would give directions to head back on the Alternative Olympic Route Network. She didn't and whilst I couldn't profess to know exactly where I was in relation to where I wanted to be, I began to get jumpy as I waited for vans to park and buses to pull out as the traffic limped through Willesden. I turned into Kilburn High Road.

Kilburn.

'Kilburn. Full of Irish navvies it is.' Dad's words came back to me as I stop-started in the busy traffic. His opinion was very often expressed as he sat at one end of the settee with me at the other watching the telly. 'Go in any pub and you'll hear the Mick's and Paddy's. It's the same in Hammersmith too.'

'In the Queens?' asked Mum who sat between us. Dear Mum, always piggy in the middle but not without her own streak of spirit for the question had a hidden sting in it; Dad's portrayal of his lonely weekday life in Hammersmith lodgings heating up baked beans on one burner often didn't ring true when he let slip who he'd been talking to of an evening.

He grunted, shifted forward and over exaggerated tilting his head to catch the news. It was enough to disturb the equilibrium of our positions on the seat. I gathered my legs up, clasped my hands around my knees.

'Does it matter?'

He pointed at the screen. 'It does when all this bloody lot is going on in Northern Ireland.'

'Dad says they'd never post our David out there, he's too hot-headed. Like somebody else I could mention.' She nudged me and nodded at Dad, the innocent mention of David, their son, my brother, sometimes proving another bone of contention. Over a pot of tea and a packet of fags with Mum or confiding to me in my bedroom more about his scrapes than I wished to know, David was normally amiable and quietly spoken but after a week at home on leave, his and dad's voices raised in anger were indistinguishable. They talked the same, walked the same, responded to the same triggers; firing bullets of old hurts and sleights at each other, only to turn the guilt and regret they felt afterwards back at themselves with equal vehemence. It was not a pretty sight.

'You're talking rubbish, Dad, you can't blame all the Irish people in London, in the entire world, for things that are happening there. It's only a very small minority.'

'Listen to me, I know a lot more about the Irish than you with all your books will ever know.' He shifted in the seat and I knew he was looking at me whilst I broke off the split ends of my long hennaed hair. 'I'm telling you, there are people of Irish origin sending money back to fund all these bombings.'

'Ugh,' Mum shuddered. 'I can see and smell those horrible flats where we lived in Victoria Barracks and Alan and David used to put on an Irish accent to save them getting picked on by the other kids for being British.'

'And it's religion, religion, that's at the root of it. Always was, always will be and there'll never be an end to it. '

'And as true as I'm sitting here, Carol,' Mum prattled on, 'it was always raining and my word, I never thought we'd survive the sea crossing. We've still got that photo of Alan and David looking ill on the boat.'

Naturally, with the wisdom of youth, I felt it my duty to remind Dad that his father had arrived in England as an orphan from Cork (a legend later disproved) and Jim and Ena, his landlord and landlady of whom he was very fond, had Irish connections and were of the religious persuasion that he was so vehemently against. 'Perhaps you ought to ask them what they do with the money you give them as rent.'

'What did you say?' he rounded on me.

'I don't know,' said Mum, 'we can never watch anything on the T.V. without there being an argument about something.'

'I'd have got the back of my father's hand or the belt for speaking to him like that.'

'And knock one devil out and ten devils in,' Mum moved forward to block the confrontation.

I got up, stretched, yawned, left an antagonistic 'huh?' in the air before making my escape upstairs, letting the fallout rumble on till I was called down so we could all wash it away with cream crackers and drinking chocolate. 'She was the teenager you wouldn't wish on your worst enemy,' Mum used to say of me years later, the comment always provoking laughter from her audience and protests of misguided disbelief.

Imprisoned in the car, outpaced by pedestrians, I wondered what mothers said of their teenagers ambling down the Kilburn High Road, the girls in ditsy tops and leggings, the boys with their jeans low slung so as to show just the right amount of underpants. What did fathers say of their daughters coming home with tattoos or, descending from other cultures, adopting western mores? Were they all as bolshie as I had been?

Such thoughts on the High Road brought my father back to life, or near as dammit, dressed in dark grey trousers, white open necked shirt and black blazer with regimental badge he joined me in the passenger seat. I pulled up short at traffic lights to let pedestrians spill across the road, his feet shifting and twitching as mine do when I'm a passenger.

'Looks to me like every nationality under the sun.' I could hear Dad say.

'Yes, there's something like over three hundred different nationalities in London. Being up here has certainly made me think about cultural differences and the Olympics committee are very keen to promote diversity and inclusion.' God, I sounded pompous and was using terms which would have been quite alien to him. I saw him circling his moustache and chin with thumb and forefinger and had that familiar sinking feeling in my stomach as I hoped against hope that he wouldn't start voicing his views.

'We've come a long way from the old days, Carol.'

'Yes, thankfully we have.'

'We're not arguing, we're debating, aren't we, Carol?' he'd always say, it blindingly obvious that both of us rejected the other's point of view. But in the end I came to acknowledge, even respect, the fact that his views came out of the times in which he lived, the Army that he'd served in. Hotheads both, Dad and I had clashed in my youthful, angry phase but he had been tolerant and forgiving in heaps of ways others would have found impossible to believe.

I looked up at the windows above the shops. Who worked in an office which screamed its contact details at you in big bold stick-on letters, or toiled in a room protected from the world by vertical white blinds? What lives were led in the dark shadowy rooms behind grubby windows? I pondered the imponderable; why was I, like Mum before me, making judgments about people based on the whiteness or greyness of their net curtains. What life had Dad led in the capital?

The lights changed. He smoothed the dashboard, studied the controls. If he went to open the glove compartment I'd have to tell him not to. 'This would certainly be one in the eye for Jim, Carol. He was a chauffeur, a chauffeur to some posh nobs as well.'

'I know, you've said it before.' I swerved to let an impatient, sleek, black car with flags on it zip past.

'What the hell!' His phantom foot, much quicker than mine, reached out to use the brake again. 'Was that one of yours?'

'I couldn't see if it had a logo on the front.'

'Bloody hangers on the lot of them.' For sure that's how he would have viewed everyone, the Olympic committee, the delegates, the security people, the government departments, and the whole damned shooting match. And he'd have questioned why I'd volunteered in the first place but, without doubt, he would have bragged to others about my role, exaggerating and embellishing it till I was driving the Head of some world organisation in a bullet proof Rolls. A proud father who, forgiving of my mistakes and misdemeanours, engendered, by accident or design I wouldn't like to say, hurts and jealousies in others.

In that traffic I reflected on how we had reached an accommodation and now, with the wisdom age, instead of arguing the point with him I changed the subject and pointed up to the whirring police helicopter overhead. 'That's a sign of the times, Dad, a sign of our surveillance society. Have you noticed the cameras in the streets?'

'And what are those things that look like saucers?'

'Satellite dishes. You need one of those, Dad, to receive that.' I pointed at an advertising hoarding and I thought of the fun he'd have had with a Sky planner and remote control, watching all day and all night, and recording too, to get his money's worth. Leaving Kilburn to enter leafy St John's Wood he had me laughing.

'Would I need a Wiffy?'

'A Wiffy?'

'Lots have places seem to have them, especially cafes.'

'It's Wi Fi, Dad. I'll have to add that to your other mispro-nunciations.' But he never did take kindly to being laughed at, didn't like to be told. A cloud came over my ghostly visitation, a thickening cloud as I proceeded through Maida Vale and he got cross at not understanding my feeble attempts to explain computers and the Internet. Satellites in the sky would be as a fairy story on a par with the first moon landing which my not unintelligent father curiously considered an elaborate hoax filmed in a TV studio.

'You'd better tell me how to pronounce what it says in that shop window in case I get it all wrong, AGAIN.'

'It's the Lotto. Do you want me to explain or not?'

By the end of Edgware Road his brain had worked overtime calculating whether a pound Lotto ticket had more favourable odds to his usual twenty pence each way bets on the gees gees or the weekly money he handed over to the football pools man. 'I'd spend my winnings on a trip back to Malaya, buy a boat and Captain's hat and surprise Alan and everyone by sailing into Polruan. And I'd buy you a sports car.'

'I wouldn't want one Dad, not driving in London, certainly not here.' Marble Arch was manic. But he was full of pipe dreams of fine cars and swish hotels as we hurtled down Park Lane; pipe dreams and a pocketful of stories.

'Talking of Jim, did I ever tell you the yarn about...?' And the first line of the story was, as always, lost in his chuckling. 'The one about...' He'd shake his head, coughing and choking, trying to get the words out against the tide of emotional energy engulfing him. I'd laugh at his laughing, wondering what he was going to come out with next. 'People will think we've gone mad.' He'd wipe his tears away but it was hard at times to know, despite the mirth, if they were tears of joy or sadness just as it was hard for me to decide in which direction to go as Hyde Park Corner loomed up.

'Aah, this is my old stomping ground.'

'Go straight across the square,' Helga cut in. I hadn't given her a thought for miles. I didn't understand what she meant so I followed the road round.

'I'd better let you go, Dad, otherwise I'll keep going round in circles'

'Drop me off near the Park and I'll see what's what with the barracks.'

'I don't think the flats in the tower block are occupied anymore.'

'Your Mother never wanted to move up and live in them anyway. Things might have been different if we had.'

'You can't keep looking back, Dad, at what you should or could have done.'

'That's rich, coming from you.'

We were on dangerous ground but circling the Corner there was no time or place to stop and reflect. 'You'd better go, Dad, before I do or say something I'll regret.'

'Tell Roger he's still my favourite son- in-law won't you?' It was an old joke. 'And tell him to try The Queens for a lunchtime pint.'

'Go!' A taxi hooted. I shouted at the car in front so that I could switch lanes and circle the Corner again. It wasn't at Helga's insistence. It was at mine for I wanted to catch one last glimpse of the lone figure of Dad, hands behind his back setting off to take a constitutional in the Park. It wouldn't be long before he'd stop to smile at a child, scowl at a cyclist or pass the time of day with those who'd care to. Pressed by the traffic, I had no time, no cause, to linger save to catch the last reflection of a ghost, a once big and bruising military man who aged to stoop and mellow into the softest man Roger said he'd ever met.

There wasn't time to think of anything else but getting back to Excel by four. Aided and abetted by Helga I shoved and merged as belligerently as the rest of the vehicles only to find myself in Whitehall. A nifty right turn had me down on Victoria Embankment and feeling happier for being with free flowing vehicles on familiar territory. Upper and Lower Thames Street was fine but I rushed headlong straight into the jaws of Tower Gateway and the dull ache of a traffic snarl up. My mobile rang, and then it stopped. The bleep of a text came through. Inching along, I pulled the phone out of my bag. Hemmed in by a white van with the male passenger staring in at me, I read the RING ME from Robert. It rang again. I dropped it like a hot potato into my lap as a second white van man at the rear hooted for me to move forward a metre. But for my uniform and the logo stickers on the car I would have made an unladylike gesture at him. The phone went again.

'Robert. What do you want?'

'We've forgotten the tent and have got to go back and...'

'I can't talk. I'm stuck in traffic. I'll text when I can.'

I threw the phone onto the passenger seat and glared in my rear view mirror. Man in van was yards away, chatting merrily on his phone; man at side had edged away, his passenger's arm hanging out of the window drumming on the door. I opened the window, choked on the fumes and closed it. Hot, tired and dawdling past East Smithfield I questioned why I had ever thought I could hack driving in London. It was so huge, so busy and so slow. How was anyone going to get anywhere? Was I capable of getting that someone somewhere? Those questions niggled and gnawed all along The Highway and Aspen Way, into Excel and through the screening process. As I pressed the button to fold the wing mirrors in I prepared my speech of resignation.

'Had a good day?' Kay asked as I staggered in. She made no mention of it being past 4 o'clock. I dumped my stuff on Jack the Dispatcher's desk. 'Long,' I said. 'I didn't get all the trips on the list done.' Take it, take it all and burn it, is what I meant to say.

'Where've you been then?' Jack asked, whilst maintaining an eye on the computer screen.

'Lee Valley and Wembley. I'm not sure I programmed the Sat Nav correctly.'

'In what way?' Jack frowned.

'Would you normally have to go through Willesden and Kilburn?'

'Oh, yes, The Sat Nav will take you that way sometimes, won't it, Jack?'said Kay.

'But how long should it take you?' I pressed.

'Weren't you late starting? Didn't you have some instruction?'

Jet seemed a lifetime away and despite Kay's encouraging noises, Jack was looking a bit sceptical. 'Carol's been a long way, hasn't she, Jack?'

'If you're not used to London,' he conceded.

'And don't forget that there'll be Olympic lanes.'

'Yes, I saw the men painting the hoops, the rings, on the road.'

'And for a mile, the golden mile, from each venue there will be volunteers directing you where to go.'

'Mmm.'

'You seem uncertain, Carol?' said Jack.

'No, well yes, in a way. It's just that...'

'Yes?'

'I was just wondering, what with me being late and all that, whether you would actually want me back on the next shift?' I don't know why I phrased it as I did. It came over in the vein of someone fishing for a compliment whereas I was in reality trying to give them and myself a get out. And I don't know what answer I wanted or would have been satisfied with.

'Oh, how sweet, listen to her, Jack, bless her.'

I could cope with the 'bless her', used as it is in an endearing way by family and close friends but SWEET!? Not in a million years could I be thought of, and not to my knowledge have I ever been referred to, as sweet before but I had now been called it twice in less than twelve hours. I felt like an old lady arriving back in the home after a day trip out. Was their response activated by the dotty dithering role I cast myself in or was 'sweet' a word that Jet, Kay, Jack and all the crew had been trained to use, a catch-all for the ladies of a certain age. Had something changed about me that I wasn't noticing in the mirror every morning?

'Of course we want you, don't we Jack?'

'Really?' I looked to Jack, conscious of my glowing armpits and a spill of tummy filling the overhanging folds of my top. He took his glasses off, closed his eyes and pinched the bridge of his nose. The pregnant silence was filled by Kay who explained that it had been a long day for everyone.

Jack's smile began before his eyes opened and it is only as I write this that the cynic in my soul questions whether it was prescribed in section six b of Appendix C to the Dispatcher and Schedulers' handbook. 'Of course we do. Sort your things out.' He waved his hand over the things I'd dumped on his desk and sprang out of his seat. 'I'll make you a cup of coffee and you can have a sit down before setting off home.'

'Thanks but just one other thing. I wonder if you can answer something that's been on my mind all day?' It was a concern born out of an experience from my car hire days. After an hour or more explaining to a Norwegian gentleman that we drive on the left and some rudimentary principles of the highway code, I was encouraged by his smile of assurance that he knew what I was talking about, and gaily handed the car keys to him. I was no sooner back in the office than the call came through that he had pulled out of the airport car park onto the wrong side of the road and written the car off. It followed that having witnessed with my own eyes another dotty ditherer going in the wrong direction in the Excel car park earlier that day, I had to run the risk of being called a busybody and enquire if she had returned to the Depot safe and sound.

'Do you know if everyone has returned, in particular a lady called Ruth? I gave Jack a description which would have fitted quite a few of the ladies.

'There's no Ruth on the system.'

'There must be!' Kay had sidled off so couldn't verify the business with the radios and Tommy had gone off duty so couldn't back me up on the mobiles and Bluetooth business but Jack was very patient with me as I went through the strange thing of Ruth wanting to be known as Hilda. 'Or was it Gillian?'

'Time for home, I think, Carol. When are you down to come in again?'

'Monday, late shift.'

He gave me thumbs up.

Waiting by Custom House Station I felt very conspicuous in my uniform as people came and went. I wanted to sit down but thought it inappropriate for a Seb Coe disciple to perch on the kerb. I gazed at the seats on the platform, read the notice forbidding people without a ticket from proceeding onto the platform then remembered the Oyster card that I had been given with my uniform. The card was given to every volunteer, was valid on the day of your shift and covered six zones, but I never had cause to use it.

A train pulled in at the opposite platform. Discharged of passengers, the train left for Prince Regent and there on the platform were Robert and Hannah, lighting up my universe with their wide smiles and happy faces. I waved, struck a pose, did a little athletic jig and immediately felt silly in case I had embarrassed them.

'I'll understand if you two don't want to walk with me,' I said when we met up. 'This uniform is, what would you call it, pants?'

'Don't be silly, Mum. It's a uniform. It means something.'

'Was this your first day?' asked Hannah.

'Yes, day one, one of the longest days of my life and four days to reflect on whether I make it to the next one.'

'You can't give up on it now, Mum!'

'No way,' said Hannah.

They trailed their suitcases across the road and I told them about the cable cars and explained where we had to go to collect the car and my estimate of how long it would take to get to the Blackwall Tunnel. 'And that's one of ours.' I pointed to a three series with London 2012 emblazoned on its side. I put my hand up in acknowledgment of the driver. 'Don't fancy his chances on the A12 this time of day.'

I laughed. I was sounding like a pro.

CHAPTER 14

Checking in

Working on two consecutive days, from two till midnight on each, meant a hammering of our little red car and potential meltdown in energy levels for me so I made a reservation at a hotel within striking distance of neighbouring Excel and my parking space across the water.

'Jumping on the bandwagon,' that's what Dad would have called the way the Hotels hiked up the price of accommodation for the duration of the Games. And it wasn't only Hotels as my contretemps with Fast Buck Francis and the letting of his parking space plus luxury apartment had revealed. Who could blame them and at least they told you when the bandwagon would start rolling which, fortunately for me, was the day I would be checking out.

At twelve thirty p.m. I parked the car. I wasn't in the most upbeat of moods, feeling I had only got to shift day two and already had proved how easy it was for me to slip back into crusty 'get a move on' work- life mode. How had this come about? I had just deposited Hannah at Silvertown DLR station and had enjoyed her bright and breezy company but the prelude to it had been a constant badgering by me to rouse her and Robert from their post Festival weekend slumbers. It had been oh so reminiscent of the days when I had knocked progressively louder on Robert and Sophie's doors and shouted, 'Right, that's the third time, I'm not calling again and if you're late, you're late,' my words motivated by wanting to get into the office promptly and not wanting them to get into trouble at school. There it was, the obsession with time again and my assumption that others take as long as I do to get ready whereas the festival goers took a more chilled out approach.

I feared I had come over as a right old harridan and what had been the point of it all when there was an hour and a half till the beginning of my shift?

An hour and a half to psyche myself up to be the happy, welcoming Games Makers that Seb wanted us to be and, in that way of mine that is so infuriating to family (grouchy with them, personable with the outside world), I switched from introspective indulgence to bubbling bonhomie in a matter of minutes as I walked up the central reservation between the houses. What brought about this change of mood and expression? It was the look on the faces of the two men I met at the waterside end of the Close. One man was in a wheelchair and not looking in the best of health but his carer looked very chipper.

'I hope the weather is going to hold,' the carer shouted over to me.

'It's a bit cloudy, isn't it?' I replied walking over to them. We had quite a little chat and in amongst the conversation I learnt that they had moved into the Close when the houses were first built and loved being so close to the Dock and all the amenities it provided. 'I can certainly see why you love it so much. Where are you off to now?'

It was the man in the wheelchair's birthday (to my shame I have forgotten his name, it could have been Ron) and they had organised a trip on the Emirates gondola for the occasion. 'That's very brave and adventurous of you both,' I said, touched by the way they had been looking forward to it so much, concerned that Ron might not make it to his next birthday. 'Can I help you in any way?' It was partly the uniform talking and partly that, for the duration of my parking space rental, they were, very loosely, close neighbours of mine. 'You've got quite a way to go.'

'No, thanks, I've got used to it.'

'Enjoy the day.'

My overnight case rattled behind me as I pulled it along the dockside promenade. Ahead of me the gondola bubbles were floating high in the sky on their journey to the O2. I walked round the bend, past the Wakeboarding area and the Thai restaurant and weaved in and out between the workmen at the Crystal. A fine rain began to fall as I passed the gondola ticket office and made my way up Western Gateway. I looked across the water and, for all his optimism, Ron's carer was making slow progress pushing the wheelchair along on the other side. It would be a day to remember for them and I was at once sad and yet concerned whether I had followed the code of behaviour set out in the Workbook. I was to hear others complaining of how condescending they thought the contents of the book were. I too had screwed my nose up at certain things that had been included. Did we really need to be told to wash and care for our uniforms and not to exchange uniform items with other workforce members? In some matters it did make me sit up and question how I responded to people especially in the area of disability. I recalled a radio programme once called something like *Does he take sugar?* Had I treated Ron with the respect he deserved or conducted all the conversation with his obviously committed carer?

My thoughts moved on as did my footsteps. I looked away and concentrated my efforts on getting to the Hotel which declared it had the best bar prices in the area, food served late into the night and, one for Dad, a Wiffy connection. There were customers at the reception desk so I hovered at a discreet distance, entertained by their antics yet fearful of being swept into the maelstrom of their hyper family whose bodies and luggage were sprawled across the furniture and floor of the compact lobby. Above the hubbub I watched and listened to the painful dialogue of a guest with a map trying to squeeze directions out of the glacial receptionist. Uniform or no uniform, I was sorely tempted to step in, gently take possession of the map and show the guest that at least I was interested in his plans for their day. I didn't, though, for fear of being turned to stone.

At the other greeting station a man in heavy duty jeans and boots, check shirt and plastic fluorescent tabard was having the tariff explained to him. 'Yeah, that's alright then.' He delved into his back pocket, produced a wodge of banknotes, licked the tip of his thumb and forefinger and proceeded to count them out on the desktop. The look on the receptionist's face was not dissimilar to the kind accorded to me as a chambermaid going through the Motel lobby with a stack of tea towels for the kitchen.

'Yes?' I was summonsed. I stepped forward, pleased to have been noticed by someone but not unfortunately by the foyer family who nearly mowed me down in the method and manner of their departure.

'Phew, you're busy,' I said, as my booking was mechanically processed and I was handed the key card to my room.

'You are on the top floor.'

'Lifts, stairs?' I asked, having slipped into the stylised pattern of hotel communication. My eyes followed a pointed finger and I said sorry on realising they were only a matter of a few yards from me. I scoured the walls for a button to call the lift but couldn't find one. A housekeeping services lady pointed at a wall mounted console and made a slicing action with her hand then cluttered off. I swiped the key card every way but which but the lift doors stayed resolutely shut.

'The lift, I'm having trouble with the lift. Is this card alright?' I asked one of the desk staff.

'Have you put your room number in the keypad?'

'Keypad? What keypad?'

Alone in the compact lift, I concluded that it was probably all for the best that I hadn't been allocated to guest or accommodation services because I wouldn't have had the right mental attitude towards how to dispose of guests as crisply and efficiently as appeared to be required. On the second floor a couple got in. It was all the man could do to wrest his eyes away from his beloved to press the button for the lobby. I prayed I wouldn't be taken down to the bottom, unable to bear the ignominy of the desk staff thinking that I couldn't even make it to my room. Thankfully, the lift kept to its bargain to go up and I shuffled past the couple and stepped out. I caught my breath, the long panel window immediately to my right emphasised how high I was above the ground and just as heady was the view of the Olympic Park and the Orbit sculpture on the skyline. I stepped well away to enjoy the view then turned round and, passing the stairway on my left, walked along the long corridor checking the numbers on the doors.

It has been said that my sense of smell is at times a block to rational thinking, on a par with my sensitive eyes that can be offended by the colour and design of carpets. There had been no offensive carpets shown on the Hotel's website to put me off but I hadn't allowed for the smell of stagnant water that came to greet me. It was like the smell of a muddy wet dog or our porch when wet coats have been left out there. It made no sense for the floor level was high above the water in the Dock. The carpet beneath my feet didn't squelch or look water damaged. Had someone let their bath overflow? Was my room going to be pong free?

I turned left. It was certainly quiet, the only sound that of the rolling wheels of my suitcase lagging hesitantly behind as I made my way down the corridor. My room was at the far end, at the furthest point away from the lifts, from the reception, the bar and restaurant. If I was to holler in the night there'd be no-one to hear me. I swiped the key card and went in.

There was no noxious smell and it was far better than I expected for the price, with its décor and furnishings welcoming and on trend. I wheeled my case over to the fitted desk under the window. I overlooked the water and across to the estate where my car was parked. I quickly retreated to sit on the bed, needing to shake off irrational fears linked to being on the corner of the top floor of the building. The LED display on the wall mounted flat screen TV reminded me that it was just after one so I'd been lucky to get in before official check in time, lucky to get a room before the prices increased, lucky to have a husband who was willing to back me and more. And yet, a familiar sinking feeling came upon me, a dread whirling in my stomach, a panic playing in my head as I counted the long hours ahead of me. It was good old fashioned homesickness making an appearance. On holidays and trips away it had sometimes lurked in the background as a vague sense of unease, especially if I thought about the cats holed up in the cattery. But I had come to realise that it stemmed deeper than that, for when the days of leaving Robert and Sophie at their Halls arrived, I had relived the sense of dread, the empty ache I felt at their age of going back to an empty room. 'You've got to go away to come home again,' Dad had always said by way of encouragement. Only in very recent times had I admitted the homesickness gene but it didn't stop me chastising myself as I sat on the bed in that anonymous hotel, the collywobbles growing by the minute at the thought of coming back to the room later where the only sound would be from the TV.

The en suite, skilfully disguised behind a curved wall, was a curious affair. Innovative it may have been but it took me a while to work out where the handle was. The door slid round to reveal a circular pod housing the loo, shower and basin. Stepping up into it I felt I was entering something that had been transported through time travel. I pondered on how it had been constructed, how it had arrived there and what came first, the pod or the internal walls. Wherever it had come from, however it had got there, it possessed a life force of its own within its claustrophobic confines. Turning the tap on, the water trickled slowly at first bringing with it the smells of Dickensian drains, waterways and labyrinthine passageways and then a gush of fresh water swilled them away. The toilet flush brought a whoosh, clank and a knocking akin to the sound of a ship going down so I made a mental note to avoid using it after midnight for fear of disturbing my neighbours and spooking my half asleep self. And there was no need and no way that I was going to wrap the door shut behind me.

Unpacked and freshened up I left the room to get to my two o'clock shift. I knew a baguette etc would be provided for teatime but had forgotten whether we'd get something at lunchtime and I was starving. No problem, it was only twenty past one. No problem, that is, until I decided I'd go down the stairs rather than use the lift. At what I thought was the ground floor all entry to the reception was barred. I followed the stairs down again only to come face to face with a dead end and fire exit. So I climbed back up and miraculously found a short corridor. I peered through a glass panel to an empty restaurant which looked out over the water. A couple of waiters came into shot and instinctively I pressed my back against the wall in case they looked up and saw me lurking. I ran back up three flights of stairs, caught the lift down into reception and fled the premises. Hot and flustered

I rushed over in the drizzly rain to the convenience store to grab a sandwich.

A lot had happened in the area around FDX since my first shift. The main open space leading up to Excel had been taken over and fenced off. A part of me felt intimidated, not necessarily by the individual service personnel themselves but on account of the obvious public security and safety reasons they were drafted in for. It was comforting and yet unnerving how quickly they could set up a security zone and as the troop numbers increased with every passing day, their presence gave a surreal edge to being in the heart of London. I could only imagine as to how civilians in other parts of the world felt when the military moves in.

'Can I still get round to Fleet Depot that way?' I shouted over a metal barrier to a soldier in his combats. He looked confused and came over. 'Is it okay to go that way?' I pointed to the walkway by the water's edge.

'Okay.'

Keeping close to the perimeter of the fenced off area I made towards the water, turned left and, conscious of time ticking, walked briskly along all the while grappling with my accreditation card tucked inside my jacket so that I would be ready to show it at the checkpoint I had been through the previous week.

'Can we help you, ma'am?' Two soldiers peered at me through the mesh of a tall newly erected gate.

'I want to go over there to FDX.' My hair frizzing in the drizzle, I looked longingly over to the promenade outside the Depot where some of my ilk were having a damp cigarette.

'You can't ma'am. You'll have to go all the way round and up the steps as if you were going to Custom House.'

'But the soldier back there said it was okay.'

'What did he look like?'

The description I gave wasn't the best.

'Ah, yes, sorry about him, Ma'am.'

As I scurried back round the corner and along past the perimeter fence I toyed with the idea of beckoning to the soldier who had led me astray and tell him that there was access only to the bridge and not the Depot. Some might have seen correcting the soldier as a duty to other Games Makers to make sure they didn't get sent on a fool's errand as I had been. I inclined to the view that it was the remit of the soldiers I had spoken to take him to task. How I had changed. My natural inclination to get overly involved in sorting things had been tempered by the influence of the Workbook with its emphasis on the delineation of duties and knowing your boundaries. I smiled at the soldier who had misled me, hurried round the corner, along the pavement that had been encroached upon by the military boundary and up the steps. I was directed into a large marquee set up outside the main entrance to Excel. It was manned by civilian security personnel. A 'well made' lady relieved me of my bag, coat, accreditation and freezer bag containing the lunch I'd bought. She separated my belongings out into two trays. It then occurred to me that whereas we were able to collect food at FDX and take it out, I wasn't sure whether we were able to take food in and I couldn't check my handbook because it was in my bag in the tray.

'Don't you dare confiscate my sandwich,' I said light-heartedly, thinking it best to admit guilt in anticipation of the problem rather than be found red handed with tuna and sweet corn on brown bread. She remained expressionless as she pushed the trays along the rollers and into the scanner. It was then that I said something so odd, so stupid in the circumstances that I still find it hard to fathom why. I don't know whether it was a run-on from my anxiety about the Hotel or agitation at the possibility of being late or whether, changing places with her, I would have been inclined to ask if I was particularly hungry or was there something special about the sandwich. It could have been that I was nervy about being left in limbo, in a state of indecision as to whether it was indeed permissible to take a sandwich in. Was it some perverse unconscious desire of mine to extract a reaction from this woman who I was now beginning to suspect was sadistically waiting to see if the camera would show up any other items of foodie contraband? My steps mirrored hers as she went to wait for the trays coming through the other side. I repeated my warning not to confiscate my Londis lunchtime special. She deigned to lift her eyebrow and in reply I told her straight; 'Because I'm starving and if you do I'll kill you.' KILL! I had frightened myself, remained speechless as a security man signalled with the palm of his hand to step forward and remain still under the body scanner.

It seemed an eternity that I was stood there, an eternity during which I remembered a comical friend of Robert's from his teenage days who was excluded from school for repeating a phrase from either a film or a PlayStation game which was construed as a death threat by a particularly sensitive member of staff. I watched as the first tray nosed its way out the other side of the scanner and even worse came to mind; the recent report of a famous author who had been detained for making a similar explosive remark as mine at an airport. I wanted to achieve notoriety for writing an outstanding story about Frank, not for being the first prisoner taken captive by Group 4 Security.

I was told to step out from the scanner. I waited for the sirens and alarms to ring when the second tray appeared but nothing happened. Were they playing cat and mouse with me? Without risking a glance at the lady, my potential accuser, I collected my things from the trays and proceeded to have my accreditation swiped so that the likeness of my photo could be checked against the real life me.

I left the Marquee and with each step expected to feel a heavy arresting hand pounce on my shoulder. Five yards out I sneaked a backward glance at the woman I had threatened to kill. She showed no signs of distress, no sign of anything. I carried on making my way down the ramp access to FDX and two soldiers were coming the other way. Had the woman pressed an alarm button and summoned part of a crack squad of combat troops to ambush me? Was this how the people in charge of the civilian and military security planned to deal with such incidents? Would the arrest be low key and away from the scene of the crime?

'Afternoon, Ma'am.'

'Afternoon,' I replied.

'You look in a hurry.'

'Do I?'

'You do, Ma'am.'

'I don't want to be late for my two o'clock start.'

'You'll just make it then.'

They parted to let me pass, to get on with the rest of my day.

CHAPTER 15

Less than my Obliging Self

I left the trials and tribulations of my runaway mouth and all the sober-sided people of the world outside at the door of the Depot. It was such an easy thing to do because a range of smiley faces greeted me at check-in and I was given a gift of a green rubber bracelet.

'And I'll just put this sticker on the back of your card for you.' The enthusiastic young lady reached up with her hand to take hold of my accreditation.

'Does this work on the same principle as a coffee shop loyalty card when you get one free cup after every six purchased.'

'It's our way of saying thank you and there'll be other gifts to come your way.' And she was right because I've kept them in a cardboard box (donated by a leading sponsor) that Sophie decorated at Primary school in 2007 when the original bid for the Games was successful. Not dreaming for one moment that I'd ever become part of London 2012, I'd put the box in the cupboard to join the rest of her artwork, swimming badges, brownie sash, keepsakes and mementoes. It wasn't until I hoiked it out to house my gifts that I saw that if, all those years before, she had completed the maze on the side of the box and sent it off to the sponsors' address she might have won a prize that included tickets to the Olympics.

In the box, the green band is a striking contrast to the white one that I was given at the original selection event. I also earned a blue Games Makers pin from a leading presenting partner and at intervals thereafter this leading presenting partner followed this up with bronze, silver and gold coloured pins. There's also a white Thank you/Merci (English and French the official languages of the Olympic movement) pin from Jacques Rogge the International Olympic Committee President given 'in recognition of your commitment to the Games of the XXX Olympiad London 2012'. But the best pin of all came later, merits its own little box and marked a pivotal moment in my driving career.

I accepted the green band with much good grace and then carried on to the Dispatcher's desk where the welcome received was equally as warm as warm could be. The earnest young man still stood guard by the canteen kitchen to take the meal ticket and offer a cold ice pack.

'Do you know what to do?' he asked. 'Or would you like me to run through it with you?'

'You stay there. I can sort myself out.' I was embarrassed, concerned that he might see the sandwich that I had bought earlier. I don't suppose he would have been too fussed for he was one of little outward emotion but Gino was at the other end of the spectrum. Gino had the patter, an emotional temperament and much as Jet could have you slavering over an automatic gear box, Gino could have you believing that the hot enhancements offered up from the tin trays on the hot counter were signature dishes of the world's finest chefs in disguise.

'I can recommend the vegetarian Mediterranean slice to you today,' he ventured. 'It's oozing mushrooms.'

'What's the alternative?'

'Corned beef slice.'

'Mm, tricky isn't it when they both look so tempting.'

'It is so.'

'I know I shouldn't but I am partial to corned beef so I'll go with the pasty.'

'One SLICE coming up for you madam. Enjoy.'

Enjoy it I did, even if the fat which sweated into the serviette should have been a warning to me that a dose of one deliciously tempting dangerously fattening thing leads to another, the culinary experience of the following weeks proving the old joke that a tubby person often has a thin person inside desperate to get out, works in reverse in my case.

When I eventually took a seat at the T2 table Tommy the Beard was in conversation with two of my fellows. There were no clients to take out but we were to have another day driving the routes specified in our plastic wallets. I merrily tucked into my repast and listened to one of the men, Stu, suggesting that delegates ought to be paired with drivers who had an interest in the delegate's particular sport. Tommy said the proposal sounded very sensible and it did to me too until, with the pasty sinking in my stomach, I got to thinking back to my first interview when even the word athletics eluded me. If pressed, what sport could I hold a conversation of more than a few sentences with anyone on? But why worry? It was unlikely I was going to be asked because Tommy hadn't even acknowledged my presence let alone canvass my views and Stu had his own agenda to pursue.

'I've been given the Fencing wallet today which, don't get me wrong, I don't mind but I am a keen cyclist.'

I wiped my mouth, got ready to speak, to say that after more years than I cared to mention, I had suddenly remembered that at school I had had a number of fencing lessons. But Stu went into the fact that he had boned up on the venues that the cyclists were going to compete in and contended it would make sense for cycling delegates to be allocated to him.

'You could always have a word with the Schedulers, Stu,' said Tommy, still giving me the cold shoulder.

I'm afraid I took umbrage at this point. I didn't take too kindly to Tommy's attitude and whilst I was later to discover that Stu was a decent soul, at that moment in time and despite the logic of his argument, I thought it arrogant of him to try to dictate what he wanted. It seemed to me that, albeit it was an open conversation, there was an element of boys own stitch-up going on and, on all counts, it was enough to make me depart from my usual obliging self. I could have offered it there and then, could have taken Stu's hand and led him to the Dispatcher's desk and done a deal but I didn't.

'At least we'll get more time in the automatics,' Stu continued. 'These don't respond in the same way as the one I drive at home.'

'You are all back to driving manuals.'

'What? How come?'

'People's preferences, etc, etc. The automatics have gone back.'

'That's incredible,' I said, and now totally cheesed off with lack of eye contact with Tommy, I forced a reply out of him on the need to check we had the right contact numbers in our mobiles and the code number for the Bluetooth.

'They should be sorted but I agree it's best to check. And are any of you going up to the Olympic Park?'

I nodded because the Velodrome, BMX and Basketball were on my daily schedule tucked into my plastic wallet which bore the word CYCLING on it. I began to feel a smidgeon guilty that I hadn't disclosed it but, just as with the soldier and the directions business outside, I couldn't take it upon myself to go and sort everybody out.

'You will have to go through the VSA to get into the Park and we need to know how long it is taking the soldiers to process people so keep your eyes and ears open and make a note of timings because we need to know of any delays or hold ups and the reasons for them. Any questions?'

The only question I had was one for Donna the Dispatcher who, with bloodshot eyes, hunched shoulders and arms folded across her middle shuffled through the T2 section of the car park, ostensibly checking to see if anyone wanted assistance. I'd done all the checks on the car but after the business with the chequered flag the previous week I wanted Donna to explain how to override one destination and set the Sat Nav onto a new one without any backchat from Helga.

'You don't look so well, Donna,' I said as she twiddled with the control.

'It's the early mornings getting to me.'

'Do you work every day?'

'Yes, it's a regular job,' she yawned.

I felt happier that we had swapped back to manual cars and had every hope that with a different Helga and Donna's assistance the day would prove to be less stressful than my first. I had a hotel to find and as I set off through the car park felt quite confident and even unconcerned that Helga was unresponsive when I got outside. I assumed it was a temporary loss of signal but even if I had decided to stop and check the setting, it was much harder to find a place to do so on account of the military having erected fences, gates and checkpoints for the purposes of putting Excel into lockdown.

Out in the open I drove past the car park on my left with the railway line and Prince Regent Station on my right. I had to hold my accreditation up to a soldier hovering on the roadway and then after him, to another soldier who opened a high fence gate and a little way on there was another soldier and another gate. Tasting freedom, there was a temptation to zoom away but this was tempered by the speed limit, the watchful eyes of soldiers waiting for cars to go through the VSA on the other side of the road and the number of pedestrians going to and from Custom House Station, the next stop on the DLR.

I expected Helga to instruct me to turn right onto Western Gateway. Not a dickie bird was said. I felt slighted as I drifted along Lower Lea Crossing, bereft slinking along Aspen Way and kicked in the teeth by the time I was motoring The Highway. By the time I turned right into Dock Street there was a taxi so close up my tail the driver was virtually my back seat passenger. The traffic was busy and harried me through the narrow street network till I was channelled into Prescot Street. I was sure as hell chuffed that the hotel presented itself to me on the right but with the pressure of cars behind me I couldn't see where the main entrance was nor where to park if I had to pick up a Lycra clad delegate. Despite the car behind snapping at my heels I thinking quickly, took a sharp right and a further mini circuit of right turns until I found the hotel again.

I pulled up on the yellow lines and fiddled with the dials and, lo, Helga spoke. So cock-a-hoop was I that I'd got her up and routeing that I set off on my next journey without a second thought or second glance as to where I might need to collect a speed helmeted delegate. Instead, with Helga back to life, I did all the rights and lefts to get to Whitechapel Road and lurching from one set of traffic lights to another mused once again on Dad's Uncle George who'd had a pub in the area. Dad had said his Uncle was a boxer but with no-one else in the family remembering him, had he been a product of Dad's fertile imagination? And if Dad had visited him, what had he, a boy from Plymouth, thought of the East End which, even in my lifetime, had been held out as a run down and poor area to live in but was now changing with the times. Yes, changing with the times as the car pushed along in the mid afternoon traffic towards the Olympic Park.

CHAPTER 16

On a Mission

Tommy the Beard wanted information about the military and I was prepared to get it for him. Arriving at Eton Manor VSA in a car emblazoned with the Olympic Logo wasn't exactly covert but doing the middle aged female Games Makers bit with overawed look on face was a good ploy to start with.

I turned right off Ruckholt Lane and was met by security personnel who directed me round the roundabout and up past the security point. A short stretch of road lay ahead, a number of cars, a double Decker bus and a coach in front of me and there were tented bays to my right. A soldier signalled to me to a stop. Shaven head at one end, big black boots at the other, a belt supporting his skinny frame in between, I put him at just over the edge of twenty. I wound down the window.

'Afternoon, Ma'am, how are you today?'

'I'm fine, thank you.'

'That's good. Can you switch off the engine for a moment please?'

'You're busy today, aren't you?' I was stating the blindingly obvious but it was a canny smokescreen for my surreptitious investigation.

'I like it like this.' I could understand that because he said they were doing twelve hour shifts.

'I expect I'm going to have a long wait, aren't I?' I gestured to the coach who had by now pulled round into one of the bays and a string of men, all in similar polo shirts with identity cards round their necks, hopped off with much laughing and chatting as if they'd arrived at a football match. There was part of me that wanted to warn my soldier that he should be careful what he said, that I wasn't as benign as I might appear, that I would be including what he said in my report, but as part of Team Tommy I couldn't.

'We'll try and get you through as fast as we can.' He gave me a lovely smile even though it smacked of a fully briefed answer. It occurred to me that the military might be one step ahead of Tommy's quest to find out whether some VSA's were taking longer than others and if there was disparity between the different checks that were being carried out because I, for one, was a sucker for being more tolerant about waiting if an apology and a smile was given beforehand.

'Don't worry. I'm only on a recce, I mean I'm here to get acquainted with the Olympic Park.'

'I understand, Ma'am.' He backed away and switched his attention to the car arriving behind me and I was content to watch the coach party and those trained to play their part in what Seb, Tommy, Jet, all of them, had said amounted to the largest peacetime mobilisation ever. And that mobilisation gave rise to so many opportunities and, if I knew then what I know now, I would have grabbed Tommy's fact finding mission with bigger hands than he could have ever imagined. I would have made it a goal to visit every VSA and written a book about them, a handy pocket sized novelty version to add to other books of nonsense that are displayed by the till at all good bookshops in the run up to Christmas.

Of all shapes and sizes, the majority of the soldiers looked so young, some still sporting teenage spots and pimples, some still adolescently awkward. I recalled the description of Dad in his service records. At age seventeen he had a sallow complexion, grey eyes and was five foot nine with a girth of thirty three inches which had a range of expansion of three and a half inches. And, by contrast, Uncle Bill's Naval records showed he had a fresh complexion, was two inches shorter than Dad but gained an inch in height and chest size between boy's and man's service. Skinny wretches both it seemed. No working out at the gym in those days. I wondered what it said in the service records for Alan and David.

At the VSA there were a couple of older soldiers, clearly the ones in charge. Why had any of them, young or old, joined the Services? Was it a case of getting away from home, secure employment, good money with accommodation sorted and food on tap? Was it the camaraderie long associated with the Forces, the attitude of 'civvies' never measuring up to the bond formed in the Services? Or were they simply adrenalin-seeking body pumping action men? Watching the soldiers I also wondered what proportion of them had signed on the dotted line with a burning zeal to protect the country.

Of course it was a matter of circumstance with Dad, his time with the Territorial's handy target practice for the little matter of World War combat. And perhaps staying on after the War was more a career move than anything else bearing in mind his antipathy towards the Royal Family and his little respect for politicians who he gnashed his teeth at for lining their own pockets,

'Why bother putting your life and limb at risk for them then?' I'd argue with him and David too, even though I was really proud of walking down the street with him and Alan both guaranteed to turn a few heads in their respective uniforms.

'Brainwashing and bullying others under the guise of protecting them,' I'd say tartly. 'I don't think that's anything to be proud of.'

'Your generation haven't a clue. They wouldn't stand five minutes ducking the bullets would they, David? We need a good war to shake all these long haired types out, don't we?' On that topic father and son were more or less agreed so I don't know why I wasted my energy in arguing about it. And in bleaker moments, when I have given thought to how David's time in the Army and later life panned out, I wonder if the barbed comments of my youth contributed in any way. Roger would maintain not, but Roger was once a long haired type and were they ever to be trusted?

Whether Roger had had long, short or speckled pink hair he smoothed troubled waters, took the sting out of the 'debates' between father and daughter and such was his calming influence that I didn't feel the need to draw Dad into a debate on the desirability of a good war for our generation when the Gulf War started.

'You'll be alright Rog, nothing to worry about. When they see your qualifications they'll have you down as a shiny arse in the Officer class.' It was Dad's way of glossing over his concern that his favourite, his only, son-in-law might be called up if the War escalated.

Wars. How far away was the Olympic Park from Afghanistan? How many of the soldiers checking vehicles would be sent out to war zones and trouble spots and return home with severed limbs or not return at all? I shuddered, thinking of their mothers and loved ones waiting for them and yet I'd never given a thought to how Mum had felt when her sons were away.

'Ma'am? Are you alright Ma'am?'

I turned to the soldier's concerned face peering in at me.

'Daydreaming, sorry.'

'If you would proceed into the second bay please.'

I fumbled getting started again, took a few seconds to work out that another soldier up ahead was gesturing to me to pass the bus and pointing me to the bay where another soldier was beckoning to me. I pulled in then inched along until the flat of the soldier's hand told me I had reached the line and had to stop. I made a face at him that said I was glad I hadn't run over his toes though no-one, but no-one would want to run over the toes of such a big lad as him.

'Afternoon, Ma'am. Can you please open the bonnet, boot and doors and take all your possessions to the desk.' I knew this was the correct procedure so there was no excuse for his words to put me into a flap but they did. Poor lad, he wasn't to know that I am jinxed with locks or that I had forgotten that they weren't allowed to help me with anything in or about the car. It took me two go's at pulling the catch for the bonnet and for a supposedly expensive car it sure made an unhealthy clunk when it sprung open. Conscious of several pairs of eyes on me, I had the same problem with the boot, scurrying from front to back pressing the button in the car then the one on the key fob, confirming and countermanding the release of the spacious luggage compartment. The older wise owl of a soldier ambled over. Had he cottoned on that I was a Tommy the Beard mole? Would the concerns that Tommy had serve only to turn round and bite him in the bum because the delays were caused by whirling dervishes like me?

'The doors, Ma'am?' The owl said, as if I needed reminding, when I was already going into orbit round the vehicle, madly grabbing at the handles as if trying to beat the clock on a TV game show. The soldiers hovered, unable to do their job till I'd scrabbled about in the passenger well and seat to pick up my bag and bits and pieces.

The car was searched, in and out, and with implements that looked like water diviners under the car. Meanwhile I and my goods were searched. 'Step through the scanner please, Ma'am.'

'My, I'm quite exhausted after all that,' I smoothed my hair down after putting my accreditation back over my head.

'Do you know where you're going?' the owl asked as I gathered my things out of the tray.

'Yes. Velodrome, BMX and Basketball,' I said confidently, turning on my heel to get back to the car because the soldier behind me was shouting for the next car to come forward.

'Enjoy the rest of your day.'

'And you.'

As I was directed away from the area I held my hand up in farewell then was asked to slow and wait for the bus in bay one to leave before me. It was only then that I remembered that I should have kept an eye on the time and the performance of the soldiers. Had I been there five, ten or fifteen minutes in total? How many cars had been in front and behind, how many soldiers had been in attendance in each bay? Wouldn't it be simpler just to make something up? I was good at making things up.

It all came flooding back; me as part of a travel survey team, a grandiose term for being a member of a disparate group willing to do anything to avoid drawing dole money. Yet waiting in a dole queue held a certain charm when I had to get up at the crack of dawn on cold winter mornings and pound a mile of hard unforgiving pavement to catch the first bus out on the target route. Invariably the driver was grumpy, had a hacking cough and resented my presence counting the passengers on and off at each stop. No amount of preliminary guff from the Survey Supervisor about it being a survey to help with the development of an integrated transport system would persuade the driver that there wasn't a risk to his job if he was carrying too few passengers. And the passengers themselves weren't overly enthusiastic about answering questions about the duration and frequency of their journeys as the bus juddered through the streets.

On the rural routes it was far too tempting to snuggle down into my coat, lay my head against the window and have a snooze. I came to rely on the bell, a shout from a passenger or the noise and strain of the engine beneath my feet to wake me up and prompt me to mark the survey forms with a tick for an 'on' or an 'off'. Failing to add or subtract the odd passenger from the tally was permissible but there came the day when, deployed to work together as a small team in and around a small market town, someone mislaid the file containing the passenger numbers for that day. Despite the cold and damp, the company of disgruntled, bleary eyed bus drivers and the morning chorus of catarrh riddled throat clearers, there were none among us who were prepared to contemplate rejoining the ranks shuffling towards the Social Security counter on account of a silly oversight. Indeed, the prospect of such a reversal of fortune ignited such a flurry of pragmatic creativity that the most ardent of knockers of transport surveys would have been impressed.

Quick thinking proved the best thing once all the figures, whether manufactured or not, were in for every route and we then had several months of collating the figures. Housed in a dim and dismal red brick building under a railway bridge, more omissions and errors were inevitably made on Mondays when tales were told of weekends lost to hangovers. Drowning in a sea of paper, midweek boredom brought office contests for best thrower of spittle soaked paper missile that could stick to the ceiling. It was Russian roulette on Friday because no-one could predict what might happen after lunch at the pub, the wrong entry of numbers could mean the difference between redundancy notices on route fourteen or a doubling of its drivers.

The noise of the bus engine pulling out from bay one of the VSA brought me out of my reverie. If I'd remembered the survey when I'd been out with Driven Everything with Wheels on and More Jet I would have told him that I'd wheedled a drive of a bus on a country road out of a driver who felt the writing was on the wall for him anyway. But now the writing was on the wall for me as I edged forward to enter the Olympic Park.

So much coverage had been given to the Park that I expected to feel something momentous beneath my wheels as I drove in but there was nothing heart-stopping about the first mini roundabout I came to. The first exit was blocked, the second led to an open gate and straight ahead the third stretched to goodness know where. Helga was in a sulk and there was no road signage to help. I decided that human contact, albeit in the shape of civilian personnel running round like headless chickens just beyond the gate, was better than nothing. My arrival caused some consternation but they couldn't deny I was in the right place for BMX and so let me through. It was a risky business. Navigating a slow straight course, I was harried by a lorry from behind and another came careering down towards me from my left. I kept my head held high and carried on past dumper trucks and men in hard hats, my heart sinking with every yard covered.

There was frantic building activity but it was a dead end. I turned round and made it back the way I had come and bore left after the gate onto the third exit off the mini roundabout. I drove at much less than the twenty miles an hour limit along the straight dusty roadway because I was, quite frankly, stunned. On my left scaffolding was being erected or was it stands? I checked my map. Where was I? It was hard to make out. A staunch proponent of the Olympics, I was dismayed that there was so much construction work going on. With less than two weeks to go till the Opening Ceremony I couldn't see how any of it would be finished. The critics would have a field day and, foolish me, I had put such faith in the whole enterprise.

I bore round to the left. There was an uninviting, seemingly empty building to my right and then round to the right, left and left again was a dreary construction and round again to a curiously shaped affair. Yet none, as I could make out, had boards or signs to say what they were. I turned right then bore left and to my complete surprise was driving parallel to a waterway. Across the water I saw the back of restaurants and cafes. The car climbed an incline. There was an access road to something but couldn't make out what from the sign and so I carried on, winding round and round and passing another slip road and another, but I still hadn't a clue what these places were. A board loomed. It mentioned a Southern Loop and a Northern Loop.

I went one way anticlockwise on one loop and then one way clockwise or at least I thought I had. And then I came upon a section of two way traffic and somewhere amongst it all there was a bridge and a multi storey car park and a fenced off area which I thought could be where I had started from once I had left one of the loops. I wondered if I could retrace my steps but, desperate for human contact, I tagged on behind an empty double decker bus and went over the bridge and ended back down by the waterway again. I lost track of how many times I circumnavigated the Park, but was it circumnavigation if I wasn't seeing the same things in the same order? I felt like the lead character in The Prisoner T.V. series and like him I wanted out, believing that once I got back to the Depot I could marry up where I thought I had been with the map.

Escape wasn't easy but I made it out onto the Lea Interchange and back onto the A12, determined to get at least one easy venue out of the way. London City Airport was certainly easy. I marvelled at how the planners had fitted it in and promised myself a trip from there in the future. I holed up in a space meant for hire cars and under the scrutiny of a string of drivers at the taxi rank I argued with Helga who mithered at me to do all sorts of things that I didn't want to do.

I drove back to Victoria Docks, parked up in the waiting area by one of the hotels and managed a fair imitation of waiting for a guest by intermittently raising my head and peering through the windscreen as if trying to catch a glimpse of someone in the lobby. In between times I got aerated with Helga's controls and how to set them to ignore the last destination and think ahead to the next one.

I leant back against the headrest, frustrated with myself that I couldn't work out what I had or hadn't done wrong. Was it my cross face that made the doorman leave me undisturbed whilst I wrestled with making a decision? Should I return to Excel and sit quietly and calmly in the car park and work it out for myself or ask bleary eyed Donna for another dollop of assistance? Should I simply rely on traditional methods of map reading, head out to Hadleigh Farm and take a chance I could find the right bit of the country park where the cycling was going to take place? A third option was to take up a suggestion of Judy's on the second training day, which was to hole up somewhere till darkness fell then drive round to Excel as if all was ok. Did my nodding acquaintance with his neighbour qualify me to hang out in Triton 29's neighbourhood? But I wouldn't be able to alter the milometer reading and, unlike in my transport survey days, couldn't massage the figures on the record sheet. To add to the theatricality of the moment and for the benefit of interested hotel staff I pushed my hair back behind my ear and exposed my Bluetooth earpiece, my lips silently moving in conversation with my errant pick up. I shook my head at the lack of consideration of fictitious clients and pulled away. Who would think I could ever be lonely living in my imaginary world?

Engine off, bonnet, boot and all doors open, I cleared the car of my belongings and put them on the table at the VSA.

'Pardon me Ma'am, I need to look in your bag. We'll be getting electronic scanners soon.' The soldier was so polite, so respectful of my things.

'Oh I forgot about them!' I said when he opened my lunch bag and there were the sandwiches I'd bought and the baguette Gino had recommended to me to counteract the effects of the corned beef slice.

'You can't go without eating Ma'am.'

'No, that's true.'

'Permission to search you, Ma'am?' I turned round and a female soldier had me stand with my arms out, legs slightly splayed. Acutely aware of my wobbly waist bits I said nothing while she frisked and patted me.

'Is that it for today, Ma'am?' asked the soldier as he handed me back all my things.

'No, the shift finishes at midnight. I've come back for a break.'

'Have a good evening.'

'And you.'

When I got back into the Depot Tommy was nowhere to be seen because he had finished his shift. I would have to save giving him a verbal report on how I had found the VSA's till another day. Tommy's duties were now in the hands of Bryn, an ex copper of plump proportions with hair cut to within a number one of an electric shaver. I had him down as Welsh.

'Taffy was a Welshman,' Dad used to say in the manner of it being the opening lines to a poem, though I've since discovered that it was a nursery rhyme linked with pagan gods and the failure of crops but farming had little to do with it in Dad's mind. 'I've come up against some tricky Welshmen in my time and slippery beggars they were as well. You've got to watch them, Carol, remember that.'

'My Mother had a Welsh name, Lillian Sophia Lewis,' Mum would interrupt. 'Lovely she was.'

'She was,' agreed Dad. 'One of the loveliest women I ever met.' And such was my not wanting to spoil the memory that I'd sit and listen to the warming tales that would inevitably follow.

Bryn's tales and instruction on the first training day had been entertaining, direct and down to earth. And on this, my first evening back at base, he was similarly full of confidence and conviction as he leant back in his seat strumming his fingers on the table whilst telling us the history of the cars he had owned. When I say us, I include Graham who had been the calm voice of reason on the second driver training day. I hadn't noticed it so much when he had been in his smock but Graham was so precise; a hair not out of place, his shirt tucked neatly into his trousers. Eating the salad placed squarely in front of him, he listed all the checks on the car he carried out before setting off.

The list sounded over and above the ones we had originally been told about but if it made him happy, so be it.

'Did you manage to visit all the venues on your schedule?' I asked him, taking a chunk out of my baguette.

'Of course.' He dabbed the corners of his mouth and folded the soiled paper napkin. 'Did you?'

'Did you have any problems?' I mentioned the first hotel on my list and its problems with picking up and dropping off in Prescot Street.

'Prescot Street?' Bryn stopped strumming. 'Let me look at your sheet.'

Graham looked over the top of his glasses at me.

'You went to the wrong place,' said Bryn.

'I couldn't have done.' I reeled off the relevant road and street names of my journey without having to refer to the route book and in the face of their disbelief I reminded Graham that we hadn't had it easy locating the hotel where he and Madame Judy had gone to the toilet.

'That was at St Pauls,' Graham said with a sigh, probably thinking I was going to reopen old wounds about the Sat Nav.

'I'll have to go check to see if the postcodes are right but you've got to be careful because the Met have some crack undercover people in offices in the Prescot and Dock Street vicinity.'

'So what are you going to do now?' asked Graham.

'I've still got Hadleigh Farm to do.'

'Don't go tonight,' said Bryn 'It'll take you two hours there and back. You wouldn't be back till after ten. I should go home.'

'I've got no home to go to,' I laughed, all melodrama, the long evening ahead filling me with dread.

CHAPTER 17

Corner Shop

How many times had I bemoaned the fact to Roger that there were never enough hours in the day, never enough long evenings with no distractions to enable me to finish Frank's story? I had begun to sound like a broken record. So, with two printed-off chapters in my writing wallet back at the hotel, why wasn't I grabbing the opportunity of finishing my shift early to rush back and start editing?

I thought of phoning Robert to suggest we meet and go for a 'couple of beers' but I knew that having to leave him and journey back on my own would be worse than going back to my room immediately. I told myself that fresh air would clear all the venues and postcodes out of my head. I walked round the apartment blocks and noticed that on the balconies there was a wide range of small garden tables and chairs and occasionally a child's trike or doll's pram. Behind the windows of these costly apartments there lived real people living real lives. I glanced into the restaurants, cast an eye in an estate agent's window, and then looked across at the other apartments and houses across the water. What could I do? Here I was in London, the great Metropolis, and the most exciting thing that came to mind was to mosey along and to buy something at the local shop.

There were convenience stores at either end of the road, handy for those with the large salaries and high accommodation costs that needed to nip out for a ready meal or top up on the essentials they had forgotten. In a strange way I found that comforting, as comforting as rooting in my purse for the loose change that the shopkeeper preferred for my magazine, bar of chocolate and the postcards for cousins who I had been meaning to get in touch with. Give the shopkeeper his due, the store was well stocked but it didn't have the cosiness, the frayed round the edges feel and blend of smells I associated with traditional corner shops of years gone by. Shops like the one friend Ann's mum and dad had for donkey's years and as I crossed the road and headed back to the hotel with my goodies a corner shop from the past came to mind.

Mr. and Mrs Truscott's shop was on the corner of two roads and directly opposite the Methodist Church, whose grey façade was set in a permanent frown against its Sunday opening hours. On a couple of weekday evenings I was the shop assistant in an apron standing behind the counter and large glass display cabinet which took up most of the shop. I didn't dispense ready meals and plastic containers of pasta but would shave a quarter of ham off the bone and furnish a tin of garden peas for someone's dinner. On Saturdays I was the waitress in the café out the back, my hair soaking up the early breakfast smells of crispy bacon and two rounds of toast. Later in the day my skinny wrists picked up the teatime perfume of home baked scones and raspberry jam. But on Sundays, to the disgust of those prurient Church goers, my feet danced in attendance to both; to the tinkle of the shop's bell and the clatter of tea cups in the steamy kitchen. Sundays, remembered always for selling blocks of pretty Neapolitan ice cream from the freezer cabinet and scooping out hearty dollops of clotted cream from a huge glass bowl into dainty dishes for the lady up the road who wanted to impress her visitors.

Black haired, straight backed and flat footed, Mrs Trustcott ruled everyone with her steely blue eyes. A thin cigarette invariably hanging from the corner of her mouth, she was a toughie whereas her husband was mild and more obliging and unquestionably fragile. Of hobbit proportions with a halo of thin hair covering his protuberant skull, the little purple veins in his temples forever stood proud against his translucent complexion. In the early days of my employment he'd sit on the shop stool gazing out of the window watching the cars drive by, sucking air through his thin lips if a lorry took the corner too wide. To stretch his legs he'd potter about, grinding his teeth as he checked the jars of sweets behind me. I think he preferred it in the shop with me talking about nothing in particular because in the cafe he was a piece of inconvenient clutter, his untimely interventions causing friction with his wife as he duplicated food orders or wasted time separating the knickerbocker glory glasses and the banana split dishes in the china cupboard.

With orders for poached eggs and tea cakes coming in thick and fast, Mr. T was often banished to their upstairs flat and after a while he came to spend more and more time up there on his own. It wasn't that she didn't care for him. Her painted eyebrows were ever raised to the ceiling, her ears ever alert to the creak of the floorboards from his wandering between the small rooms above. Sometimes when the floorboards stopped creaking she'd despatch me up the narrow flight of stairs to see if he wanted anything. There he'd be, standing silently on the landing, his voluminous black trousers doing nothing to disguise his distended stomach, his deathly pall screaming out against his white shirt, black tie and black cardigan. Half an hour later I'd be back upstairs with a tray of tea and a snack and he'd be sitting on his chair in the poky sitting room waiting for me.

I had the young legs for ferrying things around but when her old legs were ready to go upstairs she'd prefix the journey with, 'I'm going up to change his bag, dear.' I turned to my parents for a possible explanation of what she meant by this. Mum, with her pathological fear of medical matters, shook her head and shivered. Dad was not much better because he said talking about it brought back unhappy memories of his father. A coward myself, I should have pressed the point, should have known what he was referring to but came away not much the wiser, my imagination running riot as to what had happened to Mr. Truscott and what his wife had to do to him. It was one of those things that as a family we never talked about, not even when Dad's bag was hanging on the side of his hospital bed.

There had been no running away from Dad's bag, or the grey circles round Mr. Truscott's eyes that hinted at something painful, something that tortured him over and above his illness. That something, or rather someone, was Howard, their son. There wasn't any evidence of him in their flat; no photo, toothbrush or pair of slippers under the made up spare bed. They lived in mourning for him but for all their sombre clothes, Howard still lived. He lived but something had happened with him, to him, because of him.

That something had happened before I came on the scene and as far as I could make out it involved Howard and the baker. It was something bad enough to have Mrs. T shoot a blazing scowl at the baker when he was out and about in his green van doing deliveries and she was out brushing the front step. I gathered there was a female component to the difficulties that had arisen in the shape of either Howard's wife or the baker's wife or perhaps both? It was certainly something very serious and whilst I never got to the bottom of it I was drawn into the practicalities of their sorrow because every month or so Mrs. Truscott would take a trip to visit Howard.

The visit was usually of a weekend. She'd stand ramrod stiff glaring out of the shop window waiting for the taxi. 'And you know who I don't want over the threshold don't you?' she'd say through a slash of red lips.

'Yes,' I replied.

'And your Mum will come up later on to help in the Café?'

'She will.'

But Mum helping out was a double edged sword for whilst she was much in awe of our erstwhile employer she couldn't help being friendly to everyone. It didn't matter who it was; Stan the milkman, Norman the butcher, the chemist, Mr Smith in the Bank, the Insurance collections man. She always wanted to please, even a bunch of morons who came in the café one day and were rude to her. I can still feel the imprint of her hand on my arm restraining me from running up the hill in a blind temper to confront them. So life could be problematical with Mrs Truscott away because if there was a run on cottage loaves and morning rolls, it was hard to stop my obliging mother from waving the baker down for fresh supplies.

The taxi would draw up to take Mrs T to I knew not where. She'd pad past me, the clasp on her crocodile handbag now tightly closed after all the checking and re-checking she had been doing in the previous few minutes. 'And you'll keep checking on Mr Truscott, dear, won't you?'

'Yes.'

I'd close the shop door behind her and watch her exchange a few words with the taxi driver, her pugnacious bearing a front for all the gossips who could guess where she was going from the way she was dressed in smart clothes from the expensive Ladies and Gents Outfitters in the town.

Somehow Mum and I would muddle through and, with the premises closed for the night, I'd keep the little man upstairs company by the electric fire which was always on whatever the weather. A day left to tend to his own needs in the bathroom combined with the warmth of the fire meant an unpleasant smell drifted to the rafters as we spent the evening awaiting his wife's return. Cold air shaken from her coat helped flush the stagnant atmosphere away, hope flickering in his pale watery eyes when he asked her how her day had been.

'He's fine.' Then she'd turn to me and ask what I was doing that evening.

'I've got plans.'

'You're welcome to sit with us, dear. We'd like that very much.'

'I can't. I'm sorry.' I'd say, backing out of the room to leave them to their own private misery.

'Stay for tea in the week then, but you'll be here tomorrow, won't you?' I never heard them speak of any other family or friends and for all their little foibles they were very kind to me. Kind is one thing, trying to take me over as their daughter is another. I felt in danger of being consumed in their family tragedy. We parted and not on good terms. I can't say I didn't care because I did, especially when the news came that Mr Truscott's bag had been emptied for the very last time.

I pressed my room number into the lift keypad, still pondering the mystery of the corner shop, with Mrs T going on to marry the Manager of the one and only supermarket in the town. It was a supermarket not much bigger than the convenience store I had just been to but Mum and I had mischievously seen the marriage as part of Mrs T's wider plan, her jaw set square in a mission to use the power of the supermarket chain to put the baker out of business.

What of Howard? His predicament and whereabouts had been shrouded in mystery or, with the arrogance of youthful disinterest, had I simply failed to listen. Had he been detained in some institution? Did he live his days out in a single room, cell or ward? His mother had had a plan but had he? And what plan did I have as I scuttled along the corridor to my London hotel room with a magazine and a bar full of dairy milk goodness?

CHAPTER 18

A Room Like any Other

'We finished early, Rog.'
　　'Any clients?'
'No.'
'So what are you doing now?'
'I'm sitting on the bed. What's happening at your end?'
'Sophie's out and I've just finished watering the plants. Busby's on the prowl looking for a lap to sit on.'
'He would be.' I bit my lip at the thought of Busby's super clean white paws padding round the house, lost and lonely without Barney to keep him in tow and lick his head incessantly when they used to snuggle up together. How daft I had been over Barney. I looked down at my feet and wiggled my toes in my trainers. 'I did think of coming back home tonight.'
'It's not worth it now, is it?'
'No, probably not.'
'I'm just going to have my pud and cup of tea.'
I glanced over at the tray on the desk with the tea bags, sachets of coffee, sugar and plastic pots of UHT, the type of milk Roger had a real dislike of. 'I suppose I could always make myself a drink.'
'You've got a telly haven't you?
'Oh yes. It's a wall mounted flat screen.'
'Very nice.'
'That's if I can work out what button to press. It's always been the kids who've grabbed the remote and known what to do.' Given five minutes in the hotel room they'd have made it very lived in as opposed to me who had contained all my possessions to one chair. I would be able go anywhere at short notice.

'And you've got your writing.'

'I know. I mustn't neglect Frank.' The next instalment of Frank that I needed to edit was still in the suitcase, tucked up in the zip up wallet that Roger gave me when the writing bug first bit me. 'He'll keep me occupied,' I laughed. 'This was going to be my little spot of self indulgence away, wasn't it?' Me and my ideas.

'You'll feel better for a good night's sleep and tomorrow you may have a client.'

'I may indeed.'

Later, washed and scrubbed, I stood in the middle of the room debating what to do next. Behind me the flushed toilet clanked away in the shower pod like a boat trying to break free from its chains. I pondered the odds of it crashing through the floor to the bedroom below, opening up a chasm between me and the corridor and then pod after pod plummeting down in a domino effect. At least I'd had the forethought to pack my red, long-sleeved Christmas pyjamas just in case the hotel was evacuated in the night.

The wall with the TV on it disturbed me more than the pod. If the wall fell away those of us on the corner of the building would be instantaneously exposed to the thin air reaching to the sky above and seven floors plus below. The odds of that happening were infinitesimal, as was the possibility of a plane taking off from City Airport and careering into it. I rushed over to close the window and draw the curtains against the sound of aircraft noise and mad thoughts toppling me off balance. And I was mad because this was summer and I had closeted myself in whilst people were still out enjoying the remains of the evening light.

A few pages of script were spread out on the desk. I skimmed my fingers over them. If I was to be sent crashing into the drink where would that leave my dear widowed Frank Luscombe? Fictional he might be but without me he would eternally be left stranded in a hospital bed with no chick or chiel to visit him. He would be forever locked into the hours that dragged by him, unceasingly repeating the same observations on the comings and goings of fellow patients and visitors. His lapses into reminiscences of earlier days with his sweetheart of a wife Ruth and back further still to when his father left home would be frozen in time as would his confused feelings for the Ward Sister. If the catastrophe I was stressing myself up for materialised, the future I had planned for him would be unfulfilled, left on the shelf until the end of time. *A Week at the Most*; a story of ordinary people, sad in places, happy in others, a story where not much ever happens, but a story nonetheless.

Frank demanded I look at the printed pages and concentrate on where we were at. If nothing else, he said, we owed it to Linda. Linda (not to be confused with Lynda, the training/group dynamics friend) is one of my and Frank's greatest allies in the venture to get his story down on paper. Without Linda's grammatical corrections, considered contribution and unswerving encouragement there had been times when I had thought of abandoning Frank to a pile of papers on the study floor. But, no, in the words of the great James Taylor, through winter spring, summer and fall, Linda had kept me focused and accepted the chapter attachments to my emails without complaint. During our last proof reading and editing session, Linda and I had agreed the required revisions and amendments to the chapter where Frank and Ruth are on their coach journey. As a consequence, an excited Frank and his gentle wife sharing a bag of sweets had been elevated from first draft status to join the other chapters stored in the computer's memory as completed. The next sequence of events revolved around Frank and Ruth's holiday and, ironically considering where I was at that precise moment, a scene in their hotel bedroom. It made no difference to the plot but I made a note to check if I'd put a tray of tea things into their room at the Hotel Majestic. I smiled, knowing that these simple luxuries were things that Frank and Ruth would delight in and it was this attention to detail and minor tweaking of everything I'd written that was needed to get my Frank on the road to publication, to get the world to love Frank as much as I do.

I leant over to the far end of the desk, switched on the mini kettle and sat down. I took my Games Makers pen out of my bag and held it aloft over the first page where my secretary (the other me who writes notes to me) had scribbled *For Revising* at the top. I worked through it line for line and at the bottom of the page remembered the bar of chocolate I'd bought earlier.

I popped a square of dairy milk in my mouth and held it there to let it soften then started moving it from the inside of one cheek to the other till it was time to swallow the melted chocolate. I'd never bite into it. It never lasted long enough that way and sure enough the bar took me through one scene and onto the middle of page two of the next. I could tell Frank had something else he wanted to say, that he wanted me to add to the words on the page so I reached out for my lined A4 notepad.

The sun had finally slipped away by the time I'd finished my scribbling. It had been a long day but when I looked in the route book at the places I had been to, I hadn't travelled far at all. Was it always like this in London? What would tomorrow's daily schedule bring? Would it contain a historical fact and a saying thought to be interesting to launch us drivers on our way? How fitting it was, that as I lay on the bed with my arm outstretched pointing the remote control at the telly, I recalled the quote from David Frost on the schedule for the day that had just passed; '[The television is] an invention that permits you to be entertained in your living room by people you wouldn't have in your own home.'

The word entertainment was stretching it that night because it took me only ten minutes to decide that I didn't want the people who were on the screen in my room. I pressed the red button and, poof, they were gone. I turned to my magazine which was high gloss and glamour but little else besides, then challenged Clovis, Mark and Laura on the Nintendo DS to our nightly game of classic Scrabble. Clovis, my old adversary, beat me two games to one so I switched him off. I visited the frail and lonely Duchess of Windsor on my Kindle but her story was not one to usher in a good night's sleep. It was the most comfortable hotel bed I had ever slept in but it didn't stop me tossing and turning, throwing the duvet back off then drawing it back up again. Wearing my long sleeved pyjamas would be eminently respectable if the hotel was evacuated in the middle of the night but hadn't allowed for the sparks from the material's static adding to my disorientation. By three a.m. the warmth of the room was stifling so I got up and opened the window. The noises of the metropolis breezed in without a by your leave. I lay back down on the bed, my heart throbbing just as the city's heart throbbed in the clear still air outside. I listened to its pulse easing into the background as other sounds coursed through its veins; the hum of traffic, sirens and bells, clanking and banging as from a shipyard or hammer on anvil. From across the water there were shouts of merriment, the shrieks of homeward bound party goers gate crashing into the orderliness of my room. Then it subsided and I was glad I was sober and safe, unenvious of the revellers who would no doubt wake up with thick heads. And yet the night air, the buzz of the world outside had an intoxicating effect, my imagination interpreting distant noises as that of people on the move, as if the city was emptying. Punch drunk from my driving experiences and tiredness, my mind played tricks, casting me in the role of the only person left in a deserted 2012 London. The film set my imagination projected on the ceiling had me, resplendent in red, trapped in the hotel because I couldn't remember my keypad number and the stairs led to nowhere. I knew it wasn't real, that even in films women are never given parts like that so I got up, staggered over to the window to close it and my imaginings down.

I slept. I woke. I stood by the window as the shower Pod gushed and gurgled, discharging its waste into the new day. The capital hadn't been emptied overnight. A family of ducks bobbed about in the middle of the Dock. After taking a breather the mother broke ranks and, buffeted by ripples of mossy green water, the ducklings swam in a line behind her to the other side. They were minute and fragile compared to the immovable and indestructible towering iron cranes on the promenade, markers for a man cycling and another out on an early morning jog.

London; dismissed by some as grey, dull and dirty. It depended on your perspective. I thought back to the David Hockney Exhibition that I'd visited earlier in the year with a friend. If DH could capture early morning landscapes using his thumb why couldn't I? Because I have no artistic talent and no iPhone or iPad to draw on. It didn't stop me. I reached for my beautiful Paper Blanks notebook and sketched. Sketched!

They were making such hard work of getting across to the other side of the water that I didn't include the ducks in the sketch but got to work on the cranes. In the west the thick black lines of crane number one were drawn in great detail, the structure bearing a sinister aspect, indicative of its commanding presence sitting in front of and between two blocks of housing with carefully delineated windows, mock chimney tops and no vegetation to ease the eye. Crane number two, sitting closer to the middle of the page was only drawn in outline and could have been mistaken for a gnome with a generously proportioned pointed hat. In the east I managed to capture a fluidity of movement in the cranes and with the lightest of pen strokes gave the buildings behind them only a hint of structure, a glimpse of windows and the suspicion of trees in piggy tail squiggles.

The Tate and Lyle factory floated above the open rooftops with the words *Baking Britain Golden* clearly visible and if I'd had a box of coloured pencils to play with I could have drawn the Tate and Lyle logo in its green and golden yellow colours. Colours would have enhanced the trains which were represented in two parallel rows of square boxes; the liquorice allsorts black and blue train that ribboned behind and above the backs of the houses and the longer thread of the Docklands Light Railway train in red below it. If I'd had the pencils I could have sharpened the yellow and coloured in the sand that cascaded down the flimsily constructed gravel chutes in a nearby ballast depot. Mixing the yellow of the sand with the red of the DLR train I could have made the Tuscan orange and Sienna red of the fascias on the apartments and penthouses perched up high in my representation. I needed green, lots of different shades of it, to fluff round the houses and flats, to fill in trees and greenery, to disguise my inability to draw the church whose steeple was captured on the page like a flame on a candle rising symbolically at the top of the page.

I looked at my handiwork. I would stand a thousand times more chance of getting Frank published than ever getting *A View from Room 749, an interpretive landscape of random squiggles and wriggly lines in black biro,* exhibited at The Royal Academy. As with my writing I was trying to cram so much in, trying to capture the moment. And did the differing styles in my artwork, the contrast between the east and west on the page, show two sides of my personality? A click of the camera would have sufficed, would not have been so telling but as I closed the notebook I had half a notion that one day I would get the sketch copied, framed and exhibited on our landing as a reminder of that time.

I glanced through my A4 scribbling from the previous evening. I shook my head contemplating what Linda would say if she could see what Frank and I had been up to. The first draft done, I was supposed to be tweaking each scene in turn. But Frank, being Frank, had taken advantage of the long hours I had spent away from home and persuaded me that he wanted me to add a little more to his story. I should have stuck to making only minor adjustments to the poignant hotel bedroom scene but no, I had allowed my pen to be guided by an inner voice telling me that the reader would want to see a bit more of Frank on his first full day at their holiday destination. I had obliged and my pages of A4 confirmed that he was feeling very chipper and had had a joke with the young man on reception about how long it was taking Ruth to get ready. Then he had ensconced himself on the green leather Chesterfield settee, happy to watch the comings and goings in the lobby area. I had crafted a sympathetic smile on his face in recognition of the plight of a column of grey and silver haired residents with rickety knees side stepping down the stairs. His face changed momentarily as he grabbed hold of the side of the settee to stop his backside slipping on the leather. I laughed at him, his antics as real and as clear as the ducks in the water. And yet it was no laughing matter because I knew that if I kept listening to Frank I would never let him reach a final ending.

The sound of voices and banging doors along the corridor was a timely reminder that I needed breakfast. I got dressed and, so as not to draw attention to myself but in clear contravention of the Workbook style tips which said not to wear any other clothing items with your uniform, I put on Games Makers trousers and trainers and civvy T shirt and cardigan. At least I hadn't committed the Workbook misdemeanours of rolling up my trouser legs into shorts or put my jacket round my waist or slung it over my shoulders.

The smell of eau de stagnant water wasn't as bad as I walked along the corridor. After the experience of the day before I thought better of trying to get anywhere down the stairs so joined a couple of self absorbed canoodlers in the lift. It was a good job I didn't expect the type of sunny greeting I had accorded Frank from the receptionist at the Hotel Majestic because I sure as hell didn't get one in real life when the lift doors opened and I stepped out into reception leaving the cooing lovebirds behind.

Breakfast; pour out your own cereal, burn your own toast, make your own tea. It was no better, no worse than many hotels that have opted for self service. I tried to be organised and methodical with my selection but I was up and down like a yo yo. It didn't matter. I felt totally anonymous, invisible and everyone just got on with what they were doing whilst I slid in and out from the red padded leatherette seat behind my table. It was busy and cosmopolitan with families, couples, singles and a gang of men split between two tables shouting loudly across at each other. I came up with several theories as to why they were gathered there but I didn't see the man in the lumberjack shirt with a fistful of money from check-in the day before. I read the newspaper amongst the clatter and the chatter and another wave of breakfasters appearing, and then I gave my table up so that I could get back to spend some writing time with Frank.

I'd left him settled on the green Chesterfield settee but I had to make the interlude fit in with what I had written in the first draft. To do that, I'd have to focus on Ruth who looked and felt dreadful after the long coach journey and a restless night's sleep. Writing a book in the first person is no easy task especially when you know that the wife of your main character is in a poor state of health and you need to convey that she, Ruth, knew that Frank knew that she knew that Frank was putting so much store on the holiday bringing a healthy glow back to her cheeks. I could paint a picture of Frank in denial but Ruth's feelings were as relevant too. I gazed at the sky and the landscape for inspiration, the same landscape I had so lovingly replicated in my notebook. Frank and Ruth, they were a worry to me as was the sound of knocking on my door.

In less time than there was to put my pen down and get up from the chair, the door opened.

'Hello?' I said to the young woman in a housekeeping assistant's apron who stood partway in my room.

'You not finished?'

'No, not yet.'

'I sorry.'

'Don't worry, it's no problem.'

I went back to Frank and had him making light of Ruth's comments that the dark rings round her eyes made her look like a panda and that she'd fit in well with the animals at the miniature zoo he was planning on taking her to. I hoped the reader would see the humour and irony in Ruth having to help Frank out of the settee.

There was another knock on the door and I got to it before the handle started to turn.

'Hello, I'm still here.'

'I sorry.'

I tapped my Games Makers Swatch watch. 'I don't need to check out till twelve, do I?'

She smiled. She glanced at the shower pod.

'I'll leave at about half eleven.'

She stood fast by her trolley laden with linen.

'Okay, I'll leave at eleven, is that alright?'

'Thank you, thank you.'

I closed the door behind her, exasperated by my own stupidity in feeling pressured to vacate earlier than I needed to. It was not as if she had been unpleasant or demanded I leave but after two interruptions the zing had been taken out of my pen and Frank and Ruth would have to wait awhile before I could find the words to describe the complex emotions attendant upon them waiting for the bus to take them to the Zoo.

I changed into my Games Makers top and packed my clothes and odds and sods into the suitcase. There was one last thing I had to do. I stepped into the pod and closed the door behind me. The floor squeaked and creaked beneath my trainers and as I sat in trepidation of the pod breaking away and joining its mother ship I took a leaf out of Mum's book. We always used to laugh at her, the first few words of a song followed by a tra la lee and then a tuneful hum acted as her warning that she was in the toilet. There wasn't anything remotely laughable or melodic about my tra la leeing which fell flat against the toughened plastic of the pod but I had to do something in case the overzealous assistant appeared again and trusted to fate that my soulful wailing would ward off any aliens wanting to take possession of a lonesome Games Makers.

I wheeled my case along the corridor past the housekeeping trolley and heard the sound of hovering behind a closed door. I wasn't sorry to leave. My stay had seemed never ending and there was over two hours still to go before my shift began. Met by strewn suitcases, bags and excited jabbering people in reception, my thoughts turned to home where the Olympic torch would be paraded along the seafront in the evening.

I handed my key card in, negotiated two fifty pence pieces in exchange for a pound coin and strode with purpose over to the computer station.

Hello my dearest.

Can you believe that this is Mother sending you an email from a Hotel in Docklands? I feel very 'WITH IT' sitting here in reception at the Internet bar in my uniform. I look frightfully important and am looking over the top of my glasses when people come in. OH MY WORD! JUST LOOKED OUT OF THE WINDOW AND THERE IS A BALD MAN in his car WITH HIS WINDOW DOWN. He hasn't a top on and is lighting a fag. I've given him a look because after all, I am on this red stool with my accreditation on and who does he think he is motoring round this area like that. Honestly, what is the world coming to? Anyway my darling, must fly before my pound runs

out and I get caught in mid sentence Have fun flag waving tonight
with Papa. Missing you.
   Love Mumsy wumsy.

Mumsy wumsy? What a daft message but I thought Sophie
would see the funny side of it. I walked round the Dock to the
car, dumped my suitcase in the boot and walked all the way
back again to FDX Excel for shift day three. I was tired before
I'd even begun.

CHAPTER 19

Ag'in us

'From today T2's have their own break area,' said the lady on reception.

'Oh, where's that then?'

'Go out through the double doors at the rear into the car park and go straight across the roadway and you'll see the double doors into it. You'll be having your briefing in there.'

'But it's the same procedure about collecting our food, is it?' I waved my cool bag at her.

'Exactly the same. Have a good day.'

For 'break area' read 'bunker' because that's what it felt like; one large white walled and windowless room plonked in the middle of and accessed directly from the car park. I stood just inside the doors to take it all in. I had been in the room, albeit briefly, on the first training day and then it had held a stack of tables and a collection of chairs but now these were set out and organised into specific areas.

Straight ahead and side on to me was a desk for the Dispatchers, the last people you'd see before going through the opposing double doors into the main section of the car park. Donna and Maureen were by the desk, along with Mefi who I'd had a long chat with the day before about the life he had made for himself and family in England. Beside them were the boxes of plastic wallets and, on the wall behind, a clean as a whistle white board marked out in sections for details of clients, pick up times and destinations. To the right of the Dispatchers and against the far wall from me was the drinks station, the tea and coffee area above which there was a mounted television streaming news in from the world outside. In the middle of the room were rows of chairs facing the Dispatchers and then behind those rows, were tables and chairs set up either singly lengthwise one behind the other or in twos set up in a T shape. On the other side of the room, on the wall behind me and directly opposite the tea area there was another television and a seating area consisting of the blue foam benches I recognised from my interview day. Several computers also lined that wall and the fourth wall held another television and a door out to the area where we had all had our first introduction to the cars. Remember Isabella?

After the same kind of indecision I employ when walking into an empty restaurant, I eventually found a table, deposited my bag and Route Book (I'd labelled with my name and number) and headed back into the main building to collect my food. With baguette, drink, fruit and cereal bar stashed in my cool bag, I came out of the canteen clutching a pastry slice of vague description in a napkin.

'Hello. You don't remember me do you?'

I looked down at my assailant. Since our last meeting I had studied the Workbook further and had discovered another test that could be applied to suspect persons. It was the triple A test of Access, Appearance and Avoidance but now in full uniform with accreditation and a confident no-nonsense air, she passed it with flying colours.

'Yes I do. You were wearing a fluorescent jacket.'

'Oh, that. Being as I'm so small UDAC didn't have my size. You were a bit agitated.' I thought of myself back in the car park with sweaty armpits whilst she hadn't had a hair on her head out of place and her makeup had been, and still was, immaculate.

'Me, agitated? Don't think so, only concerned about that other lady driving the wrong way out of the car park.'

'Which lady?'

'Don't you remember her sailing past us? She was called Hilda but went under the name of Gillian and I asked after her under the name of Ruth. Oh, it doesn't matter.' And because I felt silly for being a prattler and because she had a certain way about her I bowed to her command to sit down at the nearest table with her.

'Do you know what I'm supposed to do with this file?'

I was surprised she had a file because we were waiting for the morning shift cars to come back but for all my pique and pang of envy for her many attributes, I went into first day at school befriending mode and told her what the driving schedule was about and what I had been up to on my first two shifts. 'You'll soon get the hang of it but you can't stay in here because this is the T3 break area. These are T3 tables.'

She flipped her hand up as if it was of no consequence.

'I'm going over to the T2 area now. Do you want to come with me?'

'I'd better look at all this,' she said, leafing through the paperwork. I felt dismissed, a bit silly and I'm not sure she even noticed my leaving.

Back in the bunker I tucked into my lunch and watched the steady influx of afternoon shift drivers come in.

'Hello again, can I join you? Sorry, I'm awful with names but we met...'

'I know we did. I'm Carol, you're Chris.'

'Looks like we've been booted in here by the T3's,' grumbled another man who came to sit with us. 'No air, no sunlight.'

'But it is exclusively ours and not a main thoroughfare,' I said in its defence.

'And looks like everyone's ag'in us,' said another, gesturing to the T.V. The screen showed a sea of black cabs mounting a blockade in protest against the use of volunteer drivers who were viewed as an attack on their livelihoods. And what with questions being asked as to whether the Olympic Park was going to be ready and one paper calling it a shambles we all agreed with the man's conclusion that the organisers were cutting everything a bit fine.

'But it's not been so bad since the Olympic Torch has been going round the country,' said Chris.

'I'm just worried someone is going to throw a pot of paint over me.' I said jokily, though there was a kernel of truth in the comment because, outside of the cocoon of Excel where most of us enthused with Olympic spirit and gung ho smiles, there was a daily drip drip of negative press coverage and T.V. reporting which, to me, wasn't doing much for drumming up the nation's support or our profile overseas. The others laughed, then all eyes fell upon Bryn promenading the room with a clipboard in his hand.

A briefing being a briefing, I thought he would have wanted us seated in the rows of chairs facing the white board. Instead he took the storyteller approach, drawing the faithful to his side as he ambled over and sat on a chair in the gangway between the two main sets of tables and chairs. It meant the people on the tables behind him either had to lean forward to catch his authoritative but not particularly loud voice or else had to get up and stand or perch on the ends of the tables. Quite a crowd gathered as new arrivals gravitated over to see what was going.

Bryn reiterated that this was our very own T2 area and that come Games time the changeover of drivers would take place between two and four in the afternoon and clients would be made aware of this so that journeys were planned to avoid this two hour window. It was imperative that we obtain details of our clients' plans for the following day so that the Schedulers could co-ordinate journeys. 'And make sure you have a note of your pin number for fuel and the car wash and the local locations of the BP garages. Don't let the petrol tanks go below a half and don't assume the person before you has had time to fill up or clean the car. And though the taxi drivers are protesting about us and the press are making a fuss about the Olympic lanes, the lanes aren't operational yet so anyone can use them.'

'Have we got any clients yet?' a man asked. You could have heard a pin drop.

'No,' replied Bryn. 'We are awaiting calls from them to activate the service.'

'So what do we do in the meantime?'

'I want you all out there getting familiar with the routes, especially the one to UDAC where you got your uniforms from. It's in Stephenson Street and you may have to take clients there to pick up their accreditation passes.'

'That's all of a mile away!' A joker with local knowledge shouted.

There was tinkle of laughter which Bryn chose to ignore. 'And do try to bring the cars back undamaged. Four have been damaged already.' He paused whilst the word four rippled round the room. 'I know some of you have had a bit of trouble parking out in the car park.' He paused again and I thought back to the second training day and the state that my fellow female co driver had got into at the thought of having to park at Excel and how she had dithered and prevaricated in the supermarket car park. 'But can anyone tell me,' Bryn continued, 'how a man can reverse the car and not hear or feel the scraping of metal against concrete until he stops the car, switches off the engine and finds he can't get out of his door because he is pressed up against the pillar.' Expressions of disbelief spread round the room and someone even dared to suggest that Bryn was making it up because surely no-one could be that senseless. 'I only wish I was.'

'At least it was a man who did it,' a woman sitting behind Bryn called out. Bryn didn't turn round but kept his eyes and his response aimed at those gathered in front of him. 'Did you notice that I only referred to one man and yet there were two other reversing incidents and a fourth of an unspecified nature?' He waited for pockets of gentle laughter to subside then stood up and I imagined that before the extra weight had crept up on him he would have been a useful rugby player. 'Any problems, you know where we are.' A few Games Makers sidled up to him with queries and the comments flying around the tables indicated an unease, a disquiet, part induced by the move to new premises, an influx of first timers and the scenes on the telly but I sensed that it was more the feeling that, like me the week before, the great majority had assumed that we would be transporting clients from day one of our shifts. Of concern to me was that thinking too much about something usually does for me so that driving around in training mode was more likely to chip away at my confidence rather than bolster it. But there was nothing I could do about it save contemplate the day ahead, the day as set out on the schedule that I now extracted from my plastic wallet.

'What have you got lined up for today?' Chris asked.

'This lot,' I said, showing him my Daily Schedule.

'There's a one way system to think about at number two,' he said, pushing his glasses up over his nose. 'That one's in a field but you can put your foot down there and back and that one's tricky because of the work that's going on.'

'Anything else you wish to add?' I stood up and gathered my stuff together.

'No.'

'What were the words of that song? Wish me luck as you wave me goodbye?'

'That shows your age.'

'And yours!'

It took the customary ten minutes to rejoin civilisation and accustom myself to the daylight. I followed the schedule and turned left into Western Gateway. Complying with the twenty mile an hour limit, I took in the wonders of a convenience store, the hotel I had holed up in to get my bearings, the apartments that I had passed in such wonderment on the day of my interview and my equivalent of a corner shop where I had purchased my guilty pleasures of chocolate and magazine the previous evening. There was frantic building work going on at the corner premises of the block, workmen of all trades trying to get it converted into a diner before the Games began. I carried on up into the dead end and did a u turn by the hotel that, despite my silly gripes, had served me well. Silly as it might have seemed to the likes of Chris, I had programmed Helga for that shortest of journeys but her 'you have reached your destination' was music to my ears as was the confirmation of the next destination an affirmation that I had pressed the right buttons. Success was followed by failure when no amount of pressing the buttons inset into the driver's door would adjust the wing mirrors to suit my sitting position. Bar returning to the Depot, I'd have to put up with it.

You can't do much by way of speed on the Lower Lea Crossing or the East India Dock Road but going north on the A12 I maintained the maximum of forty as the car alternately guzzled up then spat out the five Olympic rings painted on the road in the outside lane. It wasn't hard to do yet it felt weird considering I was the only car in the lane. Was it misinterpretation or misrepresentation that had other drivers on the road complying with a prohibition that didn't exist?

I was the only one, that is, until a white Range Rover appeared in my rear view mirror. It was making such good ground on me that I wondered if it was the undercover cops. My fears were despatched when I saw that the flashing headlights weren't flashing sequentially in a row and I was tailgated so close that I could make out the dark roots in the driver's blonde hair and imagine the tone and tenor of the words she mouthed at me.

In ordinary circumstances I would have bowed to this pressure and some might argue that I should have shown the courtesy of a Games Makers and pulled over into the other lane. But who was this woman to think that she could intimidate me with the type of vehicle which I personally didn't like the design of. I knew Sophie wouldn't put up with being bullied and Jet had told me to stand my ground in such circumstances. If I was going to have to put up with City swervers, seasoned bus-cutters-in and disgruntled taxi drivers I might as well cut my teeth on someone snarling through their shiny dental implants at me.

Madam finally got the message that I was not going to move and, hooting and flashing, switched into the left lane, undertook me and shot off at the speed of light. I think Helga had been momentarily stunned speechless by my implacability for I hadn't heard her dulcet tones whilst my power struggle with the woman had been going on but now she was telling me to go left. And that was always the problem with the Olympic Lane. You could steam ahead in it but invariably you then had to take a left and have to rely on the drivers who were inching their way along the inside lane to let you in.

I managed to get over into the next lane and caught sight of an Olympic car shooting off away from the main carriageway, the male driver giving me the most awful smug look. Helga came out in sympathy with him, emphatically telling me to bear left but I wasn't quick enough and overshot the turning at the Bow Interchange. Helga, as she was prone to do when reprogramming, fell silent and sulky.

I put the mystery Games Maker and his sneer behind me, pressed on and came off the main road at the Ford Interchange, doubled back, turned off and chuntered along Stratford High

Street. It's a busy road and I needed my eyes all about me with the traffic lights, buses and jaywalkers. Cruising past the bus station Helga piped up and said I had reached my destination. It was, by no stretch of the imagination, the Aquatics Centre but before I had time to think, I was accosted by some black and green uniformed marshals who, arms waving wildly, directed me off the High Street and before I knew it the car had of its own accord taken me into a small VSA. I did their bidding and stood by the side whilst they completed their search.

A shiny black Lexus pulled up in the bay next to my car. A man in a grey suit got out. He did as men in suits do; he breathed in, ran his hand round the waist of his trousers to check his shirt was tucked in, gave his arms a little flap to make sure his jacket was resting okay on his shoulders then adjusted his tie. Perhaps I studied him too closely as he twisted his accreditation pass round the right way to show the soldier because he looked over at me.

'Hiya,' said I, a fifty eight year old star-struck teenager flapping about in size nine grey trainers.

'Good afternoon,' he nodded and smiled.

'You can get back in the car and proceed,' said my soldier. The Lexus had arrived a smidgeon later but had been processed more quickly and the driver was back in his car ready to leave at the same time as me. I assumed he was a visitor to our country and to compensate for the 'Hiya' and with some good old fashioned courtesy I indicated to him that he could leave first. It was only then, as the sleek black vehicle purred slowly away attracting admiring glances from the soldiers that, it dawned on me that I didn't really know where I was in relation to the Aquatics Centre.

I kept a discreet distance, wondering if the Lexus exhaust pipe siphoned out the type of luxurious fragrance that I reckoned its smooth driver would wear. Our association was short lived and determined by the wave of the hand of a volunteer directing the Lexus to the high road, me to the low road. I went at a snail's pace, all the while keeping half an eye on the Lexus as it glided in front of a building where flags were hanging from the windows in greeting.

On the low road there were Olympic vehicles galore queued up and I slunk into the only available space in a rank of cars. Such was the power of the seductive Lexus that I'd strayed into the Olympic Village. A number of Games Makers, standing in two's or three's, were having a chat. The others, like me, remained behind their steering wheel watching an Olympic team roll in, the black people carrier vehicles and accompanying minders in dark suits with earpieces more associated in my mind with the arrival of a bunch of rock stars.

I looked at my schedule. It was marked up for Basketball which didn't explain the abortive trip to the Aquatics Centre but did explain the next trip to a hotel. However, there was something I had to do before setting off and when in need who better to ask than a man slouched nonchalantly in his driver's seat with the window open and his fingers strumming on the door. I peered in at him. 'Hello,' I said, interrupting his evident enjoyment of a muffled Five Live. 'I hope you don't mind but would you be able to help me out with my wing mirrors?' He stopped strumming, withdrew his hand and sat up. 'I'm a danger to myself and other road users the way the mirrors are set.' He took his sunglasses off, gave me the once over and glanced back as if checking that I actually had a car.

'Have you knocked it? Is it broken?' He got out of the car.

'No, of course it isn't. They're tilted downwards too far.'

He clocked my call sign in the windscreen. 'You're not a T3 then?'

'No, a T2 but I can't see a T2 rank.'

He grunted, which I took to mean that there either wasn't a rank or I was incompetent not to have found it. He manoeuvred himself into my seat and gave me a demonstration.

'I've been doing that.'

'But not in the right order or forcefully enough. These cars are built to last.'

'You should think about your sitting position,' he added. 'The lever is...'

'I don't want to be put in a racing driver position thank you very much.' If only I'd listened and moulded the car to me and

186

not the other way round I would have saved myself a lot of discomfort. I'd mastered the basics, not the intricacies but perhaps that's what I always do.

Wing mirrors corrected I gave up on finding the Aquatics Centre and headed back down the A12. I admonished myself for drifting into a mindset that saw T3's as different beings. Whilst not excusing it, it wasn't hard to analyse how that had happened. There'd been the comments on the training days about them being a glorified taxi service and, making the sign of the cross to ward off dark thoughts, I recalled Merv the Swerv during the driving assessment boasting that he was going to be a T3. He'd implied that to be a T3 you had to be that extra bit special, a go anywhere with anyone at any moment kind of kid rather than being tied to the same client. I thought back to my first shift the week before, when I'd mistakenly found myself with some T3's who hadn't been that friendly towards me and yet I had sat with my eyes open wide in wonderment at the talk of who'd been where and how they'd got there and back. And even in the space of an hour spent in the bunker some T2's had made unflattering comments about the number of T3's congregating in the room we passed through on the way to the canteen and the toilets. It was all very silly and by feeling intimidated by the swollen ranks of T3's at the Village I was giving in to a culture of them and us, and us and them would never do.

To lose one's concentration on Helga's favoured route of Aspen Way, Limehouse Link and Highway wouldn't have been a good idea but I kept a steady hand on the tiller until I lost faith and got in the wrong lane and instead of heading for the City, set off across Tower Bridge and had to cope with Tooley and Tanner Street and back over the bridge again till all was well along the Embankment. It was textbook from thereon in till I pulled onto the Square with the heavily guarded American Embassy on my right, the Maze restaurant on my left and Helga confidently saying we had reached our destination even though there was no hotel to speak of. In seconds I was going to run out of straight road and have to make the decision to either bear left or veer round to the right. My powers of deduction relied on trusting the fact that

Helga would hardly refer to a destination if the hotel was somewhere else on the Square and I also recalled Sophie telling me that when she had dined at the Maze another customer had walked through from an adjoining hotel. Bear left it was then and bear left I did, having to pull up short to avoid shooting past the hotel's entrance. There was a slipway taking you up to the door but with room for only a couple of cars I didn't risk it. The main thing was to see if they had a car park. In Sherlock Holmes mode I reasoned that it couldn't be straight ahead and I certainly didn't want to get snapped up in the jaws of the traffic in nearby Oxford Street. I kerb crawled the remaining few yards of the Hotel's miserly frontage and turned left. In my rear view mirror I saw one of OUR cars moving slowly past, the driver looking across at me. I guessed he was on a reconnaissance prowl like me. His, like many others, was a face I would never see again, but if I had I would have told him that there was no car parking adjacent to the Hotel. I would also have told him to forego a smile at the cluster of employees who liked to stand outside the side entrance service doors puffing away at their cigarettes, sniggering and scowling at those, like me, who had blithely turned into Georges Yard. And my third piece of advice would be to try and turn around in Georges Yard and go left back into Duke Street rather than take the zig zag route that I did. The roads were narrow and the car's wheels hard and unyielding against the kerbs as I ploughed left then right and finally surfaced at the junction with North Audley Street. My exit blocked by a taxi, I had to wait for a real chap of a chap to get out of the vehicle and witness him perform an arms outstretched welcoming ritual to two women who advanced on him swinging Selfridges carrier bags. Off for a spot of lunch I thought as, chatting away merrily, he guided them in the direction of a restaurant across the road. I waited while the taxi driver took his time sorting his money and meter out and then retraced my steps back to the hotel so that I could reset Helga. A couple of other London 2012 cars sidled past me and a taxi driver gestured at me for taking up a taxi space. I mouthed 'sorry', smiled widely and took myself back into the traffic to stop, start, stop, start along streets whose names were already familiar to me from life in general; Wigmore, Mortimer, Goodge and then left into Tottenham Court Road so as to turn right and join Euston Road.

I was fearful of taunts and jeers from the herd of taxis making for Kings Cross and St Pancras. As it turned out, the attack wasn't mounted from a taxi and the incident itself was of such a momentary and fleeting nature that I'm sure the lorry driver involved had forgotten it by the time he had crossed over from Euston into Pentonville Road whereas I, merely the residuary beneficiary of someone else's anger and of a less forgiving nature generally, was not so generous in letting the matter go.

There we both were, the lorry in the left lane with his window down and I was next to him in the right, both waiting for the lights to change. Out of nowhere comes a big, beefy and baggy T shirted lump of manhood on a bicycle to take up the gap between us, his legs barely inches away from the car. The lights changed and I admit I remained momentarily motionless, scared stiff to move too quickly and risk harming the cyclist who wobbled as the lorry began to pull away. Conscious of the traffic snorting behind me I inched past the lights and then, who knows why, the pedalling cyclist charged ahead, reached up and cockily smacked the lorry's wing mirror. I can't convey how quickly it all happened and it was a wonder the cyclist didn't topple over. Instead he veered away from the lorry, cycled across my path and looked at me defiantly. I braked and by dint of the look I gave him, he reacted probably in the only way he knew, the only way he probably could on a bicycle. As cool as a cucumber he took his hand off the handle bar and thrust his middle finger in the air at me.

He could have made life difficult by riding slowly thereby subjecting me to harassed horn blowers behind. He could have engineered a dramatic fall and lain sprawled out on the tarmac. But what he actually did, what I observed many cyclists do in the weeks ahead, was to lift his backside off the seat and weave a path for several hundred yards till either cramp or boredom set in and he was gone, as quick as he had come, making it impossible for lorry or car alike to catch up with his hot wheels. Yes, gone, without fear of capture or reproach but his action had condemned the whole cycling fraternity in my eyes and added to the feeling that being a London 2012 driver might teach me more than I wanted to know.

I carried on along Pentonville Road and, with Helga's coaxing, across into City Road, down to Old Street roundabout where I turned left into Old Street, bore right into Great Eastern and then into Robert's stomping ground of Shoreditch, past fashionable Spitalfields Market, a sharp left and right manoeuvre into Commercial Road then East India Dock Road and, bingo, I only then realised I was on the A13 heading east out of the metropolis; destination Essex.

It should have been straightforward and to begin with as I got some speed up and sailed through the Thames Gateway and passed Thurrock I was enjoying the ride. The traffic wasn't bad either. Again there were familiar names such as Brentwood, Basildon and Benfleet to spur me on. What I still wasn't used to was Helga's distinction between 'bearing' and 'turning', the distinction blurred when it came to significant road works in the shape of the construction of a new road. Twice I went left and zoomed off along the A129, had to double back and start again at the roundabout. The penny eventually dropped and I found what I believed to be the right road. I motored on past clusters of houses and shops which had a distinct style, some boxy, others with flat roofs, others with weatherboarding. It's hard to say why, but I got a holiday feel about the area and it being a summer's evening with people out walking and gardeners mowing their lawns, I lapsed into relaxation mode. I was happy to accept whatever Helga told me, content to go wherever she wanted to take me, until that is, wedging myself between parked cars in a cul de sac of bungalows, she said we had reached our destination. 'You're talking rubbish,' I muttered, conscious of how the car stood out against all the others parked in their drives, how the rumble of its diesel engine might offend the neighbourhood.

I drove off before anyone thought to come out and see what I was doing. My holiday mood disappeared in the lifeless town but I found no neighbours to offend when I finally trundled down to the end of a lane which narrowed further into a track. There was no Olympic signage to speak of, just a gravelly car park affair and a closed up wooden building that advertised the sale of teas. Helga expressed no opinion at all on any of it, not even a whisper of a U turn. There was just me in a car in a lane in Essex.

I wound the window down to get some fresh air and looked at the dial to see whether I had put in the right address. I looked at the map to see where I could have gone wrong. I heard voices and looked up to see a man, a woman and a child coming up the track towards me. It was a track next to a field and I thought back to my conversation with Chris in the bunker earlier and realised that being near a field was a good thing and even more encouraging was the fact that the approaching threesome were pushing bikes because Hadleigh Farm was the designated venue for mountain biking.

It was obvious I was the topic of conversation by the way they were eyeing me and the car. They slowed down and ground to a halt when they were level with me. I smiled and said hello, the question as to whether I was the slightest bit close to Hadleigh Farm waiting in the wings.

'Who are you then? Security?' the man asked.

Security was good. It meant there was something in need of protecting, that I couldn't be that far off the venue, but me, a security guard?

'No, I'm not security. I'm part of the transport team getting acquainted with the routes to the various venues. Is this Hadleigh Farm or somewhere close to it? '

'It's alright for some, isn't it, being given a flash car, it makes me sick, and all this money it's costing.' From the sneer on his face, the tone of his voice, I almost expected him to spit at the car but perhaps he thought twice and considered it too good for me because he hurried the woman and child to move on in the manner of those fleeing from someone with an infectious disease.

In my wing mirror I watched them pushing their bikes up the lane. From the turn and twist of the man's head and the thrashing of his arm he was clearly having a good old moan. Conscious perhaps of my eyes boring into him, he suddenly looked round.

Our eyes met and I wondered if he was going to come back and give me the mouthful of opinions that the scowl on his face suggested he'd been wheeling up the lane. If not a confrontation, I did at least expect a hand gesture, a middle finger exercise in the same vein as the one from the man in Pentonville Road earlier that morning. I was saved both because the boy, likely fed up with his dad's world view of the Olympics spoiling their twilight ride, pushed his bike free and issued a challenge to the grownups to catch up with him.

I let a good ten minutes tick by so as to let the trio get to the end of the lane, thereby avoiding having to crawl behind them and risk an accusation of harassment. I consulted with the schedule. The afternoon shift was supposedly two till midnight but, with no clients, Bryn had said he'd like everyone to be back at Excel by ten/ten thirty. If that was his wish then there was no way I was going to have time to drive to the remaining three on the list and it wasn't as if I hadn't been to all of them previously. If I went back early, the second night in a row, would this be construed as being lazy? Should I not go ahead and do as my heart dictated by taking to the road that would lead me to mastering number five? Such was the agonising that took place in that lane in the middle of nowhere in the somewhere of Essex. But, no matter that I was feeling bruised by the tide of animosity that I perceived being generated in the world outside, I programmed Helga to kindly guide me to HA9 8DS.

On the journey up the A13 I had pinpointed a garage as one where I could get a drink of diesel for the car but I had a doubt niggling at me as to whether, being so far from London, it was on the list of approved garages. The niggle became immaterial once I realised I was now driving on the Southend Arterial Road and it wasn't as if the gauge had fallen dramatically but I was thinking ahead to the driver who would be using the car first thing in the morning. I told myself it would be unfair to go below the half a tank marker but the real time to start worrying would be if it fell below a quarter. Surprisingly, I put it to the back of my mind and concentrated on appreciating the humour of those charged with naming the road interchanges. Gallows Corner, Moby Dick,

Charlie Brown's Roundabout, Waterworks Corner and Crooked Billet flashed by as dusk began to throw its cloak over the good residents of Edmonton, Bowes Park, Finchley and Golders Green.

Humour left me as I slid down from fifty miles an hour to forty on the North Circular and, yet again, getting to Wembley became a great big muddle in my head. It wasn't that I wanted Wembley or the Arena itself but I foolishly thought of them as my markers and so I did the whole going round in circles bit again; Neasden Lane and Blackbird Hill came and went and I got in a right old twist over Forty Road and Forty Avenue, Bridge Road, Empire Way, Wembley Park Drive and Central Way and Dog Lane. I blamed the dark, the headlights and the insatiable desire of everyone to want to get to where they were going even faster at night than they did during the day. And Helga was saying we had arrived but there were bollards and diversions and a part one-way system at which I should have double backed. It was only by chance that I looked left and saw the hotel I was heading for but overshot the road and had to carry on and turn round.

One day I'll go back to that hotel. I will stand and take in its impressive features but that night, on a pretty unimpressive approach road, I was looking for somewhere to stop. I pulled into the dead end adjacent to the Hotel and apart from a white builders' van I was the only vehicle there.

Rules are meant to be broken especially in the interests of health and safety and it was my health and safety that needed looking after. I locked up and skittered across to a man loitering on the opposite corner to the hotel. I assumed he was a security man on account of his black clothes, high vis jacket and a plastic identity card round his neck.

'Is it okay to leave the car there?'

'You're not supposed to.'

'I'm going to go into the hotel but only for a few minutes, I need the toilet.'

'It's not meant to be used by cars. They're still building for the ...'

'Olympics? I know. Can you just keep an eye on it for me? Please?' I hopped from foot to foot because the need for the loo had got worse now that I was out of the car and in the chill of the evening air.

'Ok, you can leave it there but I'm not responsible if anything happens to it.'

'I understand. Thank you, thank you. I promise you I won't be long,' I called as I bounded away from him in those ruddy size nine trainers which I blame for the undignified entry that I made into the hotel reception area. I truly did feel like something the cat had dragged in and the young woman of regal bearing who greeted me did nothing to ease my self consciousness.

'May I assist you in any way, Madam?'

I flashed my accreditation at her. 'I'm familiarising myself with the area. I put my hands on my hips to suggest some authority whilst my eyes were popping out at the scale of the place. 'I'll be collecting clients from here.'

'I see.'

'But the thing is,' I lowered my voice, 'I need to use the Ladies.' I wanted to add desperately to that sentence and give her a warning that if she tried to stop me then I wouldn't be responsible for my actions. 'Where are they?' I jiggled about; scared to stay still in case my bladder misinterpreted the signal.

'Upstairs.'

I looked around. 'Is there a lift?'

'It'll be quicker if you use the escalators.'

'Escalators?'

My trainers squeaked on the floor as I rushed round to the escalator, my accreditation swung wildly as I legged it up the moving staircase. I made it into the divine toilet just in time. 'Oh thank God,' I said out loud, uncaring if there was anyone else sharing the chic and sumptuous surroundings.

Perhaps I found the Ladies so deliciously opulent because I was grateful for such sanctuary after hours of weaving in and out traffic, dodging cyclists and circling Wembley. I washed my hands with soap that turned to silk between my fingers and dried and conditioned them with luxurious lotion. I thought I'd better smarten myself up before going back out. I needed to make the right impression on the staff to ensure that, come the appointed day, I picked up the right clients. Life has taught me that it is important, at times vital, to befriend the receptionist, the clerk, steward or doorman, for it is often they who can smooth your path or have you frazzled before you've even started. And if, just if, my security man had gone off duty and, as Tommy the Beard had warned during training, the anti-terrorist squad had been called and were about to blow up my unattended vehicle, I needed to look my best for the tabloid headline *Olympic Dream Explodes.*

How many lines had been written supporting, praising, denigrating and trashing the forthcoming event? How many words were yet to be written? As many as the number of faces that stared back at me from the crazy mirror. I wondered if my blood pressure tablets were playing silly wotsits or had I been bitten by an Essex midge and suffered an allergic reaction? My reflection carried on ad infinitum, a line of simply me, the colours of my uniform clashing with the décor. I made a face, I waved, laughed, each wave and laugh replicated in front and to the side. I swear it was so; it must have been so because I hadn't even had a drink. Disorientated good and proper I left the enchanted room and came to cast an eye over the open plan restaurant. I stood taking it all in till a young lady, as cool and poised as the one in the lobby, stole up on me.

'Can I help you, Madam?'

'No, no thank you. Not this evening.' I scurried off, kept a modicum of composure on the escalator and strode back through the hollow lobby. I looked across the road. The security man had gone. Heart in my mouth I hurried along and thanked a higher being for keeping the car safe.

Back in the car I missed a major junction and ending up in North Acton came as quite a shock to me. The A40 was also unexpected with masses of traffic streaming along the West Way but at least I was going into, not out of Central London. I didn't have the memory of Dad, the memory of anyone to keep me company, my thoughts absorbed with the time that seemed to be ticking at a doubly faster rate. Yet I could do nothing but let the traffic sweep me along; through Paddington, Marylebone, Euston Road, Pentonville, so on and so forth.

'You're out late, Ma'am,' said the soldier looking through my bag when I arrived back at Excel's vehicle screening.

'I can't get used to how long it takes to get from A to B in London and the traffic doesn't ease off at night does it? In fact it some places it seems to get worse.'

'Got no idea. I don't know much about London. We've been sent over here from Germany. And don't worry about the time, Ma'am because you're not alone.' He pointed at two cars driving under the floodlights behind me.

'Thank goodness for that.'

The car park was even more eerie at ten thirty five at night. Parked in the designated bay, I retracted the wing mirrors, checked the petrol gauge, and switched off the engine. I jumped when my Games Makers mobile rang.

'Carol, where are you?' It was the unmistakable voice of Bryn.

'I'm in the car park, doing my paperwork.'

'You're the last one in.'

'There were a couple of cars behind me.'

'T3's'

'Oh.'

'I'll come out and collect your things.'

'That's it then?'

'That's it. I'll see you off the premises.'

CHAPTER 20

Superstars

HELLO SUPERSTAR VOLUNTEERS. I goggled at these opening words of an email sent out at eleven forty one a.m. on the day after my third shift.

I didn't feel much like a superstar. I felt shattered and put it down to the concentrated effort of the previous two days, the madcap night drivers on the A21, the slipping into bed at well after midnight. Drunk from tiredness, I hadn't had pink elephants haunting my dreams. I had bollards and diversion signs floating round in the air and an army of cyclists whizzing round the car making offensive gestures as I roamed a vast echoing car park trying to find a marked space. In my dreams I looked into a rear view mirror to see a thousand images of my own face glaring back at me as Helga hummed musak tunes picked up in city chic hotel toilets.

Bleary eyed, I read on. Dorothy, Fiona, Sarah and all our Team Leaders wanted us to know that we were still in training mode and it was really helpful for them to get us out on the road and learning our routes. They said that some volunteers had been picking up clients already and one had met Danny Boyle at the Olympic Park. They wanted us to know that the nature of transport was that there would be busy times and quiet periods and please could we bear with them during this quiet period. And it was only '9 Days to go to the Opening Ceremony!'

Only nine days to the opening ceremony and if I was kicking my heels till then (my words, not theirs) they had provided some reading material to keep me occupied. The body of the letter itself told me about bicycle parking, a reminder of what to take with me to a London 2012 shift and, so far as the catering arrangements were concerned, I had to remember the motto....No Bag No Lunch!

Links were given to various training handouts such as the NATO Phonetic Alphabet and instructions on Dors (Helga to me) courtesy of Sat Nav Visuals. In hindsight perhaps I should have clicked on this link but don't 'they' say that practice is always the best way of learning rather than looking at diagrams. Or is it that I don't like looking at diagrams? And, as the days and weeks went on it was almost universally agreed amongst the volunteers, certainly amongst the ones I mixed with, that, to put it kindly, Dors was temperamental; a bit fragile, tres volatile at the best of times.

If I had been a T3 I could have taken up the link to bone up on radio protocol training at TRAG/Driver Radio Brief but I did none of those things, concluding it best to conserve my energies for all that my next shift had to offer.

The nineteenth of July; the birth date of Samuel Colt (firearms manufacturer), Edgar Degas (artist), George Mc Govern (US politician), Ile Nastase (tennis player) and, last but not least, Brian May (guitarist with Queen). I know this, not because the Lord tells me so as in one of the hymns that my mother was so fond of singing one or two lines from, but from reading my daily schedule whilst having my hot luncheon enhancement. I felt a tap on my shoulder. I turned round to see Chris.

'Hello. What are you up to?'

'Reading about what happened in 1980.'

'What happened in 1980?'

'The summer Olympics in Moscow opened on this very day in 1980 but the United States and sixty four other countries boycotted it because of the Soviet military intervention in Afghanistan.'

'Well that puts the buses carrying the American and Australian teams getting lost the other day in perspective doesn't it?'

'What about all this stuff in the papers about the security arrangements and calling in more troops?'

'It sells them doesn't it?' He pulled up a chair next to me. 'How are you getting on? Where've you been?'

'I had a trip out to Hadleigh Farm.'

'Did you find it okay?'

'I'm not sure. I've looked at the map since and I think I ended up at the bottom of Castle Lane where the Castle ruins are, instead of Chapel Lane.'

'I shouldn't worry. It's only going to be used as a venue for a couple of days at the end of the Games and by then it'll be signposted with all the logo sails up. Chances are you won't be going there anyway.'

'How do you know?'

'Just do.' He shrugged. 'Been anywhere else?

'I had a second trip out to Wembley, to one of the hotels, only chanced upon it by accident.'

'Which road did you take? Did you go along Engineers Way, Stadium Way or Royal Route?'

'All of them!'

'Same here!'

'This lot weren't happy when I got back just after ten thirty.' I nodded in the direction of Bryn in conversation at the Dispatchers desk.

'Forget it. They've no cause to complain because we're only volunteers but they are getting paid till the end of the shift at midnight.'

'I hadn't thought of it like that.'

'That's the one to watch,' he said, pointing at the hotel which was number three on my list.

'Tell me about it. They said I went to the wrong place last week but it was the wrong postcode. They've corrected it up on the chart, along with the details of the Premier Inn at Putney.'

'You don't have to do things in the order they say. I'd jumble them about a bit and, for instance, lump those two on your list together. It saves unnecessary to-ing and fro-ing and there's the rush hour to think about.'

'But there must be a reason why they are ordered in a particular way?'

'Even more reason to change it!'

'Aren't you the rebel?' I laughed. He laughed too and said he was going to work it to have his lunch up at the Olympic Park and meet his daughter.

'It's number five on your list, Carol, so I might see you up there?'

'Not now it isn't and if I get into bother I'm going to blame you!'

'Hands up, it's got nothing to do with me!'

I'd been to Greenwich Park on the second training day with Graham, Costos and Judy in her anorak. Shooters Hill and Charlton Way were names I had a recollection of but as I approached the mini roundabout at the top of Maze Hill it didn't look familiar at all. I should have turned right down the Hill but carried straight on. I could have corrected the mistake and turned right down General Wolfe Way. I didn't, choosing to turn down Hyde Vale, a narrow road with beautiful houses either side, and made it safely down onto Greenwich High Road to join the traffic in a power struggle with the hundreds of visitors making a beeline for the Cutty Sark. I made it to Park Row, not the right part of Park Row for T2's but near enough. The VSA had also eluded me so I set Helga to finding the next leg of our journey.

Despite the predominance of jaywalkers in Greenwich on a hot July afternoon, I felt comfortable there. It soon gave way to Deptford and I ground on through New Cross and Peckham. New Cross wasn't new to me, not after the mercy mission to collect Robert from there once, his eye in such a gungey mess that he couldn't drive the car. Thinking about that led to a momentary lapse of concentration and, mistaking Helga's continue forward as a straight on down the A215 instead of continuing on along the A202, I veered off and twice drove along Comber Grove and Blucher Road and joining the traffic in Camberwell Road will long live in my memory.

Back on track and, in honour of cricketing husband, I nodded in respect at Kennington Oval and it was all going so well until I was sucked onto Vauxhall Bridge, roughed up in the mayhem of exit routes at the other side then thrown to the lions on the one way road system around Victoria Station; lions who took the form of bossy taxis and other impatient, belligerent drivers roaring and clawing their way between lanes. Tossed into the stream of traffic in Buckingham Palace Road there was no place to stop or hide as I was dragged along Grosvenor Place into the lair of Hyde Park Corner where other vicious specimens were waiting to pounce. No respecters of where you want to go, the traffic will, if you let it, carry you round and round like a trophy then spit you out into Park Lane where the chase between the cars and coaches begins again all the way up to Marble Arch. My heart was still pounding from the mauling at the hands of merciless Lamborghinis and ruthless Aston Martins cutting across the traffic to get to the expensive hotels that line Park Lane, when Helga flashed A40 at me.

I took her word for it, determined at all costs not to go back down to Hyde Park Corner. It was a question of mutual trust between us as I let her take me into Oxford Street, left into Portman Street and on into Gloucester Place. I merged with Park Road and then it was plain sailing to Lodge Road.

I negotiated the tricky bend into the Hotel's car park, chuffed that I had reached it without incident or trauma considering, egged on by Chris, I had demoted it from number one to number two on my daily list. And though I say it myself, it took some skill to manoeuvre the car between two lines into a tiny bit of NW8. The hotel frontage wasn't as impressive as the one at Wembley but the lack of wow factor was made up for in the dinky doorman. Drowning in a burgundy frock coat, his ears flattened by his top hat, he stepped out the distance between us at a doorman's pace, not too hurried but not too casual.

'Good afternoon, Ma'am.' Close up he reminded me of a spry Nepalese chap with a sunny smile who Robert used to work with.

'Good afternoon.' I got out of the car and went into the whole thing about being out on a training exercise. 'Have I got the right Hotel?' I showed him my list. He nodded and proudly pointed up to illustrate the full extent of the building.

'Very nice,' I smiled.

His eyes alighted on a Bentley negotiating the sharp bend into the car park. It came to a halt at a dangerous and inconsiderate angle to the other cars in the confined area. One of his colleagues rushed out to attend to the driver. The doorman's eyes flitted from the new arrival back to me. He smiled but his eyes said it all; my silver car was clogging up the place. Had the need arisen, I'm sure he would have dealt with the situation diplomatically but he was so cute I decided to relieve him of the burden of having to make the choice between offending a paying client and a lady volunteer.

'I'll be on my way now, but when I come to pick clients up from the Hotel do I park here?' The reward for my magnanimous gesture was in his broad smile.

'For you, madam, we have other parking. If you will follow me please.'

'In the car?'

'Yes, yes, yes.' He did a doorman's whistle and made a hand signal to his colleague. With the eyes of his colleague and those of the driver of the superior car upon me I felt like the driver of a funeral car as the doorman slowly walked ahead of me and led me down the slope away from the entrance. He put his hand up to stop another car approaching the Hotel and waved at me to turn right into a separate parking area. I felt so important until the bar didn't rise and a big, burly nightclub bouncer type appeared out of nowhere. Much hand waving and gesturing towards me ensued between him and the doorman as to whether I should be allowed access. I kept out of the policy disagreement, powerless to relieve the standoff between me and the car coming in the other direction. I smiled, not for the benefit of the man in the car facing me but at the sight in my rear view mirror, of the Bentley driver making an absolute pig's ear of a three point turn to squeeze into what had been a perfectly adequate space for me.

The bar was grudgingly lifted. The doorman performed windmill signals to guide me into a space. It was guidance I normally object to with a snarl but he was so lovable that the thought of kidnapping him for the duration of the Games crossed my mind. He could be my sweeper, my own personal sorter outer. The uniform might be tricky but if others of my acquaintance could get a Games Makers uniform altered it would be small fry to get a four star hotel uniform done. Getting through a VSA might prove difficult but there was so little of him under the great coat that attaching him to the underside of the car was a possibility. The idle day dream was replaced by concern; not for his safety or well being but for mine.

'Your colleague will lift the bar for me when I want to leave?' I called to him.

'Yes, yes, yes.' He tipped his hat at me and I chuckled as I watched my new friend scamper back up the slope to welcome new guests. I hadn't actually wanted to park at the Hotel for any length of time but at least I now knew what to do and where to park when I visited and could pass the info onto Chris. My dilemma now was how long should I stay? If I shot off too quickly it would seem ungrateful for all the help I'd been given but if I stayed too long Mr. Big and Burly might have something to say about it.

I consulted the schedule and elevated number four to number three. I consulted the map and, having second guessed which route I might be directed along, I switched on the engine. With my head held high to retain some dignity, I slowly drove towards the bar. My suspicions that Mr. B and B had been watching me were confirmed when the bar went up immediately and I was released into the traffic of St John's Wood.

Second guessing worked well along Baker Street, left into Marylebone and then Euston Road. I expected to follow it through Pentonville Road so the direction to turn right into Tavistock Square was unexpected. I went with it, trying to visualise where it might be leading to; Southampton Row and Kingsway, that's where it led to. Aldwych and the Strand came into view and I argued that if I had my bearings right I could take a left up Fleet Street, go up to St Paul's and risk getting lost in the myriad of roads and streets in the City where people always seemed to walk faster and with more purpose than normal folk. But no, I eschewed the speedy walkers and talkers of the money markets and did as I was told; I headed for the river and turned left onto the Embankment. And as with the walkers and talkers, the traffic seemed whizzier and busier in Upper Thames Street which leads, as everybody knows to Tower Gateway and on into East Smithfield.

The previous week, when Bryn had said I'd gone to the wrong hotel, he'd hinted that somewhere along Dock and Leman Street's there existed a body of specially trained policemen who one wouldn't necessarily want to run into or double park in front of. Yet turning into Dock Street there was a thrill of excitement in imagining covert operations being planned behind every window of that inauspicious area.

I didn't get to go the full length of Leman Street because of the one way system and I was so busy looking out for undercover policemen that I shot past the Hotel and had to go down and round Royal Mint Street and back into Dock Street where surveillance cameras may well have picked me up coming round again into the bottom of Leman. To shake off any suspicion that I was planning an attack on national security, I cruised along Prescott Street, negotiated a nifty set of turns and inches away from the junction that would have tipped me back over into the one way system again, I stopped and did the most confident of speedy reverses up onto what I thought was the forecourt of the Hotel.

I should have guessed from the presence of only one other car, a slim sleek model with an equally slim sleek owner, that the forecourt wasn't for any Tom, Dick or Harry to fetch up onto. And the doorman who appeared at my side like a ball out of cannon was as different as different can be from the one I would earlier have been prepared to smuggle away with me. Exceedingly tall, exquisitely elegant in his grey frockcoat and tailored trousers, the man sniffed as he bent down to peer at me through the open window.

'Madame?'

I was in buoyant mood, refused to wither under his piercing stare, and reeled out the training spiel, rounding it off with an innocent, 'Is this the pickup point?' Haughty and thin lipped he may have been but his French accent made a soothing serenade of his account of having, only moments before my arrival, unlocked the retractable telescopic traffic post. In short, it was only by luck that I had managed to foist myself on the forecourt

'Is there a separate parking area?'

'I will need to put the post up again in a few minutes.'

'So do I come here, to this spot, if I have to collect someone?'

'Your people will help.' He straightened himself up, took a step back and, cold as ice, stood pointedly waiting for me to move. I cast a glance at the page that was open in the route book.

'And just one other thing...' This wasn't me just wanting to listen to his voice. I had a legitimate question to which he replied politely enough and, just as I had been kindness itself to the little man in the burgundy, I put him out of his misery by engaging the gear. As I pulled out into the road I gave him an unsophisticated wave leaving him to resume his relationship with the retractable post.

Guzzled up by the cars heading up the A1211, I applied my mind to what the ice man looked like in ordinary clothes? Did he live at the Hotel or did he brush up his airs and graces cycling in from a poky flat? Did his superior air come naturally, did he have to pedal some to achieve it before each shift or was disdainful deliberation sewn into the cut of the uniform he put on when he arrived at the Hotel? Turning into Aldgate High Street I concluded that his was only a job like any other, that I should put the experience behind me and concentrate on the mission I had hastily conceived under his Gallic nose.

The mission was to satisfy myself as to the location of the hotel that Bryn said I should have gone to the previous week. It wasn't on the daily schedule. This was a frolic of my own. Frolics are meant to be kept secret. I didn't let Helga in on the unscripted trip. So there I was, Sat Nav freewheeling down Minories, a little apprehensive about what would happen if I was found out.

But how could they find out? Was there a volunteer assiduously cross checking the mileage sheets against the BP receipts so as to account to Lord Coe for every drop of diesel? Was there a margin for error, a tolerance for the odd unavoidable or incompetent detour? There had been talk of the cars being tracked but was that only coming into operation once Games time arrived? But what about Helga and others like her? Whether they were called by their proper name of Dors or given a nickname such as Doris, Bert or Fred, were they actually spies in the cab? Was there a record, a sophisticated tachograph that the fuel monitors also had to check? Would they find out about my shenanigans along Blucher and Camberwell Road's? I shuddered at the recollection and what about my shenanigans round Wembley and Hadleigh Farm?

I was cut up by a bullfrog of a man compressed into a Maserati who croaked some comment at me in his wing mirror as we entered Crosswall. I contemplated the repercussions of getting caught up in some ugly incident. What if Bryn hadn't been just full of macho guff and the police who hid behind two way glass in Leman Street were called out? How would I account to them for the ten minute gap in Helga's input without appearing that I was surreptitiously sussing out joints on behalf of people intent on wrecking the Games; people possibly like the toad in front who cared only for himself?

Anxiety is as anxiety does and one 'what if' was rapidly replaced by 'what now' as I hugged the kerb thinking Maserati man had distracted me so much I might have missed the road I needed. But he stuck with me as we were both swallowed up by the gloom underneath Fenchurch Street Station and no sooner was it dark than it was light again and flash Harry disappeared and I brought the car to a stop across the entranceway to the hotel's garage.

I looked at the map. I had taken a longer route than needed. After parting company with Gallic the Grey I should have taken the road straight ahead instead of turning right. In turning right I had travelled nought point seven of a mile in distance terms instead of nought point three. Theoretically that longer journey should have taken three minutes but in practice I'd taken double. Nonetheless it was no small achievement that I had survived six minutes of coping without Helga. Six stolen moments; it was hardly a capital offence for the fuel checkers and the Leman Street gang to cause a fuss about and if I could survive six miles without her why not sixteen or twenty-six? But I felt guilty and, at the risk of being pinched for illegal parking or obstruction, I pressed the button and the last journey for which she and I had been on speaking terms came up, our last communication denoted by the solitary chequered flag planted slap bang in the position of Gallic the Grey's post.

The break from each other's company did us well because the A1203 produced no terrors and I was in East India Dock Road and merging with the A12 before I had time to think where I was. And unlike days earlier when I'd felt belittled by the snotty look I received from a fellow Games Makers shooting off at the Bow Interchange, I kept faith with Helga, trusting her to take me off at Hackney Wick, lead me down to the Lea Interchange and thereon guide me to the soldiers at Eton Manor.

'Do I detect a West country accent?' I asked the plumptious soldier, older than the rest, who was controlling the flow of vehicles into the bays.

'I hail from Bristol.'

'That's close enough. Where are you stationed?'

'I'm part of the Territorial's drafted in for the next few weeks.'

'Enjoying it?'

'It's different.'

Three circumnavigations of the Olympic Park later I felt no wiser as to where the Aquatics Centre was but, conscious of not wanting to be late back, I pointed the bonnet in the direction of the A12, giving a nodding hello to the advert encouraging me to buy an apartment in Poplar. I went to London City Airport then over the Connaught Bridge to find the entrance to Excel East but took the wrong turning and ended up in a hotel car park. It was close enough and I wanted to get back at a respectable time that no-one could grumble at.

Back at the Depot I poured myself a coffee and parked myself on a row of chairs near the drinks station. It was with some satisfaction that I ticked off all the completed destinations on my sheet. I'd managed them all bar one.

I turned and there in the seat behind me was the white haired man I'd met on the first day, the one who'd been given the cold shoulder by the T3's.

'Had a good day?' I asked him.

'I've been out with Colin.'

'Colin?'

'He's up there now, sorting out some extra shifts.' I looked over at the Dispatchers' desk. The man I took to be Colin, of slight build with a beard and cap on head, was deep in conversation with Pauline whilst others were handing in their plastic wallets and being wished well by Mefi till reunited on the next shift.

'Are they short of cars?'

'He offered to take me out. There's so much to take in isn't there? What with getting used to the car and the traffic and the Sat Nav. It's not what I thought it might be.'

'What do you do in real life?'

'I'm retired now but I was a chauffeur.'

'A Chauffeur?'

'Yes, I even drove Rolls Royce's.'

'Isn't this a cinch then?'

'No, it isn't.'

And mean as it sounds, the conversation gave me hope, hope for a lot of things, one of which was that I would eventually find the Aquatics Centre.

'I'd better get going,' I said getting up. 'I've got to drive back to Hastings.'

'Hastings? Colin comes from Hastings.'

'Does he?' We both looked over to the Dispatchers' desk. Colin had vanished.

'Colin, that man who you were just talking to, do you know where he's gone?' I asked Pauline.

'Home I guess.'

'I expect you're not allowed to divulge his details but can you give me his surname please? He comes from Hastings.'

I drove out of London feeling it had been a good day and that, come the next one, I might have someone other than Helga for company. And by that I wasn't thinking of Colin even though his surname was scribbled on a note in my bag.

CHAPTER 21

The Barb that Makes it Stick

'There's no possibility of being witty without a little ill nature; the malice of a good thing is the barb that makes it stick;' so said a little over two hundred years before London 2012 and not the kind of motivational quotation that would appear on our daily schedule. Indeed, on the day of my fifth shift, the organisers had fallen back on the bard himself to fire up those of us who needed firing up. In Will's immortal words we were enjoined to '*be not afraid of greatness.* 'Some are born great, some achieve greatness and some have greatness thrust upon them.'

Not that I needed firing up. It was a Saturday and I like Saturdays, my mood generally pretty upbeat. Sundays I'm not so keen on, the slightest thing can knock me off balance. Mondays and Tuesdays are Mondays and Tuesdays and I very often get muddled up with Wednesdays and Thursdays but Fridays are distinctive; the weekly local rag, a glass of wine and a handful of peanuts smoothing our passage into the weekend. And on this particular Saturday, whilst not reaching the lofty heights that Shakespeare was referring to, I was nevertheless feeling good, my confidence helped by the small successes I had had on the previous shift.

I rattle on in my recollection, an indication of how buoyant my outlook was even before I picked up the schedule. Others, notably the guys and girls at the pedestrian screening area, weren't so buoyant. Who could blame them? Every aspect of their antecedents, training and employment had come under scrutiny and their boss had come in for a proper drubbing from MP's in the previous week, one notable newspaper referring to him as having come across as someone who couldn't organise a tea party at Twinning's, or a pig-out in a pie shop.

It was serious stuff and only right that security planning had to be investigated, though I felt uneasy that operational strategies or, looking at it another way, dirty linen had to be aired so publicly. Okay, it was fifty years on and there were different threats to the civil population to contend with, but I could remember the trepidation engendered by the Cold War and, whether tongue in cheek or not, the suggestions of building nuclear shelters at the bottom of the garden. Cynic that I am and with no evidence to back it up, I felt that the politicians and planners, and no doubt press as well, had known a lot more and for a lot longer about the situation than they would admit. Someone somewhere had probably thought it would all come right on the night but as the days drew ever closer to the opening of the Games, realisation had struck that it might not. Did it therefore suit that someone somewhere to cause a fuss so as to cover themselves? And after all the probing and pontificating, who were getting it in the neck? The people on the ground! It was ever thus. Admittedly the bearing, sheer professionalism and atmosphere created by the soldiers at the VSA's wasn't matched by the civilian security force but being held up as untrained and incompetent made them easy targets for criticism which had a knock-on effect on how they conducted themselves and how they were viewed by some in the bunker. If you give people a label won't the vast majority choose to wear it? And I'm not blameless in that regard because, after my faux pas with the death threat over the sandwich, I rarely made any attempt at breaking through their reserve, did nothing to distract their attention from the job in hand and watched closely to make sure that they had done what they were supposed to do with the person in front and the one behind as well. So much for my 'speak as you find' mantra, so much for suspicion and scaremongering.

I ate my lunch with Chris. We compared notes as to where we had been and, to my satisfaction, he confirmed that my trip through Deptford and Peckham etc the previous shift was a perfectly acceptable way to get from Greenwich up to the West

End. He pointed out that the route was coloured in grey and marked in the key to the Route Book as part of the alternative Olympic route network. I cleared the table of our rubbish and we were on the verge of going up to the Dispatchers to see what excitements the day held for us when Bryn sauntered in and perched himself on the end of the opposite table.

'Hey up, I think the cabaret is about to start.'

'Let's see what he's got to say for himself today.' Chris sat back in his seat and folded his hands behind his head.

Bryn reminded everyone that we had to be careful of the traffic cameras. 'There's been a few drivers issued with penalty notices already and it's no use you looking to us to pay the fines for speeding or for any other road traffic offence.' I looked at Chris who made a face and then I scanned those assembled to see if there were any guilty faces.

'And watch yourselves at the Olympic Park. The speed limit is twenty miles an hour. Stopped once and you'll get a ticket, stopped a second time you may not be allowed back in and the clients won't be too pleased about it.'

'It would help if we had some clients. Where are they all?' a man standing close to Bryn asked.

'Activations are slow.'

'What does slow mean?'

'Slow as in not everyone is here yet and some might decide to make other arrangements.'

'What arrangements?' the antagonist pressed.

'Well, see now, there was a delegate who rang to say that although she's entitled to a car she lives close to London and has decided to make her own way to and fro.'

'But that's one person. They can't all be like that.'

'There's less than a week to go,' someone else chimed in. 'They should be arriving in droves by now.'

'Yeah,' said another. 'The papers are full of reports of a mass influx of athletes and officials arriving at Heathrow.'

'That's right but until the delegates ring and confirm they have arrived and want to use the service then there's nothing we can do. In the meantime you can familiarise yourself with the routes but remember that some roads will be closed because the Olympic Torch arrives in London today.' He straightened up and attracted a few who had queries that they wanted to put to him.

'Well that's us sorted for the day then,' said Chris, leaning forward and drumming his fingers on the table. 'I'm going to see if I can swing a trip to Wimbledon.'

'How can you do that?'

'I'll sort it somehow.'

I said hi to Stu (the cyclist fanatic from shift day one) and Sam (from training day two who was mates with John, and Andrew and Ian (muckers from the tables) and a couple of ladies (acquaintances from the food queue) and to any number of others because that's how it was, all of us swirling round the tables like eddies, keen to acknowledge and be acknowledged, some going to, some coming back from the Dispatchers' desk.

I stood in the queue waiting to collect my wallet with Giles. 'They've got another thing coming if clients think I'm helping them with their luggage,' he said, his lofty, bordering on Thespian caricature, delivery on the most ordinary of subjects always guaranteed to make me laugh when we occasionally bumped into each other at the drinks station.

'What makes you say that?'

'Keep up with it. That fellow up there has just asked the dispatcher what he should do when collecting a client from the airport.'

'What do we do?'

'Sweet nothing because I'm a driver not a bell hop.' Shorter than me, bald on top and with a physique of someone who was not a gym Club aficionado, Giles could not be mistaken for anything of the kind. His hands in his pockets, he had the air of someone who was king of all he surveyed

'Quite right,' I said, my tone reflecting his indignation yet at odds with my natural inclination to want to assist without giving any thought to the issue of being seen as subservient. And there was also the issue of how far to go with the physical demands of the job though recourse could be had for useful advice on Lifting,

Pushing and Pulling on page twenty one in the 'My Role' section of the Games Makers Workbook.

'And I'm certainly not staying over my time just to please some puffed up jackass who can't organise his technical commitments or is out on the piss.'

I cracked up, delighting in his licence to be so forthright, being 'out on the piss' not something I'd thought of in relation to the delegates. From what Bryn had said there was no danger of any of us being subjected to an alcohol fuelled delegate that day but when I picked up my plastic wallet and saw my schedule it fuelled a concern in me, a concern that I confided to Chris who, on his way to the cars, stopped to see what routes I had been given.

'I don't know but I'm feeling a bit paranoid that since my late return last week I'm getting lots of short journeys.'

'I don't think they're being that sophisticated in working out who goes where.' He looked over his glasses at me. 'If you talk to most people I think you'll find everyone's doing more or less the same routes.'

'Are you going to Wimbledon?'

'That would be telling!'

And it was telling, throughout the whole experience, how, as in life, for some inexplicable reason you get on with some people but not with others. Telling also how friendships can be seeded in the most unlikely of places.

A trail of grey trainers squeaked on the floor and the metal locks on the doors to the cubicles clicked and clacked behind me as I stood at the wash basins in the ladies' toilet. The mirror above reflected my smile and also the smile of the much smaller, slimmer and trimmer lady standing next to me, the prelude to a conversation that flowed as freely as the water from the taps.

'I'm not going to wear the hat if I can get away with it.' It was quite a confidence for me to share with someone I had only just met.

'Why not?'

'It's hard to tame this lot!' I shook my head, the manufactured blonde highlights in my thick wayward hair in contrast with the straight mid-length pepper and salt grey of hers. She turned and looked at me, her glasses ill disguising the mischievous twinkle in her eyes.

'You could tie it back.'

'That would look horrible, wouldn't it?'

'Not if you sorted out the side bits.' Her rolling Scots accent refused to be drowned out by the roar of the hand dryers. That was it then, the easy familiarity, the type of chat I would have had in my teens in the ladies' powder room on Wednesday disco nights.

'I'm Carol, by the way.' I said as we headed out to return to the bunker.

'Hi, Carroll.' That Scottish roll again. 'I'm Florence.'

Half an hour later, the glare of the sunshine struck through the windscreen like a violent headache as, part of a veritable posse of cars, I slunk out from the shady car park into the road that ran between it and the railway line. Progress was slow as every driver had to show their accreditation cards to the soldier on duty and wait for the signal to carry on through the metal gates.

It might have been the sun that caused the Dors system to go down, a reason no more implausible than any other. Reliant on postcode directions, I cruised along Aspen Way, right into Butcher Row, left into Commercial Road to Aldgate and into Commercial Street. The pavements of Spitalfields were alive with young people talking and laughing, the first floor windows of the Commercial Tavern open wide to show others eating and drinking. It made me glad to see them having such a good time for that's how it should be. It made me mighty glad and maybe a little sad for I was probably no more than streets away from Robert who was either working or playing. Feeling very middle aged I had to leave vibrant youth behind to motor up Great Eastern Street and beyond.

A sunny summer's afternoon and who would want to wear a burgundy frockcoat and hat? The dear little man whose acquaintance I had made two days before? He might have thought me a stalker if he had been on duty and seen me driving up to the Hotel again so I sidled past the turning, pulled into the nearside pavement and programmed in the next venue. It was a mere hop skip and a jump and I was in the shadow of world renowned Lords cricket ground.

Whether it's something in the air in North West One but even the Games Makers possessed an aura of exclusivity about them, making it seem as if something was going on but they didn't want outsiders joining in. A South African chap came bounding up to me when I came to a stop at NW8 8QN. He was polite enough as he hurriedly told me I was at the T3 pick up point in Cavendish Close and there was nothing aggressive in the way he flicked his fingers in the direction of where he thought the VSA was going to be set up near a hospital. But he didn't want to talk, his attention diverted by something amusing going on up the road behind us. He looked at his watch, tapped on the roof of the car as if to say, 'that's it mate' and waved towards a road to get me on my way. It didn't necessarily matter that we didn't have a long conversation and I did work out approximately where I would need to be should I be called upon to collect or drop off an Archery delegate. It was the manner of his shooting off back to where some other action was without making sure I was heading in the right direction which made me feel I was being a nuisance. I pressed on and passed some very attractive houses and got myself back onto Grove End Road and snuck up to the gates of the ground. My wheels were barely pinching the kerb, my eyes had only a fleeting glance of a gang of volunteers when a young lady flew out to see me. I wound the front passenger's window down. Again, the young person was perfectly polite, confirming that this was the T1/ T2 point.

'So I just pull up here?'

'Yes.' Her body twitched in response to the sound of laughter beyond the open gates where I caught a glimpse of tables and a garden umbrella.

'But this is a main road.' I looked down at page 231 of my Route Book. I couldn't work out the logistics of how the VSA was going to work in practice.

'It'll all be signposted and there'll be people directing you where to go.'

Instead of having to learn the mnemonics of safe driving as we drivers had done I suspected that the Games Makers at Lords had received instruction in HAFF, namely hand, arm and finger flicking because the young lady used the very same gestures towards a vague destination that the young man on the other side of the Ground had used not five minutes before. I only hoped that the gestures would not be open to misinterpretation by people of other nationalities nor would the way she maintained a smile whilst backing away before giving me a little salute in farewell.

Farewell it was and off I went down Lisson Grove, left into Marylebone High Street past Great Portland Street Station, running free and easy into Euston Road. I got a bit cocky in Pentonville Road knowing it would fold out into City Road. But Helga, in postcode as opposed to Olympic route mood, had a surprise for me as we made our approach to the Angel traffic lights in Islington. She implored me to turn left. I didn't know whether to trust her or go by my instinct, rely on my memory. I drove straight across the traffic lights but she wasn't going to overlook the transgression and I, of feeble will, gave in to her admonition to turn right and right again and was led by the nose back to the Angel traffic lights. The lights on red, I still had time to conceive an alternative plan which was to either go left into the wilds of Finsbury or go straight on to Pentonville Road where I could double back the way I had come from. So what did I do? I turned right into Islington Upper Street.

Islington. I was thankful for the traffic going at a snail's pace so that I could have a gander at the shops and people enjoying the café culture; people of every shape and size and it didn't matter what you looked or dressed like, people just were. I was enjoying it too much and when I saw more shops in the distance I took the instruction of straight on as a bearing left to continue along Upper Street when in fact I think Helga would have preferred me to bear right along Essex Road. She didn't make an issue of it, not straightaway at least. The sting came in the tail in the command to go straight across at Highbury Corner. To me the Corner was more of a square and straight didn't marry up with a little swerve to the left which would take me to

Holloway or the minor road I saw immediately ahead of me. My state of indecision had me drive round the central wooded island five times. I wondered how long it would be before someone took note of a woman in a London 2012 vehicle and green faced from motion sickness, driving round and round the local landmark for no apparent reason. Would they alert the police or possibly a medical team? Should I take the A1? I knew it led to all things Arsenal but at least I recognised the name. Helga was advocating St. Pauls Road which was the road to the right. I did as she said but a crisis of confidence descended. A dead end, a three point turn and a cruise round the island later brought me back into St Pauls, the road I should have been in ten minutes before. The caper made me wonder why on earth I had been so worried about the secret police asking me to account for my movements on the day of my last shift when I'd gone AWOL from Helga.

What had eroded my senses? I had coped with Hyde Park Corner and Marble Arch, and Old Street's roundabout had been a cinch. Was it the sun, the intoxication of the young people in Shoreditch, the colourful sight of singles and couples and babies in buggies promenading Islington Upper Street? Was there something sinister lurking in St Pauls Road that my sixth sense was telling me to avoid? Was it the influence of the film I had recently watched which showed alternative courses of events set in motion by the main character arriving a minute earlier than planned? If I ended up a mangled mess would I live or die for prevaricating or, coming upon a pile up of cars, would I end up thankful for biding my time? I heard sirens but sirens are the songbirds of the metropolis and nothing swooped past me as I trundled along Balls Pond Road. I crossed over Kingsland High Street and bore round into Dalston Lane and tried to take in the area where Robert would soon be working. Less affluent, less busy than Islington, the road wound round into a tricky little intersection where I felt a pull to go straight ahead into Pembury Road but held fast against such temptation and did as I was told and turned right into Lower Clapton Road then right at the traffic lights into Urswick Road to bumble along Homerton High Street.

The hurly burly of city life going on all around it, a hospital fronted the road. I looked up at the darkened windows of offices or weekday clinics. I thought of the wards swelling with Saturday afternoon visitors. Frank pricked my conscience. Why, with my fear of hospitals, had I set his story in one and how was it he could make me feel guilty for swanning around? And I thought of all the people in the hospital who, like Frank, had no one to bring flowers and magazines to them. Yet the story of Frank allowed contained people who cared for him back in the town where he lived but what of people in London who could live and die without anyone giving them a second thought? Where had the spirit and vitality of the pub goers and shoppers in Spitalfields and Islington gone? Had I left it back at Highbury Corner?

Homerton High Street gave way to Homerton Road and its traffic calming humps. Lea Interchange gave way to Eton Manor VSA and the soldiers going through the car and asking if I was enjoying my summer Saturday afternoon. It did look very much like a Saturday afternoon at the Park with tables, chairs and umbrellas set up at various points to shade the Game Makers from the sun. They needed them, to rest their weary legs either from standing about for hours on end or from running alongside the cars to stop drivers going to places that weren't quite ready or where access wasn't permitted. Not that anyone had to run alongside me, for access to the Olympic Stadium was still barred and I don't believe I ever got the hang of where T1/T2's were supposed to go for the Copper Box. I might not have been alone in that for there were so many cars cruising round. On a slip road to nowhere or somewhere of which I was unclear I stopped to wind the window down and have a few words with Giles who had come out of nowhere and was looking for somewhere, as was Stu who, everywhere he went, was hoping for a glimpse of the BMX track or Velodrome. An observer from outer space, ignorant of the fact that we lived in expectation of a momentous event, might have seen us all as the last remnants of some forgotten tribe who had failed to escape from the Park, forever condemned to circle it looking for pick-ups who didn't exist. Films had been made out of flimsier stories so why couldn't I develop a vision of a disused and decaying Olympic Park with the likes of Stu and Giles running feral to siphon the last dregs of diesel from abandoned cars? Another idea, another storyline, the fine details of which I'd have no time to fashion until after I'd finished with Frank and certainly not before I had finished in the Park that day and followed the schedule.

North Greenwich Arena. What memories of Dirk, Merv and Richard the place brought back and also of Costos who had sped Graham, Judy Anorak and me back to the haunt. On that trip out I had had to cope with the confusion of Costos using a different approach road and the dismissive attitude of Judy to Graham's meticulous record keeping. Going solo I had to keep a clear head.

I'm sure many of the drivers of the umpteen other Olympic cars that were driving up and down Millennium Way, West Parkside, East Parkside, Edmund Halley Way, Phoenix Avenue, and Cutter Lane, up to and down from the Arena, were trying to keep clear heads as well for certainly those roads weren't as I remembered them from previously. The members of public enjoying their day of sunshine seemed unperturbed by the circus of performing vehicles. Two sombre policemen were parked on the perimeter surveying the cars as they converged, circled, exited. They looked on as Sam and I stopped side by side and wound our driver's windows down.

'Do you know where to go for the pickup points, Sam?'

'No. Do you?'

'No. And where is the VSA going to be?'

'I don't know. Are you going back to Excel?'

'In a while.'

My 'while' incorporated having a chat with a lady I already had a passing acquaintance with. My car bonnet pointing one way, her bonnet pointing another, we tried to connect through our open windows.

In the 'well being top tip's' that Seb had included in our workbooks he urged us to take care in the sun; keep in the shade, apply sunscreen, wear sunglasses with 100% UV protection, wear a hat and cover skin. He didn't want us getting sun stroke but said nothing about tans; were real tans, fake tans, all over body or just arms and face tans okay?

I'd have staked all the pound coins in my money box on the fact that this lady, who was propping her stylish sunglasses on the top of her head, hadn't got her tan from a bottle nor endured standing naked in a pair of plastic pants whilst a complete stranger sprayed her. And I'd have bet all the Tesco Clubcard vouchers I'd accrued that the burnt umber colour of her skin wasn't of the pottering round the garden genus. If home grown I'd have hazarded at a daily set of tennis or round of golf, perhaps a sailing from Marina to Marina which allowed the salty breeze to brush it deep into her pores. Yet it was more likely worth putting all my coins and vouchers together to bet that this was a foreign climes tan, perhaps of the annual three weeks spent in Southern France variety. And a tan was the best compliment anyone could give the colours of our uniform along with wearing it with a smile that oozed confidence as hers did. My missing teeth, glaring fillings and obvious crowns were no contest.

'I'm off to Greenwich Park.' She played with the several gold chains round her neck, the wearing of chains a blatant contravention of the restriction to wear minimal neckwear. And why had the enforcers, Bryn or Tommy the Beard, not said anything about the diamond earrings.

'It's busy.'

'Bound to be.' She fiddled with her collar to make sure it's edges were turned up, a departure I felt from how the uniform designers had envisaged the uniforms being worn. Her ill discipline didn't stop there. No specially commissioned red Swatch watch with an extra loud tick graced her arm. I thought of how grateful I had been when the young lady had given it to me on uniform pick-up day, how childishly I had reacted, behaving as if it was every birthday rolled into one. I felt almost embarrassed to be wearing mine as I watched her swivel her worn-a-fraction-loose gold bracelet watch round to look at its face.

'And afterwards, are you back to the ranch, to Excel?'

'Yes, then no more training runs for me. My client's in.'

At times I'm pretty good at underplaying, overplaying, recovering my composure as befits the occasion (is that a case of she who speaks with forked tongue or an adept mistress of containing one's feelings?) so I played it cool, I played it casual.

'Who is it?'

'That's all I can say.'

And that was all that could be said, the limits of our conversation and mutual understanding reached. She slipped her sunglasses back onto her nose pushed back into the seat, stretched out both her arms, gripped hold of the top of the steering wheel, and fixed her eyes on the road. And on the road there was a further influx of comrades cars which made our continued presence bordering on an obstruction in front of the two boys in the panda car. We needed no better excuse to part.

When I got back to Excel there were no visible signs that there had been a rush of delegates clamouring for cars. It was all very chilled out and I sat with Giles who was doing the crossword in his paper.

'It's just not Saturday without my husband and I doing the crossword.'

'It's the same with my wife and me.'

'And I always have a glass of cider of lunchtime.'

'You really know how to live don't you?'

'Would you like some help?'

'No!'

Chris rolled up after an uneventful day. So did Stu and another mate, Harry. Over mediocre coffee in plastic cups we strangely and seamlessly leapt very quickly from non events to *Fifty Shades of Grey*.

'I only read the first chapter, if that,' I said. 'Just to see what all the fuss is about.'

'The things that are done in the name of market research,' said Giles.

'I wasn't impressed.'

'Why not?'

My views were no match for Giles' and by the second round of coffees Giles had demonstrated how well read he was and how ignorant we all were of the sheer volume of erotica published. In fact he knew a lot about publishing and though I never mentioned

Frank by name, his gloomy Eeyore view on the chances of anyone unknown getting published was a bitter pill to take. But on the subject of racy novels, on sexual mores generally, poor perplexed Stu was saying that men didn't know where they stood in relation to women anymore because they thought that they wanted to be treated in one way but apparently not and the advice he dispensed to his children now seemed naïve, irrelevant and out of date.

'And reality hits when they go off to university,' Stu was warned by one of the gathering. 'Especially when they come back home and the packs of contraceptives are left in the bathroom alongside the toothpaste.'

'My wife and I never had children but we have kept up with what goes on through contact with family,' said Giles.

I had been less than charitable in my heart towards Stu on shift day one but I warmed to him as the discussion opened out to the banking crisis and employment and what to do with aged parents and so on and so forth. It all got pretty deep considering we'd only known each other for such a short time. Or was it that I had forgotten the art of conversation when merely keeping up with the everyday occurrences in the lives of friends?

'Well it doesn't look like we are going to be given anything else to do this evening and I've got a life to lead,' announced Giles, folding his newspaper up.

'And me.'

'And me.'

'I'm going too.'

'And me.'

'Are you back in tomorrow, Carol?'

'No, it's Pirates Day in Hastings.'

'My word, such wild living.' And then we took Giles's lead, got up and dispersed. I handed my wallet to Pauline, a third of my shifts completed.

CHAPTER 22

Just the Beginning

It was late Sunday evening and Rog and I were sitting on the sofa having a cup of tea. He had finished recounting his cricketing exploits of the day and I was reliving the moment when it was announced that Hastings had trounced Penzance's record for the highest number of pirates gathered on the beach. 'Sophie was so embarrassed by my screaming and clapping but I got so caught up in the excitement of it,' I laughed. 'Over fourteen thousand pirates, Rog, can you believe it? You couldn't move for them and George Street was heaving with men with long black beards and cutlasses and a few buxom wenches as well.'

'A good day then?'

'A good day, very memorable but now I've half a mind not to go up to London tomorrow.'

'But haven't you made arrangements for lunch?'

'It's stretching it a bit to say 'arrangements.''

'So why don't you want to go?'

'I hadn't allowed for feeling as weary as I do. If I'm like this after only five Games Makers shifts, what am I going to be like after fifteen?'

'You'll get into the swing of it and I bet if you asked them, all the other drivers would say they are feeling exactly the same.'

'I doubt it. Some of them are holding down full time jobs in between shifts.'

'Never mind them. Go tomorrow or you'll regret it. Have you got to wear your uniform?'

'No, it's not an official duty.'

As is so often the case, all my hesitation and prevarication was hot air and the following morning I was to be found standing at the ticket machine at the bottom of West Silvertown DLR Station with a sturdy, black leather box-shaped briefcase by my side. It was a job getting my fingers working to press the right keys after lugging the case all the way over from my parking space. I wouldn't call the place desolate but on the few occasions I'd been there or driven past, there was hardly a soul about and the concrete construction supports that hold the platforms and track high above street level act as a wind tunnel. But on that day the uninspiring place was lifted by the presence of several smiling Transport staff. Whilst no-one actually offered to carry my case, I was directed to the lifts and as soon as I stepped out onto the upper level a bright and breezy young man was there to ask if I needed any assistance in planning my journey.

'I can't say at the moment, thank you, because I need to make a phone call to find out where I'm going.' He sidled off but must have kept me in his sights because he was by my side as soon as I'd put my mobile away.

'Old Street?' he repeated after me. 'Change at Canning Town for the Jubilee Line to London Bridge and change again to the Northern Line for Old Street. Is there anything else I can help you with?'

I thanked him kindly as the train pulled in and if I thought West Silvertown was well staffed, Canning Town was awash with guards and helpers, some literally falling over each other to make sure everyone knew where to go. There were a couple of overly authoritative assistants but they weren't unpleasant with it. A few gruff passengers grumbled and barged past them but the majority of us, being the sheep that we humans are, responded with quickened steps and spread out along the platform to prevent the bunching up that the staff were anxious to avoid. Had there been a recruitment drive for extras or was it, as one seasoned cynic later surmised, that indolent established staff had been booted out of their broom cupboard and rest room hideaways to work extra shifts? It didn't matter where all the staff had come from, what mattered was their attitude which I took to have been based on a simple formula; if they were happy, we were happy and if we were happy, they were happy. It worked that morning and I surfaced into the daylight above Old Street Tube Station with a sunny smile etched on my face.

I sat on a concrete seat opposite a Pret a Manger with the incessant rumble of traffic trundling round Old Street roundabout behind me. The sun blazed down and, to a surveillance camera or helicopter, my presence there must have looked highly incongruous. I was dressed more for a day at the seaside in blue linen trousers, beaded top and new prescription sunglasses (bought on Seb's advice) and didn't fit the profile of a computer programmer, systems analyst or data technician, apparently the usual fodder fare of the offices that encircle what once became known as Silicon roundabout. And what would those who monitored the snoop in the sky footage make of the big black briefcase next to me and the way my flabby bingo winged arm was laid so protectively across it? Was I engaged in espionage of some sort? That theory might have been feasible in the past, the place an ideal location for a 'drop' with road, bus or underground to whisk me or my 'contact' away with files and reels stuffed into the pockets and flaps of the case, but nowadays? No way, such illicit information that I might be carrying could be stored on something the size of a pinhead.

The case itself was of a kind that I've always referred to as a Counsel's briefcase The quickest of peeks inside would have satisfied Special Surveillance Operations that there was nothing of a legal bearing about its contents that day. So why did I hold the case so protectively by my side? Even if one discounted the theory that I was at that time being vetted by satellite as a security risk or involved in some nefarious crime which entailed using the clever cover of a middle aged woman, it was highly unlikely that I was going to be mugged. Highly unlikely indeed unless the mugger believed the case was filled with bank notes and he was extremely flight of foot.

I was a guardian, an official custodian of the case which had been entrusted to our safe keeping by Roger's cousin, Jack, until such time as we could pass it on. What worthy newsprint and editorial pieces had jostled for position in the case as former journalist Jack had bombed about in his sports car on his way to company board meetings, fine restaurants, hotels and gentlemen's clubs before beetling back to Fleet Street?

Time was the operative word as I waited for the blood to return to my fingers after lugging the case across from West Silvertown. I looked at my feet to see if they were swollen. I mopped my brow and the back of my neck with a tissue, popped an extra strong Trebor mint into my mouth and read the text that had come through in my message inbox.

I watched life going on around me, especially the clutch of people being herded up the street to the left of me. Dressed in sweltering black, a woman in charge was herding them towards a black Mercedes carrier whilst she pulled an altogether lighter attaché case on wheels behind her. Such distractions made me relax my hold on the case and I would have been in serious trouble if the man who approached me had been able to snatch it and run as fast as he could talk or had a partner who could grab the bag whilst I watched matey plant his backside down beside me. I instinctively put my hand on the case and then felt a bit stupid seeing as I was wedged between it and him. And it was a very tight wedge, though it didn't seem to bother him because he was doing a bit of business on his phone. Once I'd sussed what kind of business it was I got to thinking that the reason he had to keep moving his phone from ear to ear was probably on account of his having a bit of arthritis in his fat podgy hands. And when he got wildly excited and started moving his head from side to side and the elbow of his phone-holding left arm nearly gave me a nose bleed without a please or thank you from him, I decided to shuffle the case and me along away from him. He carried on putting together the team for his new build, calling up the brickie, plasterer, chippie, electrician and building suppliers. I had no doubt, from the tautness of the bicep bulges that under the short sleeve of his polo shirt and from the little nicks and purple scars on his hands, he had once got covered in brick dust or spiked by splinters but not for a while. I found it curious that he should choose to conduct business negotiations under a frying sun. I supposed it was better than in a coffee house or restaurant where you never know who is listening and I assumed he had discounted me as a threat of any kind because I am at a stage in life when you become invisible to people. Invisible but not without guile because it would have served him right if I had actually been a mistress of industrial espionage and had a secret camera and microphone, hidden in the side of the briefcase, trained on him. I could have scuppered his plans by posting the film and sound recording on YouTube and, if I was feeling faithful to my star sign, could have gone home and typed up spreadsheet details of his costings and time schedule on the Internet.

Industrial espionage was stretching it because having been sat waiting for an hour I was beginning to feel more like a stooge for one of those T.V pranks; the camera focused on me to see how long it would take before my patience wore thin and the builder with the manicured hands next to me was the prankster's bait. Was his constant gabble (even talking to himself in between making calls) meant to test my endurance or merely the prelude to his talking about something so scandalous that my reaction was worthy of putting out on prime time T.V? I snuck a look at him. He was possibly, but only just, out of the age range of those who look back with fondness on the Candid Camera capers. He wore no rubber prosthetics, no sign of a false nose and from the way he switched his mobile phone from one ear to the other his arms looked and worked normally with no indication of one of them falling off to the sound of hysterical screaming from the lady next to him, dressed for the seaside in blue linen trousers, beaded top and Wimbledon sunglasses.

His arms were fine but mine were going pink as were my feet and the highlights in my hair were taking on a scorched blonde look. I dug deep in my bag and pulled my mobile phone out. There were no new texts. It wasn't as high tech as my builder friend's but I pressed the buttons more deftly than the stubby tips of his fingers did. The dialled number rang out once then cut into the theme tune from Disney's Robin Hood. It was a familiar tale, one that had caused me much self induced and energy sapping frustration and anxiety over the years. WHAT'S HAPPENING? I texted but, before hitting the SEND key, the phone rang.

'You alright?'

'Yes. Where are you?'

'We're just walking up from the Barbican. We won't be long.'

How long is a piece of string? As long as it took me to look up in my A TO Z where the Barbican is and to work out from which direction they would be arriving and then to keep my eye trained on the pedestrians walking in my direction.

I saw the three of them approaching through a heat haze generated by my need for a drink. They stood out against the crowd; Robert's shock of bleached hair under his trademark fedora, T shirt, black skinny jeans and leather jacket slung over his shoulder; Hannah with her dramatic hair and eyes wearing a short black skirt, braces and Doctor Martens; Connor with swept back hair and his skin bristling with tattoos beneath his singlet. I got a big hug from all three.

'Sorry we're late, Mum.'

'That's alright. I expect you're hungry aren't you? Where shall we go?'

Robert made what I term an Alan 'aah', derived from his Uncle's repertoire of similar noises. Such 'aahs' denote a thought process going on but can variously mean he's not given any prior thought to the question posed, he's given thought but hasn't come up with an answer or, having arrived at an answer, it has raised a supplemental question that you have caught him on the verge of asking.

'Where do you think?' He looked to the other two who mumbled a few places I had never heard of.

'I'm happy with anything,' I hoped it might prompt a decision. 'And it better not be too far because you'll have to carry this, Robert.' I pointed to the briefcase which was getting its own sweat on.

'Aah.'

'You did say you wanted me to bring it up, didn't you?' And my little brain was galloping ahead as to what I could do with it if Robert decided he didn't want it. What could I do with it if it didn't fit in with his plans? Aah, would it be best to take a trip back to the car and perhaps drop it round to his flat later or simply take it back home with me.

'Yes, but is there anything in it?'

'Just a few things, but if it's too heavy or...'

'Go on Rob, pick it up for your Mum,' said Connor, fidgeting to get going.

'He will,' I said, unable to bear any implied criticism of my son who was putting his jacket on. 'Won't you be hot wearing that, Robert? I'll carry it if you want.'

'I'll carry it for you, Rob,' mimicked Connor.

'Can't we eat somewhere around here?' I looked about, knowing that there would be a point blank refusal from Robert to eat in any of the restaurant chains.

'No, we'll go down towards Shoreditch.'

'That's fine by me. I'll just follow you lot.'

For a change I was a pedestrian in Great Eastern Street, Hannah at my side gaily chatting to me whilst the boys walked on ahead, Robert every now and then changing the case from one hand to another.

'What about going to the bar?' I asked. 'Isn't that quite close?'

'No, we'll go somewhere different.'

Hannah pointed out where she was working. A man in a car at a garage called out to Robert. He always manages to know someone and we paused for a few words to be exchanged and to say cheerio to Connor. I contemplated suggesting we went into the garage and got some plastic sandwiches then thought better of such a crass idea. London dust crept into my Clarks sandals as we carried on down Commercial Street. 'What about the Commercial Tavern?' I suggested, though without its windows open it didn't look as appealing to me as it had when I'd driven past it a few days before.

'No.'

The three of us ended up standing round the briefcase in the middle of Spitalfields Market. Robert was texting someone.

'Did you know, Hannah, that this is the only place that I have ever known Roger say he would like a return visit to do some shopping.'

'No way!'

'True!'

Robert put his phone away and looked around. 'Aah.'

'What's the aah for?'

'Where to eat?'

'In here?'

'No.'

'Right then, I'm going to I tell you what I'm going to do. I'm going to go outside and I'm going to go in the first pub or restaurant I see.' And that's what we did and the food was good and the conversation flowed. A man peered in through the window and Robert put his hand up in recognition.

'Who was that?'

'Sam. He's homeless, lots of problems, really nice guy. You know how soft I am, Mother.' Hannah went to the loo and I leant over and put my hand on Robert's arm.

'Everything's going ok, Robert?'

'Yeah, it's all good.'

'Well, while Hannah's not here, there's pants, socks, T shirts, a letter from the Bank and I think Dad's put a book in the briefcase for you. And there's a card so that you can get some foodie bits.'

'Thanks Mum.' He squeezed my hand. Hannah appeared and they walked me along to Liverpool Street. 'You'll need the Central Line to Stratford.'

'Okay, thanks.' I kissed and hugged them goodbye and they made off in completely the opposite direction. When I got to the top of the steps for the Station I stopped and looked back over my shoulder. I pin point Robert's blonde hair and Hannah wearing his hat, as he shepherded her through the flock of monochrome office types hurrying towards the Station. They weren't looking back. They had no need to and I knew too that it did me no good to do so either; affixing myself to the present and putting all my efforts back into writing about Frank was the only way forward. And so I turned, became invisible again and melted into the crowds.

Underground, beyond sun and moisture, a familiar whoosh of warm air preceded the arrival of the train for Bethnal Green, Mile End and Stratford. Bursts of summer clothing and Games Makers purple and red on young shoots and older hardies flashed past before the carriages came to a stop. I planted myself on a seat, my blues the colour of the moods that can take you through the seasons. As I rummaged in my bag for my lipstick holder and mirror, I heard the doors closing, the smells of nature composting quickly as the train moved into the dark where nothing can grow. I applied a coat of heather shimmer to my lips, checked I had everything I needed for the evening, closed my bag and looked up. I wished I had kept my sunglasses on because the fuchsia pink and light purple visions I saw scattered amongst otherwise drab and sleep rooted passengers was a sight I had been unprepared for. I wondered who the hybrids, wearing uniforms akin to those worn by Games Makers, were? I shuffled in my seat, not wanting to make it too obvious that I wanted to see what variety of official the lady with the trunk legs opposite was.

I peered again and saw that the fuchsias were the Mayor of London's Ambassadors; home grown Boris beauties, their heads topped off in white trilby hats. In a bunch they would have looked quite effective, as singles they looked out of place or was that just me, having got used to my own species? I was glad I was travelling in civvies because the clash of colours would do nothing to help the bloom of red rising in my cheeks, the greenhouse effect of the stuffy train.

Stratford. It was a nightmare with hundreds and hundreds of people and barricades and a pedestrian contra flow moving in the opposite direction to the way you would expect to go for Westfield and the Olympic Park. I was completely disorientated and there was no means of escape from the heat, the pushing and shoving and irate commuters wanting to get to where they needed to be. I shouldn't have taken it to heart as I did but I thought that if this was what it was going to be like when thousands of visitors had to get to the Stadium every day, the doom laden-prophecies of the Olympic knockers would be proved right and the transport system pilloried. We seemed to go round and round in circles and a fat bullish Transport for London woman shouted at us to keep moving. She barracked a confused group of German youngsters, who had unwittingly ended up going against the flow of pedestrians. I cringed at the way she spoke to them and when the youngsters tagged on behind I heard them say how rude she was. Embarrassed and cross at the way they had been treated I had half a mind to turn back and speak to her but the risk of being trampled on by the crowd gathering momentum behind me was not worth the taking. Above ground there was space to breathe and the tension eased, the shop windows of Westfield doing their best to lure people away from their chosen path. Few veered off even though it looked like another bottle neck was waiting up ahead to try the tempers of me and my fellow journeymen.

Queues there were and yet a soldier-in-chief barking at us to get our bags and belongings ready for security searches brought no complaint. It had to be done and done it had to be and ripples of excited anticipation rolled out from the Marquee, in large part engendered by the good humoured soldiers rifling and scanning through our belongings.

It was Disneyeque; the summer sun still wrapped around the thousands pouring across the wide walkways towards the Stadium. For all the driving around the Olympic Park I hadn't seen the outside of the Stadium in its glory because the road network was underneath the public areas. Now I stood in awe of its size and strength, its domination softened by the black and white harlequin design of its supports. Like me, others stopped to take it in whilst all around the business of the Park went on with good grace and good humour, from the calls of the Olympic programme sellers, and the chatty natter of the servers behind the fast food and drinks outlets who had already received a hard time from the critics, to the army of smiling Games Makers with giant foam finger-pointing gloves and the earnest security personnel directing people where to go.

There were crowds but it wasn't crowded. Everyone seemed to know someone and had food orders as long as your arm or is that how it always feels for those asking for a solitary baked potato with bean and cheese topping and a bottle of water? And where is the fun in hearing your own footsteps paddling up an iron staircase, the only tactile warmth that of the potato leeching through its cardboard casing.

'There is a lift,' an enthusiastic Stadium attendant advised. I took it, leaving the smell of baked beans wafting behind me as the doors opened onto the floor I needed to be on. If my seat had been any higher up I would have been tempted to backtrack and get home before the TV news channels reported on the success or otherwise of the evening. But I thought that there might be difficulties in trying to get out of a place that everyone was desperate to get in to and recognised that with no-one to listen and administer sympathy to me I would just have to cope with my vertiginous fear of falling forward out of the seat.

To take my mind off of my situation I listened to the woman behind me telling the man next to her all about the selection process and the training for her Games Makers role, right through to the draw she had entered to get a ticket for that evening. She focused mostly on how the Olympic movement as a whole would benefit from her extensive experience. I began to wish I had the briefcase and a secret camera and microphone with me but it would have been tricky getting it through security. I choked on a mouthful of potato. It was comical, farcical and tragic even to entertain such foolish notions. How far from reality had I come, surely the result of spending too much time in my own company and that of Frank?

In reality I had a glorious view of the inside of the Stadium and marvelled at its sheer size and the engineering expertise that had gone into it. The seats in the Stadium began to fill up, individual seats then whole rows, people clothed in mufti like me, others in the royal red and regal purple of Games Makers or the chameleon fuchsia of Boris's beauties. On the other side of the Stadium people looked like the coloured pegs on the peg art boards that Robert and Sophie used to play with.

I looked at the time. I rang home, putting on a la dee da voice. 'Hello. I'm making this call from my seat in the Olympic Stadium.'

'What's it like?'

'Amazing!'

'Anything happened yet?'

'No. I'm just acclimatising to the altitude.'

'Enjoy yourself and ring me when it's finished.'

Behind me the woman rambled on and her seating partner's monosyllabic responses were such that I took him not to be part of the Games Makers fraternity. I swilled my mouth with water to wash the last remnants of my salad accompaniment down and concluded that, despite the hunger of some critics to make a fuss about the restrictive practices imposed on the Park's catering facilities, the food was no better or worse than I would have expected. I concluded too that the woman must have taken a bite or drink of something because the man managed to squeeze a few words in edgeways.

'When did your shifts start?'

'Umm, umm, um,' she spluttered and though I wouldn't have stood up in court and sworn on it, her muffled reply, perhaps caused by an errant crumb of a biscuit illicitly brought in, suggested she hadn't seen action in the field of duty. It isn't something one should be proud to admit but I felt very smug because, unlike me with five shifts under my belt, she knew nothing of the Games Makers experience.

I gathered my empty bottle and dirty cardboard box together and looked round to see if the droning voice which I thought would probably give me heartburn by the end of the evening matched the woman's appearance. Games Makers uniforms were designed to hide a multitude of sins but nothing could disguise the flittering eyes, the jitterbug mouth of this lady who could have been a sister to Gillian, alias Hilda, back at the Excel ranch. My ranch; I wondered how many of the drivers I had made the acquaintance of were at that very moment driving to or from Excel on shift. What stories would be traded by the drinks station when they returned? I missed them and when I compared the snatches of conversation in the bunker with the Stadium woman's incessant self praise, I knew I had been lucky with my T2 colleagues.

Smug I may have been, but compassionate too, believing that all the nonsense spouted behind me while I had been eating was likely due to apprehension at what the Games might bring. None of us knew, just as none of us had an inkling what was in store for that evening. What was so surprising to me was that the man was togged up in Games Makers gear too and had been content to listen, not a shred of his experience revealed. I wondered what his Games Makers role was as I stepped down the stairs, still uncertain whether gravitational pull would have me toppling in freefall down into the centre of the Stadium. Freefall or not I had to dispose of my litter and go to the loo.

I stood by the three waste bins fiddling with my paper wrappings, conscious of a woman bearing a badge of officialdom watching me. I was trying to look busy whilst I brought to mind the relevant pages of the section on Sustainability in my Games Makers Workbook. I so wanted to help Seb reach the target of sending zero waste directly to landfill (page twenty six). For Seb's sake I had to remember what he had said on page twenty seven. For my sake I didn't want to be ejected from the Stadium. Page twenty seven; I remembered seeing a 'catch all' there, an 'if in doubt items' defence I could pray in aid if hauled before the refuse tribunal. But which colour bin was designated to take all the dross? As set out on the page was it green, red or black?

I sensed the watcher woman moving forward. I had to do something. Did a courageous heart beat beneath my beaded top enabling me to make a proper choice or should I go for the mealy mouthed safe black bin option? Mufti or no mufti I was a Seb babe through and through and as the woman's footsteps got closer I knew I had to do him proud and take decisive action. I put the empty clear plastic water bottle in the green bin and my food and food contact items, i.e. the cardboard container, serviette, knife and fork, in the red bin.

'Well done,' the woman said. 'You wouldn't believe how many people get it wrong.'

'Really?'

'Sounds like something is happening.' She cocked her head towards the stairs to the seating area and put her hand to her ear. It felt a bit phoney, a trifle over the top. It was as if she wanted to clear me away so that she could have an unhindered view of the next person who might be considerate enough to come and throw their rubbish away. Seb had obviously spread some of his magic fairy dust on her too.

'I'd better get back to my seat then,' I obliged, later wondering if her dramatic representation was all part of the carefully orchestrated opening ceremony rehearsal experience.

As a matter of fact, by the time I had gone to the toilet and climbed back up to retake my place something had happened. Pre sustainability crisis, I had been the lonesome flower in my row but others had snuck in during my absence. There were quite a few along the row from me but the principal change was that I had to dislodge a lady in the aisle seat to get back to mine, the next but one to hers. And in the course of her gathering her things together to let me in I noticed, but not without feeling giddy, that the rows above and beyond had filled up quite considerably. I suspected too that the droning woman wouldn't be able to carry on talking at her compliant neighbour because they were the gatekeepers to their row which was steadily filling too.

I sat down, my jaw dropping at the number of people seated in the Stadium. And down in the Arena there was a village scene with a cottage and a garden, a vegetable plot and open pasture. Incongruously, present day technicians and Stadium staff scurried about whilst groups of men and women, boys and girls in costumes from a bygone agricultural age ambled in. You would have thought them ghosts, oblivious to the technicians or audience and the technicians paying no attention to them. Was the country scene really there or was some supernatural power affording me a glimpse through a veil at a scene from a previous life on the ground where the Stadium had been built? Was I seeing what others were seeing too?

Then cheering and clapping broke out. I looked down and on the track people were walking around with puffy, make believe clouds suspended high above their heads. I looked at the aisle lady. 'Interesting clouds,' I said, by way of being friendly, by way of finding out if I was hallucinating on the additives in the food I had eaten.

'Very clever, they look the sort that you could float on,' she replied and I took the comment, combined with her natural fabric wide legged trousers, caftan tunic top and ethnic neck choker to mean that she was a creative type. I classified her as a teacher, probably recently retired, someone receptive to new ideas, someone who might apply her own artistic interpretation of the cloud idea in a forthcoming local drama production. I had her holidaying in Cornwall, the Dordogne or Puglia where she indulged in landscape painting.

'Do you think it will start soon?' my aisle friend asked across the empty seat between us.

'It's bound to, they can't risk any hold ups on the actual day but I'm not too sure what's going on down there are you?'

'If it doesn't, I'm going to miss some of it because I'll have to go early to catch my train.' She came from either Herts or Bucks but we both agreed that there were likely to be people from all over the country in the Stadium.

We were joined by a vigorous young woman of healthy proportions in a whiter than white T-shirt and white jeans held together by a wide sparkly belt. The sheen of her streaked hair matched the shine of her sparkling teeth, the confines of the seat no match for the enthusiasm and excitement she showed for being where she was at that time. Her phone rang and an explosion of Spanish burst from her mouth as she thrashed about, her eyes wildly scanning the massed crowds. Wild were her eyes, wild were her hands as she waved frantically at a woman far over in another section. Then she turned, her arm stretched only inches from my face as she waved to another. It was alright for the aisle lady, she had some spare air space to capitalise on, but my choices were limited if I wanted to avoid getting my teeth knocked out by the white jeaned wonder. It was either lean back and rest my head against the knees of Mrs Dronesville behind or be seen to be making advances on the chap the other side of me. I compromised and leant back slightly and was in mid tilt towards unsuspecting chappie when the white whirligig decided she wanted to stand up and take some photos.

'Your friends?' I asked once she was sitting back down, trying not to do that awful patronising bit of over enunciating the word and yet I was equally discourteous by doing the finger pointing thing at her mates in the crowd and then at her.

'Others in my delegation,' she replied. My eyes lit up. A real live delegate. This would be something to tell the others back in the bunker on my next shift.

'From where?'

'Rio.'

'Rio? Isn't that...'

'Yes, 2016.'

'Which sport?' If I struck up a rapport with her I might be able to call the shots with the schedulers to have her as my client. With her unbounded exuberance I'd be prepared to do long shifts to see what night life London had to offer, even if I was liable to be stuck waiting in an NCP car park while she cocktailed herself round the party scene.

'No sport.'

'Aah.'

'I am with others looking at what accommodation we need for the Rio Games. There's much planning to do.'

'Of course.' I nodded and lifted my hands up in supplication. 'These things don't just suddenly happen.'

If ever there was an advert for infectious enthusiasm, this young woman was it. She was on the phone then talking to us, then getting us to stand up to join in the first few Mexican Waves and then, because it interrupted her chain of chatter, we remained seated and participated in the Waves by simply putting our arms up to keep the wave rolling.

I must admit that she, Rio, did look uncomfortable wedged in between the two of us, me feeling like a dried-up blueberry against this vivacious ambassador. I wondered if the lady in the aisle seat with her wooden carved earrings felt the same. But Rio kept the conversation going and came up with some staggering facts about the size and population of Brazil and especially of the capital city's capacity to absorb the millions expected to go in 2016 and how they could draw on and benefit from London's experience and expertise.

'We'll need lots of volunteers.'

'Indeed you will but would you agree with the view, put forward by one of the drivers I've met along the way, that in certain countries the population rely on either the Church or State to organise and provide things for them and that when that is the case there isn't a volunteering culture to rely upon when organising events such as this? If that applies in Brazil, how are you going to get enough volunteers to help with the Games in 2016?' I'll never know why I leapt from using simple phrases in broken English to full blown NewsNight questioning techniques whilst the air was sparking with excitement.

Give Rio her due she responded with in diplomatic fashion. She was a great girl and full of fun and it was only natural that she would want to enjoy the evening with others of her age and without someone like me going all seriously socioeconomic on her. I guess that was the gist of the mobile phone conversation that interrupted our chat.

'I am going to sit next to my friend over there. She says no-one is using the chair.' She put her phone in her glitzy bag.

'Good thinking.'

She shook hands with both of us and we watched her clatter down the steps in her high strappy sandals. Before disappearing for ever she turned and waved up at us.

'It'll be lively and colourful at the next Games,' I remarked across the respectful distance of the now lacklustre empty seat.

The makeshift clouds were still circulating and there was so much more activity it took me a few moments to work out what was going on.

'There's real sheep!' I gasped like a child who had only ever seen them in picture books. 'And geese!'

'And look over there.' My neighbour pointed at the cottage.

'There's smoke rising from the chimney.'

'And look at him ploughing.'

'And there's a maypole.' Then words failed me, entranced as I was with the country scene and the colours of village life; the muted yellows and greens, earthy browns of the stage set and the costumes. It was glorious in its simplicity, gentle calm and inherent peacefulness. Above it all thousands of hushed people looked on and higher still an air balloon floated in the London sky.

I watched the cricket scene and people tending the vegetable plot And the light, golden with a pinkeish hue was perfect. Was it real or artificial? I didn't really care as the ladies perambulated with their parasols and reminded me of a scene in Frank's story and I knew that someone like Frank would feel the emotion I was feeling too at that moment.

'Do you think it's going to be like this throughout?' my lady acquaintance asked.

'I don't know,' I stared straight ahead, not wanting this stranger to see my misted eyes. Her question was not without merit because it set me wondering where all the pretend athletes would do their parade and would there be a firework display amongst the country folk like in the Lord of the Rings.

The drums started and the gladiatorial roar of the crowd was as nothing I had ever heard. Such was the electric atmosphere coursing round the Stadium, such was the awe inspiring spectacle of the industrial towers rising from the earth that I could have been persuaded to pledge my life to any number of causes just so I could remain part of that kindred spirit, to share in that sense of wonderment at what was unfolding before our eyes. But I couldn't share in the way I wanted to, in the way I have come to know and take for granted.

'Who's that?' my acquaintance shouted over to me. I peered at the man with the top hat striding down the hill.

'Kenneth Branagh.' I made a 'fancy that', a 'would you believe it' face. I pointed at another chimney rising and she pointed at another scene but after a while we stopped communicating. There was so much going on, so much to absorb and, in truth, little meaning in sharing it with a stranger. I followed the ever changing scenes, the words coming up on the screen at various points saying that, come the day, a film or the arrival or a ceremony/event/happening would be inserted at that point.

Without kith or kin, I couldn't point and say 'look at that', or squeeze an arm or hold my hands up and clap rapidly and excitedly like a kid. I couldn't laugh loudly or grin widely or join in the rapturous cheers for Danny Boyle. I felt it wasn't the sort of thing you did on your own. And there was no-one with me who knew how uncomfortable I found the J.M. Barrie tribute, how I had to steel myself to look at the white iron bedsteads, representative of Great Ormond Street, a legacy of childhood hospital experiences and just below par with my hatred of stilts. And there was no one to answer to when the tears pricked my eyes for no other reason than seeing the Chelsea Pensioners marching.

I felt a hand on my arm. I turned my head.

'I'm going now to catch my train. Nice to meet you and best of luck.'

'And to you.'

I'm not saying it was her departure that precipitated the gradual trickle of audience from the area but from that point on I was conscious of people on the move. Then the spectacle was over and it took me a few moments to collect my thoughts. I likened the energy of the evening to a religious fervour. I could see how at a convention, with a gathering of likeminded people, much could be done to excite and incite. As the lights from the Stadium illuminated the night sky we could glory too in knowing that of all the people on earth we were the ones chosen to know what was going to be offered to the world on Friday.

'Save the Surprise'; the words flashed round the Stadium as we filed out, and were held up on cards to us as we left the Park. For once we weren't being encouraged to go out and proclaim the news of our wonderful experience to all we met. Instead we were to say nothing and I heard no-one talking about what we had all just witnessed as we inched past the closed shops of Westfield. Was it shellshock or inspirational brainwashing?

'I'm on the way to the train, Rog, but we've come to a standstill on the bridge from Westfield to the Station.'

'They've been showing the crowds on the news.'

'We're squeezed so tight together. I don't know what time I'll get home.'

'You can tell me all about it in the morning then.'

'Oh no I can't. My lips are sealed.'

He laughed. 'Are you allowed to say whether it was any good?'

'It was brilliant, wouldn't have missed it for the world.'

'I told y ...'

'Sorry, Rog, I've got to go because we're on the move.' I couldn't talk and shuffle along at the same time because I might trip up and get trampled in the crush from the stampede behind.

What kind of headline would that make?

CHAPTER 23

Saved by a Whoopee

'Surreal and crazy but secrets kept safe'. It wasn't the headliner on their front page but that's how one leading newspaper reported on the technical rehearsal of the opening ceremony and it was a curious thing that hardly any of the other newspapers gave the rehearsal prominence either, as if they too were in on saving the surprise.

There were, however, other Olympic themed stories to report on, with No 10 Downing Street expressing unease over thirty miles of Olympic traffic lanes in London which it said was a 'requirement' imposed by organisers. Hello! Had Dave C only just woken up to the fact? Another news item reported that hundreds had been forced to queue for hours in London after the biggest overseas agency had failed to post tickets out before the start of the Games. Tut tut, but who couldn't fail to be captivated by the moth invasion of the Olympic village and, from the wording of the caption under a photo of a scantily clad female member of the Australian beach volleyball team, captivation of one section of the population was clearly on the agenda of one national newspaper.

The newspaper reports were a prelude to shift day six, a day that I liken to the kind of day I've had midpoint on a holiday, when my mind goes to mush and body into meltdown and the children would invariably get teasey after all the anticipation and initial flurry of excitement had died away and late nights took their toll. The previous few days had been busy. There'd been the long hot afternoon of scheduled driving on the Saturday, then on Sunday the fun of Pirates Day. There had been no swashbuckling pirates but only a wheeler dealer builder to entertain me the following day whilst waiting for Robert at Old Street roundabout. That had been more than made up for by the lunch with him and Hannah, the preamble to the spectacular rehearsal which would have blown my Games Makers socks off if I'd been wearing any. I'd returned home that rehearsal evening, my head buzzing with what I'd seen, only to have to get up a matter of hours later to get on the road so as to be part of the congregation giving thanks for the life of Freda.

The cool of the Chapel of the Order of St John in Winchester had provided a welcome relief from the scorching heat outside and no finer tributes could have been paid by friends and family to Freda who had been my first teacher in a far off country. Those same friends and family gathered together afterwards to offer condolences and support to John (Brother John as he is required to be known as by the Order). I thought about John and Freda as I drove up the A21; how it had come to be that the Slim School Association had brought me back into contact with them, neighbours of ours at Tanglin Flats. I thought of how I had proudly pointed out to a fellow mourner the photo of me as a little girl in a cotton frock with other children in the company of a young Freda. Then John and I had stood contemplating the photo of a drinks party, the men in suits, the ladies in day dresses with little hats and Freda looking askance at Dad with a drink and cigarette in hand. I wondered what story he'd been telling. 'It's Freda's smile I'll always remember, John,' I said. 'It really did light up the place.'

'You and Roger are welcome to come and visit anytime. I'll show you my flat and the grounds. It's the most beautiful place. I'm so very lucky.' And, from what we could see, it was and we made a promise to go back but as I drove into the Blackwall Tunnel, the colonial days in the Cameron Highlands and the few happy lunchtimes we had shared together in more recent times faded away.

I didn't have the same spring in my step as I had on previous days but went through the motions of a cheery good morning at the pedestrian screening area and to the lady at the Depot's check in desk. She handed me a bronze badge.

'I'll take it but I feel a fraud for doing so,' I said, knowing that my only contribution to the Transport Team had been to help burn a few clutches and give Helga and her clones the Sat Nave equivalent of dyspepsia on account of my deviations from route.

'How come?'

'I've not had a client yet.' Being without a client had been alright to begin with but with friends ringing and texting to see if I had picked up anyone important it was all becoming a bit embarrassing. The situation wasn't of my making but I was not only beginning to feel like a fraud but a bit miffed, miffed in the way of those who find out that someone else is getting a better deal for exactly the same package tour or some form of preferential treatment. The feeling had been prompted by the encounter at North Greenwich Arena with the lady with the gold necklaces, turned up collar and sunglasses on top of head who had announced her client was in. It was silly to feel that way as I'd seen no evidence of others bombing off to meet clients but if that's the way the mood leads you, that's where you go.

'You might have one today.'

'That's true though I'm not sure I want to go very far.' She looked at me as if there was no pleasing some people and with that I made a hasty retreat to the loo.

The state of my digestive system at the beginning of day six was a reminder of how a change of surroundings and routine can affect your constitution. However, it wasn't enough to stop me collecting my lunchtime provisions and joining the queue for my hot enhancement. The canteen wasn't the jolliest of places despite the efforts of Gino wearing his hat at a jaunty angle and intermittently calling out 'Good Morning' to ring eyed and monosyllabic colleagues who showed little enthusiasm for his quips or the food.

'And how are you today, madam?' Gino called over to me as he peered over the serving lady's shoulder to check on the levels of scrambled egg in the warming tray.

'I'm very well, thank you,' I replied, resisting the temptation to use Mum's phrase of 'all the better for seeing you'. And it was a temptation because, though I didn't have her honeyed Cornish burr of a voice, I had several times caught myself saying the things she would have said and I didn't know how or why that had come about.

'Would you like some bacon?' the lady asked.

'It's very good, madam,' added Gino.

'Yes please.'

'And mushrooms?'

'You're spoiling me.' What looked like watery tinned mushrooms was hardly spoiling but the three of us laughed as I reached over for my ration. 'Thanks very much.'

'That'll keep you going,' Gino beamed.

'I'll have bacon with mushrooms, please,' requested the man in the queue behind me.

'You can have bacon OR mushrooms but not the two together,' replied Gino.

'But that lady's just been offered them!'

'No, no, no, no, no.' My Latin friend behind the counter wagged his finger.

'You obviously don't smile as sweetly as me,' I joked with my fellow Games Maker who had every right to feel cheated. His face showed he was in no mood for jokes, would be unreceptive to any offer to share my mushrooms and, definitely, definitely, was not going to let the matter drop. Anxious to avoid getting embroiled in a great bacon butty debate I scuttled off to the bunker.

In the first days after moving to the bunker the lack of immediately accessible washrooms was something I'd not considered vital but, after dumping my half eaten butty in the appropriate bin, the trek through T3 territory to get outside and then walk several yards before getting back into the public section of Excel where the toilets were, proved an irritant I thought the organisers should have considered. It wasn't so much of an irritant that I couldn't keep my public persona in check.

'No matter what time of day it is, you're always smiling,' said Maureen, who was heading out of the bunker as I was heading back in after my second trip to the ladies lavatories.

'Am I?'

'Yes, you are.'

'Wasn't there some research or is it an old wives' tale that says you don't use so many muscles smiling as you do frowning? Or is it the other way around, which means your face doesn't get set?' A quizzical expression, a troubled look, settled on her face. It was Maureen's natural response. It wasn't that she was miserable or incapable of sharing a joke. I took the anguished look to be part of her make up just as the rush of Tommy the Beard and the swagger of Bryn was part of theirs.

I never thought to establish her exact job title. When we'd first been let loose in the car park prior to taking the cars out on our own, Maureen was the one the other employees sought guidance from when there was a problem. In the bunker she never got involved in handing out the plastic wallets but when she occasionally appeared she would hover around the desk, monitoring the situation, her hand frequently passing over her furrowed brow and short hair, One day she had looked particularly anxious about delivering a briefing to the lot on the shift after me and my educated guess was that she was a liaison person between the Dispatchers and the Schedulers, the one who took the brickbats when things didn't go according to plan.

'As they say in Gavin and Stacey, what's occurring?' She looked up at me in a way that said she wasn't au fait with Gavin and Stacey so I rephrased it. 'Have the clients been ringing in?' She made a screwed up face in reply and asked if I had eaten.

'The sausages are putting on the pounds and there's not much room for expansion in these trousers.' I patted my grumbling stomach.

'Go on with you.' She smiled and left for the main building whilst I joined the few lined up at the Dispatcher's desk. Up ahead I overheard one man asking if there were any airport runs to pick up delegates because how else would they get to their hotels. The Dispatchers shook their heads and the two men idling beside me began to mutter about T3's and taxis and what was the point of us.

'It's not the Dispatcher's fault, 'I chipped in. 'We ought to treat it as the lull before the storm.' I could be so nauseatingly optimistic but it was as much to boost my confidence, to convince myself that I hadn't been hoodwinked into thinking that I was part of an active battalion involved in a grand national campaign as opposed to being a bit player in reserve forces. As it was, those in front fared no better than me because we all ended up with wallets and confirmation that there were cars but no clients.

I decided that having no clients was probably a blessing in disguise. I didn't want to embarrass myself or others or be held responsible for a reportable incident by leaving a client in the car whilst I hot footed it to a public convenience. At least if I got caught short on the road I could always revisit one, if not all, of the hotels from previous days. The lovely man in the burgundy frock coat and oversized hat in St John's Wood was bound to welcome me and I knew the layout and could nip up the escalator at the shiny new place in Wembley. The lanky Frenchman at the city hotel might not be so obliging but I hoped he wouldn't be so cold as to turn me away completely. Such foolish notions they were when I thought about the time it took to get anywhere.

I undid the popper on the plastic wallet to see what the schedule had in store for me.

'It's the lady from Hastings.' I looked up and standing at the end of the table was tall John with Sam in tow.

'My, it's John from Bexleyheath!'

'Chislehurst, please! I told my wife I'd met someone from Hastings. She was very interested.'

'Did you tell her I look perfectly normal for all of that?'

John let out one of his deep belly laughs. 'Where did you get to on that training day? One minute you were sitting with us the next you were gone.'

'I don't know,' I lied.

'You didn't have another trip on the Woolwich ferry did you?'

'No, instead I had an experience with a woman that I wouldn't want to repeat.'

'Like us then, Sam, wasn't it?' Sam, his face as round as a moon, merely grinned from ear to ear as John took his cap off, adjusted the strap and put it back on his suntanned balding pate.

'Why, what happened?' I asked.

'You wouldn't have imagined it from looking at her. Bloody hell, her language. She was effing and blinding and shouting at other drivers. I got a bit edgy about it. Christ, if she's like that when she goes out with a delegate! It was something wasn't it, Sam?' He looked down at his stocky friend. Sam chuckled and shook his head as if reliving the experience. 'I heard a lot of people dropped out after the training days and even now people aren't bothering to turn up. It's a wonder you are coming all that way up from the coast.'

'I'm getting used to it.'

'I went on that website you told me about and I've got a car parking space with a young fellow called Rob. Thanks for that. It's only just across the foot bridge. Is that the way you come?'

'No. I don't do bridges.'

'Bloody hell, Sam. did you hear that?'

'I must introduce you sometime to Florence, John, because she lives in your neck of the woods.'

It was good to see them again and we chatted about nothing in particular and then I excused myself on account of wanting to talk to someone who was at the drinks station. I weaved in and out between the tables and bounced up to the unsuspecting man.

'Hello. You're Colin aren't you?' Little did he know that my approach had been set in motion some days before by the retired chauffeur whose cheery countenance would have seen him best suited to driving a sleigh. Eyebrows furrowed, Colin protectively took a step back and held his drink up to his chest. His close cut beard and glasses added to his serious, studious look.

'Yes, I'm called Colin.'

'You look different without your cap on.' I gabbled.

'My cap?' He glanced over to what I presumed was his bag, which had secured him a seat in the way that a beach towel thrown over a poolside lounger can. Was he fearful that I had taken his cap from it?

'I'm Carol. I was here when you came in with another man the other day. You'd been out showing him the routes.' He didn't respond. 'You left him sitting over there.' I nodded to the corner of the room to back up what I had said but the way he was looking at me suggested he was taking it more as an accusation of abuse.

'Do you mean Malcolm?'

'Could be. You were talking to Pauline about the availability of more shifts.' I omitted to say that I had also been talking to Pauline and had extracted his surname from her though I'd never reveal her as the source if Seb sent his mob down to find the leak.

'I have mentioned extra shifts.' There was still no way of knowing if he remembered me or not. Why should he? He hadn't been out training with me and even sharing a couple of hours in a car was no guarantee of recognition. I had seen fellow trainee Richard and his white hair antennae in the car park earlier in the week and I might as well have been one of the concrete pillars for all the attention he gave my cheesy grin and girly wave. And now between Colin and me there was an uncomfortable pause with him looking terrified that I had latched onto him.

'I understand you come from Hastings?' In the interval that followed I wondered if Malcolm had been suffering heat stroke that day and made it up. Had I misheard him? Did that account for the fact that I hadn't been able to locate Colin in the local phone book, on 192.com or on the online electoral roll and find out where he lived? Was internet stalking yet another skill set acquired in the years spent in my own company at home?

'I do live in Hastings.'

'I live in Hastings too,' I said with the exuberance more fitting of someone who had bumped into another in some place thousands of miles from the burnt out Pier on Hastings seafront but he visibly relaxed and I was optimistic that Colin was abandoning any ideas of evil intent on my part.

The ice broken, we ended up sitting together, with Colin explaining that he was staying with friends in London and I came out with my long saga about the times of trains and my parking space etc. Looking ahead we chatted about travelling up in the car together if he got extra shifts and then we flicked through the Fleet Drivers Route Book comparing what routes we had been on. Such was, such is, the quiet calm that surrounds Colin I felt comfortable enough to tell him of my problem with the Aquatics

Centre. My attempts had included an unscheduled trip to the Olympic village, a realisation as I motored along Stratford High Street that the Centre bore the same postcode as the street and was only a hop skip and a jump over the fence away and, in addition, I had been shooed away from what I took as the approach road to the Centre by Games Makers guardees sitting under an umbrella. It is a testament to Colin that I felt I could own up to it and he consoled me by saying that he had heard of drivers getting well and truly lost in the Park and that's why he was happy to take anyone out.

'I don't want to be taken out.'

'Let's look at the map, shall we?'.

'Yes please, I love looking at maps.'

'So do I.'

'And have you seen the amount of detail in the route book, everything that...'

'Find pages 226 and 227.'

'The Olympic Park?'

He nodded. 'It's easier to see it as two loops. See the bridge? Its cross over and under the bridge for the South and up and over for the North. Northern Loop is one way, anticlockwise. Southern loop is one way anticlockwise and the central link is two way. Pudding Mill Lane, Wick Lane and Wharton Road VSA's service the South, Pennybrook is for the Village and Eton Manor for the North. Watch the slip service road for the Copper Box and Fleet depot is up by the Hospitality Centre and the Multi storey and...'

'I think I've got it, by Jove I've got it !' He watched me scribbling on pages 226 and 227 and I suspected it was the sort of thing that would offend him just as I had once mortified a former work colleague when I turned down the corner of a page of his book.

'And the Sat Nav is only a guidance tool. You don't necessarily need it.'

We exchanged phone numbers, wished each other good luck and I made my way to the Ladies debating whether I should revise the route on the schedule so as to alleviate any stress of finding a place to stop for the toilet. I decided to see how I felt with a drive round the block.

I drove along Western Gateway. Even though I had walked along that road each day I hadn't fully taken in the size of the vehicle barricade that had only recently been put up at the end of the road. It was no mealy mouthed affair. It was a beast of a steel contraption which I guess would prevent the largest and heaviest of armoured vehicle breaking through to the hotels or the Olympic venue of Excel itself. And the alterations to the Diner on the corner of the block were coming on a pace. Could I make it out on the open road?

I came off the Bow Interchange so smoothly it wasn't true and joined the traffic heading for Stratford as if I had done the journey every day of my life for the last twenty five years, done it all on my own without interference from such as Helga who was mute and disabled. Then, pulling away from traffic lights, I realised I should have turned left up Marshgate Lane to lead into Pudding Mill Lane and the VSA which was recommended for the Aquatics centre. No matter, I'd carry on, go round Great Eastern Street, the Broadway, do a flip round the Interchange, and get back onto the High Street and, with the Porsche garage on the corner in my sights, turn left at the traffic lights. That was the plan until I was seduced by the happy faces and windmill waving arms directing me off Great Eastern Road into Angel Lane. I recovered my street wisdom and worked out that they wanted to take me to Alma Street and Pennybrook and I'd only end up amongst the T3's at the Olympic Village again. It would have been easier if I had because after that my head was in a whirl of streets as I cut down one, turned into another, moved forward, double backed, joined all the other cars top tailing it along residential streets, all the drivers looking as fed up as me. Was it like this every morning or had there been an accident, an incident that was making our progress tortuous in the extreme? Looking at the map only made things worse. If I wasn't careful the centrifugal force of a knot of little streets would suck me into their back alleys and byways. I went right, left, right again and ended up back where I started, taking heart from the fact that the growing number of white van men and their equivalents appeared as stymied as I did as we snailed along a gridlocked Leytonstone.

I looked at the clock. It was edging nine; the kids at the local schools had barely had time to get their pencil cases out so I didn't know why I was getting so demoralised. But what would happen if I got caught in a similar snarl up when I had real live clients to contend with? As I inched along wondering if there had been a mass explosion at the Olympic Park or somewhere to cause such a jam, I also reflected, just as I've fleetingly done on holiday, whether the fatigue of over exuberance was a price worth paying for all the effort. Yet I had to take the positives out of it, had to get over this hump of tiredness and look forward to the rest of my time in the metropolis.

The traffic started to flow more freely and by the time I had pushed my way into Ruckholt Road and was turning into Eton Manor VSA I was rationalising the events of the morning. I should probably have gone south of the river first but I had thought it best to avoid the Blackwall Tunnel so early in the morning. In overshooting Marshgate Lane I had taken a wrong turning and ended up taking what seemed like hours to travel a few miles but in reality I hadn't taken that long.

The security checks done, I drove round the Park with Colin's eyes in situ. Yes, I could see what he meant; that after coming round behind the International Broadcast Centre, there was a service road for access to The Copper Box. I also took note of the two way system when I came to the junction just after the Energy Centre. He'd also given me confidence to take another look at World Square and, further on, I was bold and dashing in telling the man hovering by the slip road to the Olympic Stadium that I wanted to acclimatise myself to the T2 drop off and pick up zones. He stood aside for me and, emboldened, I swept up to the Aquatics Centre and afterwards, when I came to the Bridge, went up and over into the Northern Loop. The whole experience was topped off with a drive round the multi storey car park that had been commandeered from Westfield so that I could pinpoint the T2 parking area.

Learning from Leytonstone, I reinstated my relationship with Helga. It wasn't imperative for the next destination and I had survived without her so far that morning but, when all was said and done and in the words of a Michael Buble song, we were better together than we could ever be apart. And yet I ignored her prattling on once we were approaching North Greenwich Arena because I was heeding the advices of Colin and wanted to get acquainted with the changes in the road system and experience the now operational VSA.

Then it was off to Woolwich. Memories of arriving at a dead end with Dirk and the boys and the ferry flashed before me and it is on that that I blame losing the ability to count the number of exits leading off the roundabout underneath the A102. I shot up onto the A2 then left at the Sun in Sands roundabout, left along Shooters Hill Road, left into Charlton Park Lane and then down Ha Ha Road from where I could see the perimeter fence. I glided effortlessly into Woolwich Artillery Barracks, the venue for the Olympic and Paralympics shooting events.

The next stop was supposed to be Greenwich Park which was only a ten minute drive away. I talked myself out of going there because Colin had given me crystal clear vision regarding access from Charlton Hill and the VSA arrangements. Instead I talked myself into retracing my steps back to the Olympic Park and the VSA at Pudding Mill Lane which had proved so elusive earlier.

Pudding Mill Lane proved a fraction of the size of Eton Manor, wasn't at all busy and was a recommended VSA for the Aquatics Centre. It had all I could have wished for and having come to an accommodation with Helga and asserted my own stamp on the routes, I had every reason to feel chipper as I headed back down the A12. I briefly toyed with checking out the petrol station and car wash on Newham Way because its reputation (via Florence) had gone before it. But it had turned out such a good day that I didn't want to spoil it by getting in a fluster if the car wash brushes got stuck and the clock was creeping towards one o'clock. It was best to go back to the bunker on a high note, confident in the knowledge that I was ready for anything.

What I clearly wasn't ready for was when, all smiles, I walked back into the bunker from the car and Mefi leapt up from his

Dispatcher's chair. His eyes wild, he lunged at me and snatched the plastic wallet out of my hand.

'Where have you been?' he demanded. 'You should have been back long before now.' I looked up at the clock. It was twenty past one.

'Have you filled in the form?' His hands shook as he rifled through the paperwork to check the mileage and whether I'd declared any damage on the vehicle. 'Everyone's waiting for their cars.' I looked over at the tables. It was no busier than usual and the drivers seemed relaxed eating their hot enhancements and chatting.

'I'm sorry.'

'You should have been in earlier, before one.'

My face aflame from the embarrassment of Mefi's drubbing, I did a reckless thing considering the state of my stomach earlier that day. I made a cup of coffee. I smouldered at the drinks station watching and waiting to see if Mefi greeted others in the same manner as he had me.

'Hello, Carroll.' The Highland roll of my name was unmistakable. 'How are you?'

'Livid!'

'Why?' Florence looked up at me, her eyes searched mine for a clue.

'I didn't know we had to be back by one o'clock, did you?'

'One o'clock?'

'I thought the clients were to be told that between two and four was the change over time and where are all these clients anyway?' Florence guided me away from the urn whilst I vented my spleen.

'He's usually so nice, Carroll.'

'Not today he isn't.'

'What did he say when you said about the timings of the shifts?'

'I was so shocked that my mind went blank I just said sorry. Sorry, for God's sake!' If my cup hadn't been nigh on full I would have scrunched it up. 'But I tell you what Florence, I'm not going to let this fester.' And with that I paid no regard as to whether I disposed of the cup in the environmentally correct bin or not and marched over to the desk.

'I want to clear this up,' I snarled at Mefi who was sitting down. 'I wasn't aware I had to be back at one. No-one has ever said that before and I wouldn't deliberately stay out.'

'It doesn't matter, Carol.'

'It does because of the way you were with me.'

'It's all alright. Don't think any more about it because you've finished for the day now haven't you?' He dismissed me with a smile and a friendly wave. On the long hot drive home the incident opened up a heated debate.

Why hadn't I complained about the smell of stagnant water in the hotel the previous week? Because I had convinced myself I must have been the only one to smell it on account of my ultra sensitive nose. Why hadn't I made mention of the shower pod creaking like the Marie Celeste? Because I put it down to my sensitive hearing and it had caused me no real harm. The fault lay in me for not wanting to cause a fuss, for labelling the staff dismissive and abstracted when it wouldn't have hurt me to strike up a meaningful conversation with them.

Why hadn't I stood up to Mefi when I initially arrived? Why hadn't I had the gumption to demand a full apology from him for his aggressive stance, ripped up every sheet of paper in the plastic wallet then disposed of the wallet and, for good measure, the car key in the food waste? And why had I backed off like a lamb when I returned to challenge him? Challenge? She of the gold necklaces wouldn't have been so accommodating and Merv the Swerv would definitely have manned up to him and demanded to know where the one o'clock rule was written down. And Judy? She had been spirited enough to challenge me to a metaphorical duel on Tower Bridge. I had told Florence that I wasn't going to let it fester. Me, fester? I didn't fester. I putrefied.

'Any clients?' asked Roger as he came into the kitchen where I was preparing a meal for the three of us that evening.

'No.'

'Well, did it go well?'

'The driving did but I got a rollicking for getting back late.' I repeated the sad saga finishing with a replaying of another broken record over dinner, the one that said I wasn't sure whether I could be fussed to go back.

'You're not serious?'

'I don't want to let anyone down but if I'm going to be treated like that...'

'You said he was alright to you when you went back and had a word with him.'

'That's not the point.'

'You're too sensitive, Mum,' piped up Sophie.

'She's right you know, Carol.'

We carried on eating in comparative silence, comparative, that is, apart from the T.V. news which provided us with our daily fill of recession news and Olympic titbits.

'Thanks, Mum.' Sophie put her knife and fork on her empty plate and scooted out of the atmosphere in the dining room.

'We'd best clear up,' said Rog, turning the T.V off. We did. He went and put the vegetable peelings on the compost heap. I checked my emails. There was one from the Transport team. I'd had a stack of them, had been party to the countdown; one hundred days, ninety nine, ninety five.....three days. And now they said it was 'TWO DAYS TO GO, WHOOPEE'.

I caught up with Rog wiping his feet on the back door mat.

'He could have been getting it in the neck from someone above I suppose.'

'Could be,' he agreed, well versed in me revisiting previous conversations without prior warning of going back to them.

'There might be things going on behind the scenes that we don't know about?'

'Quite possibly.'

'And I just happened to be the one walking in the door at the wrong time?'

'More than likely.'

'I'll give him a wide berth from now on.'

'Probably best.'

'And you're beginning to annoy me agreeing with everything I say.'

'Inevitably!'

CHAPTER 24

Distant Bells

Mum loved Jim Reeves, his mellow, velvety renditions of *Welcome to my World* or *I Love You Because* always turned up to maximum volume on the radio. 'He's my boyfriend,' she'd say, all dreamy eyed as Jim asked her to step into his heart and leave her cares behind. And his message that there was something beyond her sitting in the kitchen tending the boiling vegetables appeared to have an added piquancy when it was transmitted courtesy of the Two Way Family Forces Favourites programme on a Sunday. It seemed to make it extra special that a perfect stranger serving in Gibraltar, Monchengladbach or Cyprus had put in a request for one of his records and that the voices of the presenters, Jean Metcalf and Cliff Mitchelmore, were reaching into every corner of our home along with the smell of roast beef.

Mr Reeves was six years younger than Mum and the effect he had on her was made all the more poignant by his premature death in a plane accident. 'He was 'ansom, was Jim.' It was said as if she knew him well, as if they'd walked out together many a time. Usually vociferous in her dislike of 'Yanks', the fact that he was an American appeared no hindrance to her affections. 'They say only the good die young, like Mario Lanza before him.'

'I'll live to be a hundred then.' Dad's joke prompted no response. 'Do you have to have the radio up so loud? I know I'm only reading a rag of a paper but I can't hear myself think.'

'You wouldn't be saying that if it was your girlfriend Patsy Cline or Alma Cogan singing. Or that woman Harry Munsey was having a duet with down the Club last night.'

'What woman?'

'You know very well who I'm talking about.'

'With old Bert jabbering in my ear I didn't pay much attention to anyone.'

'Lie teller!'

He turned his attention to the steamed pudding boiling away on the hob, a boyish grin reflecting back at him in the saucepan lid. 'Um, this looks good.'

Her liking for Irishmen in the shape of Val Doonican, The Bachelors and Daniel O'Donnell never reached the same intensity as it did for Jim and whilst Dad was dismissive of her tuneful sweethearts they were united in their love of Tom Jones and *The Green Green Grass of Home*. Most times the song had them in tears, borne out of an association they made between the words of the Welshman and the complicated relationship they had with their errant son.

I thought about David a lot during those Olympic days. I couldn't fail to because of the soldiers who were a regular reminder of how young he was when he joined the Army. Yet when he was home on leave there was always an undercurrent of tension between him and Dad, always some scrape or incident he'd got himself involved in which you knew was going to trigger an almighty row. And when he died I wished I'd asked him how he had felt at age sixteen leaving home to join up or how he came upon his Army nickname of Chuck and what had it been like as part of a foreign force in Aden and Bahrain. None of it had been said or had it merely got lost in the swell of mixed emotions that usually marked his departures? I'd vowed I wouldn't let it happen with Alan, cajoling him to write about his time in the Navy, encouraging him to jot down his childhood memories so that I'd have a record of what our family life had been like before I was born.

Johnny Cash was David's hero, the lyrics a guaranteed tear jerker for mother and son alike but between the three of us there was joint adoration of Elvis. 'It's the words I love,' Mum would say. And driving up the A21 to start a shift I'd belt out an accompaniment to *The Wonder of You*, a lump in my throat when I got to *and when you smile the world is brighter*, recalling Mum nestled between the fridge and the twin tub washing machine alternately la, la, la-ing to the music then tutting at the salacious detail in Dad's cast off newspaper. Along with Elvis, Leonard Cohen, Bob Dylan, Bob Marley and John Martyn were brought on board the Games Makers mobile to ease the journey on the A21. Not that these artistes ever found favour with Mum, Dad or David, united as they were in their view that some of the sentiments expressed were treasonable and threatened our existence.

Equally contentious in their day, but not when piped through as a series of reports on the car radio, was a programme which explained in words and music specific moments in the history of the Olympic Games. It looked back at Jesse Owens' four gold medals at the Berlin Games in 1936, the Black Power salute controversy in 1968, Black September attack at Munich in 1972, and turned the preparations of some of the 2012 athletes into song. Walking alongside the Dock for my seventh shift I wondered what these Games were going to be notable for after all the words that had been spoken and written about them. The metal barricades and mini marquees of the public pedestrian screening area filled the concourse in front of Excel, which was itself festooned in banners and flags in the Olympic colours. It was quiet and empty at a quarter to six in the morning but that highlighted the anticipation I sensed hanging in the air. There had definitely been a change in mood for the better since the Olympic torch had arrived in London and the rehearsals in the Stadium. I walked along the narrow bit of boardwalk that skirted the area and slowed to sneak a peek in through the gates that had been erected. Beyond them a handful of Army and Police personnel were gathered together in a clump deep in discussion. Who'd want to be in their shoes, who could tell if the consequences of something going wrong in the next few weeks might appear as a feature on a Rio de Janiero radio programme in 2016? An officer with the listening ability of a bat turned his head and shouted 'Good Morning. 'Good morning,' I shouted back and hurried on and up the steps to our screening area.

'Today's the day,' I said cheerfully to the guys putting my things through the scanner. They looked at me blankly. It was an altogether different atmosphere, a genuine buzz about the bunker that morning, a realisation that this was the day that something was going to happen, that the eyes of the world were watching. There was only a matter of hours left before the ground beneath the Olympic stadium would tremble under eighty thousand pairs of feet, and the roar from eighty thousand pairs of lungs would be heard far and wide across Stratford and beyond. And because something was happening, because this would be the day that our real duties began, I decided that it was time I settled down and found a seat, a spot that I could treat as my base from thereon in instead of flitting about willy nilly as previously. And because the Dispatchers still looked to be setting up, I had the luxury of being able to do it before collecting my breakfast or instructions for the day.

I lay claim to a seat on an empty table that formed the long end part of a T with another. From that position I could see the clock, the white board giving details of destinations, the drinks station, the Dispatcher's table, one of the TV's and who was arriving and leaving through the doors at either end. I was leaving it to lady fortune as to who would be my companions for the short time we would be there before going out to pick up our delegates, some of whom I reasoned might be grouchy from jet lag and the need to rush to prepare for the festivities.

The festivities were the focus of a number of newspaper headlines; 'Greatest Show on Earth' proclaimed the Daily Mail, 'Ready Set, and Go' said the 'i' newspaper,' Let's Party' screamed the Daily Star. How many journalistic hours had it taken to come up with such headlines? Carrying my breakfast cuppa, I snitched a look at what appeared to be an orphaned copy of The Guardian. It had several pages devoted to Olympic stories ranging from a report of William and Kate welcoming the torch at Buckingham Palace to the farmer cycling to the Games from China on a rickshaw. David Cameron had apparently said it was an 'honest mistake' that the South Korean flag had been used at an Olympic football match but I didn't read on to see if he had made a comment about the NHS allegedly spending nine hundred thousand pounds on private ambulances. The paper suggested it was time to find out who we were and had picked up on a sense that it could go either way, that we might pass the mammoth test or flunk it.

'If that isn't hedging one's bets, nothing is,' I said to the man who had appeared at my side.

'That's optimism for you. Have you finished with it?'

A second look and I realised it was Robin whose acquaintance I had made on training day one. He looked so different from the man I had met in the white cheesecloth shirt, cotton trousers and cloggy things that he'd been wearing on our first meeting. His choice of natural fibres and casual unkemptness had set him apart from the norm on that day but he had carried over the relaxed style into the way he was wearing his uniform with the trousers crumpled and the shirt left fluid.

'Hello. Do you remember me?'

'Yes, indeed. I thought of you the other weekend.'

'Me?' The only thoughts I had had about him had been to accuse him of treachery for having left me with the wildcard that was Merv.

'I went to Hastings at the weekend with some friends.'

'Oh!'

'I was pleasantly surprised. It wasn't how I was expecting it to be. It's got a lot going for it in the old quarter and we had some brilliant fish and chips for lunch.'

'That's what I'm always telling people. I'll introduce you to John from Chislehurst and you can put him straight.'

'John?'

'No matter. Do you think all the delegates must have arrived by now?'

'I hope so because there aren't many routes that I haven't driven on.'

He'd either been given a great variety of routes or, like Chris, gone off to exotic places such as Wimbledon or Earls Court regardless of what it said on his sheet. I'd been nothing less than unadventurous. I'd mixed the order up at times but hadn't shot off to anywhere unlisted, thinking that I might be called back to base at a moment's notice. But it wasn't his adventurous spirit that marked him out. It was that there was nothing else I or he could think to say, no spark between us as I'd found with Chris or Florence, or indeed with Colin once I'd got past his initial reserve.

'I'd better go and see what I will be doing today,' I started to move away.

'I'm going to read the paper first.'

On the way over to the Dispatcher's desk I met up with Maureen making her way out. I stopped her and asked if I might have speech with her, my choice of words instantly inviting her trademark troubled frown to fall upon her face. 'Can you clear something up for me please?' Even as the words fell from my lips I knew full well that at my age I shouldn't take things so much to heart or sulk as I do but sometimes it takes less effort to give into such traits than to fight them. 'What time are we supposed to get back into Depot for shift changeover?' I could understand her confused look because it wasn't a question that ought to have been asked by someone who had been out on several shifts. 'No names or pack drill, Maureen, but the other day I was told it was one o'clock.' She umm'd and aah'd then said it wasn't strictly so, though it was preferred but, when pressed, agreed it hadn't ever been set as a hard and fast rule.

'It won't apply now, Carol, because with the Games about to begin it will depend on what you are doing with your clients.'

'Come Games time!' I laughed, the comment only serving to add to her worry lines and to my thinking that I was the only one who had picked up on the much loved expression of Bryn who padded past us. 'Thanks, Maureen. It was only curiosity.'

Bryn was hovering by the Dispatcher's desk when I went to collect my plastic wallet. I might have had problems with Helga, had been unadventurous in my travels, hadn't reached the dizzy heights of taking the car to a designated garage to have a car wash or fill up with diesel but my skill at easily identifying when a piece of paper is missing never fails to come up trumps. It's a skill acquired after a long apprenticeship reaching back to schooldays when the exam rash would appear on my neck and face if I'd forgotten to take the right revision notes with me for last minute cramming. I've never thought to check if the rash has appeared during the fretful nights dominated by dreams of turning over the exam paper to discover it's not the one I've revised for or waking up with palpitations to unravel hallucinatory fact from fiction in which I have sent the wrong documents to the wrong people in my day job.

As Bryn, the master of showing no emotion, was to observe, paper checking neurosis led me straight to the realisation that the only paperwork in my wallet was admin stuff, a key and a mobile.

'There isn't a schedule. Where am I going to?'

'All the cars are staying in. No more practice drives.'

'So what do we do?'

'Chill out. It'll soon be eight o'clock.'

I headed back to my table, confined to barracks, it seemed, unless and until a late influx of delegates arrived at the airports. There was cutting it fine and cutting it fine for an Olympic ceremony.

'Morning,' I said to the man in his late thirties, early forties at most, with black framed glasses who came to sit directly opposite me. They were the sort of frames that Mum had been given on the National Health and hated because she looked like Eric Morecambe. 'Morning,' I said to the lady with a set face who sat next to him. And it was another round of 'Mornings' when another man, grey haired and more my age, sat at the table that made up the T and another sat next to him.

'Well, we've all got plastic wallets,' I said by way of an ice breaker.

'Is it alright if I sit here?' asked a lady taking the chair next to me. We did the introductions and it came about that Brenda was next to me, Mandy diagonally across, Nicholas immediately across, Allan at one end of the T and Harry at the end nearest to me.

'It's nearly eight o'clock,' said Brenda. On cue we got up and assembled with others in front of the T.V by the drinks station. It wasn't a ritual early morning call to stand and listen to a piped message from Seb encouraging us in our mission. Neither Jonathan

Edwards nor Eddie Izzard appeared on the screen enjoining us not to be downhearted that the best part of nearly three weeks had been spent circling round the streets of London. All fell quiet as we waited, the minute hand on the wall clock ticking inexorably towards the moment that the Daily Mirror had prophetically captured in its knockout headline 'Ring it on'.

Then the bells started and I felt goose bumps, for all around the country T.V. cameras were capturing the moment when people took to Church bells, hand bells and cow bells to ring in the Olympics. By a quarter past the excitement had passed and we drifted back to the tables.

'What shall we do now?' Harry asked.

'Set your phone and Bluetooth up,' snapped Mandy. A hefty lady, she was the sort who went by the rule book, had to get things done sharpish and felt others had to too. I'd met the likes of Mandy in the past and whereas in younger days she would have made me bristle and rebel, now I felt rather sorry for her because the Mandy's of this world are no more responsible for their routines, their need to be in control, than I am of my sulks. Of course there was no way of communicating to her that I understood what made her tick, that I was on her side, and I knew it wouldn't take her long to belittle my efforts to set the phone up.

I pulled the phone and earpiece out of the wallet and dropped it into my lap. With my head bowed and my hair providing a curtain I kept pressing all the buttons like Billy O, hoping against hope that I'd hit the right ones. This was my comeuppance for secretly mocking Gillian's abilities in the technology department and forgetting all that Tommy the Beard had told us on day one or, the days having merged into a blob, was it day two?

'Have you done it?' Mandy barked. I looked up, the weight and thickness of my hair as much responsible for my pink cheeks as my rising blood pressure. Nicholas wasn't playing this game, more interested in his Iphone/ tablet thingamajig. Brenda was reading the paper, Allan on the T had disappeared and Harry was bravely playing with his Bluetooth earpiece in front of Mandy.

'Yes,' I said putting it on top of the wallet. 'It's now a matter of waiting for someone to ring.'

'I'll test it for you.'

'No. It's fine. You never know the Latvian technical delegate might be trying to get through to me at this very minute.' I laughed and feigned an urgent need to check on something in my bag. There was a million to one chance of anyone from Latvia or even Loughborough ringing me but I was happier to take a chance on that rather than have Mandy seeing me as a right idiot if I had set the phone up incorrectly.

'No, come on, what's your number,' she persisted. There wasn't any malice in her request, no deliberate attempt to catch me out and past experience had taught me that the ploy wouldn't work because that's another thing I've noticed about people like Mandy. They may have an unfortunate manner but generally they want to be helpful, they need to finish what they have started and yet don't have the sensitivity to give you a bit of wriggle room out of a situation. I looked at Harry to put her off the scent. It could just work, I told myself because species Mandy like to sort out trouble and whereas I looked merely ditsy, Harry appeared troubled.

Why, some might ask, was the issue of the phones such a big deal on this particular day when theoretically they should have been set up properly on all the shift days prior to this one? I had had my phone on everyday but had kept it in the well between the passenger and driver's seat. From a straw poll it seemed that most people had taken the same line in that if you were trailing around without a client to put your name to, then you might as well take the risk of having to pull over at a convenient spot to take a call from the Depot. Then there were those like Gillian who were determined to have no truck with the technology at all. The answer to the question was that this was IT. The fact that the chairs were packed with early riser pasty faces, the tables littered with table mats in the form of plastic wallets, the cars in the car park metallically melancholic; none of these factors could escape from it being Action Stations day.

Mandy clearly wasn't up for transferring her attention to Harry. I manufactured a mega crisis over my medication, sure in the knowledge that the lightning occasioned by my untruth wouldn't be able to strike me in the bunker. It still wasn't enough to quell her demand for me to disclose the number and put the earpiece in. It occurred to me that it was people like Mandy who ought to be in charge of the Government, even the world. They were the 'doers' not the 'takers' as Dad used to say.

Albeit cowed by her formidable presence, I managed to adopt a fragment of dignity in the way I read the number out to her and, to show how casual I was, continued my search for the bogus tablets. It was an agonising few seconds whilst she tapped out the digits. My phone rang. I pressed the catch on the earpiece and we were in communication. 'I've found the tablets,' I beamed, putting my hand on my heart.

'Job done,' she said, turning her attention to Harry. He was all fingers and thumbs with the earpiece but wasn't as duplicitous as me. Such is life because she ended up calling him a Muppet.

The Muppet incident put the mockers on Mandy and Harrys' relationship and he decided to go and watch the telly and Brenda was up and down like a yo-yo. Allan similarly was on the T table one minute and gone the next so I was left with Mandy and Nicholas. Mandy set and lined up her newspaper on the table in front of her, checked her watch then started to read the front page. I tried to have a conversation with Nicholas. It was hard going especially when you consider the communication and inter personal skills he must have needed to fulfil his role as a lawyer with an International Bank.

'Snap,' I said.

'Pardon?' he replied, one eye watching the incoming messages on his thingamajig.

'I'm a lawyer too. Well, was, no, I mean, I am because once you are you always will be won't you, unless you're struck off which I'm not and never have been but I don't practice anymore and don't have a practicing certificate but I've kept my name on the Roll of Solicitors and it's only twenty pounds a year and I figure that if I didn't do that and then decided to go back, which is the most unlikeliest thing in the world, then I should think it's harder to get a practicing certificate.'

There was a time delay whilst he assimilated the information. 'Intellectual Property?'

'No,' I laughed. 'That's a minefield isn't it? I was involved in family law, divorces, a bit of civil litigation, that kind of thing. The practice I was with liked to think of it as looking after clients from their cradles to their graves.' I endured another of Nichols's ponderous deliberations.

'In London?'

'No, not London, the South Coast.'

'Brighton?'

'No.' Envisaging that one word questions and one word answers might have us there till sundown and anxious to take the focus off of me, I ran at breakneck speed through how a one year sabbatical had stretched way and beyond my expectations. 'How have you managed to get this time off?'

'Holiday.'

'For several weeks?'

'Mostly and I do have a team.'

'Yes, I'd guess you'd have a team.'

'I'm fitting this in with work,' piped up Mandy who pushed her chair back and stood up. 'Do you want a refill?' She pointed at my plastic cup.

'No thanks.'

'And that's my paper.'

'Don't mess with Mandy's paper,' I quipped when she was out of earshot. 'Otherwise there could be trouble.'

'Could be.'

'I find the 'i 'paper sufficient for my purposes.' The statement might have hit the right cosmopolitan note if I hadn't blathered on and said that I'd only come across the newspaper the week before when I'd stayed up in town for the night. 'Have you come across it?'

'Yes. It's been going two years.'

'Oh. We have The Times every day. My husband likes the Sport section. What do you have?'

'It's all on this.' He pointed at his tablet.

'Yes, of course.'

I don't know what it was about Nicholas. It was hard to connect with his reserve and find a subject to have a conversation about. We sat together on a couple of further shifts which demonstrated to me that, high powered or not, he found comfort in the routine of being with the same people on the same table just as I did.

'The papers are full of speculation about what's going to happen at the Opening Ceremony, aren't they?' I said when Mandy returned. She went rigid; her eyes scoured the paper and plastic wallet as if checking they were in the same position as when she left them. Mandy found it hard to trust anyone, particularly people she had just met.

'I went to the rehearsal on Monday night. Its top secret of course but it was breathtaking.' I wasn't bragging, the revelation a way of convincing her that I'd have no need to read about what I already knew from personal experience.

'I haven't kept up with what the press is saying about the ceremony but I'm certainly looking forward to watching it at home,' said Nicholas.

'Where do you live?' I asked to keep the conversation away from possible allegations of newspaper tampering.

'Victoria.'

I thought of the houses with columned entrances that friend Sue and I had walked past in that area when we were on the Moonwalk and wondered if he owned one of those. I had a vision of him sipping whatever was 'in' in a white painted lower ground floor which housed a sleek kitchen seamlessly melting into a living area bursting with soft furnishings in primary colours. I had a property agent's description of the house running through my head with the 'light and airy feeling of the hub of the several storied house made possible by the ceiling to floor bi-fold doors opening out to the garden.'

'Have you got tickets for any of the events?'

He had and there was mention of his children being excited at the prospect and I told him how Roger and Sophie were going to the athletics one day.

'I've got tickets!' Mandy announced, folding up her paper and suspicions.

'What for?'

'The Closing Ceremony. I'm taking my mother.' It was a fact simply stated but the anxiety and anger that lay behind it was anything but simple as Mandy went through what it meant to her to be able to get something for her mother that no-one else in her family could. The story touched on sibling rivalry, jealousy, feelings of inadequacy and powerlessness, disappointment at not having children and emotional attachments that hadn't worked out. Again, she reminded me of others who, behind the barricade of bolshiness, are as vulnerable and lonely as one could ever be. I tried to be non contentious but my occasional remarks and observations prompted fresh outpourings of hurts and sleights. Nicholas took refuge in his electronic device after Mandy's first few sentences gave every indication of taking the conversation to a level above that of a couple of freebie tickets, and whether an elderly mother would prefer burger or fish and chips when they got to the Olympic Park.

I sensed there was much more to come in her outpourings but I needed to go to the loo and it was hard to know how to wrap the conversation up without appearing shallow and uncaring. Sudden movements and bursting bladders are not compatible and Mandy and Nicholas nearly had something distasteful to tell Mother and fellow bi-fold door neighbours respectively as a result of someone tapping me on the shoulder.

'Oh my word, you made me jump out of my skin,' I said to a smiling Chris who had taken Brenda's empty seat.

'What are you up to then?' he asked.

'Not much.'

'I'm going up to the Park.'

'A client?'

'No. Do you want to come along?'

'I thought we weren't allowed out today.'

'I just tell them I've got to go up there.'

'I might get a call. We all might get a call.' I pointed to the wallets.

'Unlikely. They are bussing the delegates and dignitaries up to the Stadium for the Ceremony. You can tell the Dispatchers where you're off to and they can ring if there's a problem.'

'No, I'd better not. It would just be my luck that they needed me.'

'I'll see you later then.'

As I walked through the car park into the main building, out onto the dockside and then left to the Ladies, I questioned why I was being such a goody two shoes. The Olympic Park wasn't exactly far away and I hadn't fully investigated the Hospitality Centre up there. But no, I felt comfortable with the decision and whilst there were still several hours to go I could always look at the Route Book or release Frank from my bag and continue with the story of his and Ruth's holiday.

The Route Book proved the easiest option because I decided that to do Frank justice he and I needed quality time together, not the constant comings and goings of Mandy, Nicholas, Allan, Harry and Brenda.

'Anyone would think you were doing The Knowledge the way you've got your head stuck in that book.' I turned round. It was Giles, stopping by on his travels.

'I love maps and I'm looking for the place we went for lunch on the day we came up to collect my uniform.'

'You couldn't have found anywhere around UDAC to have lunch, surely.'

'Here it is, Lauriston Road, Hackney '

'Hackney?' he wriggled his nose.

'I was born and lived in Hackney,' said Allan, who had been sitting quietly at the T. 'But I wouldn't go back to live there.'

'I bet you wouldn't,' said Giles with a shudder.

'I thought it was up and coming or that's what my son tells me.'

'Really?'

'Where do you live then, Giles?'

'Clerkenwell.'

'Clerkenwell? Isn't it an area where lawyers live?'

'Lawyers? Pah! It's much too funky for lawyers!'

271

'You wouldn't want to live near lawyers then?' I laughed and would have winked at Nicholas if I could wink.

'Perish the thought!' With all the theatre of a courtroom drama he swept off and, watched over by Allan, I thumbed through the pages to see exactly where Clerkenwell was.

'It's close to the City, Allan.'

'I know.'

'Where do you live?'

'On the Isle of Dogs.' And he went on to draw a portrait of what it was like living close to Old Father Thames and the ease of access and convenience to restaurants cinemas and theatres which proved so handy now that he had retired. The conversation moved to Allan's memories of happy childhood holidays spent in Hastings. To a boy from Hackney, Hastings had had everything and more and he conjured up hordes of perky holidaymakers spilling from the train at Warrior Square Station or from coaches down on the Old Town Stade, and of kids with buckets and spades, whooping with delight at the sight of the sea. He asked if the putting green was still at Grosvenor Gardens and the parade of shops along from them. His memories were so clear and bright and suffused with such genuine joy and contentment it was hard not to get caught up in them and seeing the place through the eyes of Allan as a child I felt a heel because of my sometimes ambivalent attitude in the face of criticism of the place.

Despite a jaunt back into the innocence of youth, the morning ground on interminably with a cup of coffee here, a peek at the T.V and a cursory look at a magazine.

'Shall we go and stretch our legs?' asked Allan. Mandy didn't respond but Nicholas and I decided to join him.

We intended to take a walk along the promenade by the water but, seeing that we could use the stairs by the toilets and get into the main part of Excel, we took a diversion to see what was going on in the building. I don't think our accreditation covered us to be there but it was such a hive of activity and one of those occasions when, if you walk and behave with an air of purpose, other people believe you are on official business. We wandered freely though there was nothing of interest to see. There were areas sectioned off by black drapes, masses of cabling and rows of lockers. We stood in a hall where staged seating had been erected and sound and camera checks were in progress.

'What do you think they'll be doing in here?' I asked.

'Fencing,' replied Nicholas. 'That's why that light is focused on the centre point of the room and the bleeper keeps sounding. It's all to do with the scoring.'

'It's not that big in here though, is it? Not what you'd expect for a world event.'

'It'll be different when all the spectators are in.'

The bleeper hit a glitch and rang continuously. 'Best get back,' said Allan

I don't know for how long the inquiry had been going on in our absence but when we returned to our tables Mandy was very disturbed.

'Did you see who took my paper?' she asked.

'No.'

'I left it here and when I got back it was gone.'

'We've been outside.'

'You didn't see anyone with it?'

I shook my head. No amount of telling her that someone had probably picked it up thinking it was a communal newspaper consoled her and I worried for the safety of the person who might seek to return it to its resting place. If it was Muppet Harry there'd be a bloodbath. Mandy went on the prowl round the bunker and I kept an eye on the door with the thought in my head to ward him off and warn him of the situation he might be walking into.

Killing time, wasting time, I hate both with a passion and yet as the time dragged on that morning I had more tolerance and patience than anyone would have given me credit for.

'Time, goes by, so slowly and yet, time can mean so much.'

'Pardon?' said Nicholas.

'It was a song that my Mum used to sing though I can't remember the name of the singer who recorded it. It was long before your time.'

With the dogged tenacity of a bloodhound, Mandy's investigations into the missing paper took her away from the bunker but such had her umbrage been about someone moving her things that I thought better of moving her empty cup. Instead I collected together the rubbish that the rest of us had amassed over the morning and took it over to the bins. It was on the return journey that I saw him. No, not Harry, who was likely despatched to a bin all of his own at the hands of Mandy. It was Jet with lunch in one hand and a cup in the other.

It might have been the prospect of food to fill his belly that dulled Jet's response to my cheery Hi as he crossed the room ahead of me. He flung himself into a chair at a table set apart from the volunteers and started devouring his food like a lion at his prey. In hindsight, it must have been the angle and split second movement of his head combined with the trajectory of the food he was shovelling in to his mouth that gave me the impression that he was trying to catch my eye. I ambled over as his table filled up with other instructors whose matching black shirts and leg wear gave them an air of exclusivity. His near neighbour saw me and gave Jet a nudge.

'Hello,' I said. 'Lunchtime?' To give him his due Jet wiped his mouth with a serviette before nodding in acknowledgment. I didn't shout but the noisy chatter of his mates and the distance between us meant I had to speak up 'I liked the car in the end but I only drove it for a day.' He took another bite out of his obviously irresistible baguette, 'They changed the cars, didn't they?'

'Why's that?' He paid lip service to me, his expression one of having half an ear to the ongoing conversation of his colleagues.

'They say they switched back to manual cars because so many drivers complained about the automatics.'

He shook his head and I guessed it was in disbelief because from our time together I knew there wasn't a man on that table who held a deeper faith than Jet's that automatics were the best for the city, being ecologically efficient and easy to drive.

'It's incredible, isn't it?' I continued, the only incredible thing being that I was still standing there being made to feel like a spare part. I was only being friendly as is always my wont or was my approach construed as that of a cougar, the older woman, the type family had tittered about at the dining table after Robert had once nearly fallen prey to one? Was it actually stretching credibility beyond all limits to think I even fell into the cougar category? I was probably ten or fifteen years too old for that and a woman dressed in two tone polyester mix top, logo splattered trousers and grey trainers with a breathable mesh and red laces was hardly going to make a stir. Unlike his powers of recall of every vehicle he'd ever driven, perhaps it was too much to expect him to remember everyone he'd taken out for a drive over the preceding few months but it was only a matter of days earlier that we'd been out. Standing there at full height with big feet in full view of his chums, I suspected I no longer qualified for the epithet of sweet. Frankly I felt silly, stupid and bruised by his lukewarm response. By my calculation, he should have been on a sun kissed beach by now but I didn't stop to ask what had happened to his holiday plans. I don't think he even noticed my departure and though Dirk in the same situation probably wouldn't have remembered me, or anyone for that matter, I was convinced he would never have treated anybody so dismissively.

The day had begun with a cacophony of bells across the country but there was no bell or whistle to mark the end of the shift. It came to a natural ending or rather I looked at Nicholas and he looked at Allan. Allan looked at Harry's empty chair then at me and I looked at Mandy's empty chair. And just as we were completing the second round of looking at each other and at empty chairs Brenda reappeared and said she was off.

'And you ought to be off as well, Carol,' said Allan. 'You don't want to get held up in traffic and miss the ceremony on the telly.'

So we switched our phones off, picked up our plastic wallets and trailed over to the Dispatchers desk and handed them in.

I bought a packet of Quavers and a bar of Dairy Milk at Tesco Express on the way back to the car and crunched my way through the curly corn snack whilst the radio news reported on the mishap of Jeremy Hunt, the Culture Secretary, whose bell fell off as he was ringing it to mark the beginning of the Olympics.

'I hear the sound of distant bells' I sang out loud and laughed recalling Mum likewise corrupting the Jim Reeves' song when the Church bells rang out, summoning Dad across the road to listen to the dull, dry sermon of Reverend Fairweather. His penance done, Dad would be back to pour himself the first drink of the day and Mum would chitter on that it wasn't the way of people who went to Church to come out and do that.

'How would you know, you never go to Church.'

'You don't need to go to Church to be a Christian.'

Then after he'd taken the first mouthful of beer he'd defend it by saying that the Reverend Fairweather was no better than others of his ilk who put on one face to the world but drank sherry behind closed doors. 'I bet if you went over and knocked him up at half past one he'd come to the door in a stocious state. You've only got to look at the colour of his nose to tell it.'

'Huh, I don't think you've got any room to talk about noses, Dick Beresford.'

I was driving home to watch a spectacle that would have been beyond their wildest imaginings, a show that Dad would have no doubt derided as being done with camera trickery and costing too much into the bargain but would have delighted Mum with its music and fireworks. And I knew that with a glass or two of wine inside me my nose would glow and I'd be the same as my father and talk all the way through it, telling Roger and Sophie where I had been sitting during the rehearsal and what had happened then and give hints as to what was going to happen next. It really would be a case of Let the Games Begin.

CHAPTER 25

Due Consideration

Early morning, shift day eight, and a definite sense of purpose pervaded the bunker. Maps of the Olympic venues now wallpapered part of the main wall and flip charts bore details of amended postcodes and revised destinations. At their desk, the Dispatchers were falling over themselves to make sure that all the paperwork tallied, their stress levels added to by the presence of Tommy the Beard who was pacing up and down watching proceedings like a hawk.

I was in the queue with Giles, his hands in his pockets and a practised look of general disinterest about him.

'I wonder if I've got a client today.' I pointed to the white board which was now replete with details of cars, times to leave the depot, pick up and drop off points. It all augured well that we would be usefully employed.

'You'll find out in a minute.'

'It's been so long in coming I think I've forgotten most of what we were told but I assume we can shake hands with our clients and don't we have to follow their lead in conversation?'

'There's no need to get so anxious about it.' Giles puffed out his chest.

'I'm not.'

'You ought to be excited.'

'I am.'

'That's what we're here for.'

'I know, I was merely saying...'

'I wish they'd ruddy well get a move on so we know where we're off to. I'm not going to be the one apologising to the client if they've got the times wrong.'

'They wouldn't do that.'

'Wouldn't they?' He raised an eyebrow and I was happy to let him go ahead of me.

'Ah Carol. Let's see what we have for you,' said Pauline when she'd finished with Giles.

'A client?'

'Yes, here we are.' She handed me the plastic wallet, looked at the white board and then at her watch. 'You've got time for your breakfast. Don't forget to ask the client what his plans are for the rest of the day and for tomorrow so that we can plan around it for the next shifts.'

'Will do.'

'And good luck.'

I bumped into Harry on my way back to the table.

'How are you doing?' he asked.

'Fine.'

'Had a client yet?'

'First one.' I patted my file. 'You?'

'Just been given my first too.'

'Where are you sitting?' I thought he was brave not keeping the file with him.

'Over there. Are you going to come over?'

'No thanks, I'm a creature of habit. I'm with Allan and Brenda and all.' All didn't include Mandy who never sat with us after the day of the opening ceremony. Indeed I only saw her once more during the whole experience and that was fleeting and awkward but she seemed content with the group she was with. 'Have you had a chance to look to see where you're going to today then, Harry?' On the verge of telling me, the inhabitants of the bunker were called to hush by Tommy the Beard.

'The Women's Cycling Road Race is taking place today. It starts and ends in the Mall so please give that due consideration.'

Due consideration was what I gave it, seeking guidance from the Route Book.

'With your nose stuck in the book like that anyone would think you were doing the Knowledge.' It was a passing comment from Giles who was sauntering by.

'I'm checking on something.'

'Just get in the car and drive.' He coolly carried on perambulating the room whilst I was joined by Harry who perched on the seat next to me. Thick as thieves, we huddled over the book and when we came up for air, looked each other straight in the eyes.

'Are you thinking what I'm thinking?' Harry asked

'I think so. Shall I go and ask?'

I approached Tommy the Beard with a carefully prepared set of questions.

'Are we expected to follow the designated Olympic routes?'

'Yes.'

'Would that still be the case today in view of the Mall being closed?'

'Yes. That's why you must follow the time they've put on the board for you to leave the Depot.'

'But look at this.' I showed him my instruction sheet which was deliberately tucked into the page relevant to my argument though it is still a source of pride to me that during the conduct of the conversation I had no further recourse to any page or grid reference. 'By my reckoning I'd be better going along Highway, turn right at Butchers Row, onto Commercial Road following into Commercial Street then up...'

'To Old Street, City, Pentonville etc...'

'You get my meaning then?'

He nodded.

'Or I'll risk a jaunt along the Embankment and do a Strand, Aldwych Kingsway manoeuvre. What say you?'

'I can't say anything because you should follow the official routes.'

I slapped the book shut and went back to Harry to scheme a little more.

'Are you going to do it?' he asked.

'If I'm going down I'm taking someone with me so I will if you will.' We got pretty darn close to bloodletting and signing each other's instruction sheets in shaky handwriting but were saved by Tommy bobbing along towards us looking pretty pleased with himself.

'I've just had a word and it's all in order if you want to use an alternative route.'

Harry and I exchanged self satisfied smiles of success and all that remained to be done was to put our plan into action.

The checks on the car completed and my paperwork done, I slid the car out of its space. The car itself was more of an estate than a saloon though the manufacturer had its own name for it. My headlights on the car in front and the lights from the car behind flashed and flickered as, at a funeral pace, each of us lurched over the speed humps in the car park. I watched the car in front, drawn, like a butterfly to a candle, left into the shafts of light outside. I slowed and even at five miles an hour the car behind was rapidly gaining on me. I stopped, gripped with the same sense of anticipation that I once had on the Snake Ride at Chessington. That rollercoaster had proved to be my last thrill ride ever and as the security man up ahead waved at me, my stomach heaved in much the same way that it had when I thought the snake cart was going to tip over the edge. The cart hadn't, it merely turned sharply and hurtled down the track and now, with infinitely more sophistication and grace, I let my foot off the brake, turned the steering wheel and gave myself up to daylight and drizzle. It was the same daylight and drizzle that fell on an enthusiastic Games Makers who was stopping the drivers to see if he could provide any assistance in operating the Sat Nav.

'Probably, but it's a bit late for that now,' I replied, knowing I had to get out on the road before the nerves got to me good and proper.

There was little traffic on the Highway. It was much as expected. The Capital was sleeping off the excesses of the weekend which had kicked off on the Friday with the Opening Ceremony. The plaudits in the worldwide press for the Ceremony were more than enough to nurse the celebratory hangovers of organisers and participants. Hardly recovered from that, the crowds in the city had downed all the excitements of the first day with the Men's Road Race, the Tennis Men's Singles and the Women's Football. Many would no doubt be suffering from their last one for the road drink and even Helga was less strident in her commands, as if the sound of her own voice reverberating round the car was too much to take.

A fair few city dwellers and tourists alike might have been rubbing their bloodshot eyes but I, of course, was as sober as a judge. Sober and a bit lonely so I summoned up the genie of Eddie Izzard to keep me company as a passenger. From the first training film to seeing him in the flesh at Wembley and, via a CD, on my computer screen, we'd been through a lot together. His acronymic spell, rendered universal in the Workbook, had been lovingly transposed in best ink into the notebook I carried in my handbag. Now, as the car glided on the alternative route that Harry and I had devilishly devised, I repeated out loud the mantra. Eddie, in whatever form he took, would surely be pleased with my performance, as he would also be with my powers of recall in relation to page thirteen of the Roles section of the Workbook which gave guidance on how to welcome the world and how to treat my client as I would want to be treated.

The Workbook said I wasn't to assume that a person from another culture can't speak English and, whatever my client's level of proficiency, I would need to slow down and make my instructions clear and brief because many people find that British people gabble away. And I was expected to greet him in a courteous, friendly and helpful way, respect his space and refrain from physical contact. There was also a ban on the use of abbreviations and jargon so I'd have to be careful not to lapse into Cornishisms or titbits of youth language that I'd picked up from the kids or venture a personal opinion on religion and politics or become embroiled in 'social issues'.

I drove into Grosvenor Square. I was early so I pulled up by the pavement rather than risk turning left into the street where the hotel was. I was the only car parked outside a prestigious restaurant in Grosvenor Square which made me even more conscious of Mr Obama's representatives watching from behind the protective fences of the American Embassy. Would combing my hair and touching up my lipstick count as suspicious activity?

I checked my phone to make sure I hadn't missed any messages or calls whilst I had been mentally running through my top tips with Mr Izzard. Even if I freewheeled it would only take forty seconds to get to the hotel but with five minutes to go to the designated pick up time I pressed the ignition. My destiny had arrived. I only had to drive round the corner and up the ramp to the front entrance of the hotel and my ambition would be fulfilled. I would have to contain my emotion at that point so as to enable the Games Makers who would be waiting with the client to effect a smooth introduction and handover. Would that Games Makers and my client be as excited about this as I was?

In the preceding days, nay weeks, I had borne witness to the frenetic activity going on up at the Olympic Park and had been fastidious in checking out what parking facilities etc there were at the various hotels and venues I had driven to. So with that in mind and with security and safety a priority, why hadn't I sussed that, come the day when this hotel was stuffed to the rafters with Olympic representatives, the ramp to the Hotel would be barricaded off? I saw the blockade. I saw and heard the drizzly rain transform itself into a summer shower. I could do nothing else but pull up short by the pavement and ignore the evil eye of a taxi driver whose wheels flicked water at me as he drove past.

I leant across the passenger seat and peered out of the window and through the gaps in the topiary frontispiece to see if anyone appeared to be waiting for me. There was no-one to be seen. The rain pelted down on the roof and I checked my instructions again. There was nothing for it, the appointed hour had come and I recalled one of Dad's sayings; 'If Mohammed won't come to the mountain then the mountain will have to go to Mohammed.'

I got out of the car, glad that I had put my jacket on though there was nothing I could do to avoid my hair being ruined by the rain. The large airy foyer with its marble columns and flooring as smooth and shiny as a skating rink was equally devoid of anyone to make me feel less conspicuous up against the sombre clothes and disposition of the clusters of people gathered round small tables drinking tea and coffee.

'Excuse me,' I said of the man who stood behind the reception podium nearest the door. 'Pardon my pronunciation but I'm here to collect a client.' My pronunciation of the gentleman's name did nothing to advance my quest so I pointed to the name on my sheet.

Nostrils flaring in the mode of Kenneth Williams he raised his forefinger in the air, peered into the middle distance of the Hotel and then turned back to run his finger down through a list. He lifted the telephone receiver, tapped out a number and was unfazed by my eyes boring into his profile as the phone rang out at the other end. He looked me up and down like something the cat had brought in as he explained to the client that I was waiting.

'He'll be down in five minutes,' he said, replacing the receiver.

'I'll be waiting outside in the car.' I chose not to give the man my name, but my car number instead.

If the weather hadn't been so horrible I would have hovered on the pavement but with my eyes trained on the entrance I sat in the car and waited and waited till intuition told me that the tall man hovering on the front step was my man. I was only halfway out of the car when he spotted my uniform and came rushing down holding a newspaper over his balding head. I skittered round to meet him. The rain stopped any long winded introductions and there wasn't time for me to open the door as Giles had couched against because Mr Z. had thrown his newspaper and black plimsoll bag into the car, folded himself into the back seat and shut the door before I had time to think through the diplomacy of the matter.

I got in behind the steering wheel, turned round and announced I was Carol whilst he brushed water droplets off of his jacket.

'Hello Carol.' The smile went with the kindly face.

I didn't want to be stereotypically British and make a comment about the weather so cut immediately to the chase and asked him, slowly and clearly, to confirm that he wanted to go to the Aquatics Centre and kept my eyes on him till I was satisfied he had put his seat belt on. Then it was his turn to watch whilst I fiddled with Helga's dial. Did I do it just because that's what I'd been programmed to do by the trainers, was I simply showing off, or did I merely need the support of Helga in the car in case Harry and I had got the plan horribly wrong?

Charged with the care of a visitor to our shores, I put the signal winker down, released the handbrake and joined the trickle of traffic heading towards Oxford Street. Bereft of its usual crowds, the Street looked as if it needed a face lift on the soggy summer's day.

'Turn left in two hundred yards,' commanded Helga. I kept spy on Mr. Z in my rear view mirror and, being all legs, he was still getting comfortable and showed no reaction to my carrying straight on ahead. But when I ignored the second instruction a troubled look started to appear on his forehead. Then, the dear of him, when I turned right he glanced round longingly at what he would have seen if I had turned left in the direction Helga had advocated. And when he turned back our eyes met in the mirror and he bore such a little boy lost expression that I decided to come clean with him.

Dilemma! If I spoke too softly he might think I was muttering to myself, if I spoke too loudly, clearly and slowly, would that come over as condescending and impertinent? And I would have to choose my words carefully so that there was no risk of miscommunication. And should I open up a potential dialogue by becoming all formal and addressing him by his name. I leant back into the seat and rolled my head to the left, ready to speak in the manner of the chauffeurs on the telly when they are on the verge of advising their masters and betters in the back of an alternative course of action. As luck would have it, I was saved from doing a female impression of Parker in Thunderbirds by the cars in front coming to a standstill.

I swung round to meet his gaze. 'There are diversions on the usual route to the Aquatics Centre.' I hoped I sounded confident, like a pro, putting a special emphasis on the Aquatics Centre in case he thought I'd forgotten. 'I'm taking you on a different route to avoid the diversions.' I gestured towards the screen. 'Please ignore the instructions.'

'Ok.' He put his hand up in the way of giving me carte blanche to do as I thought fit. Such faith! By the time Wigmore Street was transforming itself into Cavendish Square he looked pretty chilled out. I turned left and then sensed him shuffling about as if ill at ease with where we were going.

'Where are we?' he asked. Was this a test? In view of Helga's belly aching had he had a change of heart about my capabilities? He was getting more restless by the minute.

'Portland Place.' I called back authoritatively, without recourse to search for a street name. Harry and I had done our homework.

'You say Portland Place?'

'Yes, it leads up to Regents Park.'

'Our Embassy is here.' I slowed down and took his 'aah' as the signal that he had pinpointed it. And then we were into Regents Park Crescent and turning right into Euston Road.

'Do you live in London, Carol?' We were at traffic lights.

'No. I live in Hastings.'

'Is that very far?'

'About fifty miles. It's on the coast, the seaside, the sea.' It crossed my mind to say '1066 and all that' but the traffic started moving again and I wanted to get myself set up in the right lane for Pentonville Road.

'Not as busy as this?'

'No, not as busy as this.' I laughed and roared ahead to get past a bus.

He was thoughtful, closed his eyes for a little while. Another set of traffic lights proved a catalyst for another conversation during which I asked him if he was enjoying his time in London. He was.

'And congratulations on your country's success yesterday.' Was that toadying? No, I thought it right to give credit where credit was due.

'What is the secret of your success?' I immediately wondered whether that expression would come under the heading of 'jargon' on page thirteen of the Workbook and whether, translated across continents, it could in any way be misconstrued. But he was a very equable man and was happy, though in no way boastful, to explain how training in America had proved highly beneficial. We chatted and I thought we understood each other enough for me to raise the matter of what time he wanted to be picked up. He said he didn't know. Now proceeding at a stately pace along the Mile End Road, I wondered if this was simply the 'man' thing that I had come across so often at home, when it wasn't a question of not knowing but more a matter of not being prepared to give some thought to the matter at the same time as I wanted an answer. I didn't want the Dispatchers back at base snapping at my heels for info so I decided to approach the issue from another way, give him a prompt to give the matter some thought whilst sitting comfortably in the back seat, far removed from other distractions. I asked if he had any plans for the evening, any places he particularly wanted to go during his stay. Of course, I was being silly applying the criteria of my normal domestic and family life to a man with the small matter of his country's achievements and position in the medal league tables on his mind. I interpreted the way he was looking out of the window as being in thoughtful mode. At least I had got him to think! But the thinking continued all the way to the Olympic Park.

Was I glad I had sussed out the VSA in Pudding Mill Lane! It all went like a dream, from the moment I turned left at the Porsche garage to the moment the soldier said we were all done.

'Is it like this all the time?' my client asked, clutching at his plimsoll bag as we pulled away.

'Yes, but it's necessary. Better safe than sorry.' And the journey from the VSA to our destination was a dream too.

'The Aquatics Centre,' I said, with some relief and a sprinkling of pride as we glided to the designated spot beneath the Centre. I turned to say goodbye and he leaned forward towards me.

'Very good,' he said. 'It took me two hours to get here before.' He rummaged in his plimsoll bag. 'For you.' He handed me a small box.

'For me?' I was so chuffed with the little round medal, so overwhelmed, that it was a good job that we were constrained in a car and that a Games Makers had rushed over to open the car door for him, because I might have broken every rule in the book by gabbling my thanks and giving him a hug.

CHAPTER 26

Gossip Gals

It might be considered thoroughly in bad taste for a comparison to be drawn between returning fighter pilots as portrayed in the glut of films that followed the Second World War, and my lonely travail back to the Depot after my mission to get Mr Z to the Aquatics Centre but nevertheless I felt an euphoric sense of achievement that I had accomplished what I had set out to do.

So cock-a-hoop was I that I abandoned myself to what became an old VSA chestnut of mine. As the soldier guided me to the stopping point I put on a theatrical alarmed expression as if I was going to run over his feet, then held my hands up in mock relief that an accidental crushing of toes had narrowly been avoided. I had used it before at Eton Manor, Pudding Mill Lane and Penny Brook but had decided to be sparing with it at Excel in case I caught someone saying, 'Oy, here she is again. Humour her for God's sake.'

'Had a good morning, Ma'am?' the soldier asked, after we had gone through the pantomime of checking his boots for tyre marks.

'A very good morning, thank you.'

'If you don't mind Ma'am, my colleague...' he gestured to the young woman who waited in the wings to check me over. The young women were never as jovial, never that willing to participate in any banter and this particular lady was especially zealous in making sure I wasn't smuggling anything of a nefarious nature into the Depot.

'Could you please take a swig of water from your bottle in front of me, Ma'am?' I duly obliged. 'Could you please unfurl the umbrella, Ma'am?'

'If you promise to fold it back up. I'm hopeless at that kind of thing.'

'I'm not permitted to do that, Ma'am.'

The security checks completed, they waved me off and I drove through the car park knowing that I had at last earned my spurs. I parked the car, completed the checks and looked at my watch. I was well within shift time but after the contretemps I'd had the previous week with the Dispatcher I was apprehensive that I might be found wanting in not extracting Mr. Z's transport requirements for the rest of that day or the following one. I could understand why he hadn't wanted to be straight jacketed into a decision.

There was a little mutter from the Dispatcher but nothing to goad me into a speech about how easy it is to sit behind a desk and criticise those out on the front line. Incarcerated in the bunker they could give us information on possible delays and diversions but had no comprehension of the comical carry-on's taking place out on the tarmac. Chained to their desks they were unable to slake their thirst with a mission accomplished coffee or soak up the tales of daring do and escapades of others. As I toddled to my table with a cuppa in my hand I began to feel sorry for them.

I sat down beside Brenda. Georgina was on the other side of the table, the gravitational pull of her youthful energy had already prompted a collection of gals to gather round about her. I'd missed the opening bars of Georgina's refrain but it didn't take long for me to catch the gist of it.

'Was he good looking?' asked the suntan and gold jewellery lady.

'He was charming.'

'They always are,' said a lady I knew for dry wit.

'What I meant was, did he stand out from the crowd?'

Georgina thought about it, thought about it a bit too long for me to totally believe the giddy excitement she injected into her voice. 'Yes, I'd say so. He was older than me.'

'They usually are.'

'He had velvety dark eyes.'

'Like Omar Sharif?' I ventured. I met a sea of blank faces though, unless they had all been on Planet Zob during the sixties and seventies, at least three of them, including suntan and gold jewellery, must have known who I was talking about. 'You must remember Omar Sharif?'

'And you had no idea when you first picked him up?' asked suntan.

'No. He just took control.'

'They always do.' It was dry wit again.

'He made a beeline for me as I stood waiting by the car.'

'But was he handsome enough for you to have noticed him anyway?' Suntan wasn't one to let up.

'Yes, yes, he was.' Georgina's cheeks pinked.

'I thought we weren't supposed to get out of the car?' A well rounded lady with glasses piped up.

'That lady hasn't had a client yet,' Brenda whispered to me. 'It's a bit of a sore point.'

'And he was such a gentleman,' drooled Georgina.

'We've all known those.' No prizes for who said that.

Alarm bells rang when Georgina remarked that after introductions he had placed his hand on her arm and guided her to the driver's seat. I should have taken from her little shiver that she had derived some pleasure from this rather than try to be clever in venturing whether the no touching rule on page thirteen of the Workbook counted for nothing or was it simply a case of it only working one way?

We sat enthralled as we heard that the man of mystery had foresworn the seat of honour in the back and slid into the front passenger seat. Georgina defended the action on the grounds that this helped avoid her getting into an even bigger flutter than she did after he told her he wanted to depart from the scheduled itinerary. 'I couldn't argue could I? They said we had to be at the client's disposal, didn't they?'

'They did.'

'I wish,' added the punterless lady.

'And I had to be completely honest with him that I didn't know the way. He thought it highly amusing but luckily he knows London better than most. '

'He would.'

'And he was very forgiving when I forgot to stop at some traffic lights.'

'I bet!' said another woman who, in the circumstances, let out a rather ungracious yawn. Georgina, for all her airhead pretensions was intent on keeping her audience, raised her voice slightly and asked if we wanted to know where she and her suave companion had ended up. We all moved closer towards her and in a low voice she revealed where he had taken her.

'You're joking!' It was the well rounded woman who broke the stunned silence.

'No, I'm not. Can you imagine it?'

'Where did you park up?'

'Immediately outside, in the Mall.'

'How long were you there for?'

'Three hours.'

'Three hours? Didn't you know you are supposed to come back here and wait for a call to return?'

Georgina twisted and squirmed in her seat as she defended him. 'But I'd have had to go through the security cordon again and I wasn't sure if they'd let me through.' I would have bet that, right down to the yawning woman, we knew what was to come. And sure enough, with a faraway look in her eye came the admission; 'Anyway, I said I'd wait for him.'

Dry wit shook her head. Suntan played with her jewellery, no doubt thinking she'd give her eye teeth for the opportunity, then demonstrated how an older and much more sophisticated woman would have handled the experience by asking whether he apologised for keeping her waiting.

'Actually, he was a bit squiffy,' Georgina giggled.

'Where was his wife?' It was a wonder no-one had thought to ask the question before. The colour of Georgina's face said she hadn't thought to ask it either but she was resilient, knowing the power she held over us, our eyes widening commensurate with the level of importance of the international dignitary.

'What time did you get home?'

'Late.'

'Do you think that's what it's going to be like for all of us?' A spark had been ignited in the clientless woman. No one answered, our collective experiences paling into insignificance in comparison with Georgina's.

'Which Hotel did you say you took him back to?' asked sun tan.

'I can't remember.' I took that as subterfuge. 'But I hope I will see him again.'

Didn't we all?

CHAPTER 27

Bother Bromley

The good folk of Bromley will have to find it in their hearts to forgive me. Special apologies go to Tom and Erica who live in a Bromwellian leafy road with a row of shops at the bottom and also to Nick and his parents who likewise reside in this select and shady suburb.

Bromley sits like a huge spider waiting to snare the unsuspecting, its traffic lights and one way systems unsympathetic to those who make the simplest of mistakes, to those like me who fail to get into the right lane at the roundabout where Tesco inhabits what once was the site of the World of Leather store, the store which always acted as a marker for us in years past.

Just in case a smartarse lawyer is following every word of this log, I'm not holding Tesco responsible for the fact that I steered the car straight ahead towards Bromley town. I can read a signpost to a destination as well as the next man. And it wasn't as if the supermarket's window display was brimming full of tempting goodies to catch one's eye. Perhaps that was the problem; if they put a giant fudge or bounty bar in the window, the sheer ludicrous size of it might have acted as a reminder, a prompt to turn right at the roundabout. As it happened, it was a dollop of day dreaming that had me in a line of slow moving traffic with no immediate means of escaping.

Day dreaming doesn't affect my ability to drive the car *per se*, my reactions to other road users or my pretty dammed good sense of direction. In day dreaming mode I am still capable of split second decisions albeit my mind dillies on the swaying branches of passing trees, or dallies in wondering who lives behind the windows of a house that has caught my eye. But there is an unpredictability to the condition which is worrying because I can happily daydream for a while, come to my senses sufficiently enough to make remedial choices and corrective decisions, then lapse back into it thereby undoing all the previous good. Come to think of it, that applies not only to my day dreaming but also to other aspects of my personality; the predisposition to sulk, the introspection, the over analysis, the self blame which probably explains why every jot and tittle of the Games Makers experience has had to be recorded and why, along with Frank's story, there's a fair chance it won't get finished.

Floating on clouds of random thoughts or fighting my way out of the sticky tentacles of negativity that enmesh me is fine when I have the luxury of time to do it but not on a boiling hot day when, with client number one tucked under my belt, I was driving to the Depot with high expectations that client number two might be lined up for me. So when, on shift day nine, I came too from noddyland and realised that Bromley's highway was sucking the life blood out of me, I took against everyone, bad-mouthing cars and pedestrians alike whenever they looked to be impeding my progress. It never does to get like that, the anger and frustration merely feeds on itself, mushrooming into an even worse situation than the one you are trying to escape from. Or does it? Is venting one's spleen healthier in the long run? Wasn't I going to feel all the better for railing against the white vans, jaywalkers and old men in flat caps bumbling along in second gear in their low emission cars? No, because the energy involved only served to slow my reactions, to get me in a right fuddle about the changed landscape of office and apartment blocks that had been built in the years since I had last visited the place. Fortunately, some semblance of sanity told me that I shouldn't go in the direction of Catford and Lewisham even if the one way system round a shopping precinct had me thinking that I was going back on myself. How I eventually ended up practically foaming at the mouth at the Kidbroke junction with the A2 is still a mystery but at least I was on the right road and one day a therapist might unlock the traumas of that journey to me.

These things invariably have a knock-on effect and so it followed that my Bromley shenanigans not only led to me arriving later than usual at my parking space but also that some Herbert had parked a chunky four by four vehicle in it. I wasn't happy though on the Overdrive Inc website Kreety K had advertised two spaces. The second space was there but it meant I had to move the wheelie bin. It occurred to me that I ought to ask his permission but as he hadn't replied to my letter way back when, hadn't returned his signed part of the parking agreement and had shown no signs of life or intention to welcome me over the past weeks, I did what was necessary and reversed the car close up next to the tree and tight up against the step to the house.

As I sat in the car gathering my things together I thought nothing of the sound of chattering voices floating in through my open window but then became aware of a man, only feet away from the car, looking at the parking permit on my dashboard. He gave me an enquiring look before he and a dozen or more young Chinese ladies trooping behind him squeezed between the two vehicles and disappeared into the house. I shook myself wondering if what I had just seen had really happened.

In the face of an indomitable tree, my exit from the car was ungainly and distinctly unfeminine but I tidied myself up and walked the few steps to the house. I tapped on the open front door and shouted 'hello' over the babble and bustle of the women milling about in the hall. One of them called to another and that one to another till the message reached out back. The man appeared looking somewhat harassed.

'Hello, I'm hiring the parking space,' I said, gesturing towards the car. He made no attempt to come to the door but remained in the hall, buffeted by the comings and goings of the excited lady folk. 'Are you Kreety?' He looked at me blankly. I repeated the question, wondering if I should have prefixed it with Mr.

'She's away, expected back in a few days.'

'Oh, my mistake,' I said, ignorant that Kreety was a girl's name. 'No problem.' I backed away as the women swept him back down the hall, my curiosity and imagination working overtime as to who he was, who the ladies were and what exactly was going on.

I stood on the dockside, the back of my hand held to my perspiring forehead as I looked over towards Excel where the red and purple uniforms of sun- seeker Game Makers stood out like flowers in a window box. My Swatch told me I was late, or rather I would be late for my shift if I had to strut my usual stuff along the edge of the dock, past the apartment blocks, the Wakeboarding kiosk, Thai restaurant, the gondola station, the convenience stores and hotels and up the steps through pedestrian security and down the stairs to the Depot. Despite their credentials my trainers weren't invested with speed enhancing powers and my armpits were already moistening up to be antisocial. And could I be bothered to rush? Wasn't all lost anyway if I couldn't keep to time? Did I have an alternative to turning tail and going home?

The sun glinted on the water. It was oh so inviting but in the absence of a James Bond look alike turning up in his speedboat to whizz me across or the owners of the swish Cruiser moored up close by allowing me the use of their rescue dinghy, there was only one option available to me. The bridge.

I had made a token attempt at mastering my fear of heights a couple of weeks before, approaching the bridge from the ground level metal gantry on the Excel side. I had climbed up the several flights of stairs but, at the stepping point onto the bridge, had come over all giddy, turned round and hurried back down like the clappers. Now it was time to put all irrational fears behind me, to draw on the surge of inner strength that being in a mood can often give me. The therapist charged with encouraging me to recall my journey would also have a field day deconstructing the reasons why I saw crossing the bridge as the punishment I was going to mete out for making myself late.

My head began to swim as the bridge, with all its bright white paint and attractive features, came looming towards me. I thought better of repeating the stairs exercise when each passing step had been suffused with emotional torment. I stepped into the lift followed by two casual and colourfully dressed women talking in German. As a representative of a welcoming Great Britain I singularly failed that day. I turned my back on them and closed my eyes, listening out for every loose bolt and screw whilst the lift rattled and clanked its way to the top.

I stepped out of the lift and, head bowed, looked under my eyelashes at the expanse of bridge stretching to the other side. Dry mouth, churning stomach and jelly legs, all classic textbook symptoms of fear and anxiety, gripped me. I looked down at my feet and my trainers which now had all the elasticity and weight of two concrete blocks. I had to fight off all thoughts of the foot suspension bridge in Morzine because if I gave in to the feeling I had had all those summers ago I would remain rooted to the spot or, worse still, my legs would buckle beneath me with the urge to lay flat on the ground. Now it was summer 2012 and I was on my own. I couldn't tightly close my eyes and rely on Roger one side and the children on the other to walk and talk me every inch of the way. Poor Robert, I had nearly broken his hand squeezing it so tight as I put one foot in front of the other, with the movement and sound of the footsteps and voices of the other bridge users a torment in itself.

Trainers identical to mine stepped round me. I raised my head to see identical trousers, shirt and bag as the Games Makers marched ahead. I took a deep breath, freed my feet and I was off like the wind, striding out, looking ahead, mirroring every leg and arm movement of the man whose face I never saw, whose voice I never heard, whose name I never knew.

Focus, don't look to the sides. Focus, look straight ahead. But in the centre of the walkway, at set distances apart, there were white metal sections holding supports. I would soon have no option but to veer away from them to the side. To stop dead in my tracks would court another bout of leaden feet and a desire to prostrate myself. A film formed across my eyes but I had to be strong, do this for myself. I heard the gasp of a phantom crowd as my size nines took charge and moved me closer to the handrail. It was scary yet liberating all at the same time but I had no time to take a bow to my imaginary audience for I had to get my bearings. Forsaking all admirable intentions to live up to my uniform, I powered through the pedestrians coming towards me so as to regain sight of my pacemaker man. There he was, forging ahead with a confident gait. And all of this stress, this racing heart and beads of sweat were because of Bromley. Bromley, bah!

At the other end of the bridge my man stopped in his tracks and the bizarre notion entered my head that he had picked up on the energy force linking us together and was waiting for me. He wasn't. He looked at his watch and disappeared down the stairs like the proverbial white rabbit and I, virtually on my last legs and gasping for breath, followed.

Regardless of whether my intentions could be misinterpreted, I would have followed the mystery man to the ends of any bridge and if we had had a similar encounter at night I would have spun a dark tale of his presence transformed into a ghostly guide helping nervous ninnies like me across the water. But this was broad daylight and by the time I reached the bottom of the stairs he had scooted off, his rear end and back of head becoming all but a passing memory as he and I were swallowed up in the crowds of people. Some were simply enjoying the sunshine and being by the waterside but the vast majority were making their way to Excel. The public were directed to go through the tented security area erected behind the fence on the open plaza at the bottom of the steps leading to Excel. Little did they know as I tried to weave in and out the crowd that I had seen that area grow from nothing to the professionally manned hub that it was that day? Little did they know that my duties were far removed from those of the Games Makers trying to shout directions over the excited babble of snap-happy tourists but it came about that twice I was stopped by members of the public, one asking me where the Pleasure Gardens were and the other to ask where he could buy a map. I directed them both to the local shop then hurried on to get to my own pedestrian screening area. Checks done, I was catapulted out into the sunshine again where a Games Makers sat on top of an umpire's set of steps shouting instructions through a loudhailer whilst her colleagues waved pink foam hands with an outstretched finger pointing towards the doors of Excel. It was chaotic but the atmosphere was good-humoured and as I hurried down the ramp to the Depot I saw a coach load of soldiers arriving in the car park below.

I arrived at Driver check in hot and flustered. 'What's with all the soldiers teeming about outside?'

'They change over at two o'clock. You must have seen them out there before?'

'No. I'm usually earlier than this and today I had to walk over the bridge.'

'And we're very glad you did,' she smiled, handing me my meal ticket and another rubber band for turning up.

CHAPTER 28

Everybody Knows

The poster on the wall made it quite clear what the felony amounted to though I had to admit to the colleague who accompanied me up the steps from the reception area that I'd never noticed it before.

'Bad luck,' he said. 'He's a stickler on that so there'll be no grub for you today.'

'I can't believe it. I've never forgotten my cool bag before, but then everything seems to be going a bit peculiar today.'

'We all have days like that.'

'There is a God,' I said, when I looked across and saw that the young catering assistant, whose dourness was something I would be worried about if I was his mother, wasn't standing guard at the entrance to the house of hot enhancements. 'It would be wrong of them to stop me having some food, wouldn't it?' In the absence of someone to challenge me and confident I could blag my way through the potential crisis with Gino, I got cocky and stepped over the threshold whilst my compadre was dragging his heels about breaching the ice block line without permission.

'Madam, madam, your voucher please.' Luckily for me the voice belonged to a chap I'd never seen before who was hurrying through the T3 area to get back to the spot where the dour lad usually stood. And what a chirpy little chap he was. Vulnerable and exposed as I was for lack of my cool bag he nodded and smiled throughout my confession and abject apology and said I could go through to collect my daily ration.

'Would it still be alright if I took an ice pack, please?'

'But where are you going to put it?' he looked at me suspiciously, as if he now doubted my story, as if I was teasing him or trying to catch him out.

'I've at last hit upon a use for my cap!' I laughed, facing the reality that a chewy baguette from the private caterers at Excel was better at teatime than having to grab something at a garage and, depending on where I chose to eat it, possibly subject M&S Simply Food to military scrutiny at the screening station. That was always presupposing I had a car and a job to do. It didn't take long to find out.

'You've got Mr. Hazoza?'

'Yes.' I held the plastic wallet closer to my chest just in case Harry was thinking of mounting a bid for it. 'What's wrong with that?'

'Everybody knows Mr. Hazoza!'

'Do they?' To my chagrin the Dispatcher had, a few moments previously, told me to make sure I was punctual and now with Harry restlessly moving from one foot to another, there was clearly something more to the man I would be picking up a few hours later. 'The work schedule says he may need some assistance but if he was disabled wouldn't he have a WAV to pick him up?' I asked, hoping that the question might prompt Harry into a more specific disclosure. I also thought back to Judy on the second training day. She was the only WAV (Wheelchair Assisted Vehicle) driver I had ever met. What if, through some unfortunate act of miscommunication, she and I both arrived to pick Mr. H up? She probably wouldn't recognise me. Her sort rarely does. Would there be a tussle, both of us tugging at Mr. H's sleeves, his walking stick sent toppling to the ground whilst the cat fight ensued? I could distract her by telling her that there was a local coffee bar to hole up in but in my heart of hearts I knew that she'd win the contest over the frail, enfeebled client. She had been so dogmatic about everything and could probably add being fluent in Spanish to all her other accomplishments.

As for Harry, he wasn't in the least complicated or as aggressive as Judy, or a natural joker, so I had no reason to think he was being anything other than genuine in his view that everybody knew something about my client.

'What have you heard, Harry?' I narrowed my eyes menacingly.

He shrugged his shoulders. 'He can be, I don't know, difficult, pernickety, so be careful. I'd better go, I've got to get over to the West End.

The exchange of words made me a tincey wincey bit disappointed in Harry. *'Be 'careful'* could cover all manner of possible scenarios. A casual male eavesdropper on Georgina's enthralling tale during my last shift might have gotten a wrong impression of Mr. Squiffy though in reality he had been harmless enough and some, who will remain nameless, would have joined an orderly queue to go pick him up anytime. It was all a matter of perspective. I wondered if Chris had had dealings with Mr. Hazoza. He wasn't one to beat about the bush and as luck would have it I managed to intercept him on one of his perambulations of the bunker.

'How are you doing?' he asked, adjusting his glasses on his nose.

'Fine. I've got a client.'

'Good.'

'What was the name of that client you had the other night?'

'You'll have to be a bit more specific than that, Carol.'

'The one you said you were going to put straight if he mucked you about a second time.'

'Why would I do that?' He laughed, as if it was the most ridiculous thing he had ever heard.

'He wasn't a less than agile chap called Mr. Hazoza by any chance was he?'

'I'm hopeless with names at the best of times, Carol, but I vaguely recollect someone with a name I couldn't pronounce. Does that help?'

'No, it doesn't.' I was beginning to get a bit cheesed off with my male colleagues, rapidly coming round to the view that they were the proverbial all mouth and no trousers.

'What time are you out?'

'Not till later.'

'Later' meant that I had time to eat, to drink, to mooch about and feel rather important checking my e mails on one of the computers. I noticed the man at the computer on my right was looking at details of used cars and the woman to my left was typing out a C.V. I went back to my table and desultorily flicked through the Route Book to second guess which way Helga would direct me later in the afternoon. With the Games now in full swing it was bound to be on the Olympic Route Network and with all the Olympic traffic lanes open I'd sail through.

'What are you studying the Route Book for this time?'

I looked up. It was Giles. 'Someone stopped and asked me where the Pleasure Gardens were today. He must have thought me a right goon because I didn't have a clue though looking at the map they're only over the bridge.'

'But why bother?' Giles asked incredulously.

'I'll know if I'm asked that again.'

'If you want to wave a foam hand about directing people then why didn't you volunteer for that in the first place? Why don't you simply ask for a transfer?'

'Because looking at them above stairs I'm about twenty years too old!'

'You and me both, darling!'

Giles hadn't heard of Mr. Hazoza which was of great consolation because Giles knew a lot about a lot of things and if there was anything going down he was the most likely candidate to know about it. And Chris of course.

'I wonder if I ought to get the car washed for him.' The words came out of my mouth unchecked.

'You're taking the man from A to B for heaven's sake. He won't give a fart for what the car looks like.'

'Won't he?'

Florence was more on my wavelength about the need to take a pride in one's vehicle. We met at the drinks station after I got back in from checking on the condition of my car. It was my favourite, it stood out from the rest with its two tone blue streaks of logo down the side. A photograph of it is safely tucked away in my Games Makers memory box though I've since thought the grey hue of the car park setting doesn't show it in its best light.

'If you need to give the upholstery and carpets a clean, Carroll, I've found the cupboard where the cleaners keep the Hoover.'

'I'll keep that in mind though I've just picked up some flicks from the carpet and buffed the dashboard and gear stick etc up with some tissues.' I'd decided against the car wash in case something untoward happened. 'I hate this hanging around before going out.'

'How much longer have you got?'

'I'm making it thirty minutes and counting!'

'Why don't you put a few pieces into the jigsaw?'

I shook my head. 'I don't think so, Florence. I don't think so at all.'

So why was it that, within minutes, I was making a beeline for the jigsaw table, propelling myself into the hands of the two ladies searching for the chimney pot on a house nestling in the hillside of a thousand piece landscape? I'd have recognised the woman, who was standing up and leaning over the shoulder of the woman sitting down, anywhere and I bounced up to her with my own peculiar brand of Games Makers bonhomie.

'How are you getting on?' I asked with the beaming smile of a jolly hockey sticks girl I had known at school. I knew from old that I would have to refrain from instinctively mimicking the way the lips of the woman before me twitched as if she were silently repeating what I had said and rehearsing what she was going to say in response. When her reply came it was far more intimate than I had expected. It wasn't a tepid 'fine' or a conversationally lukewarm 'I'm okay and how about you'. Instead it was a real outpouring of how the routine of her normal life at school contrasted with the vagueness of this one where she was still uncertain about what was expected of her.

'We're all in the same boat.' My words were meant to be supportive. She said she'd had a few dicey moments out on the road. 'Haven't we all?' I laughed and babbled on about my love hate relationship with Helga. 'Sorry, I ought to explain that Helga is the name I've given to the Sat Nav.' For a good few minutes we engaged in convivial chit chat, exchanged views on the composition of the baguettes, the comfort of our uniforms and how tricky it was to park the car next to the concrete pillars in the car park. The lady doing the jigsaw muttered a few heartfelt opinions on the organisation and how she had been tempted to down tools and walk away from the whole damned thing because she was bored and then asked where the devil she ought to fit a particular piece of sky in.

'I do admire your perseverance especially as you could come back tomorrow and have to start again if someone has come by and finished it off in your absence.' From the look I was given I knew I had crossed the line. It was the line that Roger unconsciously drew when we did jigsaws together and I was the lowly sorter outer and he was the lofty putter together.

'I'll be staying here till it's done,' the woman replied, turning away from us.

I looked at the clock above the Driving Operations white board. 'I've got a pick up to do so I'd better get myself organised.' I reached into my trouser pocket and drew out my official mobile phone. 'Thank goodness for that. No missed calls.' I put the phone back in my pocket. 'Have you got the hang of your mobile now? You weren't very happy about it to begin with, were you?'

We had been getting on famously and in doing so her facial tics had subsided but with my last words her mouth took up its customary quiver and she dished up a frown that I guessed her schoolchildren shrank from. And despite all that, what came next was totally unexpected. 'Do I know you?' she asked. 'Have we met before?'

I laughed, used to this kind of ambivalent zaniness from a friend of mine at home. 'Yes, of course we have.' It was against the no touching rule but I instinctively squeezed her arm. 'It's Ruth, isn't it?'

'No!'

The tone of Gillian's reply had the jigsaw lady look me up and down.

'Oh,' I laughed again. 'That explains it. We started on the same day, remember?' I painstakingly went through my recollection of our initial meeting and the Hilda cum Gillian conundrum and, in trying to save Gillian's dignity by not revealing I had seen her taking off in the wrong direction in the car park that first day, I admitted that I had made enquiries about her safety and whereabouts. I saw a ray of hope, assumed her brain was rectifying the lapse in her memory from the way her pale blue eyes were flickering and flitting about.

'I've got to take the dog to the Vet tomorrow.'

'Pardon?'

'His booster.'

'Of course.' I nodded as a vision of a nursing home inhabited by lost memories, miscommunication and mistaken identities flashed by me. I looked at my watch. 'I'd better go. I've got a Mr Hazoza to pick up.' If she hadn't been as she was I would have taken solace from her blank face and assumed that his reputation wasn't as wide and extensive as Harry had implied it was earlier, that 'everybody knows' was a gross exaggeration. And then the thought struck me. Had I got my client's name wrong?

CHAPTER 29

Marking Time

I hadn't even had time to come to a stop at the Load Zone at the Aquatics Centre before a young man came rushing over to find out what I was about. I put the handbrake on and wound down the window. He bobbed down and peered in at me.

'I know I'm early for my four o'clock but...'

'I'm afraid you can't stay here. You will have to stage at the World's Square Staging Area. You'll be directed back here when the client requests you by your call sign.'

Now that he mentioned it, I vaguely remembered a hand out in the wallet to that effect. The instruction was tagged on as an end note to the procedure for 'T1/T2 Driver Check In @ FDO', the Operations Centre on the Park. It was to prevent a jam of cars at the Load Zones. The rule was eminently sensible and the young man was only following his instructions but the people of Bromley, the experience on the bridge, Giles' comments and the embarrassing and somewhat humiliating exchange with Gillian, had hardened my heart. I stared pointedly at the one and only other car in front of me then turned and looked at the emptiness behind me. He appeared unmoved.

'It says on my sheet that my client might need assistance. I wouldn't want him being inconvenienced especially as this place looks to be a bit of a wind tunnel.'

'Who are you picking up?'

I'd checked and double checked and verified the name on my schedule with that on the destination board and with the Dispatchers. 'Mr. Hazoza.' He straightened up and stepped back and, the engine still running, I reached across the passenger seat and called out to him.

'Is there something wrong?'

He ignored me and summoned up assistance. I followed the direction of his gaze, his eyes trained on the woman with unruly blonde hair who held a clipboard in one hand, a walkie talkie in the other. Her spectacles dangled from a chain and bounced on her boobs as she charged towards him. She was one of those ladies that Rog and I would describe as one of the County set.

I couldn't catch what was said between them but she fleetingly looked through the windscreen at me and checked the car call sign number with her list. Was I guilty by association, guilty of something, guilty simply on account of a piece of paper bearing a particular name? She bent down, her 'good afternoon' delivered with countryside grace before the formal request to look at my schedule. The wait was agonising as she checked out the itinerary.

'Is there something wrong?'

'You can switch the engine off and wait here for Mr. Hazoza.'

'Is there something I should know about him?'

'He's had some issues. If you stay here it'll give you a head start.' Her words did little to quell the butterflies that had started in my stomach and nor did the obvious good intentions of the young man who took her place and bobbed down and said that Mr. H was alright really, a nice man, but he'd not taken kindly to some drivers. He shook his hand in a way that implied that life with Mr. H could go one way or the other. 'Tread carefully,' he warned.

I had twenty minutes to kill and it was Helga who rescued me from introspection and doubt as to how to handle this client, who I would undoubtedly recognise immediately on account of his face which would be gnarled from years of being so difficult. Generally Helga and I had been getting on fine, the turning point being the journey with Mr. Z during which I had shown her ultimately who was in control. It cut both ways because a resultant positive mental attitude towards her meant that, instead of denigrating her at every turn, I was willing to learn of her additional attributes from others. The conversation I had had with Tommy the Beard had been a case in point.

Tommy and I had discussed how aesthetically pleasing it was to have London landmarks superimposed on the Sat Nav routes.

It made such a difference; gave definition, depth and substance to the street names and geographical contours of the city. I had only happened upon this additional feature by accident but it had certainly enhanced the driving experience. I decided that, whilst waiting for what I imagined would be the giant thundering footsteps of Mr. H, the tartar incarnate, I would reset Helga to the Hotel where he would lay his sore head later that day. Helga too may have been invested with a sense of trepidation at our forthcoming passenger and wanted me to have only basic road details on the screen so that I could give my full time and attention to our new man because, whatever button I pressed, the landmarks wouldn't come up.

Bromley, bridges and bother, I got out of the car. The parading clipboard lady looked concerned, as if thinking I was going to abandon the car and walk. I scuttled to the car in front, and her face now expressed a double dose of apprehension; was I going to cadge a lift with the driver or incite him to down his steering wheel in an act of solidarity against the truculent toad I had been assigned to?

The driver was a big, bearded lad, a youthful Hagrid and he was only too pleased to come and join me in my car. I established he was a student and had also heard of Mr. Hazoza. 'You know what some of them can be like,' he said, in response to what he had heard. I thought it wouldn't do to admit that I'd only had one client so far and he had been as sweet as cherry pie so I cut straight to the problem of Helga's lack of landmarks.

'What type of car is this?' he asked.

'It's a BMW of course.'

'It's not a standard one.'

'I think it is.'

'Look, you've got a sports steering wheel.'

'Have I?'

'And the gear shift's different.'

'In what way?'

'Longer chassis and leather seats too.'

'So they are but what about the Sat Nav?'

He came out with all sorts of facts about the car and others besides as he played around with Helga's controls then sat back with a smile stretching from ear to ear. 'That should do it.'

'Thanks so much. If it wasn't against the rules I'd give you a big hug.' I laughed and immediately regretted saying it in case I had embarrassed the lad but he laughed too.

'Can you guess what I normally drive?'

I realise I categorise people too much by their appearance but it was particularly hard to judge what kind of car this young man would comfortably fit into and still maintain his street cred. It was his extensive knowledge that swayed me into thinking that, despite his size, he would favour what I considered the majority of young men would go for but, there again, the beard was out of sync.

'I don't know, a turbo charged fuel assisted four hundred horsepower customised thingamajig that would give me kittens if either of my children had one.'

'Nope. I've got an MG BGT with wire wheels, alloy bonnet and a fully functioning overdrive.'

'A classic!'

'And do you know what I'm saving up for?' But then it proved too late for any discussion on the virtues of old cars because there were signs of movement, of activity over by the entrance to the Centre.

'I'd better go in case my client is ready. Good luck with Mr H.'

I watched the woman with the clipboard rushing to get to the lift which was expelling a group of suited men. Was Mr. H amongst them? I got out of the car and went round to stand on the pavement. I felt a complete spare part in view of the stack of cars lined up behind me, the drivers all waiting behind their steering wheels. I got back into my car believing that it would only be a matter of moments before I would come face to face with the scourge of the T2's.

I waited and waited whilst cars glided past me with their passengers. I checked my phone, concerned that he had tried to ring me but I hadn't heard. This was payback time for joking at home that I am a lady in waiting; the one always waiting for someone to get ready or return or to dish up or wash up. Most times I don't think anything of it but occasionally I feel a slither of resentment that, because I'm just there, my time isn't accorded any respect. It was my thing about time again and as I sat there watching people spilling out of the lift I examined and cross examined myself as to why I was treating it as important that Mr. Hazoza, for all his status, should keep to his appointed slot. It wasn't as if I was being hassled by the clipboard lady, I had no other pressing engagements to attend to and, for goodness sake, to be at a client's disposal was what the entire lark was about anyway. Put simply, I would just have to wait.

There were several 'possibles' that fitted the mental picture I had drawn of my client but soon I started to feel like the wallflower at the end of the ball as more cars kept coming and going. I sensed the clipboard lady and the young man were huddled together talking about me. Perhaps they didn't think I was up to the job and were going to send for Judy with her assertive ways and specially adapted WAV but after all this effort I wasn't sure I would be prepared to relinquish control over my crusty old crow so easily.

I was jump-started by my phone ringing. Cack-handed, I answered it.

'Hello. This is Mr. Hazoza, I want a car at the Aquatics Centre.'

'I am at the Load Zone outside the Centre waiting for you.'

'We will see you soon.' He rang off. I was disturbed by the 'we' part of his message though recalled that dear Richard the decorator, who had been my rock and support during my online driving assessment, always referred to himself in the plural even though he worked on his own. I looked at my instruction sheet and realised that in paying too much attention to making sure I had got his name right, I had blindly overlooked that it said Mr. H plus 2. As another grouping of three men tripped out of the lift giving the impression of having had one too many, I turned over the prospect of the principal man doing a bit of showing off in front of his mates, especially if I stuck rigidly to checking that they all had the requisite passes.

'Are you ready?' It was the clipboard lady looking in at me. 'They're on their way down.' She rushed back to the lift and I could tell from the way she fawned and the young man jiggled anxiously about that my guests had arrived. There were smiles from everyone to everybody from the moment the three of them and what I would loosely call their 'minder' stepped cautiously out of the lift onto the pavement. Mr. Hazoza was a bit unsteady on his feet and it would be a close call to say if he was supporting his wife or the other way round as they made their way to the car, their progress slowed by farewell shaking of hands of presumably other delegates and their assistants. The clipboard lady and the minder escorted them the last few yards and in between I got out of the car and summoned up the friendliest smile that I could as I introduced myself.

'It's a beautiful day,' said Mrs. H with a smile that mirrored it and I held her bag as she slipped into the seat of honour in the back. I saw a teenager opening the other passenger door and settle in next to her, all thoughts as to whether I ought to check if he was an authorised passenger or not gone to pot because of the task in hand; to get Mr. H into the front seat without him sustaining crushed fingers from hanging onto the window when he tried to get in sideways on.

'Mind his head,' I said, as soon as it looked that the backward manoeuvre had found favour. Nobody appeared to be listening so I muscled in and put my right hand over his thinning pate and the other on his left arm to steady him. Breaching the no touching rule and risking a grazed hand was a small price to pay to prevent this apparently irascible man cutting his head open or being knocked out for the count. My withering look at the minder said I'd deal with any complaints of inappropriate mishandling or assault later and with that he melted away.

'Are you quite comfortable?' I asked of my front seat passenger once I was back in the driver's seat.

'Si, thank you.' I clicked his seat belt in and after eliciting a 'Si' that the other two were firmly strapped in as well, I asked if they wanted to go back to their Hotel.

'Si. We are tired.'

'Have you had a good day?'

'Yes, a very good day.' And my nose, as extra sensitive as it is, concluded from the whiff of alcohol and glassy eyes that a good lunch had been included in whatever event or function they had attended. His mellow mood augured well for a pleasant journey but I felt I couldn't let my guard down.

'This Park. You can get lost,' he said.

'Yes,' I nodded, anxious to make sure I went down and under the bridge and not up and over.

'The lady driver before, she went too fast. She was stopped and got a letter. She can't come again. Do you slow down?'

I instinctively slowed down though a quick glance at the Speedo showed I was only a couple of miles over the limit. Was he being clever and psyching me out? He commented on the number of soldiers at Eton Manor and we agreed that they were there for our protection and agreed also that the Lea Interchange was always busy and all three were quiet and sleepy as the traffic stopped and started on the A12. The grandson's head lolled against the window and the elders looked like any set of grandparents returning home after a tiring day out.

Mr. H came to on The Highway. I looked in the rear view mirror. Mrs. H had revived as well.

'It's beautiful day,' she said with a sunny smile.

'It is.'

'Do you live in London?' asked Mr. H.

'No. I live in Hastings, by the coast. It's famous for the Battle of Hastings in 1066.'

'My grandson is interested in history.'

My puff of exasperation, aimed at the cretin in the flash car playing silly beggars and tailgating me, was not the best response but neither was the growing agitation displayed by Grandma H as we drove along East Smithfield. She kept looking out of the back and side windows. Teenage Grandson, who up until that point had been monosyllabic and more interested in his phone, said something to Grandpa and he too became very aware of his surroundings. I began to wonder if the 'difficult' Mr. H was not difficult at all. Was it more a case of Mrs. H supplying the bullets of complaint and leaving him to fire them? I'd seen that before in other relationships. If she was going to play that game, she could stuff all her beautiful days in her suitcase and push off home. It was the not knowing what was going on, what was being said that I didn't like. And I didn't like the idea that if I fell prey to the cretin in the flash car's intimidatory tactics of repeatedly coming along side of me then falling back I was likely to end up in the lane that would wash us inexorably away over Tower Bridge as opposed to carrying straight across Tower Gateway. Histrionics or no histrionics in the back seat, I had to keep a clear head and strong nerve and I'd deal with drama queen Grandma once we made it to the Embankment. It wouldn't be the first time in my life that I had threatened to turf someone out of the car. It wouldn't have been the first time either for me to employ the exact same bully boy tactics that the man in the flash car was having such juvenile fun with. How I stopped myself saying 'get over buster' in colloquial English was a miracle but I nevertheless reduced him to proverbial dust, got into the right lane, glided effortlessly across the Gateway and slid into Lower Thames Street with grace and style.

Grace and style were out of favour with hot and frazzled office workers as they crisscrossed Upper Thames Street and as we waited at traffic lights my client asked if I knew where to go. It was not what he asked but how he asked it and I got to thinking whether they had previously had an experience at the Tower junction, had been carted over the bridge into the maelstrom of Tooley Street as I had once been. Was that what had Mrs. Hazoza spiralling into a fret? It was of no consequence because my affirmative response and the cooling shade and shadow of the buildings showered us, relieving the tension that had held us in its vice like grip, banishing the hot snarling creatures we had all temporarily become on the way to the Tower so that we became one big happy family again. Pulling away to head for the Embankment I caught Grandma's eye. 'Si,' she said sweetly. 'Si,' I replied.

Passing underneath Waterloo Bridge Mr. Hazoza asked which places they ought to visit because they wanted to make the most of their time with their grandson.

'Naturally you do, they grow up so fast.'

'Si, si,' he agreed.

'There's so many,' I said excitedly, thinking ahead to where I could take them. 'The Tower of London, Windsor Castle, the National Gallery.' I came up with so many ideas, praising each one in turn, my voice full of pride and patriotism that our country had so much to offer visiting nations. The Grandson was taken with the idea of Hampton Court. He asked me to spell it out for him so that he could look it up on his phone. It sounded promising. What an ambassador I was proving to be. Given the task of escorting them I wouldn't be worried about sticking to shift hours, would suss out the parking in advance and suggest a few watering holes to stop at en-route. I'd have to have a word with the young 'un about his grandparents going in the Maze because I wouldn't want them getting into difficulties. Even without a couple of lunchtime drinkies, I thought Hazoza senior would still be unsteady and his wife was so very slight. It was an undue burden to put on the Grandson let alone me but as a budding Chief of Tourism and Leisure I came up with a solution. Mr. Z was staying at the same Hotel. What about a two for one excursion and if, being stubborn, the seniors insisted on going into the Maze, Mr. Z was younger, fitter and so tall he'd get them out of trouble in a jiffy.

'Did your father serve in the War?'

'Yes he did.' I'd answered the question but it had thrown me as we drove up Birdcage Walk. And I shouldn't have tried to do the sums in my head as the traffic rushed us along to Buckingham Palace. I worked out my passenger would have to be eighty five plus to have been in the War and he couldn't be that. So that meant I was on a par with an elderly man because we both had fathers in the war. Time, age and history had undoubtedly caught up with me. Then the thought struck me as to whether his country took part in the war and what side they were on. Such thoughts swirling in my head had me jumping the next set of lights but he didn't seem to notice, interested instead in establishing where Dad had served.

'North Africa and Italy.'

'Who did he serve under? Was it..?' He mentioned a General.

'I'm sorry, I haven't heard that name.' He might have thought that the air of despondency about me related to my failure to retain the information that my father had given me. However, my feeble reply was the by-product of me summoning up the courage to tell him that, even though he seemed obliviously unaware of what I had done, the next thing he would hear would be a siren and the next man in uniform he would behold would be a policeman because, watched on by the tourists at the top of The Mall, I seemed to be the only vehicle going the wrong way round the roundabout in front of Buckingham Palace.

'It might have been General Y not X,' he continued as I dragged the car's wheels up Constitution Hill. 'My Grandson will know.' It opened up a discussion between them for which I was glad. And I was glad too that there was no way the London traffic was going to let me sulk and skulk on account of my transgression because Hyde Park Corner has no time for sulkers and skulkers. You have to get on and do, and get on and do in Park Lane as well, making sure you get in the correct lane at the correct time to turn right and not show your ignorance in missing the turning and then having to go round Marble Arch.

I turned right at the correct place and a minute later I pulled up outside the Hotel. I had shown an unforgivable lack of knowledge about Dad's Army service record but on the driving front I felt that I had acquitted myself well. Giles would have spat at my obsequiousness in the way I got out and rushed round to make sure Mrs H could manage to get out of the car ok. She thanked me kindly and we came to an understanding that it had been a long, beautiful day for her and she should get some rest. My hand hovered like a butterfly over her husband's head as he hauled himself out of the seat. He too was tired, hazy and undecided about his movements for the following day. Danger bells rang in my head. Should I try his patience by demanding some idea of his plans to take back for the schedulers or had this proved a flash point between him and previous drivers? A coward, I willingly put the responsibility on to someone else.

'I'll get someone to ring you later on to check what you want.' It was the easiest option.

'Si,' he said, and we all shook hands and grandson and grandparents alike tottered off. And I, being a fickle soul, decided Georgina could keep her suave Mr. Squiffy and his cocktail parties in the presence of so called royalty and I'd relinquish any claim to the contents of Mr. Z's plimsoll bag for jaunts and picnics in the country with this threesome. Naturally, I'd have to bone up on the campaigns and battles of the Second World War and other major political events and that wasn't something I would find in the pages of the Workbook.

CHAPTER 30

A Matter of Perspective

When I arrived back at the VSA at Excel the soldier wasn't interested in the logic and reason behind why I had an ice pack and ham salad roll stuffed into my cap. It had made the cap soggy and pulled it out of shape but the black Adidas bag in which I now carried all of my possessions was big enough to accommodate it without causing any seepage into my other things.

It was a good move to use the bag, the bag that my uniform had been shoved into on the day I collected it from UDAC, though it wasn't my own common sense solution to keeping everything in one place thereby avoiding a scrabble to get things separately out of the car when going through the VSA. The brainwave had been communicated to me by a fellow colleague whose wife was responsible for packing his bag and seeing him off at the station every shift. 'She looks after me, does my wife,' the man said proudly after I'd congratulated him on being so organised. 'Without her I wouldn't have made it to becoming a Games Maker.'

'Nor me without my husband and children.'

But the soldier responsible for checking me through wasn't bothered about my misshapen cap, the virtues of the roomy bag or that I was on a high from having survived a Hazoza encounter unscathed. She was required to establish that I was in possession of a specific authorisation. Chris or Giles, perhaps it was Allan, had explained the reasoning of it which I'm sure was much more weighty and serious than I now imply but, in essence, there had been some hoo-ha about whether food and drink were restricted items from a security point of view. Naturally the soldiers could,

317

as they did, ask you to take a sip from your bottle but for the military to have to deconstruct the selection of fillings in our rolls etc was taking the Michael out of all concerned. So, to obviate huge queues of ham salad chomping Games Makers amassing, it had been decreed that we had to carry a letter of authorisation from someone on high in respect of edible and perishable items.

I showed the soldier my letter which we were asked to keep safe in our plastic wallets. It was all in order. She waited till she got the thumbs up that the search of the car was complete and then let me pass through. She had done her job and as I sat in the car in my allotted car park space I had a job to do as well. The checks on the car had become second nature but, despite all the good relations fostered during the car journey, I was taking no chances with Mr. Hazoza and definitely no chances with getting my message across to the Schedulers. I did what all good lawyers do, I committed his requirements to paper.

Mr. Hazoza has given no indication re his forward plans. I have told him that someone from this depot WILL PHONE HIM THIS EVENING *to take his instructions on his requirements for tomorrow.* CAN YOU PLEASE ENSURE THIS IS DONE *to avoid any issues or problems arising.* I signed and dated the sheet.

'I've written it here,' I said, running my finger under my words for the benefit of Dispatcher Pauline who was collecting in the wallets. 'You will make sure that someone sorts it out, won't you, because otherwise he might cause hassle.'

'Yes, Carol. I'll let the Schedulers know.'

'When?'

'Later on.'

'He was tired so it had better not be too late and if they leave it till the morning he might not be happy.'

'No worries, Carol.'

I turned and started to head back to my regular table and it just so happened that Maureen came wandering into the bunker. There was no let up with her worried look which I added to by repeating all that I had said in my note and to Pauline, thereby perpetuating the view that Mr. Hazoza could be *un poco dificil.*

Or was it *um pouco dificil?* I didn't know which. It was a matter of perspective.

The day had held out the prospect of a fist fight but it had turned, as Giles had predicted, into a matter of transporting three souls from A to B, on time and without incident. There was nothing much to say about it though as we gathered round a table, there was a good trade in stories that evening.

Rumour had it that one driver had been due to collect a delegate up from the nearby hotel where I had performed my waiting for nonexistent client thespian piece but had set the Sat Nav incorrectly and ended up at a hotel of the same name in Wimbledon.

Chris told of a trip he had taken to a late night store to buy some whisky for a client because the client's hotel was charging three hundred pounds for a bottle of spirit. For another of our fraternity, however, there had been an issue as to who he was supposed to have been carrying. He'd duly reported to a hotel to collect a delegate and had been greeted by delegate plus one and they were big boys into the bargain. Theirs was only a short journey to Excel but the atmosphere in the car had been tense, made all the more so by their sheer physical presence and the language barrier meant our driver friend had no way of knowing what the disagreement between them was about.

I never got to see it but above the bunker a service road ran round Excel so that coaches and cars could drop off and pick up people at given points. From how it was described, passengers had to get in or out without any of the fluffy handshaking and joie de vie that I'd witnessed when Mr. Hazoza and family had left the Aquatics Centre. Anyhow, the two men got out of the car and our diligent friend made arrangements for pick up. What he didn't know, what he couldn't have foreseen, was that on arriving back later the second man (the one not listed on the original sheet) commandeered the car, refused to let the 'delegate' in and, harassed by the vehicles building up behind, there was no option other than to drive away.

With the wrong man in the car it had, to me, all the makings of the opening chapter of a thriller though I gave nothing away on that front and asked whether my table companion had thought to go back and pick the other one up.

'No. They'll have to sort it out between themselves.'

'That's what I say,' said Stuart, who, hovering close by after just returning from a mission, bore all the signs of someone itching to tell something. If the story of the warring delegates had been enough to fire my imagination Stuart's too was one to get my creative taste buds going.

'I'd better not say where I've been or who I've been with but I picked the client up from one hotel and on the way he asked me to stop off and pick up a lady from another.'

'That's nothing,' interrupted Nicholas. I was surprised at his intervention as he rarely contributed to group discussions. In fact it sometimes felt like extracting teeth to draw an opinion out of him. In that regard he was unlike any other lawyer I had ever met. 'I know a delegate whose wife is based at a different hotel to him.'

'Really?' Stuart raised his eyebrows. 'I wouldn't like to say what the connection was between my two.'

'Did you ask to see her accreditation badge?'

'Give over, Carol. Would you have done that?'

'You're not supposed to take people in the car unless they are authorised. What if there was an accident?'

'There wasn't.'

'You wouldn't have got through a VSA.'

'They didn't want to go through a VSA. He said to take them to another hotel and I didn't need to wait around because they'd make their own way back. I've done what was asked of me and it's all fine because nobody knows.' And from the nods and gestures of those around the table it seemed, as comrades in arms, we were all agreed on that and what it meant to be fully fledged.

CHAPTER 31

Strangers in the Camp

I heard the flap of the letter box, the post flop down onto the floor of the porch and opened the front door to see my favourite cheery postman retreating down the drive. Even with his bag draped from his shoulder he looked cool and casual in his shorts, whilst the armpits of my uniform top were already feeling sticky. He had the rest of his round to complete and I had another one and a half to two hour drive ahead of me for my next shift.

I picked up the travel magazine that we subscribe to. It gives us a window on the world and ideas which, pedant that I can be at times, are stored away neatly in a file. The pull out résumé's of city and country breaks and coastal walks has come in very handy and there are some places on our hit list for the future. I shuffled through the letters and circulars and amongst the invitation to take up a new credit card and a request for donations to a charity, there was an envelope addressed in my own fair hand. It bore a post office sticker saying the letter was undelivered on account of the addressee failing to pick it up from the collection point. It was good of the Post office to let me know that the trouble I had gone to with special next day delivery prior to my shifts starting hadn't worked. It appealed to my sense of order that there were no loose ends, that it completed the circle even though by then I already knew that Kreety K was away and would probably have laughed in the face of my letting her have my part of the parking agreement anyway. But did she know of the goings on at her property, of the man and his harem, or have the faintest idea that I might be killing the roots of her tree by having to park so close to it? I put the letter away and when, ten minutes later, I pulled out of the drive, I reflected on how easily I had assimilated

Kreety into my life, had exchanged my usual set of common or garden parochial matters for another.

Bromley? I managed to steer clear of the turning to it. The parking space? The 4 x 4 wasn't there. The bridge across to Excel? They say that one swallow doesn't make a summer and one pressurised rush across the bridge to prevent me being late for the previous shift was not sufficient to prove to myself that I had the resolve to do it ordinarily. With my heart beating so fast and hard that I thought it was going to spring out of my chest with the same force and intensity as the alien who leaps out of John Hurt's chest in the film, I got into the rickety and ratchetty lift and ascended. I had the luxury of knowing that if I couldn't face walking across it, I had plenty of time that day to scoot round the dockside and up Western Gateway. I met the challenge and, eyes front at all times, strode out. The people coming from the other direction were a blur who must have made way for me because I made it to the other side and down the steps and round into the throng by the pedestrian VSA and so on and so forth until, taking breath, I presented myself and my black cool bag to the dour young catering assistant man who had returned to his post. I decided he would never need to know of my previous dereliction of duty regarding the coolbag and so I only returned one ice pack and not the extra one I had been given by his more affable stand-in. On balance, I decided that my progress thus far that day augured well and I might, just might, get the Hazoza's again, especially as the head of the H household had complimented me on my driving.

'No clients today, Carol,' said Pauline.

'Oh.'

'Perhaps it's better to say not yet and you can take this wallet in case a call comes through.' In hindsight she was just being kind and saving herself from grief, which she seemed to be getting plenty of that afternoon.

I watched on from my usual seat, a lonesome pine because Nicholas made a fleeting appearance before going to pick up someone he had driven before. Allan too was going out on a trip though couldn't see the sense in it because the amount of time it would take to get there didn't equate with the short distance between the client's hotel and venue.

There were some, mainly men (apologies to the male brotherhood), who, on occasion, stomped back into the bunker and threw their plastic wallets on the table in rage. That's not to say that the female sisterhood didn't complain, they just did it in a different way. Stories circulated that some clients weren't very amenable, some downright rude but the main frustration was when drivers went to collect a client who had gone walkabout as a result of miscommunication or impatience. Why wait for a T2 to drive across London from Excel when they could double up in someone else's car, purloin a T3, hail a private taxi or, as Allan contended, simply walk. And it followed that Pauline and her Dispatcher colleagues were the first ones at the receiving end of a driver's displeasure.

There were, as ever, two sides to the argument as to whether getting ratty with a scarlet pimpernel of a client served any purpose or if we had any right to complain about the hours spent doing nothing. After all, we had all made a decision to give up our time so didn't it follow that Seb and his underlings could do with our time as they wanted? Was it pushing the argument a bit far to say that an abortive mission did nothing for the confidence or self-esteem of the drivers who had driven out to collect someone only to be told by some haughty hotelier that they'd vamoosed?

Did the T3's muscle in and take what was rightfully the T2's? The way the set up had been explained to us way back in the beginning, it seemed that it would be impossible, inconceivable, that a delegate allocated his/her own car would want to avail themselves of the T3 service. But group bonding, group mentality, and a looking at 'them' from an 'us' standpoint exerts a powerful influence, makes you alert to others not of your ilk, makes you more watchful of 'what them others' are doing. What is that indefinable quality that sets one group apart from another?

Who was it, what was it, that had galvanised the T3's to devise a makeshift table tennis table and instigated the setting up of a league? Who had brought in a selection of books and games for the T3's and why did they always seem so busy and noisy? Was it simply an impression, a mirage? By contrast the T2's were a lot quieter or was it just that the bunker absorbed the cheers that went up if Team GB had a sporting success. And the pervading mood, apart from the stompers, was mellow, light-hearted and had less edge.

The T3's had their ping pong and we had the calming influence of the jigsaws and it was, as Colin was making his way to the jigsaw table that morning that we stopped to have a chat. A quiet, sensitive soul at the best of times, he seemed positively downhearted. Having heard that more shifts were available, he had offered to do more on top of those he was down to do but none were forthcoming.

'I made enquiries as well, Colin. Not for extra shifts but to see if I could swap to do earlier ones because I function better in the mornings.' My night time wanderings on the North Circular still haunted me. 'I also asked how easy it would be to synchronise shifts so that you and me could travel up together like we said.'

'I'm in limbo about it all. But are you going to join me and Florence to do the jigsaw? She'll be back from the Ladies in a minute.'

'No, I'll give it a miss, thank you. I don't think I'd make much of a contribution.'

Reinstated at my table I pulled out a few pages of Frank's story, a wad of additional blank paper and some Driver Information that the Transport Team had sent through with an email. The Games Makers experience was not as I had expected it to be and I felt sure that a real live Frank would have likewise joined me in relishing the thought of sitting in the corner of a fresco painted room in the Dorchester Hotel waiting for a client to call on the mobile after they had finished their breakfast. This room, generally unused because of the repairs needed to the stucco, was simply the product of my imagination, the fantasy given life by the reference at training to holding rooms where we would spend the time waiting on clients' whims. Frank, although unwell at the beginning of my book, would have sufficient energy and enthusiasm to relish an evening waiting in a holding room whilst the client showered after a day at a venue and planned his evening.

The Route Book gave a list of Hospitals, Hospices and selected Healthcare Facilities and the maps showed schools, tennis courts, mosques, synagogues, Coroners Courts, ice rinks, bowling greens, heath clubs, Doctor Johnson's House and the Church by St Andrew by the Wardrobe but NO eating places. It occurred to me that they might look to me to make some suggestions or recommendations and the London city break planners from our travel magazine had thrown up some ideas. I imagined Frank and me watching the antics of our client and friends through the window of our parked car as they wined and dined in a Chelsea restaurant.

Perhaps visions of the Dorchester and an exclusive restaurant was taking it a bit far but I hadn't thought that a picture of me slumped over my laptop in the corner of a hall attached to a sporting venue was wide of the mark. It obviously was and a laptop was an absolute no-no as far as security was concerned. So it was Frank between his A4 sheets and me and a plastic cup of coffee on day ten, which marked two thirds into my shift quotient. Of necessity I spent a lot of time indoors writing about Frank but when I sat thinking it through the majority of the scenes in Frank's story were indoors, with the ones outdoors always containing some threat or menace. Was that my view of the world, a view foisted onto Frank? Or was it that, because he was my creation, I cosseted him? Did I keep adding scenes and flashbacks because I didn't have the confidence to release him and his story out into the world? Could I remedy all of that by jollying him and Ruth along with a visit to a Zoo that I had been working on during my stay at the hotel on the night between shifts two and three? The Zoo idea now seemed fluffy and frivolous in comparison to what I really needed to do which was to tie up the loose ends of the revelations about his father. Had I made it all too complicated? But if I simplified it, would it cut through the 'things are not as they seem' thread in the story

'What is it you're scribbling away at today?' I was jolted out of my alternate world by Giles. He sat down beside me with an apple in his hand. 'Drawing your own routes?' I looked down at my doodles on the paper. Giles, with his long time connection with the publishing world, impressive knowledge of current authors and revelations regarding erotica might have been the ideal person to have a yarn with about Frank and how I ought to approach hoiking him round to prospective publishers. I liked Giles and found him amusing but did I trust him to take me seriously and give Frank the time and respect he deserved. How would I be if he dismissed my aspirations as futile or, worse still, was indulgently courteous and then yawned behind his lily white hand. I decided to play safe and reached for the driver information.

'Have you looked at this Map Pack on Hotels? '

'No, should I?'

'None of the hotels I've ever had to go to are listed on it.'

'Is that so?'

'Well have you ever had to go to the Marriott at Cheshunt?'

'Can't say I have.' He bit into his apple.

'For every hotel you are given details of entry and egress points, load zones, parking spaces and staging but for all the time it would take to read it you might as well use your common sense or get out and ask the doorman.'

'Exactly.'

'Or ask someone here.'

'Quite.'

I can't profess to have known everyone in the bunker because, even amongst the crew I was associated with, we came and went at various times and different friendship groups were made. But you knew faces and there was a sense of identity, a feeling of being with those of your own, being all in it together. I suspect that reading this Giles would pooh pooh such idealism but how else could it explain our reaction to the woman who fetched up on the table opposite us.

She was as thin as a rake (or lithe depending on how you were brought up), her slightness of being having something to do with the way she nibbled on a pot of something healthily delectable. I wondered where she had got it from. How had she managed to get that through the VSA? Did she have special authorisation for it?

As for her age? Was she, like me, in denial about it, finding it easier to live in a bubble where, though I won't lop a few years off for fear of being found out, I related to others as very much older or younger? I smiled, thinking back to a conversation with Chris in the early days.

'Looking at the average age of us lot, they ought to give us call signs relating to the medications we are on,' he'd said.

'They'd be a bit wordy to put on the windscreens. Come on in Perindopril,' I'd laughed and we'd had a moment reeling off our respective blood pressure pills.

If the question had been put to the mystery lady she might have denied the sixty plus label I'd put on the sinewy (or scrawny, again depending on how you were brought up) neck and silver threads running through her hair. And was it right for me to take her reading of the Telegraph as an age determiner or, from her arms bearing a mature unselfconscious tan, guess that she often read the paper in the garden.

'I don't remember seeing that lady before, 'I muttered, unwrapping my cereal bar.

'Nor me but that doesn't mean a thing.' He liked to be controversial.

'There are strangers in the camp!' I chuckled, recalling the often used phrase of Mum and Dad if someone new came into their local. 'She hasn't got a plastic wallet.'

'Perhaps she doesn't need one,' he said loftily.

'Don't be silly.' We all needed a plastic wallet. Without a plastic wallet we were as nothing. Without a plastic wallet you had to endure pitying looks from confident and cocksure fellow Games Makers who had a wallet plus client and from those with wallet only who, though they might not be called upon to go out in the car, knew that they had a motor allocated to them. Perhaps she wasn't a stranger as such, simply a new recruit who didn't know the drill. Chris had said, and Colin too, that training of drivers had taken place right up to the start of the Games because, with no obligation to give notice, lots of drivers had dropped out resulting in the Transport Team never knowing who was going to turn up.

'Do you think she's a new recruit, Giles?' But new recruits never looked as cool and self-composed as she did and I suspected that even Giles, mister play it cool, had had a few misgivings at the beginning. I resisted calling over and asking the lady if I could help with anything because the bunker experience had made me face up to the fact that I tend to interfere and try to sort things out, even if it was something as simple as clearing up other people's empty cups and debris from the table. I was well and truly that 'Doris', a jokey name that a friend applies to me. It was meant as a term of endearment but I was beginning to see a kernel of truth in it, a truth that carried a double-edged sword.

The mystery lady folded her newspaper, put it to one side then got up and glided over to us. I'd like to think it was only me in her sights but she was way too cultured to be concerned about asking where the Ladies was in mixed company. Her voice was as crisp as the sound of the apple Giles had just bitten into. It commanded your attention but had the quality of a Cox's, soft and gentle enough to make you feel at ease. And she wasn't off-puttingly neat and tidily dressed like some who made tucking their tops into their trousers an art form. Ever the gentleman, Giles put the apple down whilst I explained the route to the Ladies. And she made no request for us to keep an eye on her newspaper for fear of it being filched. I was impressed, seriously impressed.

My mucker Giles could have eaten three pounds of apples in the time it took for our lady to return and, in true Doris mode, I was concerned because when you're doing nothing, you have to have something or someone to be concerned about.

'Did you find it ok?' I asked brightly, catching a whiff of nicotine as she passed by.

'I did, thank you, but I found a much quieter and secluded one up on the first floor.' I refrained from cross examining her on the point of how she had managed to gain access to Excel proper because the story went that it was now being limited to only those who had authority to be there and drivers weren't so authorised. These restrictions were also being rolled out as regards the number of Games Makers being allowed access to watch events on account of the press revisiting and echoing concerns about the ticket allocations amid suggestions that Games Makers were simply there to make up audience numbers. 'I had better get going,' she continued. It's time to check in with my clients.' Her diction was perfect for one who 'checked in' with people. 'We are going shopping later.'

'She's going shopping,' I whispered to Giles as she ambled back to her table, disappointed that, having been in the bunker only a short while, she was preparing to leave.

'I heard her.'

I figured that her 'shopping' wouldn't be of the running in to grab a bottle of cheap booze from a convenience store type of shopping that Chris had been about.

'Have you managed to have the same clients each time?' I called over.

'Yes. It's been tiring but they are simply the most interesting and adorable of people.'

'You have been lucky.' The conversation could prove useful. I could pick up some ideas in case I was assigned to Mr. and Mrs. Hazoza and grandson again though it would be harder to cater to the tastes of three whereas, if I had Mr. Z, I could focus on specifics. I was in cloud cuckoo land again, thinking that I really had a choice.

'I'm a T1 driver.' Simply stated, no qualifying words necessary, T1 explained all.

'Told you,' said Giles.

'When?'

Giles didn't quite simper but came pretty close to it when she revealed where she travelled home to each night. It's a place I'd never heard of before, an area that apparently only those 'in the know' knew about and accepting my ignorance is presumably the reason that I forgot the name of the place so easily and no amount of racking my brains and scouring the map of London and surrounding environs since has revealed it.

'That's what you call real posh,' he said, after she had left us. 'You've got to be posh to be a T1,' he repeated, though his own way of talking wasn't exactly barrow boy.

'Not necessarily.' I thought back to the large young man I had met on the edge of a housing estate at Lee Valley only weeks, but what seemed like a lifetime, before. 'So you think you can't be one without the other, do you?'

'I don't think so, I know so.'

If she was posh in Giles's eyes, did that mean he wasn't because posh people wouldn't use that term regarding their own fraternity. Yet if he wasn't posh, what was he? In a previous conversation he implied he was funky, funky enough not to have a car of his own, relying on hiring a Zip car when he needed it. Did that mean that posh and funky were mutually exclusive? I didn't ask. He wandered off to conversations new.

The computers and T.V's were honey pots, particularly for the men, and I never got into the habit of sitting in a group on the blue foam cubes. It is one of the benefits of long hair, along with the experienced placement of papers on the table, which enabled me to put my head in my hands and have a little snooze without drawing attention. I woke up and drifted away from my moorings.

I happened upon John and gentle Sam. 'We didn't like to disturb you,' said John, and Sam looked on with his usual smile as John congratulated me after I told him that I had walked over the bridge twice.

'But this is a woman you don't want to make an enemy of, Sam, because she'll get you into a lot of hot water.'

'What?' I frowned.

'She introduced me to this woman who I'd never seen in my life before, Sam, as if we lived in the same street. I didn't have a clue what to say to her.'

It was true. I had introduced him to Florence a few days before. He had looked aghast but I'd assumed it had been Florence's Scottish accent that had thrown him. The introduction was a habit acquired from all the years living in Hastings where it always happens that if you drop a name into a conversation you will, in the space of seven questions, be able to find a connection in common with another, be it that person has wedded, divorced or unblocked the drain of the third cousin of the great nephew of the woman down the road whose child was in year six with the woman at the supermarket checkout's younger brother.

'But she comes from Bexleyheath.' It was the only defence I could put to Sam, the one and only member of the jury.

'She didn't, Sam, she came from Welling. Bloody hell!'

'I thought it was Erith? But it's all the same isn't it, Sam?' I pleaded.

'No, it's not,' said Prosecutor John.

'Not remotely like Bromley and Sidcup?'

'It isn't Chislehurst is it, Sam?'

Sam's verdict was expressed in a laugh and an 'excuse me' because he had to go.

Chislehurst. I'd seen snapshots of it on a television programme where two antique dealers slog it out, with each trying to get the best bargains and recoup a profit at an auction. It looked a very pleasant place and I had a note to myself to go and browse in the antique shops one day. Based on the programme, I had recommended it as place for the daughter and fiancée of a friend to move to. They hadn't and whilst talking with John I began to see why.

They say it's not where you come from it's where you end up. As I recall, John had pretty unexciting south east London roots but I was bringing to that the perceptions of my childhood when, down in that 'yer country life', London was seen as just another damp and grey city with smog filled terraced streets. I doubt he was a poor boy made good but it sounded like he had spent some time learning his craft on the lower rungs. And it wasn't where he came from or the nice house in Chislehurst that he had ended up in, it was all the bits in between that I found interesting.

Despite some increasingly vocal murmurs of bunker disgruntlement going on around us, I sat entranced as John unravelled his life story which included a rich and rewarding career during which he had married, had children, travelled and lived abroad extensively. His life, like Giles's, had revolved around the printed word but not a word was asked, and nothing passed my lips about my life or Frank's story. With little, apart from a 'Doris afraid of bridges' persona for him to go on, I don't know what conclusion he came to about me. As for the conclusions I came to about him?

I had him down as one who could talk with crowds and walk with Kings yet not lose the common touch in the way of Rudyard Kipling. He would have had to have those abilities in order to get fast and accurate information for the news agency. What of the competitive environment he worked in? I reckoned he would have had to have shown tenacity and drive, if not lean towards the tough and ruthless at times in order to make effective decisions and buffer the winds of change that had swept through his industry during his lifetime. There was more to the affable man under the cap than at first met the eye. And he was worth a bob or two because who else could boast a legend of a former pop star living as a near neighbour?

'Does she really, John? I didn't know she was still alive. My sister-in-law used to wear the same hairstyle.'

'A lot of women did.'

'I met Ronnie Carroll once.'

'He's dead?'

'I think so.'

As he talked I wondered what category John would fall into? Funky? Posh? Well heeled? Grammar school grafter made good? Which of these could afford to take his wife to Benares at the weekend?

'Is it far?' I asked, wondering which sea lapped up against its shores.

'Mayfair. You have to book months in advance to get in.'

'I bet.'

'Do you like Indian food?'

'I don't mind it.'

'If you don't mind going to Southall you can't better some of the curries. Benares is pricey, mind.'

'It would be.'

'We are going there with friends.'

'I'm sure you'll enjoy it.'

I've since looked at the Benares website. It's a very swish restaurant and you can watch the chefs at work through a glass screen. I imagine the attention to detail and waiters are exquisite and the place so clean that you could eat the food off the floor. But would it flush out the remnants of suspicion that I have carried round with me for years that things are not always as they seem even in the best of places. It stems from a tour of duty as a waitress in a hotel in another place in another time. I blagged the interview saying I was trained in silver service but luckily two fellow waiters, a really camp guy and a very well bred young man, covered for my inadequacies until I picked up the basics and improvised the rest. Three things I learnt. One, you must always put a clean tablecloth onto a table without baring the table itself. Two, never ask a guest how many potatoes they want because you'll get a complaint and a rollicking from the restaurant manager and, three, all may be diamond and dandy out front but ascertain the calibre of the kitchen porters in case the cloth that washes the floor is flipped over the food surfaces.

'Can I get you a drink, John?'

'That's jolly decent of you, Carol, but I'm quite particular how I like it.' 'I'm sure you are.'

So we sat and supped and others stopped and had a chat, moved on, came back. It was all very civilised, considering.

'Do you mind if I join you?' We both looked across the table at a man pulling a chair out to sit down on.

'Not at all,' said John. There was something about the way his uniform was thrown together that made me suspicious of this cheerful chappy.

'This coffee's not bad is it?' he commented, the words a confirmation that we had another cuckoo in the nest. This time I wasn't going to pussyfoot about as Giles and I had done with the T1 lady.

'I haven't seen you here before. Are you a driver? Where are you based?'

'Steady on, Carol!' said John, clearly embarrassed that I was showing all the traits that he would commonly associate with someone from 'astings.

'I'm not a driver. I'm the Chaplain.'

'Bloody hell,' said John, and it was my turn to be embarrassed, my companion showing all the traits I would not have to associated with someone from Chislehurst.

CHAPTER 32

Words from him on High

The presence of the Chaplain floored me. The organisers had thought of everything, right down to sending this friendly fellow round to check the emotional barometer in the bunker.

'My word, do they think it's got that bad?' John laughed, and the Chaplain saw the funny side too.

'I'm going round visiting all the depots.' He definitely wasn't the travelling showman type. There was no carpet bag bursting with herbal remedies and magic potions to ease posterior ache. There were no signs of a magnetic personality which any minute would have him leaping up onto the table with a huge bible to deliver a fire and brimstone message. 'I'm simply here to provide support.'

'Support?'

He wasn't there to enjoin us all to move the tables and chairs out of the way so we could fall to our knees on the blue carpet and offer up supplication, ask a being even higher than Seb to answer individual prayers for a client (Florence went eight shifts without one), for better food (it was repetitive but quite adequate) or summon up a hologram of Bryn or Tommy the Beard (I hadn't seen either on a daily briefing for some while). If you wanted a moment of reflection or prayer with him I expect he would have found a corner to deliver it. He was quietly spoken and interested in where we came from and how we were coping with the shifts.

'Is there anything, anything at all you'd like to discuss?'

He said he was happy to discuss anything because Games Makers were not above the rest of the population in having worries and concerns that wouldn't simply vanish during the

Olympics. He had time and an open channel to the Lord that we could make use of if we so wished.

I displayed my usual deference, brainwashed as a child into thinking that all who go to church must be good, brainwashed too into thinking that he could see something about me that needed remedying, rectifying. But even if he hadn't or didn't see into my soul I sensed he was an 'intellectual' vicar who could use an arsenal of theological arguments against my beefs, the sort of arguments that he and his wife (also an ordained member of the Church) no doubt picked their way through every evening in the nice part of London where they lived.

In hindsight I ought to have embraced the opportunity with both hands, revealed my innermost thoughts on a range of subjects, sure in the knowledge that I was never going to see this man of the cloth, this man of the forced languorous pose, ever again. After all, I had his sole attention because John didn't stay around that long. It might have been a call of nature but it was curious how others came to say hello, checked the rookie out and quickly drifted away. Even Chris, who I knew had some faith, beetled in from having been somewhere, hardly got past the introductions before shooting off again. Perhaps they had an inkling that he was the warm up act for the early evening entertainment.

I'm not good at circulating, at extricating myself and moving on from a conversation in a social setting before it gets awkward thinking of things to say. Conversely the Chaplain was adept at it and so, when he'd sussed out I had no burning issues to bring to his attention and no one else was sniffing round to see what he was about, he brought our encounter to a fitting end and disappeared as quickly as he had come. I returned to my usual seat at my usual table. Allan had been away most of the day, Chris had disappeared and John had well and truly scarpered after his brush with the Almighty's representative.

I munched on my cereal bar. I watched a group of men in civvies come through the bunker doors. There was a lead man with aides at a discreet distance behind him. The proverbial Pied Piper, they followed where he led and gathered in a circle in the centre of the bunker. Coming hard on the Chaplain's heels

335

I wondered if he had called in the heavy mob, that the men would soon be holding hands and if not looking to Excel above, looking at their feet and chanting. Some of the drivers left off whatever fruitless things they were doing and the circle widened to include them. Even Bryn lolloped in and sat on the edge of a nearby table, one leg dangling, kicking out and back again.

I had a grandstand view and felt invisible as the big bug introduced himself as the Director of Transport. An aide brought him a coffee in a plastic cup. The heat from it steamed up his glasses but not his vision that he might be in for stick from the way the male drivers were standing with their arms crossed or pulling their trousers up, a guaranteed prelude to harsh words. Wise man, he put the coffee down, cupped his elbow in his hand, held a finger to his lips and listened intently to the gripes and concerns of a fractious few.

I smiled, drawing parallels with a similar grouping I had been part of many years before. In an effort to resolve a dispute over a piece of land, warring farmers, barristers, solicitors, surveyors and land agents all had trudged around a muddy field with much finger pointing at fences and tree lines. Most had prepared for the day by bringing wellingtons whilst others, for all their learning, squelched in expensive brogues. The air was cold and bitter and we were kindly invited to have a hot drink in the farmhouse. We dutifully queued up and waited in the biting wind whilst the stereotypical farmer's wife supervised us leaving our footwear in the porch. A fine tactician, my booming voiced colleague congratulated the lady of the household on the roaring fire in the drawing room and immediately gained a conversational advantage point over our opponents. We stood in a circle, the crackle of the firewood insufficient to drown out the sound of slurps from china tea cups. Tea, coffee and small talk downed, the cups and saucers were cleared and it was back to business.

The big gun brought out to demolish our client's argument rose up and down on the balls of his feet. Rather than a demonstration of success, it signified defeat, my indefatigable vertically challenged boss with the stentorian voice keeping his little stockinged feet firmly on the ground whilst rebutting every allegation of boundary fixing and tree pollarding. And it was the stocking feet that did it, that had me spluttering and choking so much that it interrupted the flow of words and hot air rising to the beamed ceiling. A glass of water was called for, the blame duly accorded to a biscuit crumb stuck in my throat.

We were all in the blame game but, in truth, the biscuit was not the culprit. Posture as they might, without shoes how silly and vulnerable everyone looked; splayed feet or wriggling toes telling their own story, conveying what they really felt as opposed to the words being spouted. But it was the holes in the socks that said more about the individuals than any of the citations from legal texts or arboriculturist's handbooks. I thought of Mum telling me that I had to put a clean vest on in case I got run over, how Dad had a gift for put you down one- liners and how it would have been a wonderful destabilising act, tantamount to a *coup d'état*, if I had brought everyone's attention to the holes in the windbag's socks, the wrong pairing of an erstwhile protagonist. Only in my dreams could I have been so assertive, the ladder slowly creeping up my leg a reminder of how fragile we all are.

I wondered if the big bug and his aides wore the same kind of socks that had come as standard issue and therefore, to a man, were fresh, logo'd and sublimely hole-less. They listened intently to those whose sense of grievance stemmed from believing they were wasting their time hanging around for something to happen. I could see their point but I still held to the view that everyone who had signed up had already scrubbed those days out of their diary so what was the difference? They wanted, like me, to feel useful but who could tell what might be round the corner.

So what did the man from the seat of operations have to tell us? Like the Chaplain he was relaxed and informal but you could tell the smart cookie had a prepared script. I wondered if his toes squirmed and wriggled in his shoes as he told us that the number of drivers recruited had been based on the experience and accumulated knowledge of previous Games and even in the week before the Games began there were concerns that demand would outstrip supply. The anticipated uptake of vehicles hadn't taken place. They had waited to see what impact the road events on the first two days would have because it was always anticipated that these would cause significant disruption but, after two days of 'normal' operations involving the Olympic Route Network, there was still a low uptake of cars.

There was conjecture amongst the drivers that delegates were choosing to get T3's and if staying in the West End why would they choose to wait for a car to come across the city to take them to the big stores and fancy restaurants when they could walk or catch the tube in the same amount of time. Put like that, it all made perfect sense and the Director nodded in agreement with these theories but wanted us to know that we were very much appreciated and we had to hang on in there.

'What did you make of all that?' asked Harry, pulling up a chair after the Ops people had gone and the crew of drivers was dispersing.

'I suppose we are the victims of their success.'

'Maybe, but I'm not staying past nine.'

'Nor me.'

'What shall we do?'

'I've read that to pass time and psychologically overcome their appalling conditions some hostages have reconstructed books they have read in their heads. I think Terry Waite did the Bible. Imagine that, or trying to recall a Dickens or Shakespeare.'

We settled on testing our powers of recall as to the characters, weapons and rooms where the murder could have been committed in the game of Cluedo. It wasn't that easy.

'What are you up to?' It was Chris, arriving back from goodness knows where. He looked over my shoulder as I was writing 'dagger'.

'Any strange requests or mystery passengers today?' I asked of Stuart who bounced in from a mission.

'No, just an ordinary day.'

'Shall we move on to trying to remember the squares on a Monopoly board?'

'I know all thirty four of them,' said Chris. I'm sure he did but he was magnanimous enough to let others contribute to the list that I made. I've still got the piece of paper, a tribute, if ever there was one, to group mentality and endurance.

CHAPTER 33

Kid Gloves

Seb couldn't have got better weather if he'd organised it himself. Another sunny day added to the lifting of spirits and national pride in our sporting success which many in the country bore witness to as part of the Olympic phenomena. But the heat was of a type that made my clothes stick and drained the oomph out of me before I had even started doing anything. I wasn't sleeping well, my left arm giving unexplained gyp as if someone was stabbing me. A lethargy descended which wasn't helped by having to start my next shift at two knowing that others would be lazing in their gardens, sizzling on the beach or glued to their television screens watching sport. Yet it is rarely I venture to laze anywhere and very few and far between are the occasions when I find sport riveting.

I took up my seat next to Allan.

'Are you going anywhere today, Carol?'

'I don't know. I haven't asked. I'm going to eat my food first. What about you?'

'No client to speak of. Did you see that email from the Director of Transport?'

'I can go one better. He was in here the other day, full of apologies.

'It was addressed to the T3's.'

'Did you like the way he referred to the challenges to feeding solutions. Makes us sound like cattle.'

Naturally, the day I decided to play it cool and take the whole bunker business at my own pace I noticed there was a bit of a furore at the Dispatcher's desk and then Pauline was looking over and calling to me.

'There, there, Carol, if I hadn't spotted you, your client would have been allocated to someone else.' As I waited for the Dispatcher to sort out the paperwork I began to wonder if that wouldn't have been a better idea on account of the harassed driver I was taking over from.

'It's murder out there today,' he said, wiping the sweat off his brow with the back of his hand. His uniform was ruffled and his neck ribbon and accreditation card twisted. 'And the kid's a nightmare.'

'The kid?' I thought back to my first training day and the conversation I had had with Robin who wasn't keen on children and the question as to what to do if we had a car-sick child. It was much too hot to deal with vomit pouring forth in the back of the car. But what if he or she had been sick already and in a rush to return the car to the Depot there had been no time to clean it up? I would not be beyond giving a point blank refusal to fulfil my duties.

'She's about two or three and she kept taking her seat belt off.'

'For any particular reason?'

'The third time she did it I pulled over, stopped the car and refused to go any further until the client or the mother fastened it.'

'What did they say?'

'There was nothing they could say but the mother wasn't happy. What made it worse was that we got all the way down to Wimbledon and were turned away because the place was packed. I couldn't tell what was being said but it sounded like he was getting it in the neck from her.'

'A proper family day out!'

'Don't stand any nonsense and make sure you're punctual because he's been complaining about time keeping.'

'Go and calm down and enjoy the rest of the day.'

'After the time I've had that's some hope!'

He lumbered off and the Dispatcher gave me the wallet with the next lot of instructions in it. A stroppy child and scratchy parents? Lovely! But perhaps he was exaggerating. Perhaps he wasn't very tolerant or didn't understand the psychology of children but then I could never profess to be an expert on that either. After a break from the car and a drink, who knew, they might all have cooled down. After all, I'd been given dire warnings about Mr. Hazoza but when I deposited him and his wife and grandson at the Hotel we had been on the most favourable of terms. Yet I hadn't been complacent with Mr. Hazoza, hadn't trusted him totally not to be a Jekyll and Hyde (emotional scars of smiling assassin guests and clients in my past life score deep). As I made my way back to our table I wondered what Mr. H and his family were doing that sultry afternoon. No matter what they were doing, I was going to have to work out a strategy in relation to the family of bad mood bears.

North Greenwich Arena possessed its own little eccentricities as regards procedure, largely dictated by the VSA being outside of the Arena's perimeter fence. They were a nice bunch of soldiers there but by this stage the guidance as to who did what seemed to change at regular intervals. Originally we were told not to get out of the car because the sniffer dogs would be checking it. That plan was abandoned because the dogs scratched the cars and they probably didn't have enough dogs for the volume of vehicles. Then it became normal practice for us to pull the bonnet lever in the car, open the glove compartment, all the doors and boot and leave nothing in the car. The practice changed after damage had allegedly been caused to a car when a soldier had lifted up a bonnet, making it our responsibility to release the catch on the bonnet itself. I left my mobile in the car one day and was told to take it out and another day was told not to bother removing it. We'd had the drinking of liquids in front of the soldier and also the business of producing a letter of authority to carry food and drink. During the later stages of the Games, a paper tie was affixed to the boot to show that it had been checked and didn't need looking at again.

North Greenwich Arena had an added twist in that at the VSA you were given a security clearance pass that you had to show when you got to the gates at the perimeter fence. It was only a short drive between the two and I assumed that they either tracked you on camera or there would have been some communication between the two areas if you had taken a long time to get from one to the other.

It was a good job they didn't have the thought police operating in the area that day because as I turned out of the VSA into West Parkside I mulled over if it would be possible to smuggle a stowaway into the car park. It was one of my flights of fantasy, one of my 'what if's' that Stephen King has said has given birth to a number of his blockbusting novels. What if I devised a bogus reason to stop and have the car idle over a man hole cover so that a nimble saboteur could attach themselves to the undercarriage? What if I feigned a breakdown and switched identities with a Games Makers imposter coincidentally walking by. But that day, to the grumpy geezer on the security gate, who gave me an Oscar worthy scowl from the safety of his box, I was just another driver with nothing on my mind, certainly nothing as treasonous as the plot line for a future novel.

I should have parked up in the car park and waited for the call from the client. I didn't. I played bold. I snuck in a space between a mini bus and the kerb which was within sight of the pickup point so that I could get the measure of the child before introductions. I got out of the car and struck up a conversation with a man hovering by the minibus which showed no Olympic logos. It worked as a deterrent for the Games Makers with the clipboard giving me the heave ho back to the car park.

'Who are you picking up?' I asked the bus driver. 'A whole team?'

'No, I transport the luggage from one side of the Dome to the other.'

'Whose luggage?'

'The luggage of those walking across the top of the Dome. Do you fancy doing it?'

'What, now?' I laughed.

'If you want,' he teased.

I looked at my beautiful red watch. 'Sorry, I've got a prior commitment, another time perhaps.'

By the time my mobile rang the minibus had gone. I was back in the car and ready to do battle with the little miss.

'I wanted a car.' It was my client, the little miss's father. 'How long will you take to get to the North Greenwich Arena?'

'I'm waiting for you at North Greenwich Arena.'

'Five minutes.'

I kerb crawled along to the pickup area and verified my client's details to the Games Makers with the clipboard. There were no gasps of horror at either my rubbish pronunciation of the family's name or in relation to any reputation they may have acquired during the short time they had spent there. I was willing to put all prior tittle tattle about them behind me if they would oblige me with courtesy.

I saw them before they saw me. They bore all the hallmarks of a family who had spent a morning and afternoon together that they would rather forget, an experience that might seem better or worse depending on its re-telling in the months and years to come. The client's frazzled look was a look I had seen Roger wear on occasions. I could identify with the sore feet that the mother clearly had from the way she was hobbling in her high heels, and the sore arm too from the way the kid was yanking on it. They were a walking talking tinder box of disappointment and suppressed rage. I got out of the car. I smiled, introduced myself and mentally ticked off part one of my plan.

The plan, hastily cobbled together before they made their appearance, relied on a due but not sycophantic deference to the client, striking up cordial relations with the mother and communicating to the pretty little girl in the pretty little dress that I wasn't going to stand any nonsense from her.

The client was cold and correct with his response. That was fair enough. He'd had a stressful day. I tilted my head and gave a benevolent and admiring *what a lovely little girl* look first at their daughter and then at them. They weren't interested and he was irritated by my efforts to check if they wanted to put anything in the boot or assistance of any kind whatsoever. I was stonewalled by the mother and it occurred to me that I would probably have more chance of successfully walking backwards, unharnessed and blindfolded, over the Dome than I would of striking up any kind of relationship or rapport with her.

I left them to a heated discussion and slipped behind the steering wheel. The girl was helped into her car seat by her dad whilst her mother tottered round to get in the other side. In the moments before the adults got in I turned round and gave their precious princess a stare that Roald Dahl's Miss Trunchbull in Matilda would have found hard to beat. It would have served me right if either of the parents had caught me in the act or if the girl had started to blub, especially as I had no means of understanding what she might be saying about me. But whatever she had read into my flashing eyes and shaking head it worked because she was rendered speechless and worryingly rigid. The wife too maintained a grim silence, the only comment up for grabs was the father's sense of incredulity that we were only going a couple of miles, that it should only take us minutes, but a congested Blackwall Tunnel under Old Father Thames was impeding our progress. I did point out that there was the sky train gondola which would be fun and it sparked off some dialogue between them.

At our destination I turned round and the girl was still mute and immobile. I softened and smiled and the mother spoke through her husband to say she was leaving the seat in the back because they needed it for the evening.

'You require the car this evening?' I asked.

'We want you here to take us to the Olympic Stadium.'

I watched them as, tired and weary, they shambled across to their hotel. Dragging behind her mother, the little girl looked back at me. I gave her a little wave and hoped they would let her have a rest. Without a rest she'd be tired and teasy yet it was equally worrying that a fresh lease of life could make her troublesome. There was nothing for it. I had to get back to base, freshen up and get ready for round two.

We had been advised not to wear overpowering perfumes but I risked a floral spray and applied some fresh lipstick. With the hoo-ha about liquids I was surprised that they weren't sticky about bottles of perfume but, with my predilection for passing the time of day with the soldiers, I probably didn't notice the eau de perfume scanner. Neither had any comment been passed about my lipstick housed in a very pretty metal case with a mirror.

I arrived ten minutes early and parked outside the diner opposite the hotel, the diner where I had seen carpenters, painters, plasterers, electricians and all working their butts off to transform the empty retail unit into the thriving business it now looked to be. I was parked on red lines but no-one came over to move me on as there was already enough activity going on with umpteen vehicles arriving and manoeuvring in the tight space adjacent to the metal security barrier. And smart casual was the order of that August evening as guests came out of the hotels to take up London 2012 cars, taxis or sleek black people carriers.

Perfumed and lippied, I too felt I'd like to be 'going out on the town' and thought of the vow Rog and I make every summer, that we will make an effort to get out of a weekend evening, to walk the prom, to have a drink in the Old Town. But as easy as it is to make the vow, it is just as easily broken, just as easy as it was that evening for the man to break into the car and install himself in the front passenger seat.

'Good evening,' he said with a broad smile.

'Good evening,' I instinctively replied, instinctively wondered too whether he would benefit from the child's seat. Someone tapped on my window.

'Ah, there she is, I expect she's got some news. I'll sit here whilst you sort it out.' He snuggled his little bottom into the seat and I opened the door and got out leaving a total stranger in possession of the car. I carried my confusion well and smiled at the woman in uniform who stood in front of me. Under the guise of an apology for not being able to pronounce her name correctly, I looked at her accreditation tag. I'd never met an assistant assigned to individual sports delegations before but ran with the understanding that our two further passengers were bound to be running late.

'You know how children can be when they wake up after an afternoon sleep?' she said.

'Yes, I do, only too well!'

They arrived. I was ignored yet again by the mother, her smiles reserved for the assistant and my front seat passenger. The car filled with conversation as Jack, cute as a button with the zipper on his knitted jerkin done up, enquired as to everyone's health and wellbeing and expressed regret that the husband wasn't travelling with us. I nodded in agreement, wondering if he was lying in a darkened hotel room suffering from a stress induced migraine. I looked round and smiled at the girl who, strapped securely in her seat, looked as sweet as pie in her dress and cardi too.

'Could you please put your seat belt on?' I said to the mother, knowing how we can all get forgetful in the grip of chatter. She made no attempt to do it so I turned away, leant back in my seat and stared straight ahead at the umpteen other cars that were picking guests up. The engine was ticking over but our car was going nowhere. Jack looked at the watch on his chunky wrist. I repeated the request.

'Ready?' My eyes met hers in the mirror.

'Yes,' she spat. She had no time for me or me for her but fortunately Jack was adept at including each of us in turn in conversation. And he loved London and had heard of Hastings and he was so excited at what the evening held for them.

The queue of cars reached far back on the Park's loop road. I wound down the window to have a word with the young man directing the cars. He was flustered, poor love, because his clipboard said for us to go to one drop off point but the volume of traffic in front and behind us dictated another. We inched along to the brightly lit underbelly of the Olympic Stadium.

'I'll call you,' said Jack.

'And please allow five, ten minutes, for me to get here.'

'I know the drill.'

I watched my little group make their way through the ever growing crowd of people. It was bordering on mayhem, the Games Makers with the walkie talkies going hell for leather as they raced up and down the pavement trying to direct guests to the lifts and stairs that would take them up into the Stadium. There was an excitement, an anticipation of something historic in the air and whilst I couldn't see or hear them, I sensed the beating hearts of the tens of thousands people waiting above.

I was stopped from pulling away by a woman of the walkie talkie brigade.

'Can you point out your clients to me please?' The urgency in her voice suggested something was amiss. I bobbed, strained and stretched to see them.

'There, over there, by the column. The two ladies with bleached blonde hair and the small man and child. What's ...?'

'Don't move!' The woman scurried off and all sorts of scenarios ran through my mind, all scenarios brought about by my failure to double check their identity with my sheet. I knew the mother and child but wasn't it strange that the father, the client, wasn't with them? Had the girl and the car seat business simply been a ploy to distract me and my successor from detecting other aspects of their behaviour which would otherwise have been suspicious? How could I have got it so wrong about Jack? One minute I had been comparing him in my mind with Danny de Vito and the next....

The walkie talkie lady returned looking even more harassed than before. 'There's a problem.'

'Is there?' I looked across to the main area. My guests were nowhere to be seen. How could they have melted into the crowd so fast? Jack was small and strong, he could work in tandem with the girl and burrow through the air conditioning shafts and let off a noxious gas into the Stadium. On the gigantic TV screens the assistant would beguile the audience with her smile and calm manner and tell them all was well. For those who needed a little more persuasion, the facial expression that the mother had reserved for me would sublimally flash.

'It's heaving here tonight.'

'I can see that.' I could see also that her words might simply be a conversational piece, a softening up ploy before I was spirited away for questioning.

'There are too many people for the VIP Lounge. They are turning them away. Move along to the end and wait because you might have to take your clients back.'

'They won't be happy.'

'I don't suppose they will.'

Having been turned away from Wimbledon earlier in the day and now without husband/father, I started to feel sorry for mother and daughter and yet I wasn't going to have the blame pinned on me for being late arriving at the Stadium. The assistant should have worked out the times and the mother not taken so long in belting up. But I was happy to ease along to the far end of the Load Zone, switch the engine off and watch all the comings and goings. What a social affair it was. Behind me it was mainly the London 2012 cars with a few other shiny expensive vehicles, but in the reserved area up ahead the rollers and limousines alike came purring to a halt, discharging what I assumed were the higher echelons of the sporting world.

But there's always a few who want to spoil a party, who barrack and barge and demand to be let in. There was just such a scene going on in my rear view mirror. A group of agitated men were arguing with a couple of Games Makers by the entrance. Little by little they moved closer to the doorway as if practised at getting the better of bouncers, but not these dressed in red and purple bouncers who were doing it for free. No room at the Stadium or not, a few well heeled stragglers scurried in behind the Games Makers provoking more arm waving from the stroppy group.

I don't know how long it eventually took for the situation with the men to calm down or how long it would have been before I would have been directed away from the area but after ten minutes I decided to leave of my own accord. Along with the crowd in the Stadium overhead I too wanted to see the action. Drivers picking up from the Aquatics Centre or the Olympic Stadium were expected to park up at the Worlds Square Staging Area prior to being directed on by the Venue Staff. It made sense but in the case of the family Hazoza I had been saved from going there and now, perversely, I chose not to do so again. Instead I drove and parked in the T2 area of what was normally the Westfield Stratford car park and checked in with the Dispatchers at the Depot which consisted of two portakabins, one on top of each other.

I opened the door to a cacophony of chatter as row upon row of Games Makers lounged at white tables drinking tea or coffee. This was Chris's haunt on his visits to the Park but I didn't recognise anyone, I felt like a stranger in a foreign land. Then the room quietened, as all eyes turned to the TV screens showing the scene within the Stadium.

In years to come, when I relate how electric the atmosphere was in that portakabin on the night Usain Bolt tore through the finishing line to win the 100 metres Men's Final, I will probably embellish it by saying I heard the roar from the Stadium. I didn't of course but the Depot rocked with cheers and clapping and as I went back down the stairs to check out, my eyes misted over with the emotion of the occasion. Powered by the energy emitting from the Stadium I checked out and hurried back across to the car park. I tidied my hair and wiped away my smudged mascara whilst waiting for Jack's call. It wasn't long in coming. I hadn't thought it would be, not with the little one having had such a long day.

Inevitably the queue to the Stadium pick up point was as long as it had been before. Moving forward at a snail's pace I opened the window. The night air was saturated with the sound of engines running, car doors slamming and the Stadium belching its guests. And then I saw Jack at the front of his group waving to me as if greeting an old friend.

'Have you had a good evening?' I asked when he was snuggled in his seat.

'One of the best.'

CHAPTER 34

Feeding Solutions

Seen from the air that night, the Olympic Park would have been ablaze with the lights from the Stadium and the headlights from the procession of cars snaking bumper to bumper along the loop road. And passing air traffic would have felt the heat of the departing crowds, still high on the tension and excitement of the day's events. Then the magic was left behind as we spilled back into the traffic at Ruckholt Road and the Lea Interchange.

It was as busy on the A12 at ten thirty that night as it would have been during any day. The little girl dozed and I listened to the gossip bandied between Jack and the assistant. They seemed to go back a long way and relished the gossip that said a certain wife had been miffed that she hadn't got to sit where she wanted and another had had her nose put out of joint by not being invited at all. It was deliciously damning and though I didn't have a clue who they were talking about, it made me smile for it proved that people the world over are just the same.

There were queues everywhere, on the roads, outside the Hotel where I dropped them off and even to get into the VSA.

'Where've you been Ma'am?' asked the young soldier while we waited for the signal to proceed up to the checkpoint.

'The Stadium.'

'Did you see it, did you see Usain?'

'Only on the telly at the Depot.'

'Oh.' He sounded disappointed.

'Nine seconds, or whatever it was, was amazing wasn't it?'

'I did a hundred metres once in thirteen seconds.'

'My goodness.'

'I never liked reading and writing stuff at school but I liked sprinting.'

'Well done. Who knows, if you'd stuck at it you could have been up at that Stadium tonight.' I was sounding just like Mum again, could see the gangly youth cheered on from the sidelines as he burst through the finishing tape.

'No, Ma'am, I was never that good.' His words were laden with unfulfilled dreams and the split second moment of victory was lost as he waved me on and wished me goodnight.

Even allowing for the hour I had got back after my sojourn to Hadleigh Farm and Wembley, I had never been in the bunker as late as I was that night. I was tired, had no intention of staying very long but needed a reviver before setting off home. I poured myself a cup of coffee and picked out a couple of chocolates from one of the tins that had appeared in the wake of the Transport Director's visit.

Not wishing to appear offish I didn't sit at my usual table (it was empty anyhow) but wandered over to a table where a bit of plea bargaining was going on over the pickup of some exceptionally tall basketball clients. The height issue wasn't being discussed in a discriminatory way, more as a talking point of how height, weight and size could determine how many you could comfortably get into the vehicle. One driver had reported that it had been a squeeze to fit three weightlifters in a car and if my Mr Z had had travelling companions of similar build I would have had trouble seeing out of the back window. Jack, by contrast, was an ideal size; small and compact but I'd guessed not a lightweight either physically or in dealings with others. The size issue of the basketball player was also brought into focus because one of the parties to the negotiations was the petite, bubbly and savvy lady I had met in the car park on my first shift. Juvenile as it was, the encounter had sparked a pathetic and irrational jealousy that had been cemented by the rebuff I felt I later received when trying to help her with her paperwork. And it wasn't helped that she could effortlessly pirouette around the room without banging into tables or chairs whilst I still bore emotional scars of being called a baby elephant in relation to my childhood balletic qualities. Or was I simply envious of the way she used her feminine wiles to charm the gents, Bryn in particular. I watched and listened.

The deal was done, the downside and flipside of the negotiations mirrored in the faces of the parties.

I too needed to use negotiating skills in the tussle between me and myself as soon as I hit the A2 heading out of London. As if visions of large fluffy strawberry milkshakes weren't bad enough, the food devil blew the smell of thin and lightly salted fries through the air conditioning vents. I knew branching off onto the A20 had inherent dangers but I argued well and convincingly that I could prove more of a danger to myself and others if I didn't satisfy my fast food craving.

I knew there was a twenty four hour outlet in Orpington but couldn't get my bearings to work out how to get there. Houses, roundabouts, pedestrian crossings all flashed by. Tired and ludicrously ravenous, I thought I'd ring home and say I was checking into the next hotel I could find that had round the clock catering facilities. There were signposts for Lewisham and Catford and the A205. There was a restaurant in the middle of a road island but by the time I'd worked out where the entrance was I had taken the wrong lane and was borne away from the happy, self-satisfied diners. I suspected I was driving the reverse of a route that had caused me grief previously but in the dark everything and nothing was at once familiar and unfamiliar and, for all my grand posturing in the rear view mirror, I was too wimpish to take a right turn off the beaten track to a signposted fast food facility.

The unmistakable logo of all things seasoned, salsa and burgery came into view. It had taken possession of what I assumed had been a former pub. I slowed down. The place was in darkness and if that wasn't bad enough I realised I was back in Bromley. Bromley, Bromley, Bromley! What had I ever done to the people of Bromley for them to treat me this way? My hunger pangs had reached the point where I would have gladly licked a discarded greasy carton but I put my foot down and sped away, putting as much distance as quickly as I could between me and their suburban frontages.

My only hope lay at the Blue Boys roundabout. I knew the café, housed in the former pub, would be closed. But there was always the food in the chilled cabinets at the garage shop to fall back on and I was more than prepared to pay the gastric price of eating a micro waved macaroni cheese. I was salivating even as I locked the car. Undeterred by the sight of sparsely stocked refrigerated shelves in nightlight gloom, I made my way across the forecourt. The automatic doors stayed tightly shut but hope still raged within me when I made out the attendant at the other end of the store, I waved. I knew she had seen me but still the doors didn't open.

'Is it possible to come in?' I stood and looked at the woman through the glass at the night till counter.

'No.' Her dark eyes glinted in the subdued lighting.

'I'm starving.'

'At this time of night I can only take payments for fuel.'

'I don't need any fuel but would you be able to get me something to eat. A packet of Quavers and a bar of chocolate would do.' I pointed through the glass to where I knew they lay. There were no other cars, no-one else waiting to be served. It would only take her ten seconds and I hardly looked like a smash and grab a night-safe felon.

'Fuel only.'

I contemplated shredding the roll of paper used to wipe up fuel spillages and stuffing it through the payment hatch then kicking over the rubbish bin for good measure. The sourpuss would have loved that but I had a uniform to live up to. Yes, a blasted uniform, and as the CCTV cameras caught me stomping back to the car with a scowl and the footfall of an adult elephant, there was one person that came to mind. It wasn't the little girl I'd petrified to stay still in her car seat, not jolly Jack of rippling muscles under zippered cardigan fame, nor the victorious Usain Bolt, the sprinter soldier or the pirouetting pragmatist. No, it was the Director of Transport tucked up in bed with a tin of sweets whilst the paperwork on the challenges to feeding solutions was laid out on his swanky desk. And as the Sussex countryside swept by me I wished him a sleepless goodnight.

Chapter 35

Fair Warning

It was four fifteen in the morning. I was on my way to my next shift but stood by the counter in an establishment on the edges of Hurst Green. When I later retold the story at home I gave it all the hallmarks of a Bates Motel scene though there wasn't a motel in sight and the unscheduled stop wasn't caused by a broken down vehicle. That's not to say that my little car, with its defunct speedometer, faulty connection to the brake lights and rattles and clunks from the rear axle, wasn't the worse for wear.

Nothing spectacular had occurred as I made my way up the A21. The traffic had mainly consisted of lorries, their sides emblazoned with the supermarket names that competed to empty the pockets of the communities of Hastings, Battle and Robertsbridge that I had left behind in my wake. I drove unhindered through Hurst Green and had had no intention of stopping until a little voice in my head told me to slow down just in case the sign up ahead signified twenty-four opening.

Standing by the car on the deserted forecourt I saw that, despite the promise that the illuminated sign had held out, a notice on the wall next to the night payment till said after twenty-two hours p.m. customers had to make payment first before filling up with fuel. Despite the car's suspect fuel gauge readings I had no cause to top up my tank and despite the experience of a few nights' previously I walked over to the night hatch.

I peered through the window. There was no-one about but, as the thought struck that I would need to draft a complaint to the managing director of the company, I spied way off through an open door into an office the figure of a man slumped in a chair at a desk. His back to me, a reading lamp cast light on a newspaper before him. I tapped on the glass. He didn't move. I banged on the glass. There was no reaction whatsoever and, the fault of me watching too many films, it crossed my mind that he was ill or had died reading the lurid detail of a first edition news story. Even from a distance I could tell he was no spring chicken. Working at night might have taken its toll. Or had he been attacked? The thought that the perpetrator was rifling the safe in another part of the office, the getaway car round the back where the tyre pressure gauges and water facility were housed, gathered force. If I hung around much longer would the next thing I saw be a raider wielding a weapon in one hand and a swag bag in the other. It would be absolute folly to play a part in such a drama but I couldn't just let the man in the chair be and run the risk of another journey haunted by mirages. I saw a bell and pressed it. It rang out clear as anything and he jumped in his seat. I jumped too then laughed with relief. He swung round in the seat to see who it was. I gave him a jolly Games Makers wave and smile and he came rushing up to the hatch.

'Morning. You can use the main doors you know.'

'Can I?'

We stood either side of the counter inside the shop.

'You're starting early,' he said as, all fingers and thumbs, I fumbled in my purse.

'I'm sorry about this,' I gave him an apologetic smile for having to scrape together the sum illuminated in green on his till. He raised his eyebrows and his hand hovered protectively over the objects of my desire. I wondered if he really believed that I would besmirch the reputation of the Olympic movement and snatch them purely to satisfy a craving.

'I hope you've forgiven me for ringing the bell just now.'

'Think nothing of it.'

'It's not that I've got a problem.' I handed him the money.

'No, of course not.' He looked over the top of his glasses and handed me my goodies and though at that hour he probably wanted to go back to his newspaper, I bombarded him with the story of my late night experience with the woman ten miles up the road a few nights previously, bemoaning my growing dependency and waistline and expressing over exuberant delight that the shop was so well kept stocked with just what I wanted. My purchase made, I put my purse away.

'If you get stuck anytime during the night and the doors aren't open just ring the bell and I'll bring anything you want to the hatch.'

'That's kind, thank you but I can't see I'll need anything. These are only emergency supplies.'

I deceived myself because I was barely past the next garage, where the unhelpful, 'only doing her job', woman hung out, and I ripped open the packet of Quavers. I'm also thinking back to the argument I used on a dour Scotsman in an Edinburgh off licence many years before. I should have cottoned on then that Roger prefers a non speaking part in negotiations because he stood outside the 'offy' looking very sheepish and suspicious whilst inside I tried to persuade the licensee to open the bottle of wine we had scraped the money together to buy. The Scot said it would be against the terms of his licence to open it but he'd sell me a corkscrew. I'd looked in my purse and shaken my head. 'I could use a knife,' I'd thought out loud and he'd thrust the bottle of wine at me and ushered me to the door. Cast out in such a fashion, feeling the licensee's eyes upon us we knew what it must feel like to be seen as a couple of dossers desperate for a drink. We had made our way back to our tent, pitched within sight of the Firth of Forth Bridge. The wine had given us sustenance to get us through a cold and sleepless night just as my sweet and savoury treats were going to give me the spurt to walk across the bridge to Excel.

From my first triumphal walk on that bridge until the last I always had to focus on someone up ahead. That morning it was a portly man in Games Makers uniform. He looked back at me a couple of times and was waiting for me at the top of the steps.

'Are you going to Fleet Depot Excel?' he asked in a strong Irish accent.

'I am.'

'They've sent me over to help out.'

'I don't think we need any help.' I thought of the fireworks there would be if one of the ladies I had been talking to on my last shift heard he'd been drafted in. She had been verging on the apoplectic because she had had no clients and had stormed off to give Bryn an ultimatum. If he couldn't find her a client she was going to throw in the towel. Perhaps she had done as she had threatened hence the need for my walking companion that morning. Others had made it quite plain that they would only drive the same client throughout the Games and were steadfast in their resolve that they would down ice bag and leave for good if they were allocated to anybody else. Brenda, one of the two ladies on our table, was a case in point. I never had the gumption to make demands and equally, for all my weasly words, something particularly dire would have had to happen to make me quit.

Anyway, the Irish fellow and I walked on and I prattled on about the beautiful sunrises I had captured on camera. At the security screening tent he took exception to some procedure that differed from the one he was used to and I made a joke of it to pass it off. We headed down the slope and he said he'd heard that the food wasn't that good at Excel and he'd have something to say about it if he didn't like it.

'The food's fine.'

'I'm getting out on the road as soon as I can.'

'You are? I don't think you'll get much choice in the matter.'

'Well I'm not travelling all the way from Kilburn at this time in the morning to do nothing.'

'I don't blame you.' I left him at the check-in desk and sped through into the bunker, hoping he'd find another person to demonstrate the technique of how to go onto someone else's patch and find everything wrong with it. When I saw him marching towards the drinks station I didn't rush over and invite him to join Allan and me at our table because a breakfast bap in his company would not ease either of us into the day. And I wasn't sufficiently interested in keeping an eye on whether he did get a client because after my hot enhancement I had to get out on the road.

I had been assigned to Mr. Z again. It was an ordinary working day and there were Olympic events taking place on certain roads. Potentially there could be problems but I decided not to devise alternative plans. I didn't necessarily need Helga but if there were diversions and hold ups it would be good to have her on board and such was my mood I decided I would go whither Helga sent me without dissent. The traffic was slow along Aspen Way and The Highway. Tower Gateway was the usual free for all and Upper and Lower Thames Street enabled a good dekko at what to wear when going to work in the City. Black or grey with an intent frazzled look seemed to be the fashion.

Even allowing for the shutting down of some streets, I'd assumed I'd re-run the route I'd taken Mr H and family on, that is, along the Embankment until Westminster and then the twiddly fiddly bits past Birdcage Walk. However, coming under Waterloo Bridge I received instructions to turn right. Had Helga caught wind of something else that I had not been aware of prior to my departure? It was new territory and I tagged on behind a white van. With my bonnet nudging into the Strand I felt like a bunny popping its nose out of a burrow and was startled into joining the flow of traffic by the man behind beeping at me.

The Strand was busy, the pavements getting a pounding from people hurrying about their business. I too had trodden those pavements, carrying a bag laden with files and law books to and from Charing Cross Station to Chancery Lane. And I often think of the man who always got on the train at Etchingham in the mornings and would take up the seat next to mine. He was a surveyor or engineer, with wavy hair, purple and red broken veins on his face and had lived abroad a good part of his life. It helped that he was small and didn't mind my large bag edging onto his lap. Our passing acquaintanceship was a strange old business because I never knew his name nor he mine and even though I have a pretty good memory I can't remember one thing we talked about and yet talk we did until our paths stopped crossing.

Charing Cross Station came into sight. I incurred the wrath of the bus behind me as I slowed prematurely at the lights, reliving, as I was, the moment when Roger first met Mum and Dad. It was in the days when you could park immediately outside the Station. It had been so hurried and heated. Mum, unusually lost for words, kept her eyes glued on Roger's long Pre-Raphaelite locks. Dad grudgingly shook Roger's hand and made a big thing of shunning his help to get my suitcase out of his boot and into Roger's Vauxhall Viva.

'We'll be off now. Come on, Berry, get in the car.'

'But I thought we could go for a cup of tea,' I said, looking over to the Lyons Corner House perched between Duncannon Street and the Strand.

'No time for that. I've told Jim and Ena we'd be with them by four o'clock,' Dad growled, looking at his watch. 'And if we don't go now we'll get stuck in the rush hour.'

'I've never seen anything like such traffic,' said Mum, edging past Rog to give me a kiss goodbye. I burst into tears.

Waiting at the traffic lights, I saw that scene played out behind the wrought iron railings as clear as day and reflected on how Dad and I had parted on bad terms and how my first evening with Roger's family had been interrupted by my flight to the phone booth to ring Jim and Ena's number to try and make it up with him. And the traffic behind, for all its honking horns, couldn't stop me fast forwarding two years on to Dad, at our wedding, referring to my waterworks in the Strand, those salty tears convincing him that he had met his future son-in-law. Everyone laughed and Mum was joyous too, her pre-wedding sleepless nights assuaged because Rog had cut his locks off for the big day and finally looked respectable.

The lights changed and I was forced to abandon my recollections of our modest wedding as the traffic started pushing and pulling me towards St Martin's Lane. I went into survival mode in order to withstand the bullying tactics of taxis and coaches in Trafalgar Square. And Dad was back with me, puffing and sucking air through his teeth at perceived near misses. How Dad had ever coped with the rush and tear of London traffic was beyond me but he had been much younger then, even younger than I was now as I drove along Pall Mall, up St James Street to Piccadilly. He hadn't reached the crotchety stage, the stage when Mum sometimes dreaded getting in the car with him because he would rail against the traffic lights turning to red just to spite him or complain about women parking at any old angle or speeding youngsters cutting in front of him. And it didn't help that I used to voice my frustration at his impatience and tell him to wait for the blower to demist the windscreen rather than wipe it with the back of his gloved hand. Now I have friends who complain that there is no pleasure in going out in the car with their husbands and I've noticed that Roger too is becoming more vocal about road and weather conditions. Helga told me to turn into Dover Street and, as can happen in unexpected times and places, an unassailable truth flew through the windscreen at me. The truth was that when Dad's death sentence was pronounced in whatever cosy jargon his Doctor framed it, he got rid of the car, his beloved Mitsubishi with all its gadgetry. 'I won't need it. It's downhill all the way now, kid.'

There weren't many, there weren't any, thirty year old Mitsubishi's in Berkeley Square or in any of the surrounding streets. It was a good job too because the sight of one might have had me careering off in completely the wrong direction. It was enough to have to contend with the one way systems, diversions and mini road blocks that popped up wherever I went. Dizzy and disorientated, I finally made it out into the upper section of Park Lane.

I waited in Grosvenor Square a good ten minutes before coasting round to the front of the Hotel. My client was nowhere to be seen but I watched Mr Hazoza with his wife and grandson heading for the car that had pulled up behind me. I took comfort from the fact that my former clients had no picnic basket or parasols so they weren't heading out for a day in Richmond Park or the like and I didn't recognise the driver as someone from the Depot. It was their loss as the car pulled out and drove past me.

My eye was taken with a man casually dressed in a long raincoat going into a shop opposite the Hotel. I knew him from somewhere. I wracked my brains as to whether he was from Hastings or a Games Makers in civvies? He came out of the shop. He was someone you wouldn't forget in a hurry and I had half a mind to get out of the car and loiter in the hope that whatever the connection was between us, he might remember it too. Then it came to me. It was Bates, Bates from Downtown Abbey and

I laughed at what a fool I might have made of myself when my phone started ringing.

Mr. Z was checking where I was. He muttered something about coming earlier but what that was about I didn't know because after five minutes he still hadn't showed. With certainly more authority and confidence than I'd had on my first visit I waited for him in the foyer. When he appeared he looked as if he had dressed hurriedly. I walked towards him with a welcoming smile but it did nothing for my ego that he was distinctly hazy about who I was.

'We've met before,' I told him. 'You gave me a medal.' He laughed and I suspected he was lying through his teeth when he said he remembered. He fleetingly held my arm, an act that I didn't associate with the natural reserve of his fellow countrymen. I took no offence even though a little bit of the revolutionary in me said to check in the Handbook as to whether there was one rule for the bosses and one for the workers. Wasn't it ever thus?

The traffic was really bad and painfully slow in Tottenham Court Road. There were no signs of it abating in Euston Road as we discussed what an exciting city London was. He said he'd observed how over populated it had become. I puffed loudly at the plague of cyclists who had appeared as out of nowhere and surrounded us near Kings Cross. I mumbled again as they all inched forward and, when the lights changed, took off, criss crossing in front of me, some standing up in the pedals, others poking their backsides in the air.

'Cyclists!' I fumed. 'They are so dangerous.'

'I'm used to them,' he replied.

'Are you?' I was concentrating hard on not knocking one over as he swung out in front of me from behind a bus in Pentonville Road.

'Yes, Beijing has lots of cyclists.'

'Oh, this is nothing then,' I laughed, feeling such a fool as he gave voice to the TV images of a city teeming with thousands of cyclists. By then we'd reached the traffic lights at Angel and I rolled straight ahead and down into City Road. Helga said to get into the right- hand lane. I complied but it wasn't really what she meant or, rather, I didn't go where she intended me to go or did I?

I've beaten myself up unnecessarily about it ever since but, as I told myself at the time, decisions are made in an instant and so I followed the road into Wakley Street then into Goswell Street. Mr Z didn't say a word. Perhaps he hadn't noticed that we were back at the Angel traffic lights, now sitting opposite the road where two minutes earlier we had been coming from the other direction.

Wasn't I glad that I had circumnavigated Highbury Corner several times on my training drives because I might have been in a bit of a spin otherwise? I wasn't so glad that, instead of taking Graham Road and Morning Lane, I followed the road round in Dalston Lane but at least I knew about the tricky junction with Pembury Road and got on to Urswick Road. It could have been the sight of Hackney Marsh or the security men setting up signs for a twenty mile an hour speed limit on Homerton High Street that prompted him to ask if we were on an Olympic Route.

'Yes,' I said confidently but I'd only had Helga's word for that previously. However the ends justified the means because, unless he was just thoroughly relieved or being kind, when we got to the Eton Manor VSA he commented that we had only taken an hour to get there.

'Sometimes it's taken two hours.'

'Oh dear,' I said, in condescending fashion when really I should have mounted a stout defence of my colleagues' performances, come clean that there was no way of knowing if the 'detour' we had taken had been longer than if I'd stuck to the official route network. But whether it was an hour's journey or two I sensed he wanted to get there.

'What are those men doing?' he asked as we motored along on the loop road.

'I don't know.' I slowed and one of them raised his hand to stop me going any further.

'What is happening?' I heard the tremor in Mr. Z's voice.

'I'm not sure.' I had a pretty good idea as I wound the window down.

'Do you know what speed you were going, Madam?' The question from the man peeking in through the window was innocent enough but my blank face and lack of response was anything but. 'You were doing thirty.'

'I told her to go fast,' Mr. Z called over to the man. My client's representations did nothing to dissuade the man from asking to see my accreditation card whilst the other checked his radar gun. 'I have a meeting to get to.'

I thought of shooting off in the car with a shouted promise to return but all Mr. Z and I could do was watch on helplessly as the first man wrote out an Olympic Park Enforcement Notice. He handed me the yellow Offenders Copy. The transaction was conducted in the most civil and friendly of fashion, as was the giving of the warning that if I was issued with another I would be prohibited from entering the Olympic Park.

I drove on and my client, shaking his head and waving his hands, gave the impression that he thought the speed limit and the imposition of notices a matter of British eccentricity. I made light of the whole affair, anxious that I had made him late for his meeting.

After a courteous farewell I watched him scoot off pretty damned quickly to the lift. He hadn't given any indication of when he wanted to be picked up but I figured the least I could do in recompense for any apologies he had to give his fellow delegates was to have the car clean and sparkling for his return journey. It would also serve to while away some time that would otherwise be spent in the bunker.

I chose to follow the advice that had been imparted by Florence as to which was the best of the bunch of the local petrol stations. From the number of London 2012 cars at the pumps it was a popular choice. I went the whole hog and filled up with diesel before negotiating the tight turn into the car wash. I pressed the code into the machine, let the handbrake off, went into neutral gear and gently turned the steering wheel so as to line the car up between the metal rails.

In the preceding weeks I'd learnt a lot about London. Fast paced were words that always came to mind and even the car wash was intolerant of dawdlers. Much quicker than I expected there was movement beneath me. There was a bump and a bang and it didn't feel as if the rear driver's wheel had slotted into the groove but even out of kilter the washer was drawing me inside. Within seconds the car was under attack from the forces of foam and an aerial bombardment of water on the roof. This was the prelude, the softening up before the rotating brushes began their pummelling, the car shuddering and rocking with every blow. The deafening noise didn't help me try to unscramble my fear and sense of desperation as, in horror, I saw a menacing T shaped metal bar drop down and come towards me. I was frightened, seriously frightened because with the car to my mind listing at an angle the T bar was heading straight for the windscreen. I picked up my phone. There was no signal and even if there was by the time I rang someone the likelihood was that they'd be responding to a pulp. My eyes, misting over in panic, couldn't see where the horn was and, anyway, would it work without the engine on? If I switched the engine on would I get electrocuted? Was electrocution preferable to a peppering by a thousand shards of glass? Why not get out and abandon the car full stop? An altercation with a crowd of wet brushes pressed up uncomfortably close put paid to that idea. I could scream all I wanted; no one would hear me over the sound of high volume blowers which had now started up. No movie sound effect could have been better employed to ratchet up the tension as the T bar inched inexorably closer. Having always protested my opposition to the Orwellian age of the camera snoops in which we live, I was praying that the man in the garage had a camera trained on the car wash and, recognising my plight, was going to press a button and avert the inevitable super dry carnage.

I looked in the mirror. Fate had decreed that there wouldn't be any cars lined up behind me to cotton on to what was happening. It was probably a good thing, some poor soul saved from witnessing my grisly end. I ducked down, counting off the seconds, clutching at the thought that the speed, momentum and strength of the T would be powerless against the immovable force of German engineering and toughened glass. But what if, thwarted in its initial mission against the windscreen, the T took on the form of a battering ram, the sound of its relentless pounding to be taken by others filling up their petrol tanks as a sign of thorough cleaning and not the result of a glitch caused by my misguided alignment of wheels. I held my breath, my head filled with a vision of newspapers spinning round and round like in an Orson Welles film, with only a glimpse caught of a non- descript car wash in Newham. What would the headlines say about the ghastly accident? What comment would Seb, Boris or the diaphanous Dave make about it?

It wasn't a plague of locusts, a Twister or a desert sand storm but I sure as crazy knew how people felt as they cowered from catastrophe. And I also knew the sense of elation and the urge to thank someone, even a being from above, for being spared when I felt the T alter its angle of trajectory and pass over the car. And I shook, as did the car, as powerful blasts of air bombarded the paintwork leaving only the hardiest of water droplets on the logo that I had come so close to disgracing. Adoration and supplication was due to the designers of the car- wash who, allowing for every make and measurement of vehicle size and possible miscalculation by drivers had cared for me as one of their own. I'd learnt my lesson and thanked the rails beneath my wheels for easing my passage back into the outside world.

I was as composed as anyone can be by the time I drove the car into the VSA at Excel. Creature of habit, I always used the same one though there was another one at the other Exit. I'd tried it once, admitting to my novice status and that it would take a bit of getting used to to the security guy who was directing cars up the ramp into the car park. 'Nah, it won't,' he said. 'You make sure you come back to this one. We're much nicer than that other lot.' I never went back, never got into the realms of working out who was what in the niceness stakes because I was comfortable as it was with 'my boys'.

One of the boys that day was a tall skinny lad with a fair and freckly face. We were standing together waiting for the all clear on the car.

'I don't want to be rude but can I ask you something, Ma'am?'
'Of course you can.'

He nodded at my midriff and I instinctively looked at it too, wondering for the life of me what he was going to say next.

'What do all the stamps mean on the back of your accreditation card? I asked the lady in that car but she said she couldn't tell me.'

'What? She couldn't tell you?' I made one of Mum's 'Lady Muck' faces in the direction of the disappearing car.

'Do you remember at school that you got stars or merit points or certificates for being good?' From the look of him I surmised that he had been at school not that many years before.

'Him? A good lad?' said another laughing at the suggestion.

'You did, didn't you?' I looked over the top of my glasses at the freckly lad. Forced to admit it, his cheeks pinked up and his mate laughed even louder.

'The stamps are the same thing for being good and turning up and they've given me rubber bracelets and pins. It's been like getting a toy at McDonald's but I'm a bit too old for all of that.'

'You're not that old.'

'No, Ma'am, you're not,' joined in the other one, the one I would have said had been a cheeky one at school. 'You could sell them on eBay and your red watch. The watches are going for a right price especially if they haven't been worn.'

'I'm going to put a bid in for some of the stuff from the Olympic Village that's being sold,' said the freckly one. 'It's all going cheap.'

Whereas in the early days I had conjured up my own ghosts and spooks to jump out at me from the gloom, since the Games began the organisers had provided sentries to sit in fold-up picnic chairs at various points of the car park. They weren't Games Makers. I assumed from their black and green uniforms that they were security bods. It was a dull job and a reminder to me that I had been extremely lucky in being a volunteer and having duties that got me out and about. But getting me out and about had now got me in a spot of bother and I had cause to consider whether I ought to tell the Dispatchers about my speeding ticket. Was it going to make a jot of difference to anything? Would they already know because wasn't it more than likely that the men who had jumped out and surprised Mr. Z and I were as quick on sending emails to the Fleet Depot as they were trigger happy? My mind preoccupied with whether an admission would disbar me from driving again, I didn't see the security woman jump out of her picnic chair to wave me in the right direction. At five miles an hour I would have inflicted little damage but was I glad when I reached the safe harbour of my parking space.

'You do know that your front nearside light isn't working don't you?' a fellow Games Makers who had just parked his car called over to me as I was getting out of mine. 'I don't think the glass is smashed,' he said kneeling down to look. I wondered if it had anything to do with the car wash. Was this another admission I'd need to make at the desk? 'No, it must be the bulb.'

'Are you sure it isn't working?' I really couldn't see anything wrong at all with the lights.

'You better report it so the workshop people can check on it.'

The Director of Transport's words about the slow uptake of cars had reached the Evening Standard and his word in the ear of a leading sponsor was still working wonders because you couldn't get to fill your plastic cup with coffee without being accosted by an éclair or caramel from the sweet tins that seemed to be regularly refilled or replaced. I sat with Florence and Tracey, Tracey one of the paid staff who looked after the cars. People came and went and we chatted about cars and holidays and children and whatever took our fancy and was it the mix of people, the uniform, the bunker, the knowledge that ultimately we would all go our separate ways which set our tongues off loose and free?

'Has anyone checked the car?' I asked Pauline. I was about to depart but I needed to know that Mr. Z would be safe that evening.

'They couldn't find anything wrong with it. You must have been looking at it from a different angle or in a funny light.'

'The story of my life!'

Minutes later, I was walking across the bridge.

'The bridge?' There was genuine surprise in Colin's voice at the other end of my mobile phone. I told him about my concern at being late a few days earlier and how I had steeled myself to master my fear and had been walking over it ever since even though, as then, I didn't necessarily have to because I had finished my shift.

'Well done.' There was such sincerity in his voice that I grew a couple of inches then asked him if the rumour was true that he wouldn't be coming back again. It was, and I could tell from his tone that he was upset and disappointed that there had been no extra shifts available and that things hadn't worked out as he had planned.

'But I'm looking forward to my driving role during the Paralympics Games. Are you down for them as well?'

'No, I'm not. I don't think I'd have the energy.'

Truth be told I hadn't given the Paralympics much thought, thinking of the two Games more in the vein of either/or, though, after all the training etc, it would have made sense to do them. It wasn't as if I didn't have the time but I did have Frank to think about and soon it would be the run up to the annual One for the Road Club meeting and preparation for September birthdays. Frank indeed was a worry to me because, apart from some writing when I stayed in the Hotel and some minor scribbling in the bunker, the poor man had been left out in the shade. There was no excuse for it. Was I a serious writer or not?

But there was truth in my comment about energy, a truth that was to become apparent on my journey home that afternoon. Bunker sweets, topped up by a bar of chocolate from the shop on the other side of the bridge did nothing to keep my eyelids from drooping on the A21. I kept biting my lip and gripped the steering wheel till the whites of my knuckles showed to keep me awake. A couple of times I shook myself because I couldn't recollect where I was or how I'd got to a particular bend or stretch of road and knew if I carried on much longer I'd end up slewed across the road. But even then I didn't take up the opportunity of some spacious lay-bys, dismissing them as unsuitable because I didn't want to be by the side of a dual carriageway or share it with a load of truckers having a good gas. I motored on, alternately going fast and then slow as waves of tiredness washed over me. It was bad and I was mad to go on.

A little way on past Pembury I pulled into a lay-by and parked up behind a dirty and dusty open topped lorry. I turned off the engine, locked the doors and wound the window down a fraction. The last I heard, the last I saw, was the lorry rumbling its way back onto the road.

My eyes sprung open at the sound of a giant snore from the underworld. I closed my mouth and wiped the dribble from its corners. Completely disorientated I couldn't work out where I was or how I'd got there. The road was eerily deserted, no cars passing in either direction. I fleetingly thought of what I would do if it came to be that I was the only person left on a lonely road after a cataclysmic disaster.

What tricks an early morning start, an overdose of chocolate and a near death experience in a car wash can play on you.

CHAPTER 36

If Only George had been there

'Do you think it's going to be like this in the nursing home?' I asked Allan as pink eyed, yawning colleagues shuffled into the bunker.

'What nursing home?'

'The nursing homes we are likely to end up in. They'll get us up early and there won't be anything else to do in the day room except to watch others coming and going.'

'I'm not thinking about things like that yet.'

'And we'll get confused with people's names and get embroiled in mistaken identities. I've done it already, the other day with the lady called Ruth.'

'You've got your children to care for you in old age.'

I told him they might not be able to, might not even want to if I was a right handful and asked if the prospect of what might happen in the future concerned him.

'Have you had something to eat this morning, Carol? We could be busy today.'

I laughed, thinking back to a conversation I'd had with Roger one evening when giving him a précis of a day's events and who was who and what was what.

'I have to smile to myself at Allan sometimes, Rog'

'Why?'

'He's ever so quiet and unassuming and then he comes up with his reminders for me to keep an eye on the time to make sure I'm not late for a pick up and tells me that I mustn't forget the paperwork. I keep debating whether to tell him that I've got one like him at home.'

'I expect he's only trying to help!'

'I know and I don't mind. He's probably like it with everyone or perhaps he's like it with me because he thinks I'm a bit dippy.'

'Don't be ridiculous. How have you managed to jump to that conclusion?'

'I don't know. Perhaps we extract different responses from people from the way we project ourselves or do we project a different persona in response to the other person?'

'I don't know,' he shook his head. 'You are what you are. There's no point over analysing everything and saying what if this or what if that.'

'That's what he'd say.'

'And don't forget your ice bag tomorrow.'

'Grrr!'

On that early morning of my thirteenth shift Allan was more concerned with the here and now, more precisely the next few hours during which he had a job lined up for Luton airport. And with his take on the world I didn't imagine that if he had been in my shoes he would have given a moment's thought to whether my lack of an allocated client was due to my having got a speeding ticket on the previous shift. I'd said not a word to anyone about it but I suspected it more than likely that the Olympic Park's Big Brother, Big Sister and possibly the lovely Mr. Z had tipped the wink to Bryn and Tommy the Beard. I knew of people having been blackballed at Golf Clubs and adverse publicity being squashed by the hand of Brotherhoods so no-one was immune to their lives being affected by the 'quiet word.'

Of course it was nonsensical to think that I was the only one singled out because, looking around, there were more people than usual in the bunker. In one way that wasn't unexpected because with the Closing Ceremony only a day or so away many events had been completed. Allan and I with a couple of others had taken a stroll round Excel on a previous shift to find a lot of packing up going on and I'd bumped into Costos who said the T3's hadn't been that busy but were gearing up for a mass exodus from the

Capital. On the other hand I had visions of the delegates wanting to get their last minute shopping or sightseeing done. I thought of the Hazoza trio and whether they were taking a boat trip along the Thames that day even though there was still much in the way of diving going on at the Aquatics Centre.

'Have you got a ticket for the Closing Ceremony, Carol?' asked Allan.

'No. Have you?' I thought back to Mandy who had been on our table way back on the first day of the Olympics and how pleased as punch she had been at getting a ticket for it and all the family issues it had brought up in her.

'No. What are your plans for the weekend?'

'Nothing thrilling. I'm debating whether to go to a local village Fayre this afternoon but it's more a question what I do between now and then.'

The question had barely left my lips when the answer came in the shape and presence of Will who slid into the chair opposite me. I was genuinely pleased to see him though he gave no indication of having previously made my acquaintance, back in the dim and distant past of the first training day when we had ended up sitting on the same concrete bench eating our lunch together on the dockside. On that occasion his longish white hair and black printed T shirt declaring an allegiance to a rock band (or was it something gothic?) had me thinking he was an old hippy who'd spent his life fighting good and wholesome causes on behalf of the weak and oppressed. I'd leapt to that assumption because, as we munched through our food, he had impressed me with his authoritative opinion on the collective psyche of volunteers, and his C.V. of volunteering activities.

'Good morning all,' said Will in the easy way of those who can slip into any situation or conversation. 'I've got something for you.' He reached into his official Games Makers bag though I recalled he was more of a natural fibre devotee. Giles sat down beside him. Will handed each of us a narrow slip of paper, explaining that it contained details of the computer blog he had set up. He invited us to have a look at it at our leisure and add our experiences to it.

'Good idea,' I said, wondering how you set up a blog and itching to find out what he had put on it.

'Anyone fancy a game?' He reached into his bag again, pulled out a cardboard tube and tipped a series of lettered dice out.

'What kind of game is it?' Giles asked.

'It's along the lines of Scrabble but you can change your letters.'

Allan declined the invitation to play on the grounds he expected to be going out shortly though I gained the impression he wasn't really up for it anyway.

'I'm not good at Scrabble,' I confessed. 'It's a standing joke with some friends that I never win and no matter how many times they explain it to me I always end up asking the same question on one of the scoring rules.'

'You'll get the hang of it,' said Will. He went first but was clearly disappointed with his score which, in double figures, I thought was fine. Giles improved on it by a creditable twenty.

'I expect I'll be hopeless,' I said, jiggling the dice in my hand.

'We'll never know unless you throw them,' said Giles.

I went into triple figures and scored one hundred and thirty six.

'That was a fluke,' I laughed.

'Good show.' Will scratched his head in contemplation and threw the dice. There was little improvement on his existing score. Giles was consistent with his and I came up trumps again.

"I'm no good at games. I'm hopeless' or so she says.' Giles put on a whingey whiney voice, a voice in which I caught an echo of George, another mimic from years past, who would just as easily have sat there playing games, chewing the fat of the day and making me laugh as Giles, intentionally or unintentionally, did. As the dice rolled, the scores were noted down and Giles waxed lyrical on the availability and cost effectiveness of hiring Zip cars on a daily basis. I thought back to George.

We had been thrown together as co-pupils in a writers' class. I've still got a group photo; all of us huddled as close as one would respectfully get by the back wall of a Victorian schoolroom now part of a community centre. In the photo an unsmiling George dressed in jogging bottoms and T-shirt and standing inches above most, stares through his glasses at the camera. And 'he be long headed' was the complimentary West country expression Mum would have applied to George, not only on account of his intelligence but also for the fact of his high bald pate bordered by side pieces of black hair. Alan Fisher took the photo but never appeared in one with us. Alan; our tutor, our mentor, our hero, the holder of a Georgette Heyer prize for a novel set in St Petersburg, a St Petersburg Alan had never been to but had reconstructed, street by street, on a blackboard. And neither did we have a photo taken of David Gemmell, Alan's friend, mentor, hero and author of thirty four successful novels who came to talk to us, and about whom George wrote a skit in relation to the hidden power of David's wide belt. For George could do that, could see the potential writing possibilities in everything and, despite him reducing me to helpless laughter in class, in coffee breaks and on Saturday workshops he held a mirror up to what I had written, exposing the parts that were unintelligible, digging deep into the action and emotion that I hinted at but was too inexperienced to know how to express, or too reticent to reveal. Are reflections in the mirror what you truly see, what you want to see or what you think you see?

'What do you do in real life?' I had asked him one day.

'Guess.'

'I can't.'

'You can.'

I came up with three guesses, placing great store on the fact that he lived in the Old Town and wore an assortment of T-shirts with logos and designs commemorating groups on them, and not one did he acknowledge as being even close to the mark.

'I'm an Accountant.'

'You can't be.' My laughter reached up to the high ceiling.

'Why not?'

'Come on, be serious.'

'I am. I'm being deadly serious.' And he was the first person ever who explained how and why being an Accountant could be interesting, how it enabled him to play detective, apply forensic skills to figures just as some of the authors he admired had their characters do in their novels. That was George, giving a twist, changing one's perspective, always full of surprises.

Giles tapped his fingers on the table whilst Will tried to come up with a word. Would George have done that? What would George have said about my being a Games Maker? What would he have said about Frank who had been pretty much shelved in the weeks leading up to and during the Games? Would he rightly have accused me of taking up the call of duty to Seb as a tactic to divert me from cracking on and editing Frank to the point of no return on the publishing front? Or would he have seen the experience as a rich source of writing material, a chance to put where I was in some sort of context. As Giles and I waited no end of time for Will to select his letters, it came as a matter of some regret that George had had no knowledge of Frank, Frank having walked into my life some time after our last communication.

The communication hadn't been pretty. At the beginning of the call I had laughed at the way he said he had rung because he couldn't contain himself any longer.

'It's not funny, Carol. I need to speak my mind because I'm sick to death of the way you carry on.' My laughter subsided as he told me that he was heartily sick of my pathetic weasel words of not having any ability to write, of never daring to dream that I might try and get something published. 'Stop fannying about. Get on and do it. You only get one chance.' The call had ended quite civilly, even with a suggestion that we'd meet soon for another lunch but underneath I was stunned and shocked to think that he'd spoken to me as he did and, absorbed in my own hurt, I didn't think to suss out what lay behind George's words.

Words. 'They're only words,' as the song that Mum loved used to say. 'And words are all I have to take your heart away.'

'That's the best I can do,' Will sighed, setting out a four letter word.

'But you've got that one to add to it if it helps.' I pointed to a letter he'd overlooked.

'You're not supposed to be helping him,' said Giles. 'It won't amount to a game otherwise.'

'Oops, sorry, I won't do it again,' I laughed.

I didn't try to help Will out again, not because Giles had adopted a George like tone with me, but in the course of conversation Will revealed that he was a retired Headmaster, and I decided, as with George, that I needed to stop taking the content of mufti T-shirts as an indicator of someone inhabiting a less conventional box. And whilst Giles had once or twice averred to publishing, when he explained his former elevated connections with a national institution I was once again surprised but didn't show it, choosing instead to open up a discussion about whether the 'who you know' rather than 'what you know' culture still existed, the conversation prompted by relating the findings of a radio programme which said the top jobs were still given to those who went to the 'right' schools and 'right' universities and knew the 'right' people.

'I think what the programme was saying was that it's worse today than it was thirty or forty years ago,' I said, though I withheld the rant I had had at Roger about it after the programme had kept me company one evening on the drive home. As I should have foreseen, both Will and Giles spouted some knowledgeable sounding politics, shot me down in flames on the significance of the Black Power salute that I had also picked up from a gem of a piece on the radio which left me to conclude that, in life, as in the game of dice words, it was every man and woman for themselves.

We played on and truth be told I got a bit irritated in a way I would never have done with George. George had lived in London for many years before moving to Hastings and it subsequently came to light he had been held in high standing in a large firm of international repute. Yet he never bragged or belittled other people and would have understood why, over an innocent word game, I got rattled when I felt natural pride tipped over into a bit of boastfulness. Or should I have taken Will's comments less seriously, accepted with good grace that my fellow Games Makers had both been to Hastings and formed an opinion at odds with mine and George's. Why didn't I just accept that my talking it up would do nothing to educate or persuade them that their London boroughs, particularly Will's, with its apparently eclectic shops and fashionable cafes, weren't the be all and end all.

'I love the Old Town in Hastings. In fact my daughter and I had a few days in Paris last month. We stayed in Montmartre and I thought it had a similar feel about it.'

'What?' exclaimed an incredulous Will. 'There's no comparison between them. Did you get to see the Sacre Coeur?'

'Yes and it was all beautiful but I still maintain that there's a unique and individual atmosphere about the Old Town.'

'Not many artists or cobbled streets though,' observed Giles.

'There are lots of artists. In fact I had dinner with someone only a month or so ago who has exhibited at the Royal Academy.'

Give him his due, Will did say that when he'd first moved to Primrose Hill it had been nothing special but over the years the houses and location had attracted the up and coming and that opened up a discussion about what makes a place fashionable or not.

'I'd like to visit Arnold Circus,' I said, resisting the urge to grab my route book in front of Giles and pinpoint where it was. 'I saw it on a T.V. programme about London and the East End.' And for the first time that morning Allan contributed to the conversation by acknowledging that he knew Arnold Circus and how it had originally been built as social housing.

'There are so many writers and actors, from both the theatre and the cinema living round the corner from me,' continued Will. 'It's being so easily accessible to the rest of London that does it.'

I fell into the trap of thinking that I should continue to try and enhance the reputation of Hastings though it was a devil to come up with any famous people that had lived in or had connections with the place. William the Conqueror would be too obvious but did Catherine Cookson and Harry H Corbett count? And what of Logie Baird? I wondered if I should mention the filming of Foyle's War or that I once knew a lady who lived near the park who was responsible for decorating the Christmas tree at The Royal Opera House. How well connected by association could I get? But what about the trees?

The trees that, over a cup of mediocre coffee and a kit kat, George and I said we'd like to identify ourselves with.

'An oak tree,' said George, visibly adding to his length and breadth as he spoke. 'Big and strong and living a long time.' I laughed and ventured that I'd like to be a willow, gracefully swaying this way and that as the wind would take me.

'No, Carol, you're a Christmas tree.'

'Only coming out once a year?'

'There is that to it but it's all the baubles and bangles you wear.' And he wrote a skit on that as well.

In uniform I couldn't get away with being a Christmas tree and, looking at Giles and Will, to pose the question as to what trees they would like to be would be seen as pretty off the wall so I sat and listened to them indulging in some mutual name dropping. To give Giles his due he was prepared to concede that being rich and famous didn't necessarily endow someone with personable qualities and it was also to his credit that he only spoke of those he considered worthy of praise as opposed to those he could have slagged off.

The game was drawing to a close, more from lack of enthusiasm than a final burst of competitive spirit. Harry stopped by and said he was off to pick up Mr Hazoza. I liked Harry. It was nothing personal but who could blame me for resenting the fact that yet another had been chosen above me to drive Mr. H and his family. It was proof if anything was that I had been ditched by the Dispatchers.

'Mr. Hazoza?' asked Will.

'I hear he's a bit prickly,' said Harry.

'Not at all,' said Will.

'Have you had him?'

'Yes.'

'And me,' I piped up.

'He's a lovely fellow,' said Will. 'Do give him and his family my regards.'

'Ok.'

'Oh, and I have a message for his grandson. Tell him that...' The message Will wanted conveyed was to do with some historical matter that he and the grandson had been discussing when Will was their driver. Part of me was impressed that Will had managed to build up such a rapport with his clients and yet another part of me was cheesed off with Will's grandiose gestures of bonhomie. Equally puzzling was that, by my maths, the Hazoza family had had six different drivers and probably more besides.

The final game score was added up. My early successes foundered on the luck of the dice and the inner voice that sends me to pieces if I start to think I can do, or win, at something. However, there was no shame in coming in a commendable second place to Giles who recommended some other transportable games to the both of us.

'That was very enjoyable,' said Will, putting the dice back into the tube. 'Now are any of you going to sign up for the Commonwealth Games taking place in Glasgow 2014?'

'Certainly not,' said Giles.

'Nor me, but I believe Brenda said she was up for it which proves what you said when we first met, Will, about how volunteering can become a bug.'

'Did I?' He'd clearly forgotten the words, the person and the occasion but I could understand that because he was a sociable chap and then he said he had to go because he wanted to distribute his strips of paper. Then Giles got up and stretched and said he was going for a mosey round before tackling the crossword.

'Do you want any help?'

'I don't think so.' His look underlined his words, an expression of sheer disbelief that I had learnt nothing from the bunker experience, that collaboration and co-operation on something as personal as a crossword was outlawed by unseen forces.

'I'm going to see what Will's blog is about.'

I had to hand it to the man that he had been able to recall and write so much down about his experience and reproduce so much research into the history of the docklands. And yet I damned him too because he'd had the forethought to tell the story as it unfolded. Why hadn't I done the same? His journal would be on the bookshelves before the embers of the Olympic flames had had time to die down. No doubt he also had a Frank of his own that he would now resume working on. With able people like Will around why should I ever bother?

I turned away from the computer and looked across the room. Giles, hand in pocket as usual, was coming back through the opened door into the bunker and though in stature and build they were poles apart my mind played tricks in transposing a picture of George in Games Makers uniform upon him. If George was here, I told myself, he'd come over and tell me to stop those weasel thoughts, berate me for not having learnt anything from the fact that all his dreams and ambitions of becoming another Ian Rankin had drowned in the medications for the cancer that killed him. I imagined him saying, 'You've got to get on and finish writing it, Carol!' What, like David Gemmell and Alan Fisher who died one shortly before and one shortly after you? But what value would an early decision to dedicate Frank's story to George the humorist, George the inspirational, George the scold be if I never finished it? But George still lived didn't he, in the hospital bed opposite Frank's? Or was it just the name I had taken, George not anything like the irascible scallywag who plays Frank's fellow patient.

That's what sitting at a computer did to me, that's what happened when I started to think about Frank and so, to escape my thoughts, I scurried back to the table and Allan where the normality of bunker life carried on with chit chat and coffee and sweets. And all the while I had been mind wrestling with George and Frank and Frank's George, Allan had been trying to get some sense out of the Dispatchers about the timings of his Luton job. There was a fair chance he would go over the time of his shift. He wasn't so bothered about that but wanted to be at the right place at the right time.

'Well, I don't think there's going to be any jobs for me so I'll give it another hour and then I'll check out and potter on home.'

'Are you coming to the party here tomorrow night?'

'No. I would have if I'd been on shift.'

'Make sure you've got everything, Carol.'

'I will, Allan. I will.'

It was a gentle potter on the A21, a weariness again descending on me at about the Sevenoaks point. I stopped in a lay-by and closed my eyes. Once more my own snore woke me up from a ten minute nap. I turned the key and decided to put off the decision I had to make until I got past Robertsbridge.

The roundabout at Johns Cross came into view. Should I turn right and go to the Fayre where Rog would be helping out with the BBQ and Sophie and her friends would no doubt be on their umpteenth perambulation of the Tombola and other stalls. It was wearing the uniform that was putting me off indulging in the delights of village life; the not wanting to draw attention to myself and the potential breach of the rule that you should only wear uniform whilst on official duties. Or should I turn left, return to Hastings and opt for an empty house and a pile of ironing?

Left or right? I was back to being a willow tree, swaying this way and that between choices whilst the hardy wooden seat on the West Hill overlooking the Old Town and the sea, its dedication and inscription to George 'who made Hastings his home' stood immovable and steadfast in its purpose.

CHAPTER 37

The Carnival

Unbeknown to me as I strode purposefully across the bridge, a fractious, ill tempered, *'morning after the night before'* mood was hanging over Excel. Caught in another sunrise, I was self absorbed in my own feelings of sadness and regret that my once in a lifetime experience was coming to an end, a niggle of nervousness already making its presence known in my stomach at the inevitable goodbyes and farewells of the next couple of days.

Admittedly, at five fifty in the morning, there was unlikely to be much activity but even the energy and excitement left by the once bustling crowds getting through the tented public pedestrian screening area had evaporated. Had the finale to the Closing Ceremony of the previous evening siphoned off every last drop of it? If 'The Carnival is over' by the New Seekers (another of one of Mum's favourites) had been played over the tannoy at that point I think I would have wept.

With the dismantling of the marquees and barricades, the concrete plaza in front of Excel was returning to normal but there was something else changing, a change in attitude that I all too soon detected when I got to the top of the steps and found our screening tent deserted. A lynch pin of the last few weeks, I felt as confused at the lack of security as I had done waking up in the lay-by several days previously. For nothing better to do I twirled round in a circle and then back again until my eyes alighted on a familiar Games Makers rushing towards me at a speed of knots from Custom House Station.

'There's no one here,' I shouted and walked towards him, mightily concerned that, with all his wheezing and puffing, I might have a medical emergency on my hands by the time he got to me.

'No-one?' He stopped, wiped the back of his neck and put his hands on his hips, his shoulders heaving as he caught his breath.

'I don't know what we're supposed to do.' I stood by his side ready to catch his fall.

'Oy, you!' My friend had spotted a man dressed in the official green and black of the security personnel. He beckoned him over and, a bit too gruffly for my liking, asked him what was happening.

'All closed down,' he said. 'You have to go that way.' He gestured towards Custom House.

I've never seen a man recover so quickly from a state of near collapse or get up a gas of steam in reaction to the news that he had to go back from whence he came. 'This is ridiculous.' The green and black pointed at a sign no bigger than the back of a crisp packet desultorily hanging from a disused rope barricade and my friend complained bitterly about his wasted walk and why sufficient notice hadn't been given.

'There's not much that we can do about it.' I opted to walk away from the confrontation.

'They can't muck us about like this.'

'Come on, otherwise we'll be late.' I came up with all sorts of alternative subjects to talk about as we retraced his steps and then took the circuitous route along by the DLR track to the rear of a tented screening area that I had often driven past when coming out of the car park. I thought I had done a good job of calming my friend down but not so; he had merely been humouring me in my idle chatter and when we were within sight of security he was like a shot out of a starting pistol into the tent to have a few chosen words about the situation. A cowardly cowardy custard, I hung back because I didn't want to be branded a complainer by association. Yes, there had been a lack of forethought and, okay, it was frustrating having to do some extra walking but complaining to those on the ground was unlikely to achieve anything. As I passed through the airport body scanner I watched him exit the tent and, from his red face and wild eyes, doubted whether he really felt any better for having had his say.

After my bag had been searched I picked up it up, turned round and standing behind me was another familiar man. I smiled but it was plain that he too had other things on his mind, things that he wanted to get off his chest.

'I've just walked round that scanner and you've not said a blind thing about it,' he said in a loud voice to no-one in particular but to anyone within earshot, of whom there were quite a few. No-one responded until he shouted again and this time it was the supervisor who rushed to his side and invited him to step into it.

'I'm not going to!'

What was it with the men? Why were they being so crabby? From long experience I knew that, generally speaking, men liked a routine in the morning, particularly with their bowel movements, but surely a diversion to a different tent wasn't enough to upset their equilibrium. And this colleague, who up until that point I had found to be a fine fellow, was, to my mind, just being downright contrary and petty. The supervisor, at least a foot shorter and a foot narrower than my bolshie colleague, looked decidedly on edge and fell upon a 'please Sir,' to encourage compliance.

'I can't.' He tapped his chest. 'I have a pacemaker fitted. You weren't to know that but none of you were paying attention to me anyway.' He had a valid point and was happy to be frisked but as I left the tent the cloud, whilst not making me fractious or bad tempered, settled on the buggy that, because of the change in access arrangements, was on hand to take us through the car park to the bunker. The early morning men grizzled and griped and I hoped it was the result of constipation, a mood that could be flushed away and they could be made happy again and the last shifts made fittingly memorable.

But the discord and discontent didn't stop there. I signed in and the gold Games Makers badge I was given shone brightly in my hand as I made my way up to the Canteen. A shouting match stopped me in my tracks, the place brought to a standstill by a furious row going on between Gino and a T2 who, from a fleeting glimpse of his profile, I recognised as a usually genial fellow. Gino was giving his volatile temperament full rein, his hands waving wildly, his voice bordering on the hysterical. His adversary stood full square on to him, an instrument of uncertain provenance held firmly in his hand but from the way Gino kept looking at it, I guessed the dispute had something to do with this item. Then the T2 brandished the object at Gino, turned on his heel and all in his pathway stepped back to make way as he stormed through. Gino continued his rant and I decided to leave getting my breakfast for the time being. The bystanders shrugged their shoulders and dispersed and I was none the wiser as to what had precipitated the eruption.

When I got into the bunker Gino's incensed combatant was sounding off at the Dispatchers and, from what I could gather, the top and bottom of the dispute had been the bottle of coke that the combatant had in his hand. Only one soft drink per person was allowed from the fridge and, no doubt demob happy, he had dared to take a coke and a bottle of water and Gino wasn't prepared to let him get away with it.

Allan, bless him, wasn't in any way crotchety but was still holding on to the displeasure he had felt at getting to Luton on the last shift only to discover that, due to the mish mash over timings, his client had made alternative arrangements and scarpered.

'But before I had a chance to find out that it was a wasted journey I had to pay out for the car park and I don't know whether I'll get my money back.'

'You will. It wasn't your fault.'

'It doesn't seem to matter to them if it is or it isn't. You be careful today. You too might get sent on a wild goose chase.'

When I went to get my hot enhancement, Gino was in a considerably lighter mood and appreciated my concern as to whether he had got over the upset, and back in the bunker it was a relief too to see Chris mooching about and untouched by the liverish goings on.

'Have you got a job today, Carol?' he asked, his eyes boring into my wallet. I told him who and where it was.

'I had him. He's got a kid, hasn't he?'

'No idea but if so isn't he the one that Nicholas has had a few times. The wife stays elsewhere. Is that right?'

'I don't know about that but I do know that the driver he had
before me was late and because he complained they sent me two
hours earlier than he asked for and when I got there he had me
sitting in the lobby for ages because he had allowed for me being
late and given the schedulers a time a couple of hours earlier than
he needed me to be there.'

'He made his point then?'

'Not half. And he knows London like the back of his hand so
you can't take him off the beaten track.'

'I don't intend to.'

'Anyway, how comes you've got him because I'm not doing
anything?'

'Who knows? You don't want to pass on any messages of
regard to him?'

'Why would I do that?'

'No reason.'

'See you later then.' He toddled off, on the lookout for some
work, something useful to do.

Where previously there had been maps of the Olympic Park
and other venues and details of hotels now the boards had
information regarding the airports. Another sign that the operation
was winding down was that a team of people in high-vis jackets
appeared who, led by a strident woman, were organising the
movement of cars to a pound in Dartford.

Yet whilst there was a sense of an ending and a dead certainty
that you wouldn't ever see the same client again, everyone still
had a desire to perform their duties well. I think that is what was
at the root of Allan's Luton dissatisfaction; that he had been
prevented from doing what he had signed up to do because of
bungled arrangements.

'Don't forget to keep an eye on the time, Carol,' he warned.

'I am.'

'You'll know where to park won't you?'

'Yes, Allan. I've been there before.'

The little doorman whom I had met on one of my training
days, the one with the hat that flattened his ears and burgundy
coat that nearly dragged on the floor, was not in evidence when

387

I arrived at the Hotel. He had been most concerned for me to take on board that the lower car park had been dedicated for our cars. However, I didn't want to run the risk of ruffling my client's feathers if he was all set to go by being left in the hands of some Herbert being available to activate the barrier. As luck would have it there was a space in the car parking area immediately adjacent to the main entrance to the Hotel and I slipped in without the merest hint of a doorman rushing out to tell me I had to beetle off elsewhere.

Unlike Mr Z's hotel where I had stood in the Foyer feeling lost, very self conscious and yet invisible at the same time, this hotel was much more geared up for the likes of me in uniform. The young woman at guest Services politely pointed me in the direction of a small table at which a Games Makers was sitting. Engrossed in checking something on a pad of A4 paper, the young man didn't look up or acknowledge my presence until, inches away from him, I said good morning in the cheeriest of tones. He leapt up and returned the greeting.

'I'm here to pick up Mr. Gonzalez.' I showed him my accreditation and schedule sheet. He showed me his and this tall, lean and sun-tanned Paolo, who might not be given a second glance by some on account of his black rimmed glasses, looked at me through eyes that had the colour, depth and sumptuous promise of a vat of dark chocolate. 'Is he here?' I stuttered.

'Mr Gonzalez? Yes. He's having his breakfast.' He made a mark on his pad.

'I'll pop to the Ladies. Do I come back here to wait for him?'
'Yes.'

As I walked through the foyer I mulled over the fact that Paolo had been given a job, a proper Ambassadorial position, that I had seen myself doing. Wouldn't it have been good ensuring pickups and drop offs went like clockwork and getting to know the clients? And wouldn't it have been great to sit and watch the ebb and flow of guests coming and going, using them as material for my writing? Or would it have been tedious? Was being stuck in one place, at the beck and call of others, preferable to my role? As I pushed the door open to the Ladies Room I concluded that

I was lucky to be a driver because at least I had been out and about, seen the Stadium, met lots of other Games Makers and more besides.

My mobile's ringtone sounded whilst I was enthroned and in midstream. I fumbled in my bag for my phone and by a stroke of luck I pressed the answer call button.

'This is Mr. Gonzalez. I am expecting a car.'

'Yes.' My voice echoed round the marble walls. I pressed the phone closer to my ear and cupped my hand round the bottom to stifle the sound. 'It is here.'

'At the Hotel?'

'Yes. I am waiting.' And also praying that he didn't continue the conversation because if someone were to come in the Ladies Room they might have thought I was involved in some form of espionage or strange secret liaison, both of which might have merited an intervention by the Hotel security services.

'I'll be down in five minutes prompt.'

I gave him a breathy okay and, stifling a giggle, ended the call. I thought of Mum who was famous for singing 'la, la, la' to alert us, and how I used to blast out a pretty mean Barbara Streisand in a loo Rog and I once had in a cold and damp basement flat. The acoustics in the flat were a vocalist's dream, as they were in the powder room's ornate and genteel surroundings when I cursed spurting water everywhere in a hurry to wash my hands and give my hair a quick comb.

On the timekeeping front Mr. Gonzalez's five minutes was more like fifteen plus ten but it didn't matter because Paolo and I had a chat about the current economic situation. He came from Majorca and was staying in London for the summer and sending off applications left right and centre to find any kind of job in the capital. I commiserated with his theory that the current ills of Spain were down to the bureaucracy, that in some places you had more councillors than doctors and that often you had to rely on connections with councillors to get you into a trade or business.

'We have a saying; it's not what you know it's who you know,' I said sagely, restraining myself from repeating the findings of the radio programme I had regaled Will and Giles with a couple of days before because that would have done nothing to boost the dear of him's confidence. Our conversation was interrupted without a by your leave by Mr. Gonzalez who I had seen bombing through from the lifts but had dismissed as he didn't fit the mould of my previous clients. Athletic and incredibly handsome, Mr Gonzalez struck me within seconds as a man who knew what he wanted and was going to get it and whilst you couldn't say he was rude, his style commanded attention. Paolo, for instance, didn't exactly salute but came over much more nervous in his presence.

'You are taking us to City Airport.'

'Yes,' I replied and gave his son, no more than six years old, in shorts, T-shirt and baseball cap an encouraging smile.

'We are going to make a stop on the way and need to do it quickly.'

'Fine. Where is it?' I played it cool, reserved, my face betraying no signs of the 'flipping heck, he knows London like the back of his hand' thought that raced through my mind and nor did I look to my sheet and make a British bureaucratic remark about it not being on the schedule.

'A moment!' He fiddled with his Smartphone. 'This place.' He showed me the screen. I only had time to absorb the postcode beginning with an E when he flipped it away from me.

'Wait. I need to write it down.' I turned to Paolo. 'Can I borrow a pen and some paper?' I picked up his pad and my client, not exactly snappy but close to it, read the address out to me.

'Luggage?' I asked.

'Over there.' He pointed to a mound of it near the doors.

'I'll pull the car around to the front.'

Fortunately, there was a space and whilst waiting I programmed the address in telling Helga I'd visit a plague of boils on her electronics if she didn't get us there, and double checked in my Route Book on the general direction I would need to take for the Isle of Dogs. I stood by the car waiting and Paolo came out to say it would be a few minutes more but his smile said otherwise.

When Mr. G finally came out of the Hotel his face was like thunder and, clasping his son by the hand, he charged towards the car with a doorman pushing a fancy luggage cart behind him.

At the car the doorman was summarily dismissed and so was Paolo's offer of help as Mr. G heaved suitcases and bags into the boot and slammed the lid on them. There was no doubt that this man was in a hurry so I wished Paolo the best of luck in all he did and got into my seat.

Mr. Gonzalez rained bags onto the back seat and then flung open the front door and I had to duck else suffer a nasty injury from the boards he was manoeuvring into the passenger well. Any thought I might have entertained of casting a sly look at the Route Book in the event of going wrong was rapidly exploded because my bag, route book and pad of paper were crushed under yet another bag that he squeezed between the boards and the back of the passenger seat. It crossed my mind that this man would be a whizz at packing a car after a visit to IKEA but would the BMW suspension bear the weight of whatever it was we were carrying in more bags than I had ever seen squashed into one vehicle. I probably wasn't the first to be impressed by his authoritative presence, manly muscle and expertise. And I probably wasn't the first to be so hurried that, until it dawned on me later, I committed an offence that as well as exacting a hefty penalty could have led to tragic consequences for all concerned.

But in the then and there my client told me we must go even before he had closed the door behind him. And I hadn't got out of first gear before he burst out with an exasperated 'Your country!'

'Pardon?' I looked in the rear view mirror, somewhat taken aback at the strength of feeling expressed in those words.

'I wasn't allowed to use the baggage cart.'

'Why?'

'Health and safety rules.'

'Oh.'

'I've seen such a difference in your country over the last ten years. Who'd want to invest in a country like this with all its regulations?'

'A lot of the regulations are made because we are part of the EU,' I said, sounding like a typical reader of an anti EU newspaper.

'No, no, no. You've followed the Americans. If something goes wrong you look for someone to blame.' I had to agree with him on that and graciously did but had taken exception to the lambast. I didn't have the nerve to tell him not to criticise us and took to commenting on the traffic which he said had also grown to peak capacity since he had first started coming to London. I withdrew into what Mum always said was golden, namely silence, and it might have remained that way if it hadn't been for his son tapping on the window and chanting Buckingham Palace.

'That's St Pancras,' I corrected him. It came out quite harsh, the result of my having taken to heart his father's perfectly valid points and a moment later I chided myself because the little boy might just have been trying to tell me where he had visited. 'Have you enjoyed yourselves?' I asked brightly, steeling myself to take on the chin any criticisms the boy's father might have.

'Yes. These Games were the best.' He elaborated by saying that the organisation had been superb and that London and the country as a whole had taken the Olympic spirit on board. He couldn't praise the Games Makers highly enough and aware that there had been more drivers than had been needed, put that down to the fact that London's transport system was one of the most efficient in the world. He was enthusiastic, deeply grateful and passionate about the sporting legacy continuing.

'When I was a child, we played outside all day, played football, any games we wanted. With my son, I don't let him play outside because we are afraid for his safety. We take him to clubs and sports halls.'

'I know. We were the same with our two children.'

'But only those who can pay for these activities benefit. Sport should be for all and we should make it so.' It was an impassioned plea and I would have gladly sold all my worldly goods at that point to don a pair of shorts and vest and donate all my money to whatever sports foundation he recommended. But as with all single minded and driven people he didn't allow himself to be caught up solely in the emotion of the conviction and as we approached the Westferry roundabout he focused on his next task of finding the address where we had to stop off.

Initially I had had a few qualms as to where we might end up but such had my faith grown over the weeks that, whilst keeping a keen eye on the road signs, I mainly left it to Helga to direct us through a warren of streets till our destination was reached. One call on Mr. G's phone later a man of his acquaintance appeared, bags were offloaded and I turned the car round whilst the men and the boy went into a nearby apartment block.

It was so liberating knowing one's place, not tied down by a responsibility of making sure my passengers had taken the right bags or whether they were going to stay longer than they needed to. I sat and watched the river knowing that when they returned all I had to do was drive the car to a place that I had been to several times before. Easy peasy.

Easy peasy it was because there were no hold ups and Mr. Gonzalez and I had said all we had needed to say. In his view he had no need to tell me what time his flight was though it might have become an issue if we were late. And if I hadn't asked I don't think he would have thought it my place to know where he was going. It was a revelation, a matter for further thought; could I live my life only being concerned with facts, getting from A to B, totally focused on the matter in hand, unblighted by inconsequential's and irrelevancies rather than my actions and conversations being informed by my desire to bring a smile, to make a good impression?

We drew up at the drop off point at City airport. He was opening the door before I had come to a halt. His son, with eyes like his father and bony brown knees stood silent and still on the pavement whilst his father unloaded the entire luggage from the car. I gave the boy a kindly look as his father rushed over to get a trolley. Then they were gone, whoosh, out of my life forever.

I drove back to the VSA at Excel and retrieved my bag which had taken a pummelling from the luggage that had been piled on top of it.

'Are you alright there, Ma'am,' asked the chirpy soldier who I'd originally met at the VSA though the last time we'd met it had been by the ice cream freezer cabinet at the convenience store. Then he had joked with me and said if I was buying he liked Twisters and I'd laughed and said if he was buying I liked a Feast.

'I think I've lost my lipstick and mirror case and I can't do without them. Silly isn't it?'

'No, Ma'am, it isn't' He rolled his eyes.

'I bet it was you who took it. I can tell from the expression on your face.'

'What colour was it?' He went all coy.

'Heather Shimmer.'

'Oh no, Ma'am. Coral Sand is more my colour.'

'Thought so.' And he and I laughed as did his jesting colleagues.

'Are you going out again today, Ma'am?'

'Possibly, because the delegates are making their way home.'

'Maybe see you later then.'

It wasn't until I parked the car up in the Excel car park that I realised what I had done. The matter of the lipstick and mirror was of no real consequence though it was a pain that I had probably left it in the Ladies Room of the Hotel. But how had I allowed myself to be overawed by Mr G's do this do that, so much so that that I hadn't thought to question his decisions and actions. Why hadn't I linked his tirade about health and safety with what I was doing? Had his tirade been merely a smokescreen, an attempt to make me feel like a spoilsport if I had cottoned on to what I was giving tacit permission to? The blood in my veins ran cold when it struck me that I had allowed him to take control, to load the car with luggage and I hadn't checked to make sure his lovely little lad was strapped in with a seat belt. What if we'd had an accident or the police had pulled me up for a routine and innocuous reason and found clear evidence of a breach of the law. The more I thought about it the more I was convinced that neither of them had been belted up or, worse still, had the lad been on his lap? Nothing untoward had happened and instead of fretting was it best to consign the oversight to history?

What was not consigned to history, what was still very much in the present, was my third misdemeanour. The evidence was plain to see on the passenger seat. It was Paolo's A4 pad with all the names of his clients and their pick up times, destinations and other miscellaneous information written in his fair hand. I experienced an awful feeling in my stomach, a feeling that reminded me of a dream when you turn over an exam paper and it reads like double Dutch.

I decided I would have to get it back to Paolo, my main concern being that he didn't get shouted at too much by belligerent clients anxious to leave our shores. What I should have done is gone straight back to the hotel instead of making foolish remarks about what a lovely young man he was to the Dispatchers who said they weren't authorised to make a decision on my proposition. Where Bryn was, was anybody's guess. I hadn't seen him for days and had interpreted this as his having lost interest in the whole venture. Tommy and the strident woman in charge of organising the cars back to the Pound were in and out of the bunker like the strikers in a cuckoo clock but he wasn't up for me returning it to Paolo personally.

'He's very nice,' I said.

'He must be but leave it at the check-in desk here.'

'He will get it, won't he?'

'Yeah, yeah, yeah.'

I returned to my post at the table and soon there was quite a little gathering with John, Sam, Allan, Ian, Chris, Melvin and Hilary and we swapped tales of who had been the furthest, had the nicest or stroppiest clients, the conversation salted and peppered with tales of misadventures, false trails and misdeeds. Florence flitted in and out making final arrangements because she had volunteered to take a car on its very last Olympic journey back to Dartford.

'Did everybody get the email with the offer to purchase one of the cars?' asked Allan, with the resultant discussion of the leasing terms of more interest to the boys.

'Did anybody get a parking ticket?' asked John from Chislehurst. The answer was a thumping no from everyone. 'Or a speeding ticket?'

'W...e...ll.' I said meekly.

'You didn't?' said Chris.

'It was only on the Park. I wasn't banned or anything like that.'

'What speed were you doing?' pressed John.

'Thirty.'

'Bloody hell. Of all the people you wouldn't expect to get a ticket.' He roared with laughter though I never asked why he should think it so. And I don't know why he thought he could get away with saying that I made such a good cup of coffee and would I be a grand dame and fetch him one. But he did get away with it and I made him a coffee and, silly as this is, it rankled. It still does or why else mention it?

'Let me take some photos, just in case some of us aren't around on my last day,' I said. I took a group photo and then Allan suggested I sat with the group and he'd take one on my camera so I'd have a record of being there. There were a few hugs for those who were on their last shift and someone said that when it came to our last day we shouldn't forget to collect a baton each.

'What batons?'

'We are all going to get commemorative batons,' said Chris. 'Though I'll pick mine up after I've done the Paralympics.'

'I'll get mine on Wednesday,' I said.

'Me too,' said Allan.

Being in the know Chris was right, because as I came back past the check-in desks from the loo at the end of my shift I had to laugh at two of the men in athletic pose imitating a baton changeover. And another fellow was clutching his baton for dear life as he and I made our way back into the car park to board the buggy.

'All ready?' the big and bouncy lady driver asked. The collar, top half her shirt and a sash (much like a Brownie one) was covered in commemorative pins and badges and I swear you could hear them chinking together as we zipped away from the bunker into the car park. It was a snug fit on the seat and for those in the other seats but her driving was such that I held onto the side to stop an embarrassing sideways slide into my baton wielding partner.

'What are they doing?' asked the driver. Craning my neck I could just make out the figures of two men dragging something out from one of the side lift wells. Apart from the petite lady I had come across on my first training day and an occasional soldier or

396

security bod, I had never seen anyone near the lifts. The driver slowed and whirred to a stop as the men, a small and a medium sized one, came to a standstill with a ruddy great trunk and other bags besides.

'Where are you going with that?' the driver asked them, though I would have been more inclined to ask them what was in it or just scoot off and call up security to check them out. What was equally disturbing was that they didn't seem to know where they were. That was in some ways understandable given the vastness of the car park but to my mind the small excitable one was overacting the part of someone who had got out of Doctor Who's Tardis to find they had mistakenly landed in an alien environment.

'We have to get to here.' The medium one handed the driver a piece of paper.

'Have you a lift?' asked the small one. The driver laughed.

'I can only take a limited number and what with your bags and all.'

'Please,' the small one kept nodding, his hands in a prayer like position. His taller taciturn mate looked embarrassed but I could tell our driver was taken with these waifs, so much so that I avoided eye contact with her as she walked round the buggy because, though she was protesting that the trunk was likely to be heavy, I felt she was behaving like the captain of a ship looking for likely able bodied and unencumbered victims to throw overboard.

'Can we try?' the medium one persisted. It could be said that she had already made her decision, that he knew he was on to a winner when she asked all of us to get off. Or had she? Did the clincher come when, hands on hips, she asked if either of the hitchhikers had any pins or badges.

'We may have,' the little tease replied causing her to bend over and start fiddling with something on the buggy floor.

'I may give you a ride then, if I can get this ramp out.'

It was an uncomfortable journey, mainly due to the trunk which took up a lot of space and played havoc with the suspension. I suspected that the luggage the men were carrying was camera equipment and lugging the trunk about had taken its toll on the larger man's armpit that I was unbearably close to. I felt sorry for the poor person who was going to have to sit next to him on the plane. Both I and his unwashed shirt could breathe when we emerged out into the daylight. By the time we had unwrapped ourselves from each other and the trunk and baggage had been disgorged, the driver was in deep discussions with the men regarding the pins.

One delegate's pin was better than none though there were other Games Makers who, by dint of who their clients were, collected many more. And the world of the Olympic Games Makers, as in the wider world, proved to be inhabited by people of all sorts so there were people like me who ferreted their pins away for posterity and others who did a brisk trade in swaps, turning the collection of pins into a competition. Being part of an international delegation paid dividends for the two men and if I'd had the mind to stick around I could have found out what the driver put her talents to in real life.

What with my client, the gathering of the group and team photos, I had given no further thought to the clouds of grizzle that had laid siege to the men I had come upon earlier that morning. Out on the road with Mr. G and son I hadn't noticed anyone being more car horn or road rage crazy than usual. As I dismounted the buggy and started to head back round the pedestrian VSA, the air had once more turned to Eeyoreish gloom and despondency. Those coming on shift were bitterly complaining about the extra walk they had to do. Even Nicholas, who was as placid as they come, raised his eyebrows and shook his head in exasperation when we met on the path to Custom House.

'It'll soon be over,' he said.

'It will.'

Just like a carnival.

CHAPTER 38

The Day that Never was

'Only one more day to go,' Roger said, as we ate our evening meal.

'All the time it took with the application and interview and training and now it's nearly over. I felt sad enough today so what I'm going to be like on Wednesday, in tears probably.

'But you can keep in contact with the ones you got friendly with.'

I was saved the bother of shedding tears. At twelve minutes past eight that very evening I received an email saying my services had been dispensed with. The clue was in the heading which said 'T2 GOODBYE'. A decision had been made to finish all the shifts because the demand was low to none until the Paralympics started on the twentieth. The team wanted us to know that we had crossed the line and delivered the best Olympic Games ever and we had all been brilliant, patient and enthusiastic.

I went and sat on the sofa with Rog, the man who had dared to think I was joking when I had said I had applied, the man who had accompanied me to get my uniform and had supported me in whatever way I had wanted or needed so that I could pander to my patriotic and egotistical tendencies.

How did I feel? A bit let down because I reckoned Tommy and the Dispatchers must have known it was going to happen but hadn't said anything even when I had been fussing about the return of Paolo's pad of paper. If I had known at the time that Bryn was locked away somewhere making that executive decision I would have bolted out and driven over to Paolo just for the hell of it and made Chris proud that I had eventually found the spirit in me to go on a frolic of my own.

I shouldn't have been that surprised because in the hours before I got the elbow there was something fishy about the emails which said that changes were afoot and my shift pattern had been temporarily removed from the Games Makers Zone then reinstated but I couldn't get into it. And the speed with which the security had been disbanded at the front of Excel and the changes to the Exit and Entrances to the Depot also said something, as did the fact that, like Mr. Gonzalez, most delegates had flown away.

There was a mixture of sadness tinged with relief too in that, hating goodbyes of any description, I knew I would likely blub on the last day. There was regret also that whilst I had taken a note of Chris', Allan's, Florence's and Colin's telephone numbers, there were others I would have liked to have made a note of, if only as contacts for future reference.

'But what about my baton?' I sat upright.

'What baton?'

'The commemorative baton.'

'It doesn't matter about the baton.'

'It certainly does!'

And, just as on that evening almost two years previously, I traipsed off to the Study to communicate via the computer.

CHAPTER 39

Finishing Touches

I let the news that I was now surplus to requirements sink in and then wrote to Chris.

Dear Chris,

Have you received the equivalent of a 'Dear John' letter from FDX? I had one last night which said how much they loved me but then gave me the heave ho,, or, rather, the man himself has decided to call time on the shifts (sorry about all the clichés).

In some ways it seems an unsatisfactory ending to what was otherwise a great experience. I never like saying goodbye to people but in your case I hope it would have been an au revoir because it would be good at some point in the future to meet up for a chinwag. For now though I will send you an odd (it will be odd; you know me!) email.

I never picked up my complimentary baton. Boo hoo. I'm going to email them about it and if I can work some magic on them would you be prepared to pick it up for me during the Paralympics? Is that being a bit cheeky to ask? We could do a baton changeover on the A21 at some later point!

If it is the case that actually I am the only soul who has been summarily dismissed and you all enjoy some camaraderie tomorrow, do say Hi to all (if that isn't paranoia I don't know what is!)

I'll say cheerio with a copy of the photo I took.

Best wishes

Carol

Did you take John from Chislehurst's details because I have a mug shot of him and Sam in addition to our table top one?

In Chris's reply he agreed that it had all finished on a bit of a downer but, the positive soul he is, he didn't seem so put out by the way it ended, primarily I think because he had his duties at the Paralympics to look forward to and is generally unfazed by things. I sent a message to Allan and he came back to tell me that he had sent me two texts telling me of the changes on the day of our dismissal but my phone was temperamental so I hadn't received them. I gathered he was less inclined to be sympathetic to the powers at the Depot because when he went in to collect his baton he had a wrangle with them over the parking charges he incurred on the airport job. He ended with 'The whole experience has left a gap and I'm missing you all already.' It was a sentiment I agreed with.

The gap in my life was filled by a flurry of activity in my Inbox and Sent Items. The Transport Team triplicated the messages about the euphemistically named 'changes in shifts' and continued to congratulate our patience and spirit *'Despite there being times we weren't that busy and that we had more cars and drivers outside some venues than we had sausage butties throughout the whole Games.'* They also said that Adidas were giving Games Makers discounts on the London 2012 online store and sent a reminder that BMW were offering an exclusive chance to own one of their cars. Rog thought it was worth enquiring but I dismissed any suggestion of it because of the general feeling amongst my fellows on my last shift and the troubles I had been experiencing with my arms and shoulders. I had found driving the cars a struggle during the last few shifts, blaming the position of the handbrake and gear change but, in fairness to the motor manufacturer, the heavy duty car, as against my battered Peugeot, wasn't the cause of the discomfort though the driving experience no doubt exacerbated it.

The FDX Team sent a Final Goodbye on the 14th August but I still had to communicate with them about my baton. At first they said they'd post it and then they came up with a plan which would have been worthy of an espionage novel where, on account of my accreditation being revoked, I was not allowed on the Fleet Depots premises but someone would meet me at Custom House

Station to effect the handover. In the end I had to provide a letter of authority for Chris to pick it up and eagerly awaited the nod from him that it was sitting on his dining room table ready for when we could meet.

The Games Makers Team carried on where the Transport Team left off and gave notice of the Athletes' Parade that was being held in London on the 10th September and said they would like the Games Makers to line the route in their uniforms. They gave notice too of a ballot to be held in which the successful applicants would be allocated one of the 9000 places in reserved areas at both the west and east end of the Mall where the Games Makers could take a bow in front of the athletes and the nation.

The computer activity was by no means one sided because even on the night when Seb's team were pulling the plug on the likes of me and Chris and Allan, I was pro-active, more pro-active than I had ever been before, or even since. I wrote to The Oldie magazine.

Dear Mr Lewis,

In the August issue the Editor looked ahead to the Olympics. In looking back at the event would the Oldie be interested in letting its readers see it from the perspective of a volunteer inmate incarcerated in a white emulsioned room deep in the bowels of London Excel?

This is not the stuff of young men and women waving giant foam hands or making jokey quips through a megaphone. This is the gritty story of mature and extra mature adults catching a foretaste of Games Makers nursing homes to come. It is the tale of a grand group of people, inspired by a positive vision, who find themselves slumped in white chairs at white tables watching the clock and a white board. There are bankers, lawyers, teachers, council officials and the rest. They watch, they listen and give support and encouragement to the ones who have been given plastic wallets. For within those jealously guarded wallets lies a key. It is a real key, a key to a trusty steed, in the guise of a shiny new BMW, skulking in the adjoining gloomy car park in security lockdown. The BMW in turn means a delegate, a quick revision of the Fleet Drivers Handbook and the freedom of an Olympic Lane.

I have enjoyed every moment of being a Driver and have kept a log of my time with the Transport Team. I am currently writing this up as a series of pieces for posterity and it will include the interview, the training, the temperamental Sat Navs and the wickedly termed early 'hot enhancement'. One of the sponsors has said that our efforts will be rewarded with a qualification that can be entered on our CV's. This brought a smile to those retired (especially high flying former executives and journalists) and gave me the idea for the title for my experiences The Pinnacle of a Career. I have attached the first piece, titled The Application as a taster/representation of my style.

I wondered if the Oldie would be interested in running The Pinnacle as a Diary type piece dealing with the various stages as outlined above in say 2/3 episodes or as one condensed version of events.

I would welcome your acknowledgement of receipt, your views and any feedback on the subject.

Regards,

Roger was impressed at how I'd bitten the bullet of self promotion and I was encouraged by Mr. Lewis's reply. I accepted what he said about being hidebound by the editorial policies of the magazine and I noted too that he was worried that the readers might have had a bellyful of the Olympics and it could be dated because they were already working on the October issue. But I latched on to him saying that he could promise nothing yet, 'all depends on how interesting and well written it is and whether it meets with the editor's approval.' He was so sorry to be off-putting but 'all I can say is that if you'd like to have a go I'll happily read on.'

If not exactly blown away by my piece, at least he had shown a flicker of interest in it but in the cold light of day I took his decency to acknowledge my existence as being part and parcel of the general 'jolly good egg' reputation of those at the publication. It was a good eggedness I could vouch for after being one of a couple of hundred people stuffed into the community hall at Rye to listen to a talk by two of their stalwarts the year before. It would be down to me and me only to launch myself into the world of lecture tours and book signings at art and literary festivals.

So in between doing summery things with Sophie, visiting Cornwall and with further apologies to Frank's manuscript, I had a go at paring down my Olympic experience to the required eight hundred words for The Oldie. And Rosemary (a friend made in tandem with George) asked if, for a cup of coffee and a slice of cake, I would write something that she could read and record for the talking magazine for the blind. Roger's Rotary Club requested a memoir for their bulletin. I duly obliged but drew the line at going to talk to them, or the Inner Wheel.

The Athletes' Parade on the 10th September soon arrived and it just so happened that Sophie and I were going up to London because we had tickets to be part of the T.V. audience for a recording of a Piers Morgan Life Stories show.

'Do you think it's going to be busy, Mum,' asked Sophie as we got off the train at Charing Cross.

'There may be more people about than normal but not hordes because it is a working day.' How wrong could I have been as we were sucked from the platform into the buzz and bustle of the Station concourse. Outside the pavements were already showing more than their fair share of pedestrians and a sea of people came up the road from Embankment Station. And right in the midst of being jostled by the crowds surging ahead, we were thrown into the pathway of Colin who gave me the warmest of hugs and explained that he had won a ticket in the ballot and was on his way to the Mall.

'And I believe you enjoyed the Paralympics?'

Colin's beaming smile said it all. 'And we're meeting soon aren't we, Carol?'

'Definitely.'

'I'll be in touch,' and he was carried away in the tide that was flowing towards Trafalgar Square.

Sophie and I weaved our way between pedestrians as we made our way along the Strand which boasted a healthy showing of people lining both sides of the street. Young and old were sitting on the pavements, some getting into practice waving their union jack flags, others holding or still in the process of making banners of congratulations. There was an air of anticipation, of unsuppressed excitement and in amongst it were Games Makers in the uniforms that would never again be seen en masse on the streets of London. I'd shied away from wearing mine, my perfectly valid excuse being that Sophie and I were later going to become part of an audience where I certainly didn't want to draw attention to myself. As we dodged in and out of dawdlers and deferred to workers walking with purpose I scanned the faces of the Games Makers in the crowds.

'Sophie, Stop!' I yelled, because she was doing her usual trick of striding on ahead. She turned and sauntered back and we stood on the edge of the kerb whilst I waved madly to catch the attention of the man across the way. He waved back and trotted over and the pecks on the cheek and the embrace were as warm as if I'd known him for years.

I introduced Sophie. 'I'm Michael,' he said, quickly enough to save any embarrassment caused by forgotten names though he wasn't the Michael of the Santa Claus physiognomy that I'd met via Colin. He'd been to the Closing Ceremony party at the bunker though it hadn't been much cop but his time as a volunteer at the Paralympics Games in Weymouth had been fantastic. He had been busy but the atmosphere had been relaxed and he said what a difference the experience at Excel could have been, would have been, if it had lived up to what we were originally told.

'And my wife's over there.' He pointed across the road and waved for her to come over but I didn't blame her for shaking her head because she didn't know us from Adam. 'We got married in the church along there.' We had more of a chat then than we ever had done but I said we were going to walk up to St Pauls so that we would see everything before going for a late lunch.

'He seemed like a nice man and Colin too,' said Sophie as we tried to make headway.

'Yes, they all were.' And I wondered if coming across Mark, Mark, Mark or Chris and Chris or Giles or Will or Sam, John,

Lesley, Melvin, Mervyn, Hilary, Linda, Lesley, Sharon, Kath, Christina, Bob, Martin, Nicholas, Stuart, Ian, Andrew or Robin et al, we would remember and greet each other in the same glad way. We walked along Fleet Street. I gave a nod to the building which I assumed John from Chislehurst would know inside out and then we were down at Ludgate Circus and being shooed up Ludgate Hill by office people showing their impatience with tourists and the incongruity of Games Makers doing relay races in the road.

We stood outside Strada opposite the front apron in the road to St Paul's which was crowded to full capacity and above the ground floor shops and restaurants people were hanging out of windows. An enormous cheer went up and whistles blew and I craned my neck to see what was going on.

'It's the motorbike outriders, Sophie. The parade must be coming soon.' The motorbikes stopped parallel with St Paul's, the riders greeting the crowds with a wave. When the wild cheering and clapping started we knew the crowd had caught sight of the cavalcade of open-top buses carrying the athletes. It was an event like no other and I waved and clapped as I'd done for no other as the flotilla juddered by on a sea of goodwill. And when the last bus had moved off the crowds at first seemed reluctant to disperse as if, like me, they wanted to hold onto the atmosphere we had been caught up in.

The Athletes Parade was the finale, the culmination of the summer of sport. But there were a few finishing touches to be applied to my experience before I should have, by rights, packed away all my things, including the Commemorative Certificate from Jacques Rogge, the President of the International Committee, and let the episode be.

First up, on the day I was recovering from the exertions of the Parade and seeing Roger Moore interviewed, I received an email saying that my 'fantastic contribution as a Games Makers to making London 2012 such a success has been widely recognised by the athletes, by your colleagues and by the country at large'. It went on to say that a presenting partner of the London 2012 Games had designed a nationally recognised qualification that was only available to Games Makers. The qualification was aimed at developing the skills and experience that had been used, would give a tangible qualification to reflect them and would act as a unique signal to employers that I had been part of the Games Makers team. It was all good stuff but not for me.

Second up, I drew on the confidence I had gained during my Games Makers stint and the universal gratitude coming the Games Makers way and decided to chase The Oldie up on the refined piece I had resubmitted the week before the Parade under the title Bunker Tales. What a cheek I had, considering that the magazine receives dozens of submissions every week but, once again, the recipient of my nudge was gracious enough to say he would read if I sent another copy. I took the view that where there's life there's hope but, as they say, the first rejection hit the hardest when I read the final email which said 'no' because the poor darling had read more than enough about the Olympics in every shape and form. I understood, kind of, sort of, especially if he had had sixty nine thousand nine hundred and ninety nine others bombarding him. I wondered if he had sent a similar letter to Will who was bound to have joined him in his blog and if I should simply accept his apology and give up.

Seb sent me an email expressing his gratitude and not to be outdone, the Prime Minster also put pen to paper to personally thank me. And as Rog, Sophie and I travelled up to Dalston (the place where I'd last spent some happy moments with Mr. Z) to celebrate my birthday, a six page spread, thanking all seventy thousand Games Makers fell out of our newspaper.

It was done, it was finished, normal life could resume.

CHAPTER 40

Keeping the Flame Alive

Normal life resumed. Barely had the Olympic rings been expunged from the roadway tarmac than the newspapers had moved on to other stories. But I hadn't.

In late September I met up with Florence and Chris and Colin at Knole Park, the day memorable for the easy camaraderie, the ginger beer, cherry cake and docile deer.

An item appeared in the local paper calling Games Makers together for a social evening. As the arrangements regarding venue, date and time were batted around I watched the emails bouncing back and forth between people who found they had performed similar roles or been based at the same place. I had a run of emails with a Games Makers who I'd never met but a connection was made by the very tone and manner of the conversations we had. Whether our long distance relationship would have thrived or spluttered through a couple of hours at a nearby pub was never put to the test because my newly acquired friend lived abroad and couldn't fit it in with family visits on his return to the old country. It might have been fun but I wasn't exactly distraught about his non attendance, nor was I nervous about making an entrance to the local event because, having been cooped up with a bunkerful of rookies, a glass of shandy with a dozen or so seasoned campaigners would be a cinch.

Some arrived in uniform and most appeared to know each other either from ties prior to the Games or due to acquaintances formed during and since. I vaguely recognised one man and it turned out he had been a T3 and I, little hypocrite me, came to the defence of Helga when he started slating the Sat Navs and of Gino when he had a pop about the food. A few had had support roles with Badminton and I thought back to the lovely young woman I had sat next to during Orientation Training and that by then, by October 2012, she would have graduated and be guaranteed to be still so full of joy and energy at the future that lay ahead of her. Others too at our gathering were looking to the future, to the prospect of volunteer roles locally or at Glasgow 2014. A former team leader in the Olympic Stadium no less was having more than a dabble with the idea of flying to Moscow for an interview for the Winter Olympics in Sochi.

I stood listening intently to the personal testimony of others, to stories that would pass into the teller's family legend, all the while trying to capture what they had experienced, to get a rejuvenating shot in the arm of the way I had felt only months before. But I don't know what it was about the evening, for the more I tried to integrate the more I felt strangely disconnected from the experience, hovering ghostlike on the edge, trying to be part of something that I didn't feel I'd been part of, though obviously had.

I looked at photo albums of venues I'd never been to, of people I'd never met.

'Look at him there, next to Jim,' a man next to me said to another. 'It was taken on our last shift.'

'You have to give it to him, he was determined to achieve what he set out to do.'

'He did that and they made mention of it at his funeral.'

I scanned the smiling faces in a group photo seeing if I could detect who the man was. There were no tell tale signs of someone who knew his time was coming to an end, nor traces of pity in those around him. In the space of only a few months, times had already changed, time had already moved on and I drove home that night with morbid thoughts of my own mortality. What was it all about? Would the handful of photos I had taken of sunrises over Excel and the Dock, my favourite car and John from Chislehurst and crew be enough to encapsulate London 2012 and all it had come to mean to me over the previous two years?

The team leader with Sochi aspirations emailed everyone suggesting we write down our experiences. Nought came of it. Come Christmas time I bought Roger a novel written by a famous thriller writer who had centred the plot round the Games. I stood in awe of the book, it having been published even before the Games began. It knocked my feeble efforts into a cocked hat and I wondered what former Games Makers cum budding authors writing the next bestseller in their latte breaks in Canary Wharf thought about the novel too.

2013 rolled in and come the March I welcomed Allan, Florence, Colin and Chris to warm themselves in front of a blazing fire before setting off for the Old Town in Allan's BMW. To a man and a woman, we endorsed Allan putting the Sat Nav on so that we could once more hear its dulcet tones, childishly giggled at the mention of hot enhancements and squealed in delight when he programmed the car to park itself.

'Does this remind you of your holidays in Hastings, Allan?' I asked, whilst we finished off the last of our fish and chips, mushy peas, bread and butter and mugs of hot steaming tea in a café overlooking the beach.

'Oh yes, we had such good times.'

'I'm writing about it, you know.'

'My holidays?'

'No, the Olympics.'

'I wondered why you were always scribbling.'

'I don't think it was that. It could have been to do with Frank.'

'Frank?'

I realised then that even though he was always tugging at my coat tails I had kept Frank under wraps. Why was that? Was I ashamed, embarrassed, the guilt I felt akin to that of someone who gradually sees less and less of a relative in a nursing home because it's easier to make excuses why they can't visit than to facing up to why they don't. How telling it was that I hadn't been forthcoming about his or, apart from prattling on about the delights of Hastings, my place in the world. Had I spent those weeks, as one friend said I am adept at, of deflecting attention away from myself by asking questions of others?

'I'll tell you about Frank another day, Allan, but I'm putting everything I remember about the Olympics down because perhaps in fifteen, twenty, maybe fifty years from now, my children, or anyone else for that matter, might find it interesting.' I stood up to put my coat on. 'Now would you like to have a drive along to where you used to stay as a child?'

'Maybe, but mind yourself on the edge of the table when you get out.'

Since then the original eight hundred words I thought sufficient to capture the experience has been multiplied a hundred and fifty fold. Does that say something about me? Does it compound how over the top I was in making a big fuss about clearing the household decks, forsaking all social events and declining all visitors during my Games Makers stint? Does it mean that whilst other Games Makers have taken their volunteering roles as a few weeks doing something different, I have accorded it more value than it deserves or can live up to?

Has the experience taken on a life of its own? Has it changed in its retelling? Has it reinvented itself as London does, the London I used to know not the same as it was then? The Olympic Park is not as it was and in and about the Metropolis old buildings have been demolished and new ones rose in their place. Plastic sheeting and scaffolding have been taken down to reveal facelifts that I had only had glimpses of from the car. And if we are to believe what we read and what we hear, the spirit that boosted the country during those summer days was all too soon replaced by something meaner and less welcoming.

I have changed; changed because I took on something that I would never have previously dreamed of. I have been changed by the people I met yet they have also confirmed my view that on the whole people are good, that people are the same the world over.

But now can I let it all go and return to Frank, whoever he is, wherever he came from? Or should I let him be, for fear that when I get my red pen out and start editing again he will have changed too?